A STATE OF CR

The Changing Face of British Politics

Restructuring Britain

Uneven Re-Development: Cities and Regions in Transition
edited by Doreen Massey and John Allen

Divided Nation: Social and Cultural Change in Britain
edited by Linda McDowell, Philip Sarre and Chris Hamnett

A State of Crisis: The Changing Face of British Politics
edited by James Anderson and Allan Cochrane

The following are the associated Open Texts published by Sage Publications in association with the Open University:

The Economy in Question
edited by John Allen and Doreen Massey

The Changing Social Structure
edited by Chris Hamnett, Linda McDowell and Philip Sarre

Politics in Transition
edited by Allan Cochrane and James Anderson

Open University Course D314 Restructuring Britain

Restructuring Britain

A STATE OF CRISIS:
The Changing Face of British Politics

A Reader

edited by

James Anderson and Allan Cochrane

at the Open University

Hodder & Stoughton

A MEMBER OF THE HODDER HEADLINE GROUP

British Library Cataloguing in Publication Data

A State of crisis : the changing face of British
politics : a reader. – (Restructuring Britain)
1. Great Britain, Politics, 1900-1980
I. Anderson, James, *1941-* II. Cochrane, Allan, *1948-*
III. Open University IV. Series
320.941

ISBN 0-340-50160-X

First published 1989
Impression number 10 9 8 7 6 5 4 3 2
Year 1999 1998 1997 1996 1995

Typeset by Wearset Ltd, Boldon, Tyne & Wear.
Printed in Great Britain for Hodder & Stoughton Educational, a division of Hodder Headline Plc, 338 Euston Road, London NW1 3BH by Athenaeum Press Ltd, Gateshead, Tyne & Wear.

Contents

Acknowledgements

The editors and publishers would like to thank the following for permission to reproduce copyright material in this volume:

The Open University for 'Britain's century of decline: a world-systems interpretation' by Peter J. Taylor and for 'Devolution with consensus: the experience of Northern Ireland' by Liam O'Dowd both © The Open University (1988); Macmillan for 'Britain in the post-war world' originally published as 'Britain's international decline', Chapter 6 of *The World Economy Since the War: The Politics of Uneven Development* by E. A. Brett (1986); Nevil Johnson for 'The failure of the post-war political order' first published as 'The domestic economy and the providential power of government' and 'Equality and welfare in the static state', Chapters 1 and 2 of *In Search of the Constitution: Reflections on State and Society in Britain*, Methuen (1977); Verso for 'From the paralysis of social democracy to the crisis of the 1970s' first published as 'The paralysis of social democracy' and 'Into the new crisis', Chapters 5 and 6 of *Politics in Britain: An Introduction* by Colin Leys, Heinemann (1983); Oxford University Press for 'The economic borders of the state' by Dieter Helm reprinted from *The Oxford Review of Economic Policy*, Vol. 2, No. 2 (1986), pp. i–xxiv © Oxford University Press; The Institute of British Geographers for 'The geography of military industry in Britain' by John Lovering and Martin Boddy published in *Area*, Vol. 20, No. 1 (1988), pp. 41–51; The Department of Local Government and Development, University of Birmingham for '"A squalid and politically corrupt process?" Intergovernmental relations in the post-war period' by R. A. W. Rhodes published in *Government Studies*, Vol. 11, No. 6, November/December (1985), pp. 35–57; Mike Savage for 'Whatever happened to red Clydeside?', published as a University of Sussex Working Paper in Urban and Regional Studies (1988); The Lancaster Regionalism Group for 'The changing political environment of Lancaster' by Jane Mark-Lawson and Alan Warde, originally entitled 'Industrial restructuring and the transformation of a local political environment: a case study of Lancaster', Working Paper 33 (1987), pp. 26–34; Chatto and Windus for 'Local politics and the economy: the case of Sheffield', an extract from *Democracy in Crisis: the Town Halls Respond* by David Blunkett and Keith Jackson published by the Hogarth Press (1987); the editors of *Politics* for 'Union, party and class in Britain: the changing electoral relationship, 1964–1982' by Paul Webb published in *Politics*, Vol. 7, No. 2 (1987), pp. 15–21; Unwin and Hyman for 'Media influences on voting in 1983' reprinted from *British Democracy at the Crossroads: Voting and Party Competition in the 1980s* by Patrick Dunleavy and C. T. Husbands (1985); Pergamon Press for 'Ideological change in the electorate' reprinted from *How Britain Votes* by Anthony Heath, Roger Jowell and John Curtice (1985).

Introduction

This book is concerned with political change in the United Kingdom since 1945, and particularly with developments since the mid-1960s. This period is not only of interest as a piece of recent history, but also because it is one in which the processes of change themselves have come under a great deal of scrutiny. It is widely accepted that important changes have taken place, but it is more difficult to find agreement as to which are significant and which more ephemeral. The extent to which taken collectively they amount to a more extensive set of structural changes – a restructuring of the British political system – remains a matter of contention. These wider issues underlie a great deal of the debate in the chapters which follow.

Despite a widespread belief that some of the important ground rules of post-war British politics were rewritten in the quarter of a century which began in the late 1960s, the implications of this remain unclear. Some commentators would argue that the extent of change has been much exaggerated in popular (and academic) writing while others identify more fundamental shifts. The papers selected for inclusion in this collection were chosen on the basis that they will help the reader to make judgements about both the extent and direction of change. It will be clear that the range of issues covered do not arise from any narrow theoretical starting-point or any single academic discipline.

Although the book is principally concerned with political structures and relationships, and can be read quite independently of others in the series, it is part of an Open University course – *Restructuring Britain** – which aims to explore contemporary debates about change in the United Kingdom. The course is divided into three parts, concerned respectively with the economy, society and culture, politics and the state. For each part, there is an Open Text and a Reader. This is the Reader for the third of these parts. The course starts from a position which acknowledges both the individuality of the United Kingdom and its position within a wider international system. Uneven development is an important concept in this context because it highlights the importance of spatial differentiation and the different tempos of economic, social and political change, while also directing attention to the complex interrelationships between apparently independent social phenomena.

This helps to explain the particular selection of topics which has been made here. So, for example, not only is the changing position of the United Kingdom in a world system an important issue for consideration, but, within the United Kingdom, the changing positions of its component regions (and nations) and their own relationship to the world system are

* Details of this course, D314 *Restructuring Britain*, are available from the Student Enquiries Office, The Open University, PO Box 71, Milton Keynes MK7 6AG.

understood to be important, too. That the United Kingdom itself is characterized by division and fragmentation, rather than being an unproblematic unity, is a basic starting-point for analysis.

If global changes are important in determining the context for developments in Britain – as the arguments in Section I of this book confirm – it is often at local and regional levels that the processes of political change are most apparent. It may be that processes of 'globalization' at one level and 'localization' at the other are beginning to undermine the old orthodoxies which encourage a concentration of attention on the politics of national governments. Section IV is particularly concerned with the politics of locality, placing it both in the context of change within the UK, and the context of international restructuring. Chapters 8 and 9, in Section III, are more concerned with the relationships between national and local politics, national and local governments, within the UK state.

The discussion, in Section II, of Britain's political crisis of the 1970s builds on the 'global' analysis of Section I, by locating key features of UK politics in their international context. But it also explores their 'Britishness', by looking at those aspects which make it a British crisis rather than simply the British response to some international economic (and political) crisis, or the working out in Britain of an internationally determined agenda. The experience of Northern Ireland, for example, is considered not as a special case separate from the wider UK political crisis but as a vital component of that crisis. The move away from the structures of the post-war social-democratic state, which is approached in the first chapters of Section III through an examination of changing state/economy relations, cannot be understood solely through the arguments of the policy-makers without some reflection on the spatially differentiated impact of the policy changes.

Identifying the relationship between political, economic and social factors in explaining political change and state restructuring is a concern which runs through the book. It is of more importance in some chapters than others and is explicit in some and implicit in others. Many of the arguments in the earlier Sections – although this is not true of all the chapters – tend to stress the importance of economic factors, particulary where they focus on the international level. In Section IV local politics and local social relations are linked, but political explanations for political processes are also extensively developed. Chapter 8 explains central—local relations largely in terms of pressures arising from the structures of the UK state, while Section V charts the end of narrowly based class voting and confirms the continued importance of ideology and political communication.

A wide range of different approaches to recent British politics is reflected in the chapters of this book. Their different theoretical and disciplinary origins often leave them separated (and sometimes in contention) in the academic literature. It is dangerously misleading to minimize genuine and important differences and to suggest that it is possible simply to merge different approaches in some unholy amalgam which seeks to identify a 'middle' ground acceptable to all. Yet it is equally dangerous to imagine that no fruitful debate is possible between different approaches (not all perspectives are always and everywhere 'competing' with each other). Important debates are reflected within and between the different chapters, but many of these only serve to confirm the complementarity of apparently alternative approaches in the analysis of political change. We believe that placing these arguments side by side makes it easier to see the value of encouraging communication between them.

Allan Cochrane

Section I The international context

Introduction

The chapters in this Section start from a shared acceptance of the importance of the international level for developments in Britain. Both chart a changing role for the UK within the world system and note the replacement of the UK by the United States of America as hegemonic power, particularly since 1945. In their different ways, both also acknowledge the importance of setting post-war developments within a longer-term historical context, stretching back to the nineteenth century and earlier. But their theoretical starting-points are significantly different: Taylor's analysis assumes the existence of a world-economic and social system within which individual states play different roles largely as a junction of the requirements of that system, while Brett's approach suggests rather more autonomy for the various states and attention is directed to the relationships between them as well as the processes of global change. Using Doherty's terms, Taylor's approach looks for 'exogenous' explanations, while Brett's is basically 'interrelational' (Doherty, 1989).

Like Wallerstein, whose theoretical approach provides the basis for many of Taylor's arguments, he relates the shifting patterns of national prosperity and power to global processes of economic and social change. The modern world, Taylor argues, is best understood as one (capitalist) society rather than many (national) societies, and the emphasis of analysis is placed on relationships between core and periphery within that society, rather than relationships between national states. Within this model, change takes place in the context of a series of long-term economic cycles (often referred to as Kondratiev cycles) which operate on a global rather than a national scale and at different points of these cycles different national powers will tend to be dominant, or hegemonic. Individual states continue to be important areas for analysis, but only because it is through them that more general political and economic conflicts are often expressed (including those based on class – a global phenomenon – and household – a local one). A key conclusion of the argument presented here is that the British welfare state is only one example of a series of 'welfare states' created in the core countries after 1945, which contrasts sharply with later arguments (see, for example, Johnson in Chapter 3) which stress the special features of the political compromise which underlies it in Britain.

Although the world-systems approach focuses primarily on global processes it clearly can and – at least as developed by Peter Taylor – does make important connections to the analysis of change within particular countries. Taylor, for example, in his analysis of Britain's 'hegemonic' century (1790/98–1890/96) and his discussion of its legacy in the context of US dominance, stresses the continued importance of the British financial sector, an issue which is frequently raised in other discussions of the British crisis (including Brett which follows). Taylor stresses the fragility of Britain's apparently strong political position after 1945. He implies that there is little which could have been done to reverse it by political initiative at the national level, although one legacy of past hegemony seems to have been a desire to sustain an international role which was unsustainable and which only made it more difficult for the UK fully to share in the post-war European economic 'boom'.

Many of Taylor's conclusions would probably be shared by Brett, despite a rather different way of reaching them. If Taylor stresses the importance of global processes, Brett stresses the importance of uneven development and the difficulties it generates for the process of global economic management. He focuses on the relationship between Britain's domestic policies and the external constraints within which they have had to develop. From the start, therefore, he emphasizes the tension between the attempt to build a social-democratic state in Britain and an effective dependence on the USA for financial support, coupled with a continued commitment to playing a major role in the international economy. Brett clearly charts the problems of reconciling these two through the 1950s and into the 1960s, convincingly showing how Britain was left behind in the broader experience of European growth. After the mid-1960s, when, according to Brett, some attempt was made to adjust to changed realities, that attempt coincided with a substantially different international economic environment. Brett suggests that Britain's problems in the first twenty years after 1945 stemmed largely from misguided attempts to play a central role in the world economy from a position of relative strength, whilst after the mid-1960s not only was the world economy weaker, but Britain's position within it was weaker still compared to its European and Japanese competitors.

The tension between trying to pursue full employment policies within a welfare state and a commitment to liberal economic policies on a world scale is one which Brett places at the heart of the British crisis, and he weaves political and economic explanations together to support this argument. He concludes his analysis with a scathing critique of economic policies pursued since the mid-1970s, suggesting that some sort of choice has now been made between these two elements, and that, despite some inconsistencies, the external orientation of the British economy has been reinforced at the expense of full employment and the welfare state. Since individual nations – such as the UK and more recently the USA – cannot be expected to carry the weight of international economic management, Brett argues that some system of international management is required but he gives little indication of how this might be achieved. This is likely to be a major problem, particularly when – as Taylor suggests – countries which take on this role actually appear to benefit substantially, at least during the period of their initial dominance.

Brett and Taylor are agreed that Britain's position within the world system has changed substantially since 1945 – or, perhaps more accurately, that it is possible to identify a process of rather incoherent (and sometimes contradictory) adjustment to that changed position. The changes they identify provide the context for a wide range of adjustments made within the British political system. The structural changes they identify at the international level have changed the possibilities for action at the UK level, but the fit between those broader changes and restructuring in Britain has been less than perfect. Both would suggest that for much of the post-war period British politics has been conducted as if little fundamental had changed, and it is only since the mid-1970s that more substantial breaks with the past can be identified.

Allan Cochrane

Reference

DOHERTY, J. (1989) 'Britain in a changing international system', Chapter 1 in Cochrane, A. and Anderson, J. (eds) (1989) *Politics in Transition* (Restructuring Britain, Open Text 3), London, Sage/The Open University.

1 Britain's century of decline: a world-systems interpretation

Peter J Taylor

Britain's century of decline as a great power can be said to have occurred between 1867 and 1967. In the mid-nineteenth century Britain was the undisputed leading country in the world with the most innovative and productive modern economy. This achievement was symbolized by the Great Exhibition at the Crystal Palace in 1851 where Britain demonstrated the wonders of the new industrial world it had created. Sixteen years later in Paris another International Exhibition showed clearly for the first time that other countries were challenging Britain's technological-industrial leadership. The first hints of doubt for Britain's continued world supremacy were voiced. Exactly one hundred years later, as part of a major economic reassessment, the British government decided to withdraw British troops from east of Suez. All pretence at being a world power was abandoned. Henceforth Britain would be a regional (i.e. European) power. A century of decline of Britain as a great power was complete.

The purpose of this chapter is to analyse this century of decline from a world-systems perspective. This means interpreting Britain's changing role in the world-economy using the concepts and analysis developed by Immanuel Wallerstein (1979, 1984a). He provides a particular theoretical framework that combines political and economic processes into a single, integrated argument (Taylor, 1985b). This is very important for understanding the case of Britain since its decline is neither solely economic nor political but both. Furthermore Wallerstein (1984a) identifies Britain as a special case in the history of his world-system. In this interpretation the decline of Britain is not just a 'national tragedy', it is at the heart of a far wider set of international changes.

Within our chosen theoretical framework the relative decline of Britain is no ordinary affair because it represents the demise of a once hegemonic power. The rise and fall of states is, of course, endemic to the inter-state system but the descent from hegemony is a rare phenomenon. (The only other cases are, first, possibly the decline of the Hapsburg realm after the sixteenth century and, second, the decline of the Dutch Republic after the seventeenth century. The fourth case, the decline of the United States, is in all probability just beginning.) These hegemonic declines are important because they represent a change in the political leadership of the inter-state system.

The key concept is *hegemony*. This term is usually associated with a class analysis whereby one class is able totally to dominate a society. In this context we are applying the term to a state rather than a class so that the former totally dominates the inter-state system (Cox, 1983). Hence hegemony is much more than mere leadership; it implies a pervasive dominance so that the hegemonic state's world political agenda is generally accepted as the framework for the political activities of most other states: the ideas of the hegemonic state are the pre-eminent ideas of the inter-state system. For instance, after 1945 the United States was not just 'leader of the western alliance', it was the hegemonic power dominating the world-economy and creating world institutions such as the International Monetary Fund and the United Nations in its own image. We shall argue that Britain was similarly hegemonic in the mid-nineteenth century.

The reason why understanding Britain's decline is important today is because the legacy of Britain's hegemony is still with us. It has been argued that British politics suffers from a 'post-hegemonic trauma' that continues to influence the foreign and domestic policies of Britain (Taylor, 1989a). This 'trauma' is a short-hand term to describe the necessary adjustment that takes place in the political self-image as the hegemonic state is relegated from number one to number two and beyond. The trappings of world power are hard to forget, as the Falklands/Malvinas War – and public reaction to it – perhaps more than any other event reminds us.

1.1 World-systems analysis: an introductory outline

One of the basic assumptions we usually make about the world is that it consists of a large number of distinctive societies – British society, French society, US society etc. Notice that such 'societies' are normally equated with countries. Since there are some 160 states in the world it follows that our 'common-sense' world model consists of some 160 separate societies. Most social science treatments of the world accept this general model and have concentrated on 'societies within the states'. World-systems analysis does not accept this multiple-society world model. It attempts to build an alternative social science on the basis of a one-society model of the world. This is the basic assumption of world-systems analysis.

The one-society assumption

The one-society assumption is derived from an analysis of social change. The question to be answered is 'what is the basic unit of social change in the modern world?' For most people the answer is obvious – societies within states. If we break away from this multiple-society assumption we can soon find indications of crucial elements of social change that occur at a scale beyond the state. The prime example is the existence of Kondratiev cycles (Research Working Group, 1979).

The idea that economic growth is cyclical rather than linear has a very long history. The particular cycles we are concerned with here are the 'long cycles' generally named after their discoverer, the Russian economist Nicolai Kondratiev. He argued, in the 1920s, that since the original industrial revolution in the late eighteenth century, a wide range of economic statistics showed a cyclical pattern of approximately fifty years per cycle. In each case there was an 'A-phase' of growth in production based upon a particular range of innovations to be followed by a 'B-phase' of stagnation when the economic stimulus of the innovations had worked its way through the system. Kondratiev was writing during a 'B-phase'. His ideas are popular today because the subsequent pattern of economic growth seems to fit his model remarkably well: the period of about twenty-five years after 1945 clearly constitutes an 'A-phase', with our more recent economic experiences having all the hallmarks of a 'B-phase'.

The main point about Kondratiev cycles for our argument here is that they are worldwide in their scope. The relative stagnation since about 1970 is not just a British problem or a US problem, it is a Polish problem, a Brazilian problem, a Nigerian problem and so on. Similarly, the 'post-war boom' although starting in the United States eventually spread to other parts of the world in the 1950s. In world-systems analysis these Kondratiev cycles represent the fundamental rhythm of the capitalist world-economy (Wallerstein, 1984b). It is this world-economy that constitutes the 'one society' of this form of analysis and is the basic object of social change.

The capitalist world-economy

The capitalist world-economy is 'capitalist' because the dominant process is ceaseless capital accumulation and it is a 'world-economy' because it consists of a single division of labour that transcends individual states. It has been global in scope since about 1900. The process of capital accumulation and the pattern that is the division of labour intersect through the operation of commodity chains (Wallerstein, 1983). These are made up of a series of production nodes which brings together labour and materials in production. Every chain begins with the conversion of some element of nature into a commodity and concludes with the final consumption of the product. There will normally be several production nodes between extraction and final consumption and these may well involve movement of commodities across political boundaries. The type of production processes at each node can be categorized as either core or periphery. In the former case production involves relatively high-technology practices carried out by relatively high-waged labour. In the periphery case the obverse obtains. Core production and periphery production processes tend to be concentrated in different geographical areas so that the world-economy consists of core zones and peripheral zones. In addition there are zones where both types of production processes occur; these are designated semi-peripheral zones.

A simple example will help clarify these ideas. Historically perhaps the most famous commodity chain in the world-economy has been that which linked the southern states of the United States with Lancashire in the period before the US Civil War. The cotton grown in plantations with slave labour constituted a peripheral process and southern USA was a key part of the periphery at this time. In contrast the processes of turning the cotton into cloth in the Lancashire mills represented the most advanced technological production process of the time. Hence Lancashire constituted a key part of the core of the mid-nineteenth-century world-economy. Note that the important feature was not that textiles were 'industrial' commodities but that they were produced under relatively advanced conditions. Today, of course, textiles are typically produced as peripheral production processes: core and periphery do *not* equate with industrial and agricultural production.

The sum of the millions of commodity chains produces a world-system that is the capitalist world-economy. In this system there is a basic dominance relation between core and peripheral zones (Taylor, 1985a). This has sometimes taken the form of formal imperialism when core states have taken political control of peripheral territories as colonies. Most of today's semi-periphery and periphery have been through formal imperialism. An alternative form of domination is informal imperialism where there is no direct political control of the periphery territories but they are economically dependent on the core. The classical case is again associated with nineteenth-century Britain when Latin America was seen as 'the informal empire'. The situation is epitomized by George Canning's statement in 1823 on the revolt of the Spanish American Colonies: 'Latin America is free and she is ours.' Today formal imperialism is almost ended (Namibia and Hong Kong are the major exceptions) but the former recent colonies of Africa, Asia and the Caribbean continue to complain about 'neo-colonialism'. This is today's common phrase for informal imperialism which consists of the combination of political independence and economic dependence.

This introduction to world-systems analysis can be summarized as follows:

(a) the basic assumption is that there is one object of social change which is the capitalist world-economy;

(b) the rhythm of this world system, the pattern of social change, is cyclical and can be described by Kondratiev cycles;

(c) the world-economy is defined as an integrated, hierarchical division of labour with commodity chains linking core, semi-periphery and periphery zones;

(d) domination by the core has taken two forms, formal imperialism and informal imperialism.

1.2 World-systems analysis: a critique

The world-systems analysis described above is derived directly from the work of American sociologist Immanuel Wallerstein (1979, 1983). As would be expected for a new form of analysis, there have been many critics of this particular theoretical framework: Wallerstein's new 'historical social science' is highly controversial. Hence before we go on and use his analysis we must consider the debates surrounding this work. In fact we will concentrate upon one particular critique, that of Robert Brenner (1977). This is usually considered to be the most important criticism of Wallerstein's work because it goes right to the heart of his analysis. The debate is commonly referred to as the modes of production controversy (Foster-Carter, 1978).

Brenner approaches Wallerstein's writings from a Marxist perspective. He designates Wallerstein a 'neo-Smithian', meaning that an emphasis on the world-market and the distribution of commodities locates Wallerstein in the political economy framework before Karl Marx, to that of Adam Smith in fact. Hence Wallerstein fails to incorporate into his analysis the secrets of production unveiled by Marx in *Das Kapital*. Brenner concentrates on Wallerstein's treatment of the early modern period. Wallerstein traces his capitalist world-economy to the 'long' sixteenth century (*c.*1450— *c.*1650) when western Europe began its global expansion. The origins of modern capitalism are located in a 'European world-economy' with Western Europe as a core zone, Spanish America and eastern Europe as two periphery zones and the declining European Mediterranean region as a semi-periphery between core and periphery. Brenner objects to calling this trading system, as he sees it, a capitalist entity. For Brenner, and Marxists generally, capitalism is a mode of production that is to be found only when a particular social relation, capitalist-proletariat, defines the process of production. Here the capitalist owns the means of production and buys labour power from the proletariat as 'free labour'. In Wallerstein's early world-economy, however, although such a relation can be found in the core zone, very different coercive social relations of a 'pre-capitalist' nature are to be found elsewhere. Hence, for Brenner, Wallerstein has most definitely not discovered, in the sixteenth century, a capitalist world-economy. Furthermore, since the 'capitalist social relation' has still not penetrated all production processes even in the late twentieth century, it follows that even today in the 'Third World' pre-capitalist modes of production survive alongside capitalism (Taylor, 1979). Hence the idea of an all-embracing capitalist world-economy cannot be justified.

Wallerstein defines capitalism in a different way. The first step is to identify an integrated division of labour as a social system. Then if the dominant logic of the system is ceaseless capital accumulation we can speak of it as a capitalist system. This assumes a much broader definition of mode of production. Hence in Wallerstein's early modern world-system, the slavery of Spanish America, the 'second serfdom' of eastern Europe and the share-cropping of Mediterranean Europe are all part of one integrated division of labour along with the 'free labour' of north-west Europe. Since the dominant logic behind this whole material edifice is ceaseless capital accumulation it follows that we have a capitalist system whose expansive nature results in the incorporation of the rest of the world by about 1900. It does not matter that some production nodes continue to have what seem to be a 'pre-capitalist' form, the important question is whether they form parts of commodity chains within the integrated division of labour that is the world-economy. Since the answer to this question is invariably yes, it follows that in Wallerstein's terms we are living today in one world-system based on the capitalist mode of production – the capitalist world-economy.

The mode of production controversy is important because it is about fundamentally different conceptions of social change. If there are several modes of production operating in parallel together then there will be separate processes of social change. If there is one mode then there is only one overall process of social change: Britain, for instance, can only be understood as part of a wider system. This is a very important debate that we cannot do justice to here: for further discussion see Arrighi *et al.* (1983) and Taylor (1985b).

In summary, the orthodox Marxist critique argues that Wallerstein misunderstands the fundamental nature of capitalism as a mode of production based upon the capitalist-proletariat social relation. In reply Wallerstein argues that capitalism should be seen as a system whose logic is based upon capital accumulation and which can bring together several forms of production relations within integrating community chains.

We are now in a position to consider the politics of the world-economy as a prelude to discussing Britain's changing role in the world.

1.3 World-economy politics

The study of politics has been the prisoner of the 'multiple-society assumption' more than any other area of social science. After all, these proposed 'societies' were generally politically defined, as we have already noted. Hence the application of a world-system 'single-society assumption' in this field is particularly innovative. But it is also problematic: if politics is largely about states where does an overarching world-system fit in?

Although it is very easy to perceive the world as consisting of 160 or so states each with a relatively autonomous 'politics', a little thought soon enables us to query the degree to which each 'politics' is really separate. Although the details of every state's politics are unique, the concepts used to create such 'politics' are always quite general. This is shown in the names give to political parties – the plethora of 'Liberal', 'Christian

Democrat', 'National', 'Socialist', 'Labour', 'Conservative' and 'Radical' parties in liberal democracies for instance. In other contexts who can doubt the 'linkages' between the repressive Latin American regimes of the 1960s and 1970s or the 'contagion' in the sequence of military coups in Africa since independence? Quite simply, political movements and ideologies have never been contained by political boundaries: they are larger than states; they are phenomena of the world-system itself (Taylor, 1986).

This is not to argue that states are not important in world-economy politics. The states have become the most important arenas of political action. As such they are one of the key institutions in the world-economy (Wallerstein, 1984a). They provide the formal framework through which the other key institutions – peoples ('nations', ethnic groups), classes and households – attempt to achieve their goals. In this process winners manipulate and losers are manipulated. Hence the states can never be neutral arenas since they have been and remain the prime instruments in the political struggles of the modern world-system.

An instrumental theory of the state

In most interpretations of international relations the states are 'actors' in an international arena of co-operation and competition. In our interpretation they are instruments, the political expression of the power of class forces. As such they are also deeply implicated in the domestic politics within states. Let us see how Wallerstein (1984a) derives these two scales of politics.

(a) Classes are defined in relation to the mode of production. Since the mode of production is system-wide then it follows that objectively classes are 'world classes'. It is true that they have often consciously thought of themselves in state terms as 'national classes' but this is a subjective definition of classes 'for themselves' rather than classes 'of themselves'. In this analysis system-wide classes are divided into national sections, state-by-state, but these sections are not themselves complete classes.

(b) At the heart of the capitalist world-system are the two major classes, bourgeoisie that own the means of production and proletariat that provide the labour power. The prime motive of the dominant class, the bourgeoisie, is ceaseless capital accumulation. Failure to adhere to the requirements of accumulation results in elimination of such renegade bourgeoisie from the system.

(c) The bourgeoisie has two basic strategies for accumulation. At each node of the commodity chain either the prices can be manipulated or the cost of labour power can be reduced.

(d) Manipulating prices means attempting to create quasi-monopolies to 'distort' the market. This is achieved by use of the state. All the bourgeois want to 'buy cheap and sell dear' in their part of the commodity chain. The more powerful have always attempted 'vertical integration' of chains to control the market. This has often been associated with imperialism of different forms. But the classic use of the state as an instrument to control prices is through fiscal policy and tariffs in particular. It is no accident that the prime political conflicts of the late nineteenth century were over tariffs and protectionism.

(e) It follows that international relations – politics between states – is the major form that intra-bourgeois competition takes in the world-economy. Each 'national section' of the dominant world class uses its state to provide market advantages in division of the world's surplus.

(f) The process of reducing labour costs involves a very different and more fundamental politics. The nationalization of labour has meant that bourgeois–proletariat conflict has largely taken place within arenas defined by the states.

(g) It follows that domestic politics – politics within states – is the major form which inter-class conflict, bourgeois vs proletariat, takes in the world-economy. It is no accident that conflicts over trade union activities and welfare issues have dominated domestic politics in the twentieth century.

(h) Hence both international relations as intra-bourgeois competition and domestic politics as inter-class conflict can be derived from the existence of world classes and the accumulation prerogative.

It is not suggested that these are the only politics operating in the world-economy, but they are the most crucial. This is because they operate to change the form that the system takes at any time – the pattern of bourgeois dominance and the pattern of proletarian resistance. The world-economy is continually changing and these two politics are at the very heart – the accumulation process – of the reproduction of the system.

The variety of politics

Wallerstein's interpretation of world-economy politics provides a solution to one of the major conundrums of the modern world – the contrast between the similarities of the economic processes across the world-system and the great variety of political processes (Taylor, 1985a). One economics (even including the 'socialist states' as the world market takes hold there) and many politics: why?

The bourgeoisie has always acted more like a world class than the proletariat. Whether formally in international congresses and alliances or informally as transnational corporations, the whole history of the world-economy is littered by bourgeois co-operation that has been much more powerful than the efforts at proletarian internationalism. Hence when the sections of the bourgeoisie class have operated through their states to enhance their positions they have always combined strategies of international relations with their domestic politics. A major consequence of this in the twentieth century has been a vast difference in standard of living between direct producers in different parts of the world.

The bourgeois within their states are faced with two challenges – their local proletariat and foreign bourgeois competitors. In core zones of the world-economy they are strong vis-à-vis other bourgeois sections but have to face in turn a stronger domestic proletarian challenge. In contrast in periphery zones the opposite obtains: they are weak bourgeois competitors but are stronger in relation to their local proletariats. This differential bourgeois competition and proletarian resistance is reflected in the range of politics found in the world-economy (Taylor, 1989b).

In the periphery the variety of forms of politics is limited to alternative means of coercion even where the facade of elections is maintained – remember that election statistics in these countries always include the number of deaths on election day, in the campaign and in the aftermath. The variety of political forms includes traditional monarchies (Saudi Arabia), military dictatorship (Chile), one-party states (Tanzania), Marxist-Leninist regimes (Ethiopia) and plural multi-party systems (India). In many cases the politics is quite unstable with elections following coups and vice versa. The archetypal form of periphery state was created in Latin America in the 1960s. Their 'national security states' combined an illiberal, repressive domestic politics with a liberal open economy for its international relations, perfectly illustrating where periphery bourgeois strengths and weaknesses lie.

In the post-1945 period under US hegemony, core states have exhibited far less variety. Although electoral systems vary, the archetypal core regime is now the liberal democracy associated with a welfare-state economy. This reflects a history of proletarian resistance culminating in concessions providing for the highest ever standard of living for any large group of direct producers. But this benefit remains only for a minority of the world's direct producers, those fortunate enough to live in the core zone.

Britain under the 1945–51 Attlee Labour government was a pioneer creator of the welfare state. This was the post-war domestic political settlement. Notice, however, that the politics producing this new form of state was by no means limited to Britain. Welfare states in different forms were created in all the core states as we have already noted. This provides another example justifying our world-economy politics argument. The politics that created the welfare state were not a particular state politics, rather they were a politics general to the world-system at one particular phase of its development in one particular zone. It would be wrong therefore to view the British welfare state as a specifically British achievement – it was part of a far wider process.

We can summarize world-economy politics as follows:

(a) states are key institutions in the world-economy: they are the instruments through which classes and other groups attempt to formally control the processes of the world-economy;

(b) inter-state politics largely reflect an inter-bourgeois competition over control of prices and intra-state politics are largely concerned with inter-class conflicts over labour costs;

(c) the variety of politics in the world-economy is based upon differences between core and periphery states: in the former the bourgeoisie is strong internationally but relatively weak domestically, in the latter the opposite is the case, resulting in liberal democratic 'welfare' states and a range of coercive state forms respectively.

1.4 A model of hegemony and rivalry

We are now in a position to bring together elements of the above discussion to bear on the question of Britain's changing role in the world. As we noted at the beginning of this section we need to take a perspective that covers Britain's nineteenth-century hegemonic pre-eminence. The rise and fall of hegemonic states is a clear expression of the use of the state as an instrument to further the ends of the most advanced sectors of the bourgeoisie.

In world-systems analysis hegemony is built up in three stages: we begin with one state which incorporates the most efficient production processes within the overall system; this leads on to the development of commercial supremacy; and, finally, financial dominance is achieved. When all three supremacies coincide the result is full hegemony (Wallerstein, 1984a). This sequence can be related to the changing pattern of the material base of the world-system as reflected in Kondratiev waves. Wallerstein and his associates have proposed an outline model of hegemony and rivalry built upon the paired-Kondratievs of the last two centuries (Research Working Group, 1979).

This very simple model is shown in Table 1.1 and proceeds as follows (Taylor, 1985a). Starting with the A-phase (growth) of the first cycle there is geopolitical rivalry for world leadership. In hindsight we can see that one of the rival states already has a material lead not yet translated into a political lead. This state has the most efficient production processes within its boundaries giving it a long-term advantage over its rivals. This stage is termed *ascending hegemony*. In the B-phase (stagnation) of the first cycle opportunities are restricted throughout the world-economy and only one state is able to take full advantage of what is available. The merchants of this leading state building upon the production edge come to dominate the world-market. It is now clear to all which state is dominant; this is the stage of *hegemonic victory*. In the A-phase of the second cycle the dominant state consolidates its position in the new growth era to become the financial centre of the world. This is true hegemony, in the stage of *hegemonic maturity*. But the other states, their producers, merchants and financiers,

Table 1.1 State hegemony and Kondratiev cycles

Great Britain's 'Century'			*'The American Century'*		
	1790/8			1890/6	
Kondratiev Cycle I	A_1 Ascending hegemony	Rivalry with France (Napoleonic Wars) Productive efficiency: industrial revolution	*Kondratiev Cycle III*	A_1 Ascending hegemony	Rivalry with Germany Productive efficiency: mass production techniques
	1815/25			1913/20	
	B_1 Hegemonic victory	Commercial victory in Latin America and control of India: 'workshop of the world'		B_1 Hegemonic victory	Commercial victory in the final collapse of British free trade system and decisive military defeat of Germany
	1844/51			1940/45	
Kondratiev Cycle II	A_2 Hegemonic maturity	Era of Free Trade: London becomes financial centre of the world-economy	*Kondratiev Cycle IV*	A_2 Hegemonic maturity	Liberal economic system of Bretton Woods based upon the dollar: New York new financial centre of the world
	1870/5			1967/73	
	B_2 Declining hegemony	Classical age of imperialism as European powers and USA rival Britain. 'New' industrial revolution emerging outside Britain		B_2 Declining hegemony	Reversal to protectionist practices to counteract Japan and European rivals
	1890/96			?	

Source: Taylor, 1985, p. 57

are not standing still. In the B-phase of the second cycle the hegemonic state can no longer maintain its production edge and we experience a period of *declining hegemony* setting the stage for the next A-phase's geopolitical competition for the succession.

Decline from hegemony is the inverse of the earlier rise: first the production edge is lost, followed by commercial supremacy, with financial leadership the last to be surrendered. Thus Britain's decline in this model can be summarized as follows. As the former hegemonic state Britain lost the production edge in the late nineteenth century, commercial supremacy in the early twentieth century and financial leadership in the inter-war years with the failure to return successfully to the gold standard. The decline of sterling as the major world currency and its replacement by the dollar after World War II is symbolic of the transfer of hegemony. Nevertheless the financial sector, as the last part of Britain's lost hegemony to decline, remains unusually powerful within the British economy. In the current period when the USA is beginning its decline and the dollar is no longer as powerful as it once was, Britain's erstwhile hegemonic financial sector has been able once again to enhance its role in this one section of the world-economy. Hence one very important legacy of Britain's hegemony is the continuing strength of finance capital within the national economy.

Table 1.1 shows the rise and fall of British and US hegemony. I will concentrate on just two of the stages here – hegemonic maturity and declining hegemony. In the former case 'pure hegemony' is translated into persuading and cajoling other states in the world-economy to open up their markets in a free trading system. The self-interest of the hegemonic state in such a form of world-economy is hidden under a universalistic liberal ideology. Hence hegemonic states are the great proponents of a liberal world order in which 'incidentally' they can find worldwide markets for their goods. Although never completely successful, the mid-nineteenth century and mid-twentieth centuries do represent remarkable achievements by first Britain and then the USA to mould the world to its own economic needs.

The decline of the hegemonic state ushers in a new and dangerous era of rivalry. The free trade institutions break down, protectionism rears its ugly head again and a 'new mercantilism' is born. In the late nineteenth century this was most vividly expressed in the European scramble for colonies in the 'age of imperialism'. It is not yet clear what the major expression of the current era of rivalry will be. The rise of OPEC, famines in Africa, US-Europe rivalry, Japan propping up the US economy are all features of our world today that were not even thought of in the mid-1960s when US hegemony still reigned over the world. The certainties of hegemony have all gone, leaving us unsure as to the future of the world.

There are two final points concerning this model that need to be stated. First, the two paired-Kondratievs are analogies and only that. Similarities between the British and American experience are emphasized, dissimilarities neglected. When Britain was hegemonic, for instance, there was no equivalent to the military and ideological challenge of the USSR that America has had to grapple with. In a sense Russia has spoilt America's hegemony (Taylor, 1985a). Secondly, the model should not be read as a simple base–superstructure model where the material processes of the Kondratiev cycles in some senses 'produce' the political responses as phases of hegemony. It is, of course, much more complicated than that. The base and superstructure interact in so many ways it is impossible to argue that one causes the other. Wallerstein's (1984b) explanation for these cycles, for instance, is one of imbalance between system-wide supply and demand. The former occurs primarily in the economic sphere and it is this 'anarchy of production' that generates growth and finally overproduction. Demand, on the other hand, is largely a product of the political sphere. The political conflicts of B-phases redistribute world income to provide a new market pattern allowing for the next phase of growth. Hence 'economics' and 'politics' complement each other in the overall workings of the world-economy. Both are necessary, neither one is sufficient on its own.

We can now return to the question of Britain's century of decline within the inter-state system. In the first half of the twentieth century Britain has been the declining former hegemonic state as the new hegemonic state, the United States, was rising. A British politics built around the assumed benevolence of a liberal world order (especially free trade) was to be constantly challenged. This was symbolized by the conversion of Joseph Chamberlain to protectionism and the capture of the Conservative Party by the Tariff Reform Movement at the beginning of the twentieth century. The Liberal and Labour Parties remained committed to free trade and were able to defeat Conservative protectionist platforms at General Elections in 1910 and 1923. It was left to the National Government in 1932 at the height of the 'Great Depression' to finally abandon free trade and opt for a policy of imperial preferences. Britain, the erstwhile hegemonic state, had at last come into line with the other major states in a world of acute rivalry centring upon economic blocs.

However, Britain's conversion was to last little more than a decade. The United States, long-term champion of protectionism under Republican Party dominance since the Civil War, finally made its turnaround at the end of World War II. The new hegemonic state was to become the new champion of free trade and a liberal world order. Why did Britain follow the United States and join in the new liberal world order when it had only so recently developed its imperial preferences and sterling area policy? This is a fascinating episode in the modern world and crucially illustrates the power of a hegemonic state and the use of the state for material ends. It is also the context in which Britain finds her final role as a world power.

1.5 Britain and the post-1945 international settlement

The apparent high standing of Britain in 1945 was in reality very fragile. We can interpret this fragility in terms of changing hegemonies. By 1945 Britain's hegemony was long gone, as we have seen. Nevertheless Britain had still been powerful enough in terms of international rivalry to find a new role as the world's largest empire (Taylor, 1989a). In fact with the addition of the former German colonies as 'mandates' after World War I, the British Empire was at its greatest ever extent in the inter-war period. But with the arrival of US hegemony the Empire was doomed.

The other two major victors in 1945, the USA and USSR, were both explicitly anti-imperialist in their foreign policies in the sense that they were against formal imperialism. Hence continuation of the empires of the European states was not part of either country's vision of the post-war world. The US attitude was vital and was made plain to Britain during war-time negotiations, most notably in the Atlantic Charter which envisaged 'self-determination' as the primary war aim. President Roosevelt made it clear that this call for freedom was not limited to the liberation of Europe from the Nazis but was to apply worldwide. The USA, as the very first 'colony' to obtain 'national independence', was presenting itself as a champion of all colonial independence movements in competition to the USSR as the alternative anti-imperialist force. After 1945 the USA was powerful enough to force through its anti-imperialism. Its liberal ideological commitment to colonial independence was joined by an economic self-interest for opening the world-economy to free trade. Just like George Canning, the British Foreign Secretary in 1823 quoted above, now more than a century later US Secretaries of State were pursuing similar policies of supporting colonial independence in an open world-economy: US hegemony had arrived. Europe's empires were no longer to be seen as permanent; independence became just a matter of timing – in Britain's case, India sooner (1947) and Africa just a little later (from 1957). The world power that was the British Empire was being reduced to just Britain. The imperial shield that had hidden relative decline was stripped away in the creation of the new world of US hegemony. And the focus of the US's new world soon moved beyond the fragile 'historical' challenge of Britain towards the far greater 'future' challenge of the USSR. With the coming of the Cold War the world was transformed into a bipolar situation in which Britain was squeezed out as a major player. This is the world-systems context in which Britain's changing position in the post-war world needs to be understood.

Our post-1945 experience of international politics has been dominated by the Cold War. It is not surprising therefore that most of the international relations literature on the post-1945 settlement has concentrated on the causes of the Cold War. In the orthodox view Russian expansion in eastern

Europe became a nightmare of what could happen elsewhere, hence the need for 'containment'. In the wake of the war in Vietnam a revisionist view has emerged that shifts the blame towards the USA and its need to open up and expand the world market for its goods. Of course, the processes from 1945 to 1948 that created the Cold War are much more complicated than either of these stereotyped views can cope with and a 'post-revisionist' school is struggling to emerge. For our purposes here, however, two points are important. First, concentration on the emergence of the Cold War has tended to devalue the role of Britain in the early post-war period. In 1945 the world was dominated by the 'Big Three' and Britain was still considered a major power. Secondly, the economic changes in the world-economy are treated as secondary phenomena compared with the 'great ideological clash' represented by the Cold War. In our discussion below we attempt to counter these two points by concentrating on Britain and its economic difficulties.

The geopolitical transition to Cold War

A geopolitical transition occurs when our picture of world politics is fundamentally changed: the old pattern of rivalries and alliances are no longer relevant and we enter a new geopolitical world order. This is precisely what happened in the decade from the late 1930s to the late 1940s (say from the Munich agreement of 1938 to the Berlin blockade of 1948). At the beginning of this decade world politics centred on a second German challenge to Britain's world leadership with neither the USA nor USSR party to the conflict. By the end of the decade Germany was politically defeated and Britain economically defeated leaving a completely new contest: USA leadership with USSR as the challenger. We had entered the new geopolitical world spatial order we call the Cold War.

The economic defeat of Britain is the least remembered element of this transition. In 1945 Britain was virtually bankrupt. The erstwhile hegemonic power had finally used up her global investments of the previous century and was now at the mercy of the new hegemonic power, the United States. US goodwill was expected but not forthcoming. By abruptly stopping the Lend-Lease programme in August 1945 and imposing severe conditions on the loan of December 1945, the USA was able formally to demote Britain into secondary economic status.

The United States' prime interest as the new hegemonic power was to create a liberal economic order throughout the world. The system of economic blocs of the 1930s had to be prised open and their markets made available for American business. The largest bloc was the British Empire and the sterling area. Hence the USA needed Britain's co-operation in its reconstruction of the world-economy. The loan conditions ensured this. Even Britain's chief economic negotiator, John Maynard Keynes, had doubts about the deal. In Parliament both Labour and Conservative MPs voted against, but the new Labour government had such a large majority that it was able to win the debate. The ending of imperial trading preferences and the convertability of sterling relegated Britain to number two status in the new American world.

Despite the support of Big Business in the USA the loan agreement with Britain was not given an easy passage through Congress. It was only when linked to an anti-Communist argument that enough support was forthcoming to win the debate (Kolko and Kolko, 1973). In early 1946 Cold War arguments were becoming popular in the USA just as the British loan was being ratified. In the event the conditions did prove too harsh: a run on the pound in 1947 set back the British economy and US plans for their new world. By then, however, the Cold War was nearly in place. The Truman Doctrine enunciated US support for resisting communist expansion and the Marshall Plan provided the economic arm of the new policy. British and west European reconstruction could now take place under American sponsorship as part of the defence against communism.

The deputy's demise

Britain emerged from the post-1945 settlement with the 'special relationship'. This always seemed to mean more to Britain than to the US. To some extent it was a face-saving formula to lessen the effect of Britain's political decline. But it was much more than that: Britain retained a global political role. America may have taken over the prime duties of world policeman but Britain remained an important deputy. Hence Britain retained armed forces east of Suez until the mid-1960s. In addition the new commitments of the army in what was to become West Germany ensured that the military drain on Britain's budget would continue long after the war ended. When this expenditure is added to the post-war domestic settlement – the welfare state – the money sums just do not add up.

Stephen Blank (1977) has argued that this is the root cause of Britain's relatively poor post-war economic performance. Other industrial countries without our overseas commitments were able to concentrate on their own economic growth in a way Britain was not. In contrast we suffered the famous 'stop-go' sequence of economic growth. Every short period of expansion was brought to an abrupt halt by the combined burden of our warfare and welfare states. The sequence finally ended with the 1967 devaluation of the pound in the biggest 'stop' of the post-war era. Troops were withdrawn from east of Suez and Britain finally settled for a future as a European rather than world power: the post-war international settlement had finally come to its logical conclusion.

Ironically the eclipse of Britain came just as its hegemonic successor was about to begin its own slow road to decline and the world-economy was entering a new B-phase of stagnation. Hence Britain's 'European adventure' of joining the European Community was to become quite disappointing as the Community was unable to sustain its earlier strong economic performance in the new world conditions: Britain had missed 'Europe's boom'.

In summary, we have argued that the emergence of US hegemony, as well as striking the death knell of the British Empire, had three consequences for Britain:

(a) the dependence of Britain's economy on the USA enabled the latter to produce a liberal world-economic order;

(b) Britain initially maintained a world role as 'US deputy' but this was to prove to be a massive economic liability;

(c) when the world role was finally unsustainable Britain reverted to a European role just as the world-economy turned into its stagnation phase.

Clearly the illusion of world power cost Britain dear in the post-1945 period. But such a grand foreign policy for what was only a medium power state was nevertheless a popular policy. That is the crucial symptom of post-hegemonic trauma.

1.6 Conclusion

The general premise upon which this chapter has been based is that you cannot understand any country in the modern world in isolation from its position within the capitalist world-economy. The specific premise that was developed is that you cannot understand Britain's century of decline apart from its legacy of hegemony. The struggle to remain a world power dominated British foreign policy and has even found echoes in the 1980s in the Falklands/Malvinas campaign. Using world-systems analysis we have provided a formal framework in which the events of Britain's decline can be explored.

References

ARRIGHI, G., HOPKINS, T. K. and WALLERSTEIN, I. (1983) 'Rethinking the concepts of class and status group in a world-system in perspective', *Review*, Vol. 6, pp. 283–304.

BLANK, S. (1977) 'Britain: the politics of foreign economic policy, the domestic economy, and the problem of pluralist stagnation', *International Organisation*, Vol. 31, pp. 673–722.

BRENNER, R. (1977) 'The origins of capitalist development: a critique of neo-Smithian Marxism', *New Left Review*, No. 104, pp. 25–92.

COX, R. W. (1983) 'Gramsci, hegemony and international relations', *Millenium*, Vol. 12, pp. 162–75.

FOSTER-CARTER, A. (1978) 'The modes of production controversy', *New Left Review*, No. 107, pp. 47–77.

KOLKO J. and KOLKO, G. (1973) *The Limits to Power*, New York, Harper and Row.

RESEARCH WORKING GROUP (1979) 'Cyclical rhythms and secular trends of the capitalist world-economy: some premises, hypotheses and questions', *Review*, Vol. 2, pp. 483–500.

TAYLOR, J. G. (1979) *From Modernisation to Modes of Production*, London and Basingstoke, Macmillan.

TAYLOR, P. J. (1985a) *Political Geography: World-economy, Nation-state and Locality*, London, Longman.

TAYLOR, P. J. (1985b) 'The world-systems project', in Johnston, R. J. and Taylor P. J. (eds), *World in Crisis*, Oxford, Basil Blackwell.

TAYLOR, P. J. (1986) 'An exploration into world-systems analysis of political parties', *Political Geography Quarterly*, Vol. 5 (Supplement), pp. 5–20.

TAYLOR, P. J. (1989a) 'Britain's changing role in the world-economy', in Mohan, J. (ed.), *The Political Geography of Contemporary Britain*, London and Basingstoke, Macmillan.

TAYLOR, P. J. (1989b) 'Extending the world of electoral geography', in Johnston, R. J., Shelley, F. M. and Taylor, P. J. (eds), *Developments in Electoral Geography*, London, Routledge and Kegan Paul.

WALLERSTEIN, I. (1979) *The Capitalist World-Economy*, Cambridge, Cambridge University Press.

WALLERSTEIN, I. (1983) *Historical Capitalism*, London, Verso.

WALLERSTEIN, I. (1984a) *The Politics of the World-Economy*, Cambridge, Cambridge University Press.

WALLERSTEIN, I. (1984b) 'Long waves as capitalist process', *Review*, Vol. 7, pp. 559–75.

(1986)

2 Britain in the post-war world

E. A. Brett

[. . .]Post-war British economic policy can be interpreted as an attempt to reconcile the consequences of three central and widely accepted commitments: to Keynesian social democracy as the basis for a stable compromise between capital and labour; to the full liberalization of trade and payments; and to an international political and economic role as junior partner of the USA in the stabilization of the world economy and the strengthening of the anti-communist military alliance. All of these involved important breaks with pre-war experience and the need to overcome internal opposition, but were effectively established as something close to a national consensus by the end of the first Labour government in 1951. Yet it is now clearly evident that they were neither mutually compatible nor in line with the country's diminished economic resources. The attempt to serve all of them, critically important, too, to the evolution of the liberal international order, was to disintegrate in the 1960s and 1970s and give rise to a fundamental crisis at the level of economic structures and political theory. The political battles of the last decade can all be traced to the consequences of this failure, a failure which has led the Conservative Party to attempt to rescue liberalism and the Atlantic Alliance at the expense of social democracy; the Labour Party to rescue social democracy at the expense of liberalization and military pre-eminence; and the Liberal/Social Democratic Alliance to attempt an uneasy compromise between Keynesianism, free trade and the weakening of trade union power. Each of these options involves a very different pattern of both domestic and international orientations than that which prevailed in the past, and has important consequences both for national development and for the structure of the international system. By looking at the way in which the original consensus emerged, was destroyed, and is now being restructured, we can provide an effective means of linking external and internal, political and economic factors in the evolution of the post-war capitalist system in a key industrial country.

We will attempt to do this through close examination of the relationship between domestic policies and the external constraint from 1945 to the present, trying to explain the crucial and usually negative impact of this relationship upon economic performance. This historical account will use a periodization derived from an identification of the major breaks which occurred in the building and then demolition of the consensus outlined in the previous paragraph. Four such periods have been identified:

1 the post-war reconstruction from 1945 to the outbreak of the Korean war in 1950, which created the social democratic framework but still forced the UK to operate with stringent internal and external controls;

2 the period of liberalization and centre currency status, but with diminishing success from 1951 to 1967;

3 the loss of centre currency status and intensified destabilization between 1967 and 1976;

4 the subsequent attempt, under 'monetarist' influences, to jettison the fundamentals of social democracy and find an orthodox solution to the crisis by accepting rising unemployment as the necessary precondition for the continued integration of the international capitalist economic order.

2.1 The social democratic foundations, 1945–1950[1]

The reconstruction period is often regarded as an important but somehow isolated episode in Britain's post-war economic development. In this view it is an abnormal period when old industries were rebuilt using emergency measures inherited from the war, measures which, having achieved their purpose, had inevitably to be discarded once 'normality' had been re-established. There is obviously some truth in this view, since the transition from war to peace necessarily demanded an altogether unusual degree of restructuring and gave those who managed it access to controls over economic allocation and personal freedom which was quickly done away with in the 1950s. But it also ignores much more important continuities between the 1930s and the 1940s and the whole post-war period which must be clarified if the period itself is to be adequately interpreted and, more importantly, its consequences for subsequent development properly understood.

In 1945 social democracy meant the central planning of domestic resources to ensure full employment, and a dramatic extension in the provision of health, education and social services. This meant a major break with the 1930s (though a continuation of important developments of the war itself) when direct controls had been of very limited importance in domestic economic management. But these objectives could only be achieved if they could be reconciled with a number of external obligations which could not be avoided and were likely to impose heavy additional burdens on the country's war-damaged productive capacity.

Firstly, Britain was still central to the sterling area made up of the dominions and colonies and now a substantial debtor to it. Here it obtained the bulk of its raw materials, found the main markets for its manufacturers, and sent the largest proportion of its foreign overseas investment. Secondly, and generating an important tension with the links with the sterling area, the war had produced a fundamental increase in dependence on the USA which had begun with lend-lease supplies of war materials, and had now to continue because of dependence on American finance and capital equipment for industrial reconstruction. Thirdly, as a leading element in the victorious alliance, Britain would be a major protagonist in the plans to rebuild western Europe and more especially in the administration and re-equipment of Germany, whose cities had been destroyed and whose population was on the verge of starvation. Finally, there was the threat of communist expansion created by Russian victories in eastern Europe which were quickly consolidated at the political level, and subsequent expansion in Asia, and notably in Korea at the end of the decade. It was to be the interaction between these external requirements (and most especially the need to come to terms with the Americans) and the internal commitment to the social democratic consensus that was to dominate policy-making during the period and will therefore provide us with our major focus.

While the interventionist domestic policy of the Labour government involved a sharp break with pre-war experience, its external orientation was far more consistent with both British and foreign practice. After a long and unsuccessful attempt to defend the liberal principles of its nineteenth-century heyday, Britain had capitulated to the protectionism of its major competitors in the early 1930s. In September 1931 the gold standard was abandoned and the pound depreciated by a total of 30 per cent before the end of the year. For the rest of the decade the exchange rate was deliberately managed by the Bank of England to maintain the external price competitiveness of British goods and to create the external conditions required to allow for an internal regime of low interest rates – of 'cheap money'. Then, six months later, in a second spectacular change in British policy, there followed 'the final abandonment of free trade in favour of a general tariff and imperial preference' (Arndt, 1944, p. 102).[2] Now this solution to the external problem imposed a very particular stamp upon British policy: direct controls were used to control trade with the non-sterling world (and especially the USA), but free trade remained within the sterling area, where it was assumed that the reciprocal needs of colonial and dominion raw material producers and British manufacturers would guarantee a mutually advantageous interaction combining the advantages of a global division of labour and a unified trading, monetary and financial structure.[3] During the war these arrangements were consolidated, which turned the sterling area into 'a closely integrated monetary association, almost a union', and subsequently made possible 'the post-war development of a dollar discriminatory club and a banker-customer relationship between Britain (with depleted reserves behind her) and her sterling associates' (Strange, 1971, p, 56).[4] At the end of the war this involved a banker with reserves of convertible currency and gold of £610 million, as against external liabilities (the 'sterling balances') of £3567 million, about two-thirds of which were held in the sterling area countries (Radcliffe Report, 1969, pp. 226–8). These represented 'in varying degrees a potential call on the reserves of the United Kingdom' (ibid., p. 227), and therefore served as a potentially serious constraint upon domestic policy-making.

Against this sphere of free trade, dealings between the whole sterling area and the USA were closely controlled and the supply of dollars to any user strictly rationed – in these circumstances the full convertibility of the pound into the dollar would involve not merely the loss of control over Britain's economic relations with the USA, but that of the rest of the sterling area as well. During the 1930s other leading industrial countries, and Nazi Germany in particular, had themselves established tightly controlled trading systems which were also sustained into the post-war period. In these circumstances foreign economic relations necessarily had to be based upon centrally negotiated bilateral arrangements, whatever the theoretical and ideological inclinations of the individual countries.

[The USA was committed to the liberalization of trade.] It is therefore easy to understand the broad orientation of their approach to the British problem; in addition to their general dislike of protectionism, their major exporters had always demonstrated a powerful dislike of the operation of the sterling area as a mechanism for the exclusion of their goods (see especially Kock, 1969). In order to gain access to American financial assistance, the British would have to come to terms with these views, as well as with the American desire to build a military wall around the Soviet Union and, later, China. The question which now has to be asked is whether these changes were to be compatible with the obligations to the sterling area and more especially to the maintenance of full employment and welfare spending.

What exactly were the problems? Critically, full employment required protection, because British industry could not compete on equal terms with American, so that many existing jobs would have been lost and new investment jeopardized without it. Furthermore, the resulting balance of payments deficit would have required deflationary policies designed to reduce domestic consumption, and this would have meant cuts in welfare spending. At the same time, however, rapid industrial development depended on access to the most modern capital equipment, only available from America and to be paid for in dollars. Thus access to these dollars was to be a key factor in economic policy-making, and the 'dollar shortage' arising out of the relative strength of American industry and that country's correspondingly large balance of trade surplus was the major constraint on the Labour government's freedom of action both at home and abroad. The solution to this problem was to have fundamental long-term political and economic consequences.

Two basic alternatives were canvassed at the time, one assuming that American credit could be secured to cover the whole deficit; the other that it should be overcome through an intensification of protectionism and the further extension of bilateral trading agreements to guarantee essential imports and external markets. The former position would inevitably involve coming to terms with the American commitment to trade liberalization; the latter could be seen as a continuation of the attempt at imperial self-sufficiency in the 1930s, but now associated with a socialist commitment to use it as a mechanism to escape the constraints which would otherwise inevitably be imposed upon the capacity to plan for domestic full employment. In the event, the liberal solution was to gain overwhelming support in Britain, as in the rest of the world, as we have seen. Let us now consider why this should have been so.[5]

This argument was presented with greatest coherence in a key memorandum prepared for the Cabinet by Keynes as adviser to the Treasury in April 1945 (Keynes, 1945).[6] He opened by noting that 'a prime objective of Treasury policy during the war had been to maintain a financial position which did not leave us hopelessly at the mercy of the United States', not in order to establish 'our own self-sufficiency, assisted by a chain of bilateral bargains with those countries which cannot afford to lose our markets' and the full severity 'of the present Sterling Area arrangements', but in order 'that in negotiation we should feel and appear sufficiently independent only to accept arrangements we deem acceptable' (p. 1). Keynes then set out at length the extent of actual external sterling liabilities and the continuing military and other official spending overseas, which he saw as 'wholly responsible for our financial difficulties' (p. 4). He argued that these would impose unacceptable levels of austerity on the population and 'our withdrawal, for the time being, from the position of a first-class Power in the outside world' (p. 9) if they had to be entirely covered from the country's own depleted financial and industrial resources. Most important, this would involve several years of 'rigid domestic controls and strict rationing of consumption, and with an organisation of foreign trade after the Russian model', an alternative 'certainly not compatible with the restoration of free enterprise', and which would be bound to lose the support of all but the very few countries 'prepared to denounce their commercial treaties with the United States and forgo all prospect of borrowing easy money from that country' (p. 1). Against this Keynes felt that an offer of credit from the USA, 'not so much generous as just' (p. 8), of $5 to $8 billion at 1 per cent repayable at 1 per cent a year for ten years after a ten-year grace period and 2 per cent thereafter, would enable them to meet all their internal needs and external commitments and, in the process, enable them to create the liberal financial conditions which would 'recover for London its ancient prestige and its hegemony' (p. 9). Thus an effective act of international redistribution designed to recreate the conditions for an integrated and open trading situation was here posed as the necessary alternative to the disintegration of the system into autarkic units.

The paper was prepared for the coalition government, but Keynes remained in office when Labour took over and fully accepted the strategy he had outlined. In the autumn of 1945 he was sent to Washington to negotiate the American loan on which so much depended, having argued in his paper the necessity of keeping alive the possibility of recourse to 'the disagreeable, indeed the disastrous [bilateralist] alternative' as the means of avoiding the necessity to accept excessively unfavourable terms (p. 8). Yet when Keynes reached Washington and began the negotiations he found the 'hostile forces' far stronger, and those 'of light and friendship' far weaker than he had expected. But having made so much of the negative consequences of self-sufficiency, he was unable to resist a series of dreary capitulations, well summarized by Dalton, then Chancellor of the Exchequer:

> So, as the talks went on, we retreated slowly and with bad grace and with increasing irritation, from a free gift to an interest free loan, and from this again to a loan bearing interest; from a larger to a smaller total of aid; and from the prospect of loose strings, some of which would be only general declarations of intention to the most unwilling acceptance of strings so tight they might strangle our trade and, indeed, our whole economic life. (Dalton, 1962, pp.74–5)

The loan only provided $3.75 billion at 2 per cent repayable over 50 years, starting in 1951, and involved a major concession on financial and trading policy by requiring full currency convertibility to come into force only a year after final ratification – in the event in June 1947. This seemingly technical requirement was of the utmost significance and was widely accepted, because it would make it impossible to protect the reserves through central controls since all foreign holders of sterling assets would immediately be free to convert them into dollars if they felt that they could meet their needs more effectively by buying in American than in British markets, as they almost inevitably would. To offset this the British would have to follow classic deflationary policies which would be bound to conflict with both full employment and welfare objectives.

Both Bevan and Shinwell opposed the loan in Cabinet, the latter correctly describing it as 'incompatible with the successful operation of a planned economy' (Cabinet Papers, CM(45)57, 29/11/35; Cab.218/4). But Keynes felt it was the only way of financing the government's domestic policy, and Dalton agreed that the otherwise inevitable increase in austerity and especially 'practically no smokes' would lead to 'sure defeat at the next election' (Dalton, 1962, p. 85). Access to the dollar loan also made it possible for Britain to maintain its commitments to the sterling area, despite American opposition, and with complex consequences which will be considered later.

In this regard, by providing the loan, and earlier help during the war itself, and by supplementing it with Marshall Aid after 1948, the USA had become, in Strange's words, 'the ultimate guarantor of the sterling area' (1971, p. 61), and of an area, moreover, committed to becoming an integral part of an emerging multilateral trading system, rather than a basis for imperial self-sufficiency as it had been before the war. Capitulation to American hegemony had been rapid and complete. In exchange for this support and for subsequent 'acts of financial and economic favouritism' the British gave American policy support which was even 'sometimes slavish and faintly ludicrous', and gave up the possibility of attempting to follow a more autonomous and self-sufficient line, with fundamental long-term consequences.

There was a good deal of opposition to this settlement both from the left, which believed that a bilateralist solution would have been possible, and from the old imperialist right of the Conservative Party, which had been responsible for the creation of imperial preference in the 1930s.[7] But it was passed in the Commons by 347 to 100, and signalled an important long-term commitment to liberalization and American dependence which has never been reversed or even threatened since then.

In the short-term this decision greatly eased the government's situation without appearing to require any fundamental shifts in its strategy. The additional resources enabled consumption, investment, contributions to European reconstruction and overseas defence to be reconciled without the need to make significant and politically difficult cuts. The Americans, despite widespread opposition to the 'socialist' experiment, did not apparently attempt to interfere too directly with internal policies, while external economic policy would only have to be modified in July 1947 when convertibility was to be enforced. The fact that the first two years of Labour rule are still widely seen as the most successful period of social democratic reformism in our recent history is a direct outcome of this situation.[8]

Yet the longer-term consequences, heavily disguised by a series of short-term problems which limited the impact of the original agreement, were to be far more serious. Two key elements need to be distinguished here: the extent to which American support served to underwrite Britain's overseas obligations and thus allowed them to be sustained at a level which could not be realistically maintained without undermining industrial and social investment, and the way in which it came to require an increasingly impossible reconciliation between domestic spending and production and an open foreign trading policy. The tensions involved in reconciling these conflicting objectives were to be clearly visible during the 1940s, though strongly moderated by the maintenance of war-time controls over both internal and external resource allocations. These controls were opposed by powerful elements in America, and were eventually allowed to survive with bad grace and because a major crisis was precipitated by the attempt to relax them. But even though they were directly responsible for the very considerable social and economic successes of the reconstruction period, they were increasingly seen by the Labour right and, more especially, by the Tories who were to succeed them, as a temporary and 'unnatural' expedient required to overcome the immediate effects of the war and to be replaced by a full acceptance of the American strategy as soon as possible.

If this argument is accepted, it then becomes possible to understand the events of the next thirty years as a process of gradual transition from centralized controls to liberalization backed by access to the American resources required to meet inevitable shortfalls which Britain's weakened position inevitably produced. This support turned Britain into a willing American client, while the resulting symbiosis allowed many short-term problems to be resolved with less sacrifice and stress than would otherwise have been necessary, but at the cost of creating conditions that were to guarantee a gradual decline into economic and political mediocrity, and the collapse of the system itself. Let us now look at a few of the key events in this depressing saga.

Firstly, the loan allowed Britain to take its place alongside the USA as a major supplier of the resources required to fund international economic recovery and defence against communism. Thus, while Keynes and Dalton were capitulating to the Americans to gain $3.75 billion and thus stave off an unacceptable austerity, the government was to spend almost $8 billion between 1946 and 1951 on overseas military and other programmes (Balogh, 1952). Secondly, with full employment and a desperate need for exports in a seller's market, domestic military spending also imposed a direct burden on both industrial reconstruction and the balance of payments. Yet in 1946 there were still more than 1200000 in the armed services and about 500000 in the supply industries, while expenditure 'still stood at . . . £1736 million, or one-fifth of the gross national product' (Bartlett, 1972, p. 12). After the 1947 crisis a half-hearted attempt was made to reduce spending and manpower, but the spending was still about £720000 in 1950, and Britain was still spending 'a higher proportion of her national income on defence (some 7%) than any other member of NATO' (ibid., p. 60), a proportion which was to increase dramatically a year later in response to the Korean war, as we shall see in the next section. As Bartlett points out, given the national commitment to an international role, 'only imminent national bankruptcy' would have led to a drastic reappraisal of these commitments, but the American loan and subsequent economic expedients 'made it possible for Britain to bear the heavy military burdens of a global power for many years to come' (ibid., p. 13). With Germany and Japan virtually debarred from any expenditure of this kind at all, it is hardly surprising that their levels of industrial and social expenditure soon greatly exceeded Britain's.

Thirdly, while the American loan eased the balance of payments constraint in 1946 and the first half of 1947, the enforced attempt to introduce convertibility in July, after a particularly severe winter, led to a major crisis. The drain on reserves which had been an average of $75 million per month in 1946, was $498 million in July 1947 and $650 million in the first twenty days of August, as sterling holders rushed to switch their money into dollars. Convertibility was suspended on 20 August and the full range of controls reintroduced. Because of these, and only because of them, the government did not have to fall back on the full range of deflationary measures which subsequent sterling crises were to impose on their successors, but the crisis did nevertheless require a fundamental reorientation in policy. The decision to nationalize steel was postponed in July in order to increase exports, in Bevan's view 'a negation of the principles of the party' (Cabinet Minutes, CM66(47), 31/7/47; Cab.128/10). Cripps then took over at the Treasury and introduced what he called a 'disinflationary' policy involving a cut in social services, a rise in interest rates and curbs in capital investment in sectors which were thought to be less important than others in the reduction of the dollar gap (United Kingdom, 1948). Wage and dividend restraint was also introduced with TUC backing, which led to a decline in the real wage by 1950 (Worswick, 1962), and the Chiefs of Staff were forced to accept that defence spending would be cut to less than £700 million in 1948 (Bartlett, 1972, p. 24).

Yet despite the strong similarities with subsequent deflations, the return to managed trade made its effects very different. The maintenance of the full array of external and internal controls made it possible for the reduction in consumption to be associated with full employment and a substantial expansion in investment and output. Disinflation, as opposed to deflation, made it possible to plan 'a comprehensive export programme' involving 'allocations, supplies, shipping, fuel and power, and labour being guided to the industries and firms of greatest need in the attainment of their targets' (Cooke, 1957, pp. 361–2). Full employment was sustained, domestic capital formation increased from £2.1 billion in 1948 to £2.5 billion in 1950, while the balance of payments assisted by the 1949 devaluation from $4 to $2.80, was in comfortable surplus and industrial production grew by 7–8 per cent each year, a level which has never been sustained since. Despite the excessive burden of defence, an economic performance was achieved which closely matched the best in Europe for the only time in the post-war period.

> Figures compiled for the Economic Survey of Europe show that during 1947–50 the United Kingdom increase of 29% in industrial production much exceeded that of Sweden and Belgium, and was slightly more than that of Italy and Denmark, but rather less than that of France and Norway, which reached 31%. During 1950–56, however, the British percentage increase slipped back to 21, while Sweden rose 10 points to 27, France 18 points to 49, Belgium 23 points to 36, and Italy more than doubled its increase to 63; Germany, a unique case, actually doubled total production, in these years of European recovery from which Britain opted out. (Nicholson, 1967, p. 313)[9]

Without the crisis created by convertibility, the huge reserve losses of July/August (almost a third of the original loan) would have been avoided. And although subsequent American Marshall Aid disbursements, starting in 1948, served to ease the situation, the need for them was in large part accounted for by these losses. Indeed, the favourable balance of payments stemming from the Cripps programme 'led Britain to announce that it would be able to dispense, ahead of schedule, with Marshall Aid' (Strange, 1971, p. 64). Had orthodox deflationary policies been tried without the re-imposition of direct controls, however, the recovery would almost certainly have collapsed, as it did soon after the First World War with devastating consequences for both the British and the world economy.

Fourthly, American assistance allowed the sterling area to continue, initially as an exclusive club of the old kind, but only on the understanding that the relationships involved would give way to full multilateralism as soon as possible. The effects of this intervention were to be complex and ambiguous, but undoubtedly a significant element in the long-term tendency to British decline. In 1945, far from being a source of strength, the sterling area involved major liabilities for Britain in the form of its indebtedness to its members accumulated during the war and totalling £3567 million in 1945 (Radcliffe Report, 1962, p. 228), four times the size of the eventual American loan. Most of the money was owed to the very poor Third World countries, particularly India, Egypt and the colonies. One solution to the balance of payments problem might therefore have been a full or partial repudiation of these debts, although this would inevitably have involved strong political opposition in the countries concerned and made it almost impossible for the old relationship of trust between Britain as central banker and the rest as willing depositors to have been maintained. Keynes himself recommended that some £880 million of these debts be cancelled (£500 million belonging to India), and that a further £1500 million be funded on terms which would be little short of outright cancellation (Keynes, 1945, p. 14). In the loan negotiations the Americans, too, wanted 'a drastic scaling down' of the balances (Gardner, 1956, p. 205), recognizing that if this occurred the possibility of an effective transition to convertibility would be greatly eased. In their view 'total releases to sterling area countries in 1946–50 would be limited to £200–250 million . . . [and] would be offset by equivalent contribution from the overseas sterling area and thus would involve no net drain on the reserves' (ibid., p. 326). At the time they assumed that the British had accepted this general principle at least, and that by repudiating these debts would no longer require external monetary controls in order to sustain its international position. Thus their assumption that convertibility could be established without serious problems in 1947 depended on their belief that Britain had been persuaded to repudiate a large proportion of its debts to some of the poorest countries in the world. The poorest were, yet again, to be asked to pay the price required to create the preconditions for the establishment of capitalist freedom.

The British certainly gave the impression that they had accepted this general principle (Strange, 1971, p. 60),[10] but in the event, and to their credit, ultimately failed to do so. According to Gardner, the desire to maintain their banking reputation, to ensure that sterling balances be used to finance British exports, and to ease the transition to independence in India, outweighed the immediate advantages of renegotiation (Gardner, 1956, pp. 326–7). This failure was entirely inconsistent with the commitment to convertibility, as we have seen, since sterling holders rapidly used their new freedom to switch their resources out of sterling into dollars so rapidly that the former controls had to be re-introduced and tightened up. The sterling balances had indeed proved 'a major obstacle to multilateral trade' (ibid., p. 327), as the Americans had anticipated, and a crucial element in forcing the British government to continue with its regime of close central controls.

The result of the 1947 crisis was 'closer co-operation among members of the sterling area' (Patterson, 1966, p. 70) and its survival as an organization based upon direct discrimination against American exports, the principle that the Americans were most concerned to destroy. Yet, paradoxically, it was only the access to American credit in 1945, and again after 1948 with Marshall Aid, that enabled Britain to treat the sterling balances as favourably as it did. The original obligations were run down gradually on the basis of arrangements which certainly favoured Britain and depended in large measure on the enforcement of very conservative economic policies in the colonies, which turned them into the major suppliers of dollars to the central pool (Strange, 1971, p. 67). Meanwhile, it was Marshall Aid and subsequent support to Britain under the NATO Mutual Aid Agreement that continued to underpin a system which the British economy itself was no longer powerful enough to guarantee. Yet before we make too much of this American generosity, it is important to recognize its source. We have already seen that a major part of Britain's weakness stemmed from its excessive spending on defence, both domestic and overseas. The only way in which Britain could have met its sterling obligations and sustained full employment would have been through a reduction in these to a level of its European rivals, and this would have been seen as a direct threat to the anti-communist alliance. Thus Strange is quite right in arguing that this support 'was a reflection of the American political interest in building a world-wide alliance system, first in Europe and then, after Korea, in Asia' (ibid., p. 62). It was because Britain was prepared to make so many debilitating sacrifices in this area, and because they had conceded that the controls over sterling would eventually be removed, that the Americans were prepared to provide it with this temporary support.

While the maintenance of the controls around the sterling area were crucial to the success of reconstruction, as we have seen, the willingness to allow it to operate in the particular form in which it did was nevertheless to have very damaging longer-term consequences. Firstly, it greatly encouraged a very large outflow of capital, and more especially of private capital, since no limits were imposed on these flows within the area, although they were only permitted for designated projects outside it. Thus £910 million of private investment went into the sterling area between 1946 and 1951, and a further £380 million into the rest of the world (Radcliffe Report, 1969, p. 264). Combined with overseas public investment of £345 million (£86 million to the sterling area) we thus discover a further leakage of £1635 million to support 'first-class power' status and the 'ancient prestige and hegemony' of London after financial and political independence had been sold to the Americans for far less. There can be little doubt that this leakage was an important element in the lower levels of investment in

Britain than in European and Japanese industry which began in the 1940s and became much worse later on. While British private capital now followed closely behind American in building up the multinational system, its future rivals in the rest of the industrial world were financing the productivity gains which were soon to alter the balance of economic power decisively in their favour. There can be little doubt that Shonfield (1959)[11] was quite correct in identifying this as a major source of British weakness which has yet to be overcome.

Secondly, the successful operation of the sterling area itself depended on the extent to which all the countries involved maintained a viable balance of payments relationship with the external world, and especially with the dollar area. Although their policies could be strongly influenced, they could not be controlled, so that the possibility always existed that a poor performance by Britain or by a combination of countries within the system could threaten a fall in reserves and, especially after payments had been liberalized in the 1950s, a run on sterling. Since the exchange rate was fixed (and was subsequently to become increasingly overhauled) the only defence against these pressures was an attempt to keep Britain in continuous surplus and the readiness to push up interest rates at the first sign of any difficulties. Both implied very cautious economic policies with a powerful tendency to discourage investment and hence inhibit growth. This problem only really manifested itself in an extreme form during the 1947 crisis during reconstruction, but was to become the root cause of the 'stop-go' cycle which was to become the dominant feature of the 1950s and 1960s.

Thirdly, and with far less persuasiveness, it has been argued that the lack of innovativeness in British industry can be attributed in large part to its access to protected markets in the Empire, of which the post-war sterling area was a continuation (see, for example, Walker, 1980). Now although it is very likely that a good many incompetent producers survived who would otherwise have failed as a result of their protected access, this argument leaves aside a number of crucial facts. Before the war protectionism was widespread and closely correlated with economic success, not just in Britain, but also outside, while major gains over Britain in Europe and Japan were made as Britain reduced its external controls and these other countries maintained them. Furthermore, it ignores the losses that would have been incurred with the collapse of weaker firms in a situation where high interest rates, a tight labour market and a shortage of capital equipment stemming from the commitments to defence spending and capital outflows made it almost impossible for British firms to match their foreign competitors. Without the modification of these far more significant policies, the removal of the few advantages gained in protective markets would have destroyed the least efficient without creating the resources to put anything better in its place – the direct outcome, as we shall see, of subsequent attempts to force British industry to modernize by exposing it directly to the bracing winds of foreign competition.

Having looked at reconstruction in some detail because of its significance in establishing a general pattern for the future, it should be possible to deal with subsequent developments rather more quickly. But before doing so it is important that we re-emphasize the essential ambiguity of that experience and more especially its very positive achievements. Whatever the long-term capitulation to liberal principles, the contingencies of the immediate situation forced the Labour government to plan both for domestic full employment and external balance, and provided them with mechanisms of central control which made it possible for them to sustain their momentum despite conditions which were far less favourable than those which have confronted their successors. An important shift in the balance of power between capital and labour did take place during these years, creating a legacy of full employment and welfare which was to be a major source of strength to the working class later and is only now being systematically dismantled. Although it is also essential to stress that a series of capitulations to capitalist orthodoxy mainly in the fields of foreign defence and economic policy also took place, which were themselves to become a crucial element in the processes which were eventually to destroy both that internal balance of power and the country's external strength, it is important that we should not lose sight of the fact that it was the use of methods entirely opposed to the teachings of neoclassical orthodoxy that allowed these achievements to be sustained. For it is now widely assumed that it has been the liberalization of the trading system which created the basis for the long boom, but what the British experience makes clear, and was equally the case elsewhere, is that the stability and continuity of the first and most critical phase was entirely dependent on the use of interventionist methods that were entirely alien to the principles of economic orthodoxy.[12]

2.2 The contradictions of liberalization, 1951–1968

The period from the Korean war to the Basle Agreement on sterling spans the golden years of the long boom funded by the American deficit and characterized by entirely unprecedented rates of growth in the world economy. It also spans the decisive move from protectionism to liberalization through convertibility at the end of the 1950s, the completion of the Kennedy Round of tariff reductions in the 1960s, and the establishment of the European Economic Community (EEC) and the European Free Trade Association (EFTA). It ends with the emergence of clear evidence that the underlying basis of the Bretton Woods system was seriously threatened by the British devaluation of 1967, the intensification of the Vietnam war and the establishment of the two-tier gold market in 1968.

The chief concern in this chapter, however, is not with the successes in the most successful industrial countries, but with the relative failure of the British economy to keep pace – failure which was to turn it into a chronic deficit country by the early 1960s and thus a significant threat to the integrity of the structures which sustained the liberal international economic system. We shall attempt now to demonstrate that it was primarily the incompatibility between domestic and external commitments which pro-
luced both the inadequacies in economic performance and its inevitable
ınd disastrous external consequence. Only the most central features of the
ɔeriod will be dealt with here; further substantiation of the argument can
ɔe found in the powerful accounts provided in the works of Strange (1971)
ınd Pollard (1969, Ch. 8).

During these years the dominant feature is a sharp alternation between
ɔeriods when growth almost reached that of European levels, and those
vhen it fell far short. Thus in the nine fat years between 1950 and 1951,
953 and 1955, 1959 and 1960, and 1963 and 1964, growth was more than 4
ɔer cent. During the remaining years it was not much above 1 per cent,
ɔroducing the overall average which left Britain bottom of the European
eague. We have to understand, therefore, what it was about British
xperience that made it impossible to sustain these bursts of expansion
vithout the need for equal periods of drastic and damaging retrenchment.
'he general arguments will be reviewed in the final section of the chapter;
here we will attempt to look briefly at the conditions that precipitated each
hase of deflationary policy. In each case there can be no doubt that
xternal commitments and pressures were the major factor, with the
problem of economic management continually intensifying as external
ontrols came to be progressively loosened.

Between 1947 and 1950 cuts in defence expenditure, devaluation and
external controls had sustained rapid growth and balance of payments
quilibrium; the Korean war produced an immediate regression. Respond-
ıg to American demands,[13] a huge re-armament programme was im-
ıediately announced involving an expenditure programme of £4700
ıillion over three years, after it had fallen to £750 million in 1949, the
diversion of a large percentage of scarce heavy manufacturing and research
apacity into the defence industries, and cuts in social services.[14] The
ɔrresponding expansion in imports and contraction in exports, together
ith rising raw material prices and deficits in many sterling area countries,
roduced an inevitable balance of payments crisis. Deflation was inevit-
ble, and as a result manufacturing production fell by almost 3 per cent and
NP by more than 1 per cent in 1952. Thus the first major break in
ost-war growth had been consciously engineered to enable the country to
ıeet external demands far in excess of those imposed on any of its major
ɔmpetitors. In the early 1950s British arms production 'exceeded that of
ll her European NATO partners combined', and was 'contributing more
ıan 40% to the total defence spending of the European members of
ATO' (Bartlett, 1972, pp. 64–5).

In 1953, however, the balance of payments pressures eased and expansion again became possible. Raw material prices had fallen and the world economy was expanding so that it became possible to sustain increased defence expenditure and investment while simultaneously beginning a drastic reduction in both external and internal controls. The balance of payments on current account remained in surplus in 1953 and 1954, but without creating a margin sufficient to build up the reserves. In 1955 it was again in deficit and, when the overall figures which include both current account and long-term capital movement are considered, it becomes clear that there had been small deficits in 1953 and 1954 as well.[15] Hence the end of 1955 saw the beginning of a new deflation, but now with the need for a much stronger use of deflationary monetary policy because of the lifting of controls, as Worswick makes clear.[16] The Suez war in 1956, while having a limited effect on the real economy, nevertheless produced sharp movements out of sterling as speculators attempted to defend against a possible devaluation, and this, too, intensified the need for high interest rates. Despite the resulting losses, with growth rates forced down to pre-war levels, in 1958 'the pressure from the City ensured that the final reckless step was taken of making sterling wholly convertible, so that the economy, which was already in imbalance of a long-term lending programme it could not sustain, had to carry the further strain of short-term lending also' (Pollard, 1969, p. 454).

Even leaving aside the negative impact of the increases in defence expenditure on exports, the break in 1955 can be wholly attributed to the negative outflows of private and government capital and of overseas defence. The total deficit on current and capital account was £400 million between 1953 and 1955, while private foreign investment totalled £900 million and government defence and other spending £335 billion; between 1956 and 1958 there was an overall surplus of £300 million, compared with private outflows of £1663 million and official outflows of £538 million.[17] As if this were not sufficient, the country's position as chief of sterling led the Treasury to believe that they should not merely aim to maintain an overall equilibrium, but a substantial surplus designed to build up the reserves to a point where they would be sufficient to deal with external threats to the reserves. This surplus was put at £300–£350 million in the mid-1950s, and £450 million by 1959,[18] figures which necessarily required extreme caution in economic policy-making since the underlying strength of the economy was not such that they could be achieved without cutting back on domestic consumption and investment. As the Treasury itself put it, the 'facts of the external position necessarily limit our freedom in our general economic policies, including monetary policy', and any failure to meet external targets 'even by small amounts, can have disproportionate effects on the whole economy'. As a result, on no account should they 'take risks in the management of the domestic economy of a kind that affect the balance of payments' (Treasury evidence to the Radcliffe Committee, p. 118).

Operating within this highly restrictive framework, it is not surprising that two years of expansion in 1959 and 1960 were followed by two more years of retrenchment in 1961 and 1962, when yet another external deficit led to the usual response of rising interest rates, spending cuts and a wage freeze. By this time it had become evident to at least some that the country was falling behind internationally at an alarming rate, and a token commitment to planning on French lines was introduced, presumably on the assumption that the problem could be solved through a more rational use of resources. But nothing was done to eliminate the major outflows of private and public resources, with private overseas investment totalling £719 million and military spending and other government spending £896 million in 1963 and 1964 alone (Tew, 1979).

The constraints on investment of the previous dozen years now meant that insufficient capacity existed to meet the increased output sought by the expansionary programme designed by Maudling in 1962 and implemented in 1963 and 1964, so that imports of basic materials and of manufactured goods increased much faster than exports.[19] The result was a dramatic worsening in the balance of payments in 1964, and a legacy to the incoming Labour government which was to 'dominate almost every action of the Government for five years of the five years, eight months [it] was in office' (Wilson, 1971, p. 5).

The Wilson government was directly committed to the solution of the long-term problem of relative economic decline, and of the underinvestment in public sector infrastructure which the periodic bouts of spending cuts had inevitably introduced. Yet it was entirely unprepared for the constraints which the problem of the weakness of sterling imposed on it, as is shown by Wilson's own account of his dealings with the Governor of the Bank of England in the context of the major sterling crisis which greeted his arrival as Prime Minister. By 24 November the Governor,

> Claiming that our failure to act in accordance with his advice had precipitated the [sterling] crisis, he was now demanding allround cuts in expenditure, regardless of social or even economic priorities, and fundamental changes in some of the Chancellor's economic announcements.
>
> Not for the first time I said that we had now reached the situation where a newly elected government with a mandate from the people was being told, not so much by the Bank of England but by international speculators, that the policies on which we had fought the election could not be implemented; that this government was to be forced into the adoption of Tory policies to which it was fundamentally opposed. The Governor confirmed that this was, in fact, the case.
>
> I asked him if this meant that it was impossible for any Government whatever its party label, whatever its manifesto or the policies on which it fought an election, to continue, unless it immediately reverted to full-scale Tory policies. He had to admit that was what his argument meant, because of the sheer compulsion of the economic dictation of those who exercised decisive economic power. (Wilson, 1971, p. 37)

At this point Wilson insisted that he would not accept this diagnosis, because to do so would be 'to bring down the curtain on parliamentary democracy' (ibid.), and put the control of policy into the hands of foreigners. Threatened with the possibility of a major intensification of the crisis and a threat to the exchange rate, the Governor then had recourse to swap arrangements negotiated under the General Arrangements to Borrow (GAB) established in 1962, and borrowed £3000 billions from the central bankers, thus defusing the speculative pressures (ibid., 1971, p. 38).[20]

For Wilson this was a triumphant assertion of the autonomy of his national government and presumably of the sovereignty of Parliament, but his optimism was misplaced. This easy access to foreign credit enabled the government to finance a greater programme of public spending than would have been possible otherwise, but by the middle of 1965 the underlying deficit was still there, together with far more insistent pressures from the bankers whose direct control had been greatly increased because of the money they had lent. Thus we find the usual policies of high interest rates and credit controls over consumption and private construction, and the formulation of an incomes policy on the basis of 'considerable communication between London and Washington at various levels', and 'including intensive talks between the heads of the two central banks' (Solomon, 1977, p. 90).[21]

What the bankers had actually done by putting together this package was to make it possible for the exchange rate to be held at a level that was no longer viable, given the damage which the economy had suffered as a result of the lost years of the 1950s and early 1960s. Entirely failing to recognize the negative effects of overseas leakages and never stopping even to consider the re-imposition of direct controls, all the weight had to be placed on a classic deflation – the 'Tory' policies which the electorate had rejected in electing him to office. Thus Bacon and Eltis note that the National Plan put forward by the newly created Department of Economic Affairs at the end of 1965 might have created the basis for a sustained expansion, provided that there was a devaluation. But this was strongly resisted by Wilson, who appears to have assumed that the whole problem was created by the greed and malice of external speculators, and by the establishment of the Treasury, Bank of England and the City more concerned with the country's external obligations and earnings than with industrial development and full employment. As a result,

> There were severe expenditure cuts and no devaluation. Expansion therefore ceased, the National Plan was abandoned, and nothing was done to make it possible for the spare resources released to go to exports where they could lay the foundation for the future. (Bacon and Eltis, 1978, pp. 50–1)

The contrast with the experience under Cripps, when effective measures to control the external balance were immediately adopted and investment actually increased, could not have been clearer. From this point onwards policy was again to be entirely restrictive until a surplus had been restored in 1969. A major opportunity had been lost. One can hardly disagree with

Bacon and Eltis, who claim that 'this was to prove the decisive turning point after which the structure of the United Kingdom economy deteriorated almost without interruption' (ibid., p. 51), although one would want to argue that rather more than a simple devaluation would have been necessary to produce a fundamental change of the kind envisaged in the Plan.

Yet this victory of the establishment was also to prove the last gasp of the old order. The underlying weakness that their policies had created was now so extreme that the old commitments to sterling and international policing had to be drastically revised. In November 1967 the immense pressure of speculation finally forced a devaluation and recourse to the IMF. The resulting policy negotiated with the IMF entirely foreclosed all possibilities of expansion and social betterment. The democratic will of Parliament now clearly counted for much less than the requirements of the country's creditors[22] and Wilson and Jenkins, the new Chancellor, had to cut investment and public services, enforce wage policies and, in 1968, even attempt to introduce legal penalties for certain forms of industrial action, thus breaking the most powerful of the understandings which united the trade union and constituency elements in the Labour Party. This time, however, the damage was even worse than before, since the 'stop' phase of the old cycle had to be extended further than ever, and an ominous growth in unemployment also emerged for the first time. As a result of these policies Beckerman argues:

> the 'go' phase of what would normally have been a 'stop-go' cycle beginning with the 'stop' of 1966/7 never materialised; the economy stayed in the 'stop' position. By 1970 output was over 2% below the trend level, and the trend rate of growth itself had no doubt been depressed by the sluggish growth of output over the whole period and the gradual slackening of the pressure of demand. And the average unemployment rate over the years 1967 to 1969 inclusive (2.5% for the UK) was higher than any previous consecutive three-year period. (1972, p. 58)

Although not everyone could see it, this clearly demonstrated the impossibility of a stable association between Keynesian social democracy and liberal external policies in a country attempting to sustain Britain's overseas commitments. Externally again, the devaluation of the pound was the first step in the process which soon was to lead to the collapse of the dollar and of the Bretton Woods agreement. More directly, devaluation meant considerable losses to overseas holders of sterling balances, who rapidly made it clear that they would move into other currencies unless steps were taken to safeguard their position from a repetition. As a result, the 'Basle Agreement' was negotiated in 1968, under which Britain agreed to sustain the dollar value of the sterling deposits in the event of another devaluation, in exchange for a 'standby credit to Britain of $2 billion to be repaid within ten years' (Strange, 1971, p. 74).[23] Although this still left Britain with the prime responsibility, it now made it clear that its old role as sole guardian for the monetary stability of the former British Empire had passed for ever. Finally, the spending cuts of this period also involved a serious review of defence spending, with a firm commitment to withdraw all troops east of Suez, and an acceptance that Britain's role would henceforth 'be concentrated mainly in Europe and the North Atlantic area' (Blackaby, 1979, p. 323). Spending continued at levels which were far higher than most of the leading countries, but Britain no longer foresaw a permanent defensive role in the Third World – a fundamental break with the imperial past.

These changes add up to a major shift in the country's international role and in the mechanisms which sustained it, but one which was made only after the damage to the underlying structures that had put Britain ahead of its major overseas rivals had been done. The cumulative effect of the inability to reconcile growth with external balance, and the damage it inflicted, comes out very clearly in Table 2.1.

Table 2.1

	Annual growth in UK industrial production (%)	UK balance of payments current account (£1m)	UK current account (ecluding govt invisibles) (£1m)
1953–55 expansion	5.6	+145 to −155	+211 to − 17
1955–58 stagnation	0.4	−155 to −336	− 17 to +555
1958–60 expansion	6.2	+336 to −275	+555 to + 8
1960–62 stagnation	1.1	−275 to +101	+ 8 to +462
1962–64 stagnation	5.6	+101 to −393	+462 to + 40
1964–66 stagnation	1.5	−393 to − 61	+ 40 to +411

Source: *The British Economy, Key Statistics, 1900–66*, published by *The Times* for the London and Cambridge Economic Service

Here we can see the direct connection between deficits, deflation and industrial decline, together with a long-term tendency for the deficit to worsen in each cycle.[24] By 1967 the strain had become too much, and the first steps were taken to change the way in which the system worked. But nothing could replace the investment lost during the wasted years, and the response was to be both too little and too late.

2.3 Disintegration, 1969–1976

The failures of the 1950s and mid-1960s had occurred in the context of the international boom fuelled by the dollar (and to a far smaller but still significant extent) pound deficit, and defended by the international military alliance to which Britain had made an entirely disproportionate contribution. The policy response to the 1967 crisis marked a decisive break in Britain's post-war development, involving as it did the effective surrender of the third of the policy commitments outlined at the beginning of this chapter – the maintenance of a central role alongside the USA in the management of the international economic and security system. It is perhaps not surprising, therefore, that this decline in international pretensions directly paralleled the country's uneasy relations with Europe. Rejecting membership of the EEC in the 1950s when it might have been a major element both politically and economically, Britain attempted to create a leadership role for itself in the European periphery through EFTA. Having failed, and beginning to recognize its increased international vulnerability, it attempted to negotiate entry during the 1960s, but was rejected twice on the probably valid grounds that its external commitments to the sterling area and the USA were too strong. By the early 1970s, however, these obstacles were no longer seen to be significant, and the country was finally drawn back into a union which was to ensure, for the first time for centuries, that its relationships with its nearest neighbours were to become far closer than those with its dependencies beyond the seas, a change involving not merely a geographical shift, but a fundamental switch in the terms on which these relations were to be conducted. The end of the Empire was finally at hand.

Equally important as this transformation in national status was the break in the dynamism and stability of the international economic order that was also to become visible at the end of the 1960s, of which, indeed, the sterling devaluation was itself an early sign. At the point when Britain was attempting to make a new and more self-sufficient strategy for growth, the external conditions required to make this possible were becoming dramatically less favourable as the long boom began to give way to the oncoming long recession. In the earlier period, the phases of deflation could always be followed by equally extensive phases of growth, because overseas demand was still buoyant enough to absorb even the high-cost products of British industry. As a result, deflation did not require the sacrifice of the commitment to the welfare state, full employment, complete legal freedom for the trade union movement and continuously rising wages. The commitments, together with the assumption that each period of deflation would be the last, were the fundamental basis of the compromise between capital and labour which sustained the liberal social democratic state system.

But as the international recession began to intensify, these possibilities were to disappear progressively. Competition intensified in domestic and foreign markets (and, indeed, with monetary reforms and tariff reductions, the distinction between these markets itself became increasingly unimportant), British goods were increasingly pushed into a no-man's land between the high technology output of the advanced countries and the low-wage output of the newly industrializing countries, the rate of profit fell precipitously,[25] and this in turn further inhibited the investment on which future progress depended.

Thus it is also evident that the end of the 1960s marked a significant shift in the way in which Britain's international problems related [. . .] to global economic management and uneven development. From 1945 to 1968, as we have seen, the key problems arose out of a misguided attempt to play a central managerial role, and the failure documented in the preceding sections must therefore be read as a further extension of the inherently contradictory implications of any purely national attempt at this role already explored in relation to the decline of the USA over the same period. But during these years, although British resources were poor by comparison with the USA, they were substantial by comparison with all of its other competitors, so that Britain was not having to overcome the inherent problems confronting a weak country attempting to establish its position in the face of the superior competitiveness of a strong one – the problems, in other words, of uneven development. By the end of the 1960s, however, it had been overtaken by its major competitors in Europe and Japan and had now to attempt to match their levels of performance in an international market-place from which almost all protective barriers and special privileges had been eliminated. Stripped bare of its former advantages and unwilling to concede that it would be unable to meet this challenge without external aids, British industry inevitably failed in this attempt, which generated not only a further phase of accelerated economic decline, but the destruction of the social democratic consensus and its Keynesian theoretical underpinning.

The nine years separating the devaluation of 1967 from the IMF intervention at the end of 1976 were marked by a series of vacillations in policy which culminated in the final demise of the liberal Keynesian thinking that had dominated the post-war period. Repudiation of these policies in response to external deficits gave way to attempts to restore them in order to regain the political support which they guarantee with the mass electorate, but these in turn proved to be incompatible with the economic viability of the national industrial base. The events of these years finally demonstrated that the basis for the old compromises between the social Toryism of Macmillan's *The Middle Way*, and the right-wing reformism of Crosland's *The Future of Socialism* no longer existed, with fundamental political and economic consequences both at home and abroad.

Thus the Wilson/Jenkins strategy in 1968 and 1969 involved a significant repudiation of many of the elements of the old position, notably a direct attack on the industrial working class and on welfare services. The latter suffered substantial cuts in the economic programme negotiated with the IMF in November 1967. The former suffered under the impact of record increases in unemployment (from 1.4 per cent in 1965 to 2.6 per cent in 1970), the imposition of a wages policy, which reduced real earnings and an attempt to introduce legal controls over the right to organize and strike. Thus while in the 1940s planning was based on the manipulation of the foreign balance in order to sustain full employment and welfare, in the late

1960s employment and welfare were being adjusted downwards to the point where the external balance could be sustained.

Needless to say, this change involved a massive loss of political support and caused deep strains within the Labour Party. Having established the surplus at the end of 1969, the government attempted to begin a new expansion designed to make good the losses, using this as the basis for the appeal to the electorate in the middle of 1970. But the political damage had been too great, and the Conservatives took over, a clear demonstration of the organic connections between political and economic variables and between foreign and domestic requirements.

In opposition the Tory party had responded to the evident inability of the old social democratic strategy to solve the economic problem or to sustain political support by calling for a return to traditional free market policies. Their programme committed them to the encouragement of competition, the elimination of subsidies to inefficient industries, the abolition of interventionist agencies set up by Labour, such as the Industrial Reorganisation Corporation, and the system of regional grants, and the restoration of free collective bargaining. To ensure that the latter was not to be exploited by the best organized workers, they introduced the Industrial Relations Act, which was designed to impose legal controls on union organization and industrial action. Externally they had inherited a substantial surplus, and therefore did not anticipate immediate difficulties. In the longer term, however, they assumed that the problem could be taken care of on purely liberal principles – accession to the EEC (finalized in 1973) to give free access to a very large and expanding market, and, after 1972, the adoption of a freely floating exchange rate to take care of external price competitiveness. This decision, combined with the imposition of the same controls on private overseas capital investment in the sterling area as had previously operated in the rest of the world, finally terminated the attempt to sustain centre country status.[26]

But this strategy, too, was to be fraught with contradiction. The return to free collective bargaining was followed by a dramatic increase in wage settlements and industrial disputes, which the Industrial Relations Act proved unable to resolve. Thus wage increases averaged 4.9 per cent per annum and days lost through industrial disputes totalled 3.7 million between 1964 and 1969; these had increased to 12.6 per cent and 13.9 million between 1970 and 1973 (calculated from Prest and Coppock, 1980, p. 45). Productivity increases remained far behind wage increases, and manufacturing continued to fall, at 20 per cent in 1968, 16.7 per cent in 1970, 17.2 per cent in 1972, 14.9 per cent in 1973 and 6.3 per cent in 1974 (Brown and Sheriff, 1978, p. 251).[27] In the early years the pressure on profits could be offset to some extent by reflation and, more importantly, an inflationary increase in prices, since the balance of payments constraint had been loosened. But, with an increasingly open economy this merely increased import penetration, which involved an increase in the share of the domestic market for manufacturers from 13 per cent in 1970 to 19 per cent in 1974 (Blackaby, 1978, pp. 11, 244). The pressure on marginal companies intensified, and the withdrawal of subsidies threatened some major bankruptcies and the actual collapse of Upper Clyde Shipbuilders and Rolls-Royce. Responding to the threat of industrial militancy and unacceptable increases in unemployment, a retreat was soon organized involving a restoration of direct assistance.

From 1972, the desire to push up the growth rate became overwhelming, and demand was allowed to expand rapidly. The corresponding increase in wage inflation and threat to profits and the external balance produced a reversal on wage policy, leading to compulsory controls over both wages and prices. Furthermore, while it was assumed in 1972 that devaluation would take care of the external balance, it failed to do so. By the first half of 1973, assisted by a dramatic increase in the export of private capital (£501 million in 1970, £1272 million in 1972, £2073 million in 1973 (Blackaby, 1979, p. 327)) it had begun to reach unsustainable levels; by the end of the year, greatly worsened by the escalation in oil and other raw material prices, it was out of control. The year 1973 saw what was probably the last attempt at an old-fashioned Keynesian reflation, with full employment and an open border. After the longest period of low growth in the post-war period, an expansion of 6.5 per cent was registered, but by the end of the year the combination of external deficit and domestic industrial disruption made it impossible for the process to continue. The Heath government had neither created an effective system of competition and controls over labour, nor a workable structure of centralized controls. In an external environment which now intensified internal difficulties rather than moderating them, the end result was an ideological and economic collapse. While governments up to 1970 could all claim to have 'achieved successes rather than failures', Bacon and Eltis could claim that 'what was unique about Mr Heath's 1970–4 administration was that failure was total' (Bacon and Eltis, 1978, p. 56). There can be no doubt that it was this experience that enabled the proponents of economic orthodoxy led by Mrs Thatcher to capture control of the party during the next few years, and to refuse resolutely to make further compromises with Keynesianism after they took power in 1979.

The Labour Party in opposition had also begun to retreat from the old social democratic consensus, but in this case towards policies involving a much more radical attack on liberal orthodoxy than that contemplated during the 1950s and 1960s. A new critique of the role of multinational capital in destroying the conditions under which Keynesian policies could operate had emerged, which claimed that their monopoly power and external linkages made it possible for them to evade the normal disciplines imposed by market competition and the controls over external flows at the disposal of the nation state.[28] To ensure that future reflations actually generated real increases in investment and output and to enforce price competition, it was decided that there would be significant state acquisitions in each major industrial sector, and the creation of new investment institutions, notably a National Enterprise Board. The Industrial Relations Act was to go and wages regulated through a voluntary 'social contract' negotiated between both sides of industry and the state, while spending on social services was to be restored. But although there were now important economic advisers in the party arguing for a return to import controls,[29] the lessons of the 1960s had not been generally learnt, and these were not seen to be an important element of the overall programme.

But these ambitions were to be brought to a very rapid end, and the circumstances of these early years conspired to turn this administration into the agency for the initiation of a fully fledged monetarist strategy after 1976. The leadership which took office in 1974 was almost the same as that which had presided over the deflation of 1967 to 1969, and it almost certainly had much less faith in radical measures than the rank and file of the party. Furthermore, there was no overall parliamentary majority in February 1974, and one of only three after the election held in October, so that it could be argued that insufficient support existed for radical measures. However, most important of all, they came to power in external circumstances worse than any experienced since 1945, and with none of the domestic and external controls that had enabled their predecessors to overcome those problems without recourse to draconian cuts in public spending and economic activity. As we have seen, the Governor of the Bank of England had explained to Wilson that such circumstances would require 'Tory measures' whatever the opinion of the electorate, and his views had eventually prevailed. Between 1974 and 1976 this experience was to be repeated, with even worse results for economic development and political support.

At the start of 1974 the immediate response to the escalating deficit was again to fund the promised spending programme and sustain an economic expansion through foreign borrowing. While total borrowing was £3 billion in 1973, it was £7.1 billion in 1974, £8.9 billion in 1975 and £14.2 billion in 1976 (Caves and Krause, 1980, p. 58). In the first instance this allowed spending and wages to be increased (no doubt making a useful contribution to the electoral victory at the end of the year), but without reducing external weaknesses. Instead, access to foreign borrowing allowed the Bank of England to hold the exchange rate at a higher level than would have been possible otherwise, while unprecedented increases in oil and other raw material prices and the inflationary effects of the dollar deficit [. . .] led to a surge of imported price increases. Responding to these, an increasingly militant labour force pushed wages up to equally unprecedented levels, and earnings rose nearly 28 per cent from July 1974 to July 1975. Inflation was now around 25 per cent, ahead of all industrial countries, and the balance of payments deficit was £3.6 billion in 1974 (see Leys, 1983, p. 86). Since there were no improvements in productivity between 1973 and 1975, not even this rate of inflation was sufficient to maintain profits, and those in manufacturing fell from 14.9 per cent in 1973, to 6.3 per cent in 1974, and to 3.8 per cent in 1976 (Brown and Sheriff, 1978, p. 251).

In these conditions the possibility of a complete collapse into hyper-inflation and industrial bankruptcy could not be excluded. Without access to any direct controls, the government had now to take up where it had left off in 1969 by taking active steps to contain wage increases, cut spending and restrain demand. Joel Barnett (1982) therefore records a life as Chief Secretary to the Treasury spent in a continuous round of negotiations designed to wrest spending cuts out of a succession of reluctant Ministers. An agreement was secured with the TUC to restrict wage claims to a flat rate of £6 in 1975/6, and the tax burden on company profits was significantly reduced. The only concessions to the radicalism of the manifesto were the establishment of the National Enterprise Board in 1975, though without the resources required to make a major impact on investment, the bringing of British Leyland into public ownership (though this was in response to bankruptcy, not to socialist principles), and the creation of the British National Oil Corporation in 1976 with important powers over the whole North Sea field.

But the retrenchment and wage restraints agreed in 1975 were to be insufficient to offset the effects of domestic cost-push pressures (wage increases were still at 16.5 per cent in 1975/6, despite the agreement) and the international recession which was now at its deepest. The exchange rate was still at just over $2 at the start of 1976, and was maintained there only through massive external borrowing, a lot of it in the form of short-term deposits, mainly from the Organization of Petroleum Exporting Countries (OPEC) whose holdings alone equalled the value of total reserves.[30] While the authorities accepted that this rate was too high, they did not want a very large fall, since this would have worsened inflationary pressures and led to an outflow of credit which would have exhausted the country's reserves and forced a drastic cut in imports. Whatever one may think of the nature of the concessions which came to be made to obtain the resources required to defend the pound in 1976, it is important to recognize that a failure to do so would have required even more fundamental adjustments to consumption patterns and economic organization than those that were eventually imposed.

In 1976 OPEC depositors began to take their money out on a large scale. In March the Treasury attempted a limited and controlled devaluation, but, given the lack of overseas confidence, this soon got out of hand and the pound rapidly fell into the $1.70s, and eventually reached just over $1.50 in September.[31] Rather than allow an uncontrolled run on sterling to develop, and refusing to impose direct controls, the government was to spend the next nine months negotiating external credits with the Americans, the Germans and, ultimately, the IMF. The American objective in these negotiations was twofold: to offer enough money to induce the British to sign, but to do so on terms that would tie the government into the liberal policies required to sustain the existing international economic order. Thus Yeo at the US Treasury told Fay and Young: 'We feared that if a country like Britain blew up, defaulted on its loans, introduced foreign exchange controls and froze convertibility, we could have a real depression.' In his view the British now 'had a higher standard of living than the country was earning', and the only answer was a classic deflation by 'cutting public expenditure, and thus government borrowing; and imposing strict controls on the expanding supply of money, to control inflation. If taxes could also be reduced, so much the better'.[32]

In the Cabinet there was fierce resistance to the implications of these recommendations, especially from the spending Ministries which had already had to digest unacceptable cuts. But it was now evident that a fundamental choice had to be made between accepting the highly conservative policy prescriptions of the foreign creditors within the existing framework of trading and monetary mangement, or adopting import controls to defend the border as the means of overcoming the payments crisis. The latter was strongly pressed by a minority in the Cabinet as the basis for an 'alternative economic strategy', but it was defeated by the weight of evidence presented by the Treasury, mainly based on the probable consequences of the international retaliation that it would provoke. Thus in September discussions began with the IMF on a credit package which was finalized in discussions in London in November/ December. Agreement was reached on the 14 December and the Letter of Intent was published the following day (*The Times*, 16 December 1976). High interest rates, substantial public spending cuts, wage restraint and an agreement to sell off £500 million worth of BP shares were agreed in exchange for an IMF credit of about $3.5 billion dollars, and a pretty well guaranteed line of credit to the private banking system of rather more.

This capitulation to the demands of orthodox theory has been chosen to mark the start of a new phase of economic development, because it represented a clear-cut rejection of the Keynesian full employment/ demand management principles which had continued to exert a strong, if increasingly untenable, influence over policy till then. But now demand was being savagely cut back, with unemployment at the unprecedented post-war level of 5.2 per cent and it was well understood that it would expand further before it could be brought down. The needs of the external balance had taken priority over the commitment to domestic expansion in a more thoroughgoing way than ever before, and in an international context so depressed that earlier returns to some degrees of prosperity were no longer possible. The fundamental capitalist principle that wage bargaining could only produce an adequate level of profit by the reality of large-scale unemployment had been re-established thirty years after the first majority Labour government had taken power, commited to eliminating it for ever. This commitment was to be taken over and applied far more consistently and ruthlessly by the Conservative government which took power in 1979, but it was clearly visible in the policies adopted by Labour in December 1976.

2.4 Liberalism in crisis, 1976–1984

In September 1976 James Callaghan officially informed the Labour Party conference of the government's conversion to orthodox theory:

> We used to think that you could just spend your way out of a recession and increase employment by cutting taxes and boosting government spending. I tell you in all candour that that option no longer exists, and that insofar as it ever did exist, it worked by injecting inflation into the economy. And each time that happened the average level of unemployment has risen. Higher inflation followed by higher unemployment. That is the history of the last twenty years. (cited in Caves and Krause, 1980, p. 75)

Three months later a Letter of Intent to the IMF confirmed that the policies designed to put these convictions into effect had received the official seal of approval from the international financial community, and for the next two years the government valiantly implemented them. The traditional combination of high interest rates, public spending cuts and restrictive wage policies was followed now backed by a Treasury which had finally exchanged monetarism for Keynesian fiscal policy as its dominant *modus vivendi*.[33] Earlier deflations had been more or less exclusively concerned to reduce consumption by enough to eliminate an external deficit, but this objective now had to be combined with the elimination of inflation. To do this it was necessary to stop the total supply of money in the economy from expanding and thus allowing inflationary wage increases to be turned into price increases. The necessary consequence of this was a willingness to allow unemployment to rise to the point where it dissuaded workers from demanding too much, and eliminated all those employers unable to sustain sufficient labour discipline and to meet the higher levels of efficiency required by the intensification of overseas competition.

During these years, as a result, unemployment increased, though only marginally, the real wage fell, while actual government expenditure was reduced between 1975/6 and 1978/9 by '£3100 million in current items and £4900 million in fixed investment' (Pollard, 1982, p. 62). These policies had a significant effect on both the deficit and inflation, since the former recovered from a deficit of about £1 billion in 1976 to a surplus of the same amount in 1978, while inflation fell from 16.5 per cent to 8.3 per cent at the same time. But growth was again suppressed, though the loss was disguised by the beginnings of oil and natural gas production. Industrial production excluding the latter only increased by a total of 3.3 per cent between 1975 and 1979, when it was still 4.1 per cent lower than it had been at its peak in 1973 (Matthews and Sargent, 1983, pp. 148–9). Yet despite these developments, the commitment to orthodoxy was not yet total. In particular, after confidence in sterling was restored in 1977, strong upward pressure on the exchange rate led to attempts at control through direct intervention and reductions in interest rates, while the major source of downward pressure on wages remained 'the direct though largely voluntary, restraint on prices and incomes'. Furthermore, even though the use of orthodox methods was the dominant feature of policy during these years of crisis, there is little doubt that the preference of the government (though not of the Treasury and Bank of England) would have been to return to Keynesian expansionism as soon as inflation and the external balance permitted. Indeed, in 1979 an initial expansion was attempted, but with the problem of productivity and profitability still unresolved, the effect was mainly to initiate an import boom and to push the balance of payments back into deficit.

The major damage stemming from the deflation was incurred in the relations between capital and labour, which now, in a context where wage increases had become an aspect of government policy, necessarily involved a break in the relations between the trade unions and the Labour Party. In 1978 the TUC refused to renew its commitment to wage restraint, and in the winter of 1978/9 a number of strikes among low-paid workers, mainly in the public sector, produced a massive level of public discomfort and negated all of the advantages the government had expected to derive from the expansion then under way. As a result, the Thatcher government was elected, resolutely committed to the implementation of a fully fledged orthodox policy which was to combine stringent policies to restrain demand through public spending cuts (with the significant exception of spending on army, police and prisons) with a willingness to allow interest rates and the exchange rate to appreciate to the point where rising costs would push unemployment up to the level required to bring down the wage rate and eliminate industrial militancy. Thus not only was there to be no interventionist policy to assist unprofitable industry, but wages and the exchange rate were also to be taken out of the political sphere and determined by market forces alone.

These policies were dressed up in the guise of a sophisticated advance in economic theory, popularly known as monetarism, which sought to attribute a scientific basis to what was essentially an exercise in destroying the capacity of the working class to resist wage and social and welfare cuts. Indeed, the Bank of England has itself conceded that the adoption of 'monetary targeting' was essential as a means of distracting attention from the real objective, 'for, *inter alia*, output and employment' which, if disclosed, 'would either have been unacceptable to public opinion or else inadequate to secure a substantial reduction in the rate of inflation or both' (Fforde, 1983, p. 207).[34] In a masterly critique of the strategy (and, indeed, of the failures of the whole post-war period) Pollard sees it as operating in six steps:

> Its sole objective is to bring down the rate of inflation (step 1). The key mechanism for doing that is to reduce the quantity of money (2). In turn the reduction in the quantity of money, or at least its rate of increase below the inflation rate, is to be achieved by the two parallel methods of high interest rates (3a) and a cut-back in government spending (3b); this will create more unemployment (4) and incidentally thereby weaken the unions. With less money and credit available firms will have to reduce their price and cost

> increases (5) and in particular will have to resist the unions' wage demands, on pain of bankruptcy. Once the inflation has been 'squeezed out' of the economy, healthy growth without inflation may then be expected. (Pollard, 1982, p. 166)

The results of these policies have been almost entirely negative. Although wage increases have slowed down, trade union resistance has maintained them at levels above productivity growth, so that profits have hardly improved. Thus unemployment has been the major means of cutting consumption down to match reduced output, and this is now apparently to be allowed to remain at levels only reached during the worst years of the 1930s. Output fell in 1980 and again in 1981 by about 2.4 per cent; by the end of 1981 industrial production excluding oil and gas was 19.2 per cent below the 1973 peak, and in 1982 a weak recovery of 1 per cent was recorded.

In 1983, however, with the election in mind, a strong expansion took place in consumer spending based on the relaxation of hire-purchase regulations and a reduction in savings. Interest rates were brought down and with them the rate of exchange, particularly against the dollar. Exporters have been able to take advantage of the favourable conditions prevailing in the USA [. . .] and growth has therefore risen to around 3 per cent. Yet this has yet to be established as a long-term trend, since the lack of investment has yet to be made good and serious problems still exist. Import penetration has increased sharply and a deficit on the balance of payments in manufactures emerged in 1983 for the first time since the industrial revolution. High US interest rates and the falling pound forced 2.5 per cent increase in the British rate in July 1984; should the American deficit be closed, as most observers feel it must, the deflationary effects on Britain and the rest of the system are likely to be severe.

Since 1981 the contribution to the balance of payments of oil has been about $20 billion a year, but in that year the actual surplus was about half that, declined to $6 billion in 1982, and is expected to disappear altogether in 1983 (Richardson, 1983, p. 195). Without this fortuitous contribution, the effects of monetarist policies would have been unimaginably destructive; the fact that these policies have now so weakened the productive base that a deficit is just around the corner in spite of it, merely emphasizes the seriousness of the situation.

To emphasize the fact that the worst aspects of the old habits of the 1950s and 1960s have not yet disappeared, the government has excelled its predecessors in its propensity to encourage the export of private capital and engage in military adventures of an absurdly expensive and vainglorious kind. In 1979 all controls over capital outflows were finally removed, on the assumption that this would help to keep down the exchange rate, and that, after an initial increase, there would be no large-scale outflow. In the event, despite a decline in the domestic savings ratio, these have grown astronomically, with outward portfolio investments alone totalling £4.2 billion in 1981, £5.8 billion in 1982, and £5.7

billion in 1983 (Bank of England, 1983, p. 29), to the point where the foreign earnings of North Sea oil which have not been used to sustain domestic consumption have gone to finance external investment – a decision for which the country must pay dearly before very long. This response on the part of capital is entirely rational from a private point of view, since monetarist policies have been unable to bring the domestic rate of profit into line with that prevailing abroad, but it will, of course, further reduce the competitiveness of the industrial base and worsen an already bad situation. Again, the government has also organized a conscious regression into the practices of the imperialist past, committing itself to increased spending on defence in real terms each year and, in 1982, allowing itself to be drawn into a full-scale war in the South Atlantic. At a time when the social and economic infrastructure was being drastically reduced, an armada was dispatched to fight a ruinously expensive war to retain a piece of land supporting a population insufficient to occupy fully a single city street. Yet again, long-term commitments involving significant diversions from the urgent tasks of domestic reconstruction have been entered to support an overseas role which is both dubious in its own terms and impossible to justify in relation to the resources available to the economy as a whole.

Thus, what we have experienced in the 1980s is a remarkable combination of all of the worst policy errors of the past thirty years. With the immediate balance of payments constraint temporarily lifted by North Sea oil, the government has organized a deflation more savage than any undertaken in the past to meet the most serious external crises. It has combined the inevitable loss of domestic investment stemming from these policies with the active encouragement of the foreign investment of a very large proportion of domestic surpluses overseas, thus ensuring that they should be used to strengthen further the position of those competitors whose products are driving domestic production out of our own markets. To complete this catalogue of imbecility, the further growth of these surpluses is being guaranteed by cutting social and economic infrastructure investments by the state, while non-productive investment in the weapons of destruction and in the assertion of an essentially nineteenth-century imperial role is being increased. It is little wonder that the problems of future adjustment are being created which must soon involve disruptions on a scale as yet entirely unimagined.

2.5 Evaluation

The material contained in the preceding pages is intended to substantiate two broad propositions: that the British commitment to a centre country role between 1954 and 1972 was a major factor in its international economic decline, and that its attempts to deal with the problems of decline in an increasingly open and market-determined international environment from the mid-1950s onwards have become an increasingly counter-productive contributor to yet further decline. These arguments, if accepted, then serve to substantiate the [following] central hypotheses – that no national economy can bear the weight of international economic management without undermining its own viability and thus its ability to sustain the role over the long term, and that once forced into a position of relative weakness, the operation of an open, competitive international economic system will intensify problems of uneven development rather than moderate them. These conclusions, in turn, require that we accept that the price of international integration must be the creation of a multinational agency – *a form of world government* – capable of redistributing sufficient resources from strong centres to weak to offset the tendencies to inequality and destabilization which will inevitably emerge in its absence. Where this does not exist, weak countries like Britain must either adopt protection or deflate in response to balance of payments deficit, and thus, by cutting consumption and investment, solve the short-term problem by intensifying their underlying structural weakness.

The current structure of the international economy is based upon the body of orthodox economic theory which assumes a natural tendency towards even development, and which therefore entirely underestimates the costs involved in both international management and in the deflationary policy responses which have always to be accepted by deficit countries where the government is allowed neither adequate external resources, nor the policies that enable it to organize a controlled domestic investment programme protected from the worst effects of international competition. The British case clearly demonstrates how mistaken these views are. While it is probable that Britain might have avoided the worst effects of its post-war failure by refusing to take on the international burden – by refusing to re-arm, repudiating much of its debt, prohibiting outflows of capital and rebuilding its own economy within protective barriers as did Germany and Japan – this would also have greatly increased the load on the Americans, intensified isolationism there, and possibly induced a breakdown in the system much earlier than the one that eventually occurred in 1971. Thus it is important that we should not ignore the positive consequences of the British role, but it is equally important that we recognize that a system which requires self-destructive sacrifices on the part of the centre country can hardly hope to maintain itself over the long term. Furthermore, when we now survey a society in which there is 16 per cent unemployment, a continuous reduction in the level of social provision, the wholesale destruction of productive resources, and growing and increasingly violent social tensions, we can also see that the long-term costs of constant recourse to deflationary policies are so great that they must inevitably lead to a reversion to protectionism unless some positive international solution can be found.

In Britain such a solution has already been put forward as a central plank in Labour Party policy, and it is now being seen by many French socialists as the only alternative to the austerity into which their government was forced as a result of a balance of payments crisis in 1982. Defending the Brettons Woods agreement in the House of Lords in 1944, Keynes asserted that its provisions would forever remove the need for sacrifices of this kind and therefore open up the way for international interventions capable of sustaining the conditions for full employment in the world economy as a whole (Keynes, 1944).[35] In the event, the machinery he helped to design has been proved too flimsy to bear the weight imposed upon it. Unless it can be improved, the pressures stemming from the weaker countries must induce a reversion to the protectionism of the 1930s.

[. . .I]t is perhaps worth saying a little about other arguments which some would claim are far more important than the problem of the external balance in explaining the underdevelopment of the British economy. Other accounts have emphasized the high cost and restrictive attitudes of the British labour force, the organizational and psychological inadequacies of the managerial and entrepreneurial elite, and the excessive growth of the state apparatus and of welfare provision. Space does not permit a full examination of all of these, nor is this entirely essential, given the brilliant exposition of the case to be found in Pollard's now classic economic history (3rd edn; 1983) and his monograph (1982).

Rather than go through all of these arguments, therefore, it seems more useful to emphasize not so much the superiority of an externally oriented approach, but the way in which it serves to explain the persistence of many of the phenomena identified in these other accounts. Looked at at any point in time, it is no doubt true that British labour has been paid more than its productivity warrants, that managers have not shown the entrepreneurial flair required to maintain their international role, and that state provision has been so expensive that it has crowded out the 'marketed goods' sector. Yet all of these problems, as Pollard effectively demonstrates, depend in turn upon the long-term failure to sustain the rate of investment required to ensure that innovations can be turned into new products, taxes increased to finance services without excessive pressure, and, most especially, wages increased without eliminating the rate of profit. Thus, as he says, 'the difference between British and foreign experience was not that money wages rose here; but that the increased costs were absorbed by rising productivity elsewhere, but not in the United Kingdom' (Pollard, 1969, p. 445).

Once this inadequacy in managerial performance and imbalance between wages and productivity is consolidated, of course, it has the effect of creating a vicious circle which further worsens the problem and becomes an independent variable in its own right. But what the historic record shows is that the problem of the external balance pre-dated the emergence of this discrepancy, and that it was the policies adopted to deal with it which pushed down the rate of investment to the point where these further imbalances became inevitable. We have attempted to show in some detail that each phase of deflation, inevitably involving lost production and a massive disincentive to investors, was initiated by the need to defend sterling in the particular circumstances that had come into existence after the relaxation of external controls in the early 1950s. Pollard writes:

> Thus, in the crisis of 1947–51 some future growth was sacrificed though the productive capacity was not wasted. It was merely diverted from investment to exports. Since then, however, this approach has become a permanent, and increasingly effective, feature of the British economy. Moreover, as it became increasingly difficult to market potential exports, the capacity abstracted from capital formation was no longer diverted to exports but was kept unemployed. Thus the main cause of the low investment, and hence the low growth rate, in Britain is easily stated: the whole of the considerable apparatus of Government economic power, especially as exercised by the Treasury, has been applied during the major part of the period under discussion to achieving it. (Pollard, 1969, p. 443)

The cumulative effects of the succession of deflations which external weakness imposed on policy from the mid-1950s onwards had thus reduced Britain to the status of a second rank industrial producer by 1976, and left the government with two choices: either to accept mass unemployment and further stagnation as the price to be paid for external balance with free trade, or to revert to the protectionism and interventionism which had made reconstruction and the post-war boom possible. The fact that both the Labour government in 1976 and the Tories in 1979 adopted the former has since immeasurably worsened the underlying problem and guaranteed that the final rejection must involve far heavier costs than would have been necessary if a more adequate policy had been arranged either on the basis of a more adequate system of international co-operation or, if that had failed, through a more thorough-going restructuring of the country's external policies and commitments [. . .]

Notes

1 I am heavily indebted in this section for ideas and material from Steve Gilliatt and Andrew Pople which is treated more fully in Brett, T., Gilliatt, S. and Pople, A. (1982).

2 Arndt (1944) provides a useful analysis of both the British case and of the development of the international economy during the inter-war period. Its general conclusions are powerfully argued and directly relevant to the current debate.

3 I have discussed these developments in British policy in Brett (1973).

4 Strange (1971) is a major contribution to the analysis of British policy and, so far as I know, the best general analysis of the nature of the link between external commitments and internal economic failures.

5 For an earlier version of this account see Brett, T. *et al.* (1982).

6 Keynes (1945), read in conjunction with Keynes's paper for Bretton Woods, provides us with a clear insight into the external policies required to complement the domestic policies implicit in the *General Theory*, which are often assumed to be absent from his work. They stand in sharp contrast to his earlier protectionism (see,

for example, Keynes (1933)) and must form an important part of any complete assessment of his work.

7 The classic description of the debate in both Britain and the USA is to be found in Gardner (1956).

8 Close detailed analysis of the period will be found in Steve Gilliatt's and Andy Pople's University of Sussex PhD theses.

9 It is worth noting here that the only period in recent British history when a comparable industrial performance has been sustained was the years from 1932 to the war *after* the replacement of free trade by Imperial Preference and the introduction of a policy of 'cheap money' based on a low exchange rate. 'Between 1932 and 1937 real national income increased by 20 per cent, industrial production by 46 per cent and even unemployment declined by 17 per cent while income per head rose 18 per cent and industrial production per person-year by 16 per cent' (Richardson, 1967, p. 21). For comparative figures see Kindleberger (1973, p. 280), which, incidentally, demonstrates that Germany, the worst offender in terms of economic nationalism and central controls, dramatically out-performed everyone else.

10 Strange (1971) denies this, claiming that Keynes greeted the American demand with 'incomprehension'. But we have seen that he himself had initiated the suggestion, and Gardner's evidence to the contrary is entirely convincing.

11 For the official justification of the system see the Radcliffe Report, pp. 265–6.

12 In a very helpful review of the original article on which this section is based, John Saville (1984) does, however, miss this latter point. Whatever its motives, the Labour government of the 1940s was able to demonstrate that managed trade did not necessarily lead to low growth and efficiency.

13 A few weeks before the outbreak of the war, Bevin, speaking for the Foreign Office, had told the Cabinet that 'our future relations with the US will largely be determined by the success of our collaboration with the Atlantic Treaty. Since it is the kernel of their policy it must be the kernel of ours' (Cabinet Papers, Cp(50) 118 Lab. 129/141).

14 Details can be found in Worswick (1962), PEP (1960) and Bartlett (1972). Three Labour ministers resigned over these decisions, and there can be little doubt that they were an important element in the fall of the government.

15 An excellent statistical presentation can be found in Caves and Krause (1968) p. 151.

16 In 1955, 'rejecting the reimposition of direct restrictions upon imports, and determined not to alter the exchange rate, the Government was left with no choice but to intensify the restraints upon demand at home' (Worswick, 1962, p. 35).

17 The overall balance of payments figures, and those for official flows, are taken from Caves and Krause (1968), p. 151; those of private overseas investments from Hazlewood (1962) pp. 197–8.

18 'Memoranda of Evidence submitted by HM Treasury to the Radcliffe Committee', Radcliffe Report, Principal Memoranda of Evidence, Vol. 1, p. 117; and Macmillan (1971) pp. 342 and 722. Macmillan's account makes it clear that it was the desire to obtain these surpluses which lay behind the very restrictive policies being advocated by the Treasury at the time.

19 There is a useful account of the way in which the Maudling strategy had to be financed 'at the expense of the balance of payments' in Bacon and Eltis (1978) pp. 40–6.

20 The ease with which this transaction was conducted compares favourably with the complications associated with the American loan in 1945, but its tendency to tie

the government into the international system was entirely similar. This package was put together from contributions of $500 million from the USA and the rest from ten other banks, followed a loan of $1 billion from the IMF a few days earlier (see Solomon, 1977, p. 89).

21 Solomon was a senior official in the US Federal Reserve Bank at the time.

22 At the OECD Working Party Three discussion of Britain's proposed loan from the IMF, 'the French delegate is understood to have hinted that next year's Budget should be approved by the Fund (IMF) and the OECD before submission to Parliament' (*Financial Times*, 30 November 1967).

23 Strange's (1971) account, which seems entirely plausible, emphasizes the limited nature of these moves, and the continuing inability of the authorities to recognize the real implications of the overall situation.

24 Eltis (1961, p. 197) reproduces the table and provides a more detailed comment on its significance.

25 A comparative examination of the falling rate of profit into the early 1970s can be found in Glyn and Sutcliffe (1972).

26 Good accounts of the Heath administration can be found in Gamble (1974) and Leys (1983).

27 An even sharper downward trend is shown for industrial and commercial profits by Sargent (1983) p. 84.

28 Notably in the work of Stuart Holland, an active member of policy-making committees at the time. See Holland (1976).

29 According to Joel Barnett (1982), Wynn Godley and Nicky Kaldor were calling for import controls at the start of 1975.

30 In 1975 reserves stood at $5.4 billion, total borrowing at $8.9 billion and OPEC deposits alone at more than $5 billion (figures from Caves and Krause, 1968, pp. 35, 38).

31 Much of the detail here comes from Fay and Young (1978).

32 It does not seem to have struck Mr Yeo that in 1976 the Americans were also consuming far more than they were earning. But then the special role of the dollar protected them from the need to control their deficit as the British were being forced to do.

33 The rationale of the development of the Treasury's 'political economic' theory is set out in a very revealing article by Fforde (1983).

34 It is interesting to note that the Bank is quite willing to concede that much of the argument that was put forward was quite consciously designed to negate the democratic process, and also that it is now quite happy to admit this openly.

35 Keynes (1944) in particular claimed that 'we abjure the instruments of the bank rate and credit contraction operating through the increase in unemployment as a means of forcing our domestic economy into line with external factors' (p. 374).

References

ARNDT, H. W. (1944) *The Economic Lessons of the Nineteen-thirties*, London, Oxford University Press.

BACON, R. and ELTIS, W. (1978) *Britain's Economic Problem: Too Few Producers*, London and Basingstoke, Macmillan (second edition).

BALOGH, T. (1952) 'The international aspect', in Worswick, G, and Ady, P. (eds), *The British Economy, 1945–1950*, London, Oxford University Press.

BANK OF ENGLAND (1983) *Bank of England Quarterly Bulletin*, Vol. 23, No. 1.

BARNETT, J. (1982) *Inside the Treasury*, London, Deutsch.

BARTLETT, C. J. (1972) *The Long Retreat*, London and Basingstoke, Macmillan.

BECKERMAN, W. (1972) 'Objectives and performance: an overall view', in Beckerman, W. (1972) *The Labour Government's Economic Record, 1964–1970*, London, Duckworth.

BLACKABY, F. (ed.) (1978) *De-industrialisation*, London, Heinemann.

BLACKABY, F. (ed.) (1979) *British Economic Policy, 1960–74*, Cambridge, Cambridge University Press.

BRETT, T. (1973) *Colonialism and Underdevelopment in East Africa*, London, Heinemann.

BRETT, T., GILLIATT, S. and POPLE, A. (1982) 'Planned trade, Labour Party policy and US intervention', *History Workshop Journal*, April.

BROWN, C and SHERIFF, T. (1978) 'De-industrialisation: a background paper', in Blackaby, F. (ed.).

CAVES, R. and KRAUSE, B. (eds) (1968) *Britain's Economic Prospects*, Washington, DC, Brookings Institution.

CAVES, R. and KRAUSE, B. (eds) (1980) *Britain's Economic Performance*, Washington, DC, Brookings Institution.

COOKE, G. (1957) *The Life of Richard Stafford Cripps*, London, Hodder and Stoughton.

DALTON, H. (1962) *High Tide and After: Memoirs, 1945–1960*, London, Muller.

ELTIS, W. (1961) 'Economic growth and the British balance of payments', in Aldcroft, D. and Fearson, P. (eds), *Economic Growth in Twentieth Century Britain*, London and Basingstoke, Macmillan.

FAY, S. and YOUNG, H. (1978) *The Day the £ Nearly Died*, London, *The Sunday Times*.

FFORDE, J. (1983) 'Setting monetary objectives', *Bank of England Quarterly Bulletin*, Vol. 23, No. 2.

GAMBLE, A. (1974) *The Conservative Nation*, London and Basingstoke, Macmillan.

GARDNER, R. (1956) *Sterling-dollar Diplomacy*, Oxford, Clarendon Press.

GLYN, A. and SUTCLIFFE, B. (1972) *British Capitalism, Workers and the Profit-squeeze*, Harmondsworth, Penguin Books.

HAZLEWOOD, A. (1962) 'The export and import of capital', in Worswick, G. and Ady, P. (eds).

HOLLAND, S. (1976) *The Socialist Challenge*, London, Quartet.

KEYNES, J. M. (1933) 'National self-sufficiency', *New Statesman*, 8 and 15 July.

KEYNES, J. M. (1944) 'The International Monetary Fund', speech to the House of Lords, 23 May, reprinted in Hansen, A. (1947) *The New Economics*, London, Dobson.

KEYNES, J. M. (1945) 'Overseas financial policy in stage III', Cabinet Papers WP(45) 301, ff. 251–2;Cab. 66/65.

KINDLEBERGER, C. (1973) *The World in Depression, 1929–39*, London, George Allen and Unwin.

KOCK, K. (1969) *International Trade Policy and the GATT, 1947–67*, Stockholm, Almquist and Wiksell.

LEYS, C. T. (1983) *Politics in Britain*, London, Heinemann.

MACMILLAN, H. (1971) *Riding the Storm*, London and Basingstoke, Macmillan.

MATTHEWS, R. and SARGENT, J. (1983) *Contemporary Problems of Economic Policy*, London, Methuen.

NICHOLSON, M. (1967) *The System*, London, Hodder and Stoughton.

PATTERSON, G. (1966) *Discrimination in International Trade*, Princeton, Princeton University Press.

POLITICAL AND ECONOMIC PLANNING (1960) *Growth in the British Economy*, London, George Allen and Unwin.

POLLARD, S. (1969) *The Development of the British Economy*, London, Edward Arnold (second edition).

POLLARD, S. (1982) *The Wasting of the British Economy*, London, Croom Helm.

POLLARD, S. (1983) *The Development of the British Economy, 1914–1980*, London, Edward Arnold (third edition).

PREST, A. and COPPOCK, D. (1980) *The UK Economy*, London, Weidenfeld and Nicolson (eighth edition).

RADCLIFFE REPORT (1969) *UK Committee on the Working of the Monetary System*, London, HMSO.

RICHARDSON, H. W. (1967) *Economic Recovery in Britain*, London, Weidenfeld and Nicolson.

RICHARDSON, LORD (GOVERNOR OF THE BANK OF ENGLAND) (1983) 'British economic policy over the last decade', *Bank of England Quarterly Bulletin*, Vol. 23, No. 2, p. 195.

SARGENT, J. R. (1983) 'Productivity and profits in UK manufacturing', in Matthews, R. and Sargent, J.

SAVILLE, J. (1984) Review of Brett, Gilliatt and Pople, *Socialist Register*, pp. 308–10.

SHONFIELD, A. (1959) *British Economic Policy Since the War*, Harmondsworth, Penguin Books.

SOLOMON, R. (1977) *The International Monetary System, 1945–1976*, New York, Harper and Row.

STRANGE, S. (1971) *Sterling and British Policy*, London, Oxford University Press.

TEW, J. (1979) 'Policies aimed at improving the balance of payments', in Blackaby, F. (ed.).

UNITED KINGDOM (1948) *Capital Investment in 1948*, Report of the Investment Programmes Committee, July.

WALKER, W. B. (1980) 'Britain's industrial performance, 1850–1950', in Pavitt, K. (ed.), *Technical Innovation and British Economic Performance*, London and Basingstoke, Macmillan.

WILSON, H. (1971) *The Labour Government, 1964–1970*, London, Weidenfeld and Nicolson.

WORSWICK, G. (1962) 'The British economy, 1950–1959', in Worswick, G. and Ady, P. (eds).

WORSWICK, G. and ADY, P. (eds) (1962) *The British Economy in the Nineteen-fifties*, London, Oxford University Press.

Section II The UK Political Crisis

Introduction

The chapters in the previous Section have highlighted the importance of placing developments in the United Kingdom in a global context. In this Section the emphasis changes towards a stress on the uniqueness of the UK as it relates to and is influenced by changes at the international level. The arguments in these chapters do not explicitly challenge the focus of those in Section I; on the contrary their authors would acknowledge the importance of the external constraints. It is, however, probably fair to recognize that not only is there a shift in the object of analysis, but also in the nature of the explanations which are developed. Here, the stress is on changes within the United Kingdom, and there is a turn towards political and ideological explanations in addition to those rooted in economic changes. The arguments considered show that the notion of uneven development is relevant to the analysis of political developments as well as economy and society.

All three of the chapters are concerned with the impact and development of *political* crisis. In Chapter 3, Johnson argues strongly that one of the weaknesses of most interpretations of the British crisis has been their emphasis on economic factors. On the contrary, he argues, Britain's failure has been principally a political one, since the Keynesian welfare state was based on a series of fundamental political misunderstandings, which have also encouraged longer-term economic failure. There are echoes of Brett's argument here, but both starting-point and conclusion are quite different: in the terms used by Doherty (1989) his approach would be described as 'endogenous' rather than 'interrelational' because of its stress on specifically British explanations. Johnson argues that the post-war social-democratic compromise encouraged a belief in the providential power of the state. That is, it encouraged the widespread belief that social problems, problems of poverty, prosperity, equality and growth could be solved by the action of the state. The electoral system encouraged the making of promises which could then not be met, thus bringing the democratic system itself into question. And for Johnson it is this, as much as economic failure, which has characterized the British crisis, although he also argues that the making of such promises made it difficult to introduce the changes required to create an efficient and productive economy.

Like Johnson, in Chapter 4 Leys stresses the political failure of social-democratic approaches but he is more concerned to link it directly to the economic problems with which those approaches had to deal. Far more than Johnson, Leys sets the political history of the 1960s and 1970s in the context of overall economic decline. While also acknowledging the significance of political behaviour and state policy in influencing Britain's economic position, the balance is quite different, and it is clear that for Leys Britain's economic weakness cannot be explained solely (or even largely) by the domination of social-democratic or welfare ideology in British society after 1945. On the contrary one implication of the analysis in Chapter 4 is that the success of that ideology and the particular shape it took in Britain owed a great deal to the economic context in which it was developed. It was a social democracy of relative international economic decline, rather than one of expansion and growth.

Chapter 4 charts the development of Britain's political crisis from the 1960s and into the 1970s. It combines a consideration of the economic conditions of the period with one of the political responses to it, while reflecting on the nature of the crisis itself. By the end of the 1970s, it was clear that the methods of the past were discredited, although it was still unclear quite what would replace them. Unlike Johnson, who sees the election of the Thatcher government in 1979 as marking a turning-point, when the old myths of social democracy were effectively laid to rest, Leys sees matters as being rather more problematic, suggesting that in the early 1980s at least there were still a number of other potential options. With the benefit of hindsight (in 1988) it is possible to confirm the electoral dominance of Mrs Thatcher in the 1980s, but some of Leys' critical comments on the internal coherence of 'Thatcherism' retain their force.

One element of the British political crisis which Leys points to is the challenge which developed in this period to the UK as a unified state covering England, Northern Ireland, Scotland and Wales. The growth of nationalism in Scotland and Wales was marked by a series of electoral upsets to the main UK parties, particularly Labour, in the 1970s to the extent that devolution or 'home rule' became an important part of the British political agenda. Possibly the most consistent and certainly the sharpest set of challenges came from Northern Ireland but these have often been discussed as if they were somehow completely separate from the other problems facing the British state. Throughout the 1970s, although less so as the 1980s have progressed, the attitude of the main UK political parties to the Northern Ireland 'problem' has been bipartisan. Northern Ireland has been understood as a wholly special case.

As Liam O'Dowd shows in Chapter 5, it *is* important to look at the specific features which make Northern Ireland the place that it is, but it is also clear that those features cannot be understood separately from their relationship with the rest of the UK. And the endemic crisis in Northern Ireland which stretched from the late 1960s right through the 1970s was a crucial element of the wider British crisis. It fed into that crisis and its own direction was influenced by the development of the crisis, as respect for existing political compromises was undermined. The development of the welfare state which in the rest of the UK was the basis for deep-rooted political compromise in the 1950s and the 1960s, in Northern Ireland provided the basis for major conflict over distribution and control. Northern Ireland can be seen as a particular example of the process of uneven development within the UK. The emphasis of O'Dowd's chapter is on the restructuring of politics and the state, with only slight reference to economic change, and it sharply highlights the dangers of trying to analyse politics in the UK without recognizing the extent of differentiation which exists.

Although all the chapters in this Section focus on different aspects of crisis they disagree about the scope which exists for resolving it. Because of his concentration on the political underpinnings of crisis, in a sense Nevil Johnson is able to point to the most positive resolution: the electoral defeat of social democracy suggests that a more extensive ideological defeat may also have taken place. Colin Leys, on the other hand, remains sceptical because he does not believe either that the underlying economic problems have been solved or that the class-based conflicts he discusses have been superseded. Despite his scepticism, however, he clearly gives some credence to the claims which 'Thatcherism' makes for itself if not on the economic front, at least as a political ideology. Of the three, O'Dowd is probably the most sceptical about claims made for political restructuring and the search for consensus, but, as his chapter makes clear, the restructuring which would be required in Northern Ireland needs not only to deal with the repercussions of the crisis of the 1970s, but with a much longer history of conflict.

Allan Cochrane

Reference

DOHERTY, J. (1989) 'Britain in a changing international system', Chapter 1 in Cochrane, A. and Anderson, J. (eds) (1989) *Politics in Transition* (Restructuring Britain, Open Text 3), London, Sage/The Open University.

3 The failure of the post-war political order

Nevil Johnson

3.1 The domestic economy and the providential power of government

Much has been written about what is now called on all sides 'the British crisis'. There was a time when it could be shrugged off as the expression of a national propensity to grumble introspectively about the alleged defects of political and social life, and by so doing to conceal an inner confidence in a capacity to solve problems in accustomed ways. But this is no longer possible: the malaise is deeply felt throughout the country, bringing in its train that loss of a sense of shared purposes and cohesion which has nearly always marked societies in decline.

In this condition it is inevitable that many are anxious for the future as well as being perplexed by the nature of the problem. And of course, no judgement can be made on the future and the possibilities it may hold unless an effort is first made to examine honestly the character of this crisis and how Britain has slipped into it. The aim here is to make an attempt at this by considering in some detail why it is that the authority of one of the world's reputedly most stable political orders has weakened so much that it is apparently no longer capable of resolving many of the problems of the society.

In order to prepare for what follows, it is reasonable to indicate right at the beginning the plan of attack. It has been often argued that the British problem is economic and social, but not at all political. My contention is, however, that the root of the trouble is now political: we have an old and tired political order under which it has proved increasingly difficult to solve serious economic and social problems. Perhaps the disease need not have progressed this far: perhaps at some point in time in the past a stroke of luck in the mangement of the economy might have opened the way to a new and more hopeful context in which to handle the conflicts of interest which inevitably exist. But the fact is that poor economic performance has persisted, and there are too many social tensions which we have not succeeded in removing. The explanation of this is to be found in a progressive failure of political will and method. Our institutions and the rules on which they rest, as well as our rulers, have revealed a diminishing capacity to identify the issues which are vital, to devise and pursue consistently appropriate policies for handling them, and to sustain consent. More generally, the perception of the authority vested in our political institutions has weakened, and with that the recognition of their claim to express a public interest.

If one is suggesting that the basic difficulties are of a political nature, then clearly it follows that one has to look carefully at the political procedures and methods of the society, and at the institutions in which these are embodied. This is what I hope to do: to examine the parliamentary system and the role of Parliament, the character and powers of the central government, the consequences of political and administrative centralization, the pressures for a new diffusion of authority, the question of the citizens' rights in our political order, and the character of the parties and ruling elites. But I do not intend to concentrate on describing these institutions and arrangements and how they have been used in recent history. My concern will rather be with trying to determine the principles on which they now apparently rest. This is why these reflections claim to be concerned rather more with 'the British Constitution' than with 'British Politics': they seek to reappraise the terms on which many of our political institutions are said to rest, and thereby to make a contribution to the characterization of the political order. And as will be seen, there are grounds for believing that many of the traditional accounts of the principles upon which British political life is supposedly based nowadays obscure more than they illuminate. To that extent we are uncertain about what is the constitution of our political order, what is the character of the state.

Yet before it is possible to come to explicitly political questions, it is necessary to consider some aspects of the condition of society which have conspired to weaken political methods and institutions. The underlying social disease can be best characterized as the pursuit of illusions. In particular we have fallen victim to a grave misunderstanding of the significance of effective economic performance and of the conditions under which this might be achieved, and we have remained blind to the probable consequences of the haphazard pursuit of certain egalitarian postulates in the provision of social welfare. This chapter will be concerned with illusion in relation to the economy and with one of the major political results of this. In order to pursue this theme it is necessary both to say something about the history of a long-standing misjudgement of the importance of producing more resources, and about the doctrinal foundation of post-war British economic management. It is this second point which leads straightaway to an important political consequence, the acceptance of an exaggerated view of the role of government in the steering of the economy, and *pari passu* a declining sense of the importance of private decision and responsibility, both as conditions of economic progress and as elements in the maintenance of a liberal political order.

Hardly anyone doubts that many of the weaknesses of contemporary Britain have their origin in an ailing economy and in the social difficulties which are bound to be associated with a failure of the economy to provide enough resources to meet those expectations of private consumption and public benefits which have become widely accepted in the society. And, of course, expectations have grown as fast here as elsewhere. The problem is that in Britain we have had relatively less and less resources with which to satisfy them.

More important than any specific event was the gradual retreat into a realm of economic myths which took place during and after the Second World War. It is doubtful whether it can be shown precisely when this retreat occurred. Certainly it was not like a general's decision to pull back his troops. It was more like a sliding accumulation of failures to recognize the realities of the situation. This failure is vividly underlined by a reference in Margaret Gowing's [. . .] study of the post-1945 British development of atomic energy (itself a sad record of economic unrealism). Right at the beginning of the story she records some words of Keynes, put down in a paper submitted to the War Cabinet on the day Japan surrendered. Without immediate help from the United States, Britain was, so Keynes wrote, 'virtually bankrupt and the economic basis for the hopes of the public non-existent' (Gowing and Arnold, 1974, p. 3). This was indeed an accurate summary of the situation! This country, endowed with material and human resources vastly less than those possessed by the two world powers, had impoverished itself in an effort which also, as one can see in retrospect, appears to have drained it of much of its creative energy. In sober practical terms the British people ought in 1945 to have been confronted with the reality of their economic situation. Essentially this was that their prospects were in the medium and longer term no better than those of their neighbours who had been more visibly devastated and weakened by war. Instead, as if in a great spasm of emotional relief, Britain began to move into the realm of illusion.

The primary economic illusion consisted essentially in a refusal to accept the implications of the words of Keynes just quoted. Common sense required that it should have been understood that the first priority was to renew the capital equipment of the economy and by effective social co-operation and appropriate political decisions to make this process a practical possibility. But this was never clearly understood even in the years straight after the war. And, in so far as it was understood, it was never put across in a way which would have established a keen awareness of the problem in the minds of the people. The reasons for this are rather interesting – and take us beyond economics. It was not that the Labour government of 1945–51 had no grasp of the economic weakness of the country and of the urgent need to get on with the reconstruction of much of the industrial structure. To be fair to that government, it did its best to achieve an orderly transition from war to peace and did not hesitate to preach the need for hard work, wage restraint, more investment, forward planning, priority to exports and so on. Indeed, it showed more courage and honesty than most of its successors. But the trouble was that the real economic challenge could have been faced only at the cost of raising and answering the one question which in 1945 and ever since most strands of opinion in the country have always sought to evade: What is to be the motivation for economic activity and by what mechanism is that motivation to be made effective? And, of course, this in turn becomes a question about the kind of society we want to see and the political order appropriate to achieving it.

It is reasonable to hold that there are for complex societies only two viable answers to this dual question. One sees motivation in the economy essentially in terms of individual and private advantages, and so the operating mechanism must be that of the market, even though it may be qualified in practice by various social welfare considerations. The other sees the motivation somehow or other in terms of serving the public good, and as an inescapable consequence is compelled to see the mechanism for making this effective in terms of public, which means governmental, direction.

There was a time when this would have seemed obvious to any student of political economy. Ironically, the growth of economics as a discipline in Britain has been accompanied by a steady decline in the perception of this question. Of course, the contention is not that in the real world these motivations and mechanisms always manifest themselves with such clarity and sharpness. The choice is not between a pure competitive market economy dedicated only to private benefit and a pure command economy resting on politically determined welfare postulates. The market principle has to be qualified in many ways, and, *mutatis mutandis*, the same goes for the collectivist command principle. Nevertheless, there is a real choice here and, depending on which decision is made, a society must expect to move in directions broadly prescribed by that choice. And the choice is one with political consequences, too. Part of the problem was that the 1945 Labour government *could not* make such an explicit choice, whilst its Conservative successors were too lazy and foolish even to see the need for it.

Having committed itself to the first and basic illusion that there was no need for overriding priority to be given to economic reconstruction, this country then refused to see the need for having any principles with which to shape such policies as were applied to the post-war adjustment to a peace-time economy. In other words there was no facing up to the choice between an economy founded on market principles and one based on the primacy of public welfare criteria and, *a fortiori*, on an extension of public power. Yet this may put the matter too sharply. Perhaps in reality we drifted into a decision against the market. There was an ambivalence and ambiguity about the policies of the post-1945 Labour government which has characterized the approach of all subsequent governments. Attlee's Administration faced both ways. It carried out a far-reaching programme of public ownership, it liked to assert the social responsibility of industry and it attempted to maintain and develop a pattern of administrative controls which in theory at least give the central government a capability for 'economic planning'. But at the same time it avoided the extension of public ownership beyond the public utility sector (though it later expressed the intention of departing from this position), emphasized the crucial role of private manufacturing industry in maintaining the external trading position of this country, and in the end gave up whatever hopes it might have had of imposing anything recognizable as a pattern of planning schemes on private business. In this way we achieved something usually described as 'the mixed economy'.

Whatever this phrase may mean – and thirty years on it is still hawked around by politicians and pundits of all kinds – it certainly signified a deal of intellectual confusion. The problem is that it focused attention on ownership, suggesting that a mixed economy was simply one in which there were public and private sectors (an idea which even at the end of the last century would have caused little stir in many continental countries). But, of course, the precise mixture of ownership between public authorities and private individuals or organizations is not all that crucial, though the liberal is entitled to believe that there are good reasons for trying to restrain the relative growth of the public domain. The point is rather that 'mixed economy' is a vacuous expression if it is considered to refer *merely* to ownership issues. What matters are the principles on which the mixed economy operates, and here one gets back to the basic options of which I have already spoken. The choice of principles lay between the individual benefit motive and its concomitant mechanism, the market, and the public welfare motive and its concomitant mechanism, the determination by a public authority of the terms on which productive resources are used. Fundamentally, the decisions taken by the Attlee government (1945–51) in its handling of economic questions expressed a political preference for the second option. True, the preference was often veiled and muted, but it was there and as far as can be judged, approved by many of the British people. What is more – and this is of crucial significance – this preference appears to have been shared by the war-time coalition, achieving its classic formulation in the 1944 commitment to full employment as well as in the acceptance by all parties of a major extension of social security benefits.[1]

This is one reason why the transition to Conservative political control in 1951, leading to thirteen years of Conservative dominance, made surprisingly little difference as far as the basic options were concerned. For the sake of consolidating their hold on power the Conservatives were not anxious to challenge in any fundamental way the economic and social measures of the early post-war years. Though ostensibly favouring reliance on the market, they did not succeed in giving any intellectual coherence to this view and, indeed, hardly tried to do so. Instead they were far too much preoccupied with rather irrelevant arguments about the balance of ownership between public and private sectors. Moreover, circumstances favoured governments after 1951: world trade began to expand, commodity prices fell, and for a while the British national product expanded modestly but sufficiently fast to allow a steady improvement in living standards. Much of this was achieved at the expense of investment and structural adaptation, but that was to be a problem for the future. For a decade or so there seemed to be a progressive consensus about how to manage the economy.

But let me come back to the questions of motivation and principle. A vital element in the post-war definition of a welfare economy was its ability to sustain full employment. This was slowly to have dramatic consequences. Until very recently few dreamt of questioning this orthodoxy or of recognizing that there might be other sensible objects of economic policy to be balanced against the pursuit of full employment *per se*. Sadly enough there is little reason to believe that some of those who thirty or more years ago advocated and defined this commitment realized quite how serious were its implications for the national understanding of the economic issues facing the country. Keynes and Beveridge, key figures in this movement of opinion, seem to have had a certain blindness to the connections in a free society between the principles governing economic activity and the terms on which great social ends may be pursued. Both appear to have overestimated the extent to which governments can commit a society to certain desirable social aims without running the risk that dedication to these may have very negative effects on motivation in the economy and on the way in which it operates. This is not to argue that either Beveridge or Keynes (and certainly not Keynes) was naive in his understanding of economic conditions: both, for example, accepted definitions of 'full employment' as equivalent to toleration of margins of unemployment which nowadays hardly any politician cares to defend; both had some perception of the dangers of inflation inherent in the monopoly power of trade unions. But both were naive in failing to recognize that if the major welfare objective they advocated – the maintenance of full employment – was to be pursued in isolation and for its own sake, then this was likely to distort economy policy-making and breed confusion about the principles on which economic activity was to be based and the terms in which it could be justified to the society. This point becomes clear through a comparison with post-1945 German neo-liberal economists who saw more clearly the interconnections between principles governing economic activity and the creation of conditions favourable to the satisfaction of social welfare claims than did the fathers of British post-war economic orthodoxy. And, of course, this means that they grasped more firmly the obvious fact that the successful pursuit of social ends depends heavily on the capacity of the economy to produce resources (or at any rate it does this side of Utopia).

Instead, what happened here was that much of public opinion came in a shallow way to accept the welfare motivation as morally superior to the pursuit of particular economic interests. Inevitably this meant that an understanding of the market mechanism, and of its political and social justification, atrophied. Gradually people came to accept the beneficence and the necessity of a high degree of centralized decision-making in the management of the economy. The ground was prepared for that slide into a veiled command economy which has now been achieved with its attendant political dangers. We thought that the need to make a choice between principles of operation could be avoided after 1945, but that was an illusion. The options are still basically the same, the difference being that thirty years of relative economic decline[2] have made it all the more difficult to face up to the consequences of taking that option which, as so much of the evidence shows, has generally been associated both with prosperity and the survival of a politically free society.

The theoretical basis for the post-war orthodoxy concerning the economic role of government is to be found in Keynesian economics. To simplify greatly, it was the idea of achieving full employment, stable prices and rising output through macro-economic adjustment by means of manipulation of public expenditure levels and taxation which came to constitute the core of the Keynesian heritage. This particular element in Keynes' work – though it was by no means his major theoretical contribution to economics – had at least two serious dangers implicit in it. One was that to some extent it was backward-looking, expressing a reaction to the problems of mass unemployment of the thirties. Thus it tended to distract attention from the problems inherent in a full-employment situation in which powerful unions and large enterprises were increasingly dominant. The second was that it took for granted the principles according to which a competitive market economy might be maintained, simply assuming that a single-minded concentration on macro-economic guidance through the manipulation of abstract quantities by government action would have no effect on many of the assumptions about economic behaviour in a market situation, which were to be found both in Keynes' own writings and in those of his classical predecessors.

This leg of the Keynesian orthodoxy was accepted well before the Second World War ended, and became virtually unassailable after 1945. For thirty years or so it has been the unchallenged conventional wisdom that the central government must have enough power 'to manage the economy'. From the adjurations of Sir Stafford Cripps between 1947 and 1950, to the exhortations of Edward Heath after 1970, from the benign assertions of the Plowden Report on the Control of Public Expenditure (Cmnd 1432, 1961) to the platitudes of the Kilbrandon Commission on the Constitution (Cmnd 5460, 1969–73) on the need to maintain the economic unity of the United Kingdom, from the advice of Keynes to the pleas of his latter-day disciples in the Cambridge Faculty of Economics, the same theme can be detected: the economic health of the country depends *in the first place* on the actions of government.

Without doubt the available evidence suggests that this great faith in government has been misplaced. Indeed, it is a reasonable conclusion that the effects of the primacy attaching to a government's ability to steer the economy through demand management of the now conventional kind have been pervasive and disastrous. Inevitably the postulates of the doctrine have required that an increasing proportion of what is managed, i.e. national resources, should be disposed of by government.[3] There has been a degree of febrile instability in economic policy-making which is without rival elsewhere, at any rate in western Europe. Public expenditure programmes have been constantly adjusted to suit short-term political claims. Innumerable measures of intervention by government to stimulate economic activity directly or indirectly have been devised, tried and cast aside. A taxation system has been built up, unstable, complex, oppressive and subversive of economic enterprise. We have tolerated a centralization of power which has steadily stifled the political energies of the country and now threatens to be destructive of political rights too. In sum, the harsh reality is that neither the successive groups of politicians who have held office since 1945, nor the Treasury, nor the many other administrative agencies involved over the years in British economic management have been able to impose a decisive check on the forces of decline. The best that can be said of their combined efforts is that they have imposed upon this decline a more orderly and measured pace than it might otherwise have shown, though sometimes their rotation in office has been too fast even to permit that.

Of course some would regard such criticisms as too harsh and even unjust. Surely some good must have come from the devotion and application of so many able and public-spirited people to the tasks of central economic management? But I fear the answer is 'No' and for two simple and clear reasons. One is that we vastly overestimate the level of efficiency which a centrally managed economy can achieve compared with one which is required broadly to work within the conditions defined by market principles and methods. And this overestimation has been particularly naive within the context of a political system in which the responsiveness of politicans to every breath of public criticism is taken to be a sign of virtue. The other reason is closely linked with this point. It is that the attempt to provide economic management by central government has always been marked by a generous dose of make-believe or bluff. Our central institutions of government, despite a vast increase in their formal powers, have not really been able to exercise the kind of powers which are logically entailed by the claims made on their behalf. Social forces and interests as well as inherited political habits have held them back. Even if one disapproves of it and condemns it as inefficient, the method of centralized economic management by command has a certain intellectual coherence and perhaps offers prospect of some progress, though the political cost will be high. In contrast, centralized management without adequate powers is fraudulent and rather pointless. Yet this is essentially what successive administrations have been forced to sustain.

My reason for going back to the economic foundations of the present political malaise lies, of course, in the belief that the economic system and the political system have, in certain respects, to be congruent. Much of the economic doctrine accepted over thirty years ago had a profound impact on political assumptions and expectations, and on the tasks imposed on the political system. To put the matter starkly, the failure to recognize the importance of producing more resources more effectively, and the refusal to opt for a market solution to the basic economic question, nourished the belief that in fact the economy could be safely managed only by the government, and indeed that the health of the economy depends more on the actions of government than on the behaviour of those actually engaged in economic activity. The Keynesian argument for macro-economic demand management was vitiated by its political naïvety in relation to its probable consequences for the role of government, and, *a fortiori*, for the political constitution of the country. But it had the equally harmful effect of subverting the possibility of a principled and realistic discussion of the nature of a market economy and of the conditions required for its maintenance. Thereby it frustrated any coherent statement of the responsibility of government for the regulative principles within which economic activity should take place, and substituted for that a purely expedient view of the economic role of government as an unending exercise in political manipulation. Inevitably this has resulted in an inexorable increase in the powers of government over the economy and over much else besides. Relentlessly this process has imposed on the political and administrative institutions a burden which they are inherently incapable of bearing. Yet despite repeated failures and disillusionment, despite the political dangers presented by this trend of events, the voices raised in protest are still muted and scattered. Why is this so?

The explanation is basically political. It is to be found in the failure to discern clearly enough and soon enough the tendency inherent in the collectivist solution to the economic question. Keynes and his epigoni have stood in a tradition which optimistically believed that there is a real choice to be made between liberal or democratic collectivism and totalitarian collectivism. It was held that the attenuation of the market economy in favour of decision-making by public authorities could take place with advantage to all and at no significant political cost. It was not understood that liberal collectivism is likely to be unstable, and in certain conditions (many of which have prevailed in Britain) is certain to be unstable. As a result it always runs the risk of sliding towards a centralization of power which points towards the totalitarian condition. But then we face a further question. Given the undoubted fact of powerful liberal traditions in politics why have these dangers been taken so lightly?

The answer is a simple one. It is a peculiar misfortune of the British that the continuity of their institutional development has hidden from them the dangers of tyranny. They pride themselves on traditions of limited government which have blunted their sense of the fallibility of all government and prevented them from recognizing the peculiar dangers inherent in accepting an indefinite expansion of public powers in the pursuit of economic and social welfare. Perhaps, too, they remain blind to a certain absolutism implicit in the Benthamite and utilitarian tradition which has, after all, profoundly influenced modern British political and social development. Be that as it may, to an extraordinary degree the British now exemplify de Tocqueville's grim judgement of the likely effects of an uncritical acceptance of the idea of bringing about by public action equality of social benefit in a society pervaded by what are taken to be democratic sentiments: 'The notion they all form of government is that of a sole, simple, providential and creative power. All secondary opinions in politics are unsettled, this one remains fixed, invariable and consistent' (de Tocqueville, 1959, p. 553).

It is a sad irony that it was the very strength of the political order which favoured the absorption of doctrines which have brought us to this depressing conclusion. It was widely believed thirty years ago that the key to orderly and progressive economic growth had been found. But this was an illusion fraught with great dangers for the management of political life. The underlying doctrine looked backward at least as much as forwards, and as time passed it became less and less relevant to the needs of the society. Moreover, even as Britain moved in this direction after 1945, the political and moral foundation for such an evolution had largely been removed in many other countries by the solvent of war and destruction. To most of our neighbours the benevolence of government seemed improbable, the wisdom of government questionable, and its capacity to determine what is good for the people wholly suspect. Thus our rivals and competitors escaped the deadening influence of a body of ideas peculiarly liable to over-simplification. For no matter how sophisticated some of the economic reasoning associated with the Keynesian orthodoxy, the doctrine rested on a shallow understanding of the interdependence of politics and economics as well as on a rarified view of the real world of productive activity. Its ultimate effect has been to erode, through the sheer weight of the role attributed to government, that sense of dispersed responsibility for economic decisions and of the importance of a stable regulative framework for economic activity which are the *sine qua non* of any genuine market economy. The justification for the practice of Keynesian economic management came to be expressed primarily in terms of the social welfare function of full employment: the theory became an appendage to a bundle of abstract social aims. Needless to say, any economic theory which mistakes its purposes so completely is in danger of tipping over into illusion, and that is what happened long ago. There was a steady but inexorable retreat into a dream world of effortlessly produced cakes and ale. And it is because reality eventually begins to break through even into that dream world, that the political order is now exposed to strains which it is ill-equipped to bear.

3.2 Equality and welfare in the static state

So far I have been concerned with probing some of the errors in the appreciation of economic needs and in economic doctrine which have contributed to the present situation of Britain and with identifying in broad terms their political consequences. But may be the consequences of these mistakes would have been less severe, and there might have been more prospect of counteracting the illusions to which they gave rise, had there not been certain judgements of social values and policy at work which reinforced and complemented the misunderstanding of economic reality. Underlying this was something yet more serious, the psychological aversion to any kind of change which required an explicit revision of principles. Pushed far enough, such aversion expresses the retreat into a morality which simply denies the necessities of the world. However, at this stage it is necessary to turn to some aspects of social values and policy, leaving until later the general question of attitudes towards change.

The matters to be raised here concern the pursuit of what will be called distributive social equality and the priority accorded to what is commonly described as 'the welfare state'. Equality has been for many years now a persistent theme in social analysis of all kinds in Britain and has its roots in a different ordering of values from that which has predominated elsewhere, for example, in the continental European tradition of social inquiry. The contrast can be seen when the work of Max Weber is compared with that of R. H. Tawney.[4] The former drew from his study of capitalism and the Protestant ethic precious few conclusions about the virtues of equality: that was not what he thought to be important. But the latter extracted from his meditations on the relationships between religion and the growth of capitalist economies support for some harshly critical judgements of the 'acquisitive' society in respect of its inequality. Such views helped to make a whole generation believe that the achievement of equality in the distribution of social goods was impossible within such a society. There developed a lop-sided understanding of equality, along with a blindness to the fact that the 'acquisitive' society might in some respects be a necessary condition of creating the very resources which were to be more widely distributed. By the end of the Second World War, therefore, the country settled into a new orthodoxy, according to which the preoccupation with equality in distributive terms began to set the framework for political argument. Nevertheless, a generation ago the idea of social equality was still expressed chiefly in terms of equalizing social chances and of improving the condition of the poorer sections of the community. Equalization as continuous redistributive social engineering had not yet taken root. The emphasis on distributive equality did, however, portend a declining perception of equality of civil and political rights. Indeed, we have now become oddly complacent and indifferent about rights in these senses: we hardly seem to care about the evidence of inequality of treatment before our courts and quasi-courts, we are not worried by flagrant inequalities in the operation of our electoral law, and we apparently care nothing about the discretionary arbitrariness attaching to the actions of so many of those in public office.

The concern with a particular aspect of equality, its social dimension, to the exclusion of other and more fundamental senses of the idea, owes much to our social history as well as to political factors which appeared to confer some security on equality in respect of civil and political rights. It was the very sharpness of social cleavages resting on great differences in the ownership of wealth, and the manner in which these were expressed, which earlier this century and before fed a sense of injustice which persists, even though the reality which nourished it has been substantially modified. In particular economic differences reinforced cultural differences which have proved extremely resistant to change. Looking at the matter politically, despite major social differences there seems to have been a widespread belief, shared apparently by dukes and dustmen, that an Englishman's rights were quite safe and as good as anybody else's into the bargain. Our sense of political and civil rights rested chiefly on a robust individualism, first expressed in the common law, later in Lockean contract theory and finally in Victorian *laissez-faire* economics, which simply assumed that public powers were bad, that the more they were reduced the better, and that so long as they were kept down, any Englishman worth his salt could and would claim such rights as were part of his heritage. The protection of liberty lay in the negative state.

It was this climate of opinion which persuaded so many that equality of civil rights was no problem: everything in that department was secure and always would be. Meanwhile the cause to be fought for was a more equal distribution of material resources. As always war was an engine of change, and 1939–45 initiated major changes. We began to move towards a much more equal distribution of incomes, though, of course, marked inequalities in the ownership of resources still persisted.[5] But since consciousness of social status differences cannot easily be legislated out of men's minds that has remained a problem, though of diminishing intensity for many. However, there have been many Rip Van Winkles who would have none of this. For them the world had not changed, and the more equality was achieved in the distribution of material goods with a concomitant widening of social opportunities, the more vigorously they protested that nothing had been gained. Gradually, in the years between 1955 and 1965, the notion of equality gave way to a doctrine of egalitarianism. Equality of social opportunities was dismissed as a fraud productive of inequality. Setting everybody at the same point in the scale of social benefits became the aim.

That this view has gained widespread support as the natural framework for political argument owes much to the part played by the Labour Party in modern British politics and to the peculiarities of its own internal structure. The party was committed in its early years to a composite programme of social reform which could satisfy the aspirations of different elements in it, though each could interpret the long-term aims differently. The virtual completion of thé Labour Party's post-war programme of 'gas-and-water socialism' and welfare statism (much of which would hardly have shocked Bismarck) left something of a moral vacuum. This was gradually to be filled by a reinvigorated commitment to the values of distributive social equality. By some this was still interpreted with humanity and a respect for human diversity. But during the fifties most of the older generation of Labour leaders disappeared, and a few years later the balance and forces of opinion in the party shifted substantially in favour of those who, on grounds of interest or ideology, were preoccupied with the search for substantive equality. It was then that the cause of equality quickly acquired a kind of sectarian hardness. It was preached (and practised) during the sixties in more bigoted ways, the obsession with its pursuit became slightly neurotic. Yet this happened precisely when some people at last began to realize that in the post-war years the country had been in an economic situation which rendered a more rapid creation of wealth the indispensable condition of any genuine progess towards greater equality of social chances. In other words the new egalitarianism was from the outset another example of the pursuit of an illusion: the aspirations which fired it were destined to turn to dust and ashes.

It is a sad but obvious fact that the dedication of the progressive left in politics to egalitarianism destroyed any prospect of this truth being understood, particularly as the years between 1952 and 1958 had constituted a misleading interlude in which for a short time there was the appearance of adequate economic growth. But once this fleeting period of hope had passed, the pursuit of egalitarian social policies demonstrated its devastating effects. It is hardly an exaggeration to assert that from then on to the present day every measure of economic policy which attempted to take a serious view of the need to produce more real wealth more quickly has been soured or frustrated by the interposition of the egalitarian argument. For since all effective measures directed to the increase of wealth must by definition have the consequence that some people will benefit more than others (even if only as a result of their own exertions), the same objection can always be raised by the egalitarian: how can policies be tolerated which might bring about what he and his brethren regard as an unfair distribution of benefits? That such arguments have often been motivated by envy and built on ignorance has mattered little: a degree of egalitarianism has insinuated itself into the moral platitudes of the age.

The pursuit of egalitarian aims certainly has its morally offensive side. But it is its practical absurdity which has been most important in relation to the economic errors which have already been discussed. For the egalitarian commitment encouraged and indeed deepened the primary illusion in respect of the economic condition. Not only did we fail to see the need for a more rapid rate of economic growth, we came to believe that it was laudable and rational to devote more energy to arguing about distribution than to devising means of producing more efficiently what there was for distribution. We have become like people fighting over the distribution of the eggs whilst forgetting to feed the hens which have yet to lay them. In contrast with the experience of so many other countries, there has in Britain been hardly any popular awareness of the simple fact that a more productive economy would have eased the problem of distribution: more people could have benefited by their own exertions and more resources would have been available for such redistribution as might be undertaken by public action.[6]

Not surprisingly, in view of this failure of understanding, there has been a steady fall in the national dividend up for distribution, both relative to expectations and to the achievements of other comparable societies. This in turn has added an increasingly unpleasant dimension of greed and covetousness to the arguments about distribution. Furthermore, the continuing faith in government as the engine of economic management has meant that the pressures on the political system arising from this situation have become heavier and more insistent. In this way social values have worked through economic illusion to present a challenge to the political order.

This criticism of the stultifying effects of egalitarian thinking does not mean, of course, that there are no problems in the British social structure. Indeed, I have already suggested the contrary. Certainly a social structure has survived in which the perception of class and status differences is still unusually widespread. This in turn has fed the preoccupation with equal distribution, irrational though this reaction may often have been. But class differentiation is not a vested interest only of those at the top end of the scale. Unfortunately there are innumerable vested interests at *all* levels of social organization which prefer to maintain these differences or some version of them. Indeed, this is one reason why most of the policies advocated by the egalitarian zealots are unlikely to have more than a marginal effect on the social rigidities to which they object. It may, for example, give some moral satisfaction to the middle-class progressive to witness the introduction of comprehensive schooling and 'no selection'. Unfortunately this panacea almost certainly leaves working-class self-isolation untouched, and barely affects the survival of a fiercely separatist working-class hostility to educational self-improvement.[7] In fact, as we know well enough, historical experience suggests that except in periods of genuine revolution significant social restructuring is far more likely to take place in a society subject to rapid economic growth and a high rate of technological change than as a result of any deliberate measures of social equalization. In a rapidly changing economic context social relationships become more fluid – hardly a surprising conclusion. Britain has, however, had nothing like a consistently high rate of economic growth since 1945; her record of technological achievement is patchy, and the dominant reaction to most forms of change requiring new forms of organized social co-operation has been negative and defensive. Nobody need be in the least astonished if, in these conditions, many of the social relationships and attitudes of the past survive, proving themselves resistant even to the policies of the most egalitarian-minded social engineers. Here may well lie much of the explanation for the fiercely selfish pursuit of group interests which now has such serious effects. Their intensity reflects both the slow pace of natural social change and the fears which are inspired by politically motivated equalization programmes.

It is now necessary to pass from the problem of equality and its re-interpretation to another aspect of the social situation, the priority attached to those welfare policies which, taken together, are often dubbed 'the welfare state'.

Let us remember at the outset two characteristics of the British view of welfare policies which distinguish this country from many others. First, social welfare policy has its origins in the desire to help the poor, followed by a growing conviction that the state should assume this obligation. It is a tribute to the strength of these roots as well as to the influence of egalitarianism that much of social policy is *still* discussed in these terms: it is assumed that pensions, housing subsidies, health services, even much of education, are somehow or other provided primarily for 'the less-well off', 'the disadvantaged', 'the socially weak', 'the underprivileged', 'working people' or even 'ordinary people'. We never seem to have freed ourselves from the influence of those Victorian philanthropists who had to feel that 'they were doing good' to the lower orders. As a result of this we have little idea of social services simply as the means of meeting a wide range of claims which, according to circumstance and need, are available to all within the limits of resources available. Secondly, we have the odd habit of conferring upon many of our welfare policies the status of holy cows, even though their form and content may stem from the needs and beliefs of a vanished age and the benefits they provide may be wholly unrelated to contemporary social needs. Moreover, there have always been plenty of self-appointed guardians of this or that aspect of welfare policy, tiresome latter-day saints who can be relied on to uphold past precedent and to frustrate change. The consequence of this complacent view of what has been built up in the past is that we have been reluctant to reappraise priorities in social policy and suspicious of any change of methods.

Housing policy provides a vivid example of this. The notion that subsidized or 'social' housing should be provided by local authorities, that is to say by public decision and action, has its roots in the last century, 'housing for the working classes' as it was actually called in the statutes until 1949. Despite the fact that the segregation of a large part of the community into council estates is a vital support of social division, that there is ample evidence that subsidies via local authorities have been grossly maldistributed, and that there are serious political objections to the continuing growth of local authority power and patronage in the housing sector, we adhere stubbornly to the idea that the bulk of housing made available as a social service must be in the hands of local authorities. The Labour Party accepts this as an article of faith as well as a calculation of self-interest, whilst the other parties have generally lacked the courage to challenge the policy in any fundamental way. (The Conservatives had a stab at so doing in 1972, but that was soon reversed.)[8]

Another example of the tendency to sanctify what has been achieved is provided by the National Health Service. The original motivation lying behind the establishment of a centrally controlled and financed service was undoubtedly praiseworthy – the desire to make medical services available to all regardless of ability to pay. Unfortunately the determination to adhere rigidly to this pattern has had very mixed results. As medical services have developed technically and become more costly in equipment and personnel, so the dependence on a central allocation of funds has weighed restrictively on what can be achieved. A preference for economies of scale has favoured the creation of ever larger units of service, remote from the users and requiring cumbersome and often slow administrative procedures. The principle of free access with its accompanying reliance on financing out of taxation has obscured the cost of the services provided, both to the users and to the providers. There remains little room for the expression of private preference in the choice of medical services, few incentives to economy in use other than administrative controls, and no means of encouraging a flow of private resources into the service. Needless to say, there is little if any competition in the provision of medical services, a situation which does not always benefit the user. All this is not to condemn the service out of hand, but rather to underline the fact that there has been too much rigidity in relation to the problems of adapting its structure and methods to a changing social and economic context. And the case is politically relevant because it provides so many examples of the strains imposed on government by the assumption of direct responsibility for such a major social service.

However, there is no need to offer a lengthy commentary of specific areas of social policy. My argument is that the prejudice in favour of state-provided welfare services – a public monopoly in the welfare business, justified by pleas on behalf of 'the poor' – has worked against the achievement of a better understanding of social needs and economic possibilities. It has into the bargain depressed the quality of many social services as can be illustrated in several ways. Had our social insurance policies relied more on employer financing, then maybe a more prudent approach to the wasteful use of labour would have been encouraged; if public support for housing had been channelled through a far wider range of agencies and owners, maybe the rate of provision of new housing would have been higher and the quality less uniformly mediocre; if the National Health Service had been less sacrosanct, perhaps methods might have been found long ago for diversifying the provisions of health care with a consequent raising of standards and a relative reduction in the burden on public resources. After all, there is plenty of experience elsewhere of alternative policies which might have stimulated a much more efficient use of resources and at the same time an enhanced production of new resources. The crucial point is simply that social policy has in many fields been flat and dreary, more or less designed to depress improvement in quantity and quality. The traditional methods have encouraged the belief that the state alone can and will provide, that the butter must be spread thinly and equally, and that no good can come of prompting initiatives which might escape the control of those who 'manage the economy' and act as guardians of the social conscience.

Thus there has been a remarkable correspondence between the bias of post-1945 welfare statism and the dominant beliefs about the economy and economic policy. In both sectors there was a rejection of serious change: in the economy because we eventually persuaded ourselves that none was needed, and in social welfare policy because most people believed that by 1950 or thereabouts all the foundations had been well and truly laid. In both sectors there was a failure to discern that the flow and availability of resources was a crucial problem, and that if resources were to decline relative to expectations and perceived needs, then one enters a vicious circle from which there may be no escape. And, finally, there was in both sectors a willingness to accept without question the assumption that the central political authority knows best. Welfare policy just as much as economic policy conspired to increase faith in the 'providential power' of government.

I must now try to summarize this economic and social introduction to the political analysis of our decline. The initial thesis is that this country has been the victim of serious and pervasive economic illusions. These have interacted with certain social values and social welfare policies in such a manner as finally to persuade successive governments of both parties to tolerate a steadily growing mortgage on the future in order to facilitate rising consumption standards and increasing public benefits in the present. More and more the political economy of the country has been adapted to the principles which governed the domestic economy of that sweet and feckless woman, Madame Ranevskaya, in Chekhov's *The Cherry Orchard*. Surrounded by old retainers and importunate hangers-on she maintained a state far beyond what her income would support, struggling against change and the threat to the cherry orchard. Yet in the end it had to be chopped down and Madame Ranevskaya made way for that vulgar but successful capitalist, Lopakhin. However, in the life of societies, it is rarely practicable to sell the assets to a new management: we cannot follow the advice of a professor of economics and ask the Hong Kong government to take over (efficacious though that course might be).[9] What has to be done is to work against the illusions, to try to take a few steps towards replacing them by an understanding of the realities of the situation, and to provide a coherent statement of some of the options which face us and of their probable consequences. And to do this is to keep alive the hope that political choice can become a reality.

The clichés of modern social science are against such an effort. They tell us that the really profound 'causes' of particular situations and events are socio-economic forces embedded in the texture of social life. Such an outlook easily leads to the conclusion that not much can be done about the present British crisis. Even if it were to be agreed that its treatment might require political changes, it would be suggested that these could have no real effect on the underlying social and economic determinants.

This quietist view – one which, let it be said, passes for progressive in the best circles – is both conservative and pessimistic. It accepts a downward drift no matter what may be the risks of shipwreck on the way. But more seriously it is a view which is mistrustful of man's claim to political self-determination. There is certainly an interdependence between a society and its political order, and between its economic system and its political methods. Similarly, social conditions impose many constraints on the adaptation of political rules as well as on the pursuit of substantive ends in political life. But social circumstances do not determine political choice nor can they extinguish the claim to freedom and rationality which is implied in the choice of political procedures and the pursuit of particular political relationships. Indeed, it is precisely in conditions of social weakness and confusion that the challenge of political reconstruction is most clearly presented, for it is then that it becomes possible to see that the constraints in society can be overcome only by a re-thinking of the ground rules of political co-operation and association.

Yet at the same time it is important to avoid illusions about the difficulties and dangers of trying to induce deliberate and genuine political change in a society. Political change is not to be equated with the conventional kind of measures which politicians and their officials produce in a never-ending stream in contemporary Britain. This kind of 'reform' is febrile and often pointless, a disease of societies foolish enough to treat management consultants as latter-day witch doctors. No: genuine political change must mean deliberate attempts to re-fashion the rules of the political order and to adopt new methods of political co-operation which in turn will compel those subject to them to see the world they live in differently. Historical experience suggests that political self-determination in this sense is a possibility, though it is quite rare and fraught with dangers. And naturally it is hard for a conservative political order like the British, proud of its continuity, to contemplate deliberate change which would challenge that very continuity. Yet this may be preferable to the dangers inherent in accepting a process of decline in which social tension is exacerbated, economic folly perpetuated, and in consequence the authority of political institutions dissipated.

Notes

1 The most notable papers leading to these commitments were those on *Employment Policy*, Cmd. 6527, 1944, through which Keynesian doctrine received full official approval, and the *Beveridge Report on Social Insurance and the Allied Services*, Cmd. 6404, 1942. The latter opens with a strong statement of principle on the Victorian virtues of self-help and reliance, an aspect later to be forgotten.

2 There are many sources from which evidence about the relative performance of the British economy can be derived, notably the regular surveys published by OECD. Many of the arguments about why there has been a low rate of economic growth in Britain are summarized in Denison (1968).

3 The proportion GDP disposed of in this way or another by the public sector varies according to the basis of calculation, including the manner in which transfer payments are handled. It can, however, be safely assumed that well over half the GDP now falls into the public expenditure net. Moreover, there has been in the past decade a steady rise in public employment and a decline in private investment, thus accelerating the rise in the ratio of non-marketed to marketed outputs. This aspect has been dealt with by R. Bacon and W. Eltis in several articles, including a series in *The Sunday Times*, 2–16 November 1975. In western Europe only Sweden shows a similarly high level of public sector claims on resources, though its productive base is relatively stronger than that of the United Kingdom.

4 Much of the confusion about the terms on which a market operated is revealed in Tawney's belief that the function of industry is service. It is not: its function is to satisfy expressed needs and a market represents a particular set of terms on which this can be achieved. Service in this context is merely a sympathetic fallacy which has, however, been productive of much mischief. See Tawney (1921).

5 A standing Royal Commission on the Distribution of Income and Wealth was set up in 1974, issuing its first report in July 1975 (Cmnd. 6171). This underlines the extreme difficulty of establishing reliable criteria for the definition and measurement of these matters, but the preliminary findings confirm a marked trend towards income equalization and to a lesser extent towards a diminution in the concentration of wealth at the top end of the scale. See also Atkinson (1972).

6 The point is expressed with matter-of-fact clarity by one of the founders of the social market economy in Western Germany in an essay first written in 1947: 'Only when a yield has been obtained is there any point in having thoughts abouts its distribution' (Müller-Armack, 1974).

7 This is not to overlook powerful traditions of 'working-class self-improvement' nor to underestimate what was achieved in this way. But there is hardly any doubt that these traditions are now in decay along with some of the organizations which carried them forward.

8 Chiefly under the Housing Finance Act 1972, subsequently repealed on the return of a Labour government in 1974.

9 Harry G. Johnson, facetiously no doubt (1975, p. 118).

References

ATKINSON, A. B. (1972) *Unequal Shares*, Harmondsworth, Pelican Books.

DENISON, E. F. (1968) 'Economic growth', in Caves, R. and Krause, B. (eds), *Britain's Economic Prospects*, Washington, DC, Brookings Institution.

de TOCQUEVILLE, A. (1959) *Democracy in America*, London, Oxford University Press.

GOWING, M. and ARNOLD, L. (1974) *Independence and Deterrence: Britain and Atomic Energy, 1945–52*, Vol. I *Policy-Making*, London and Basingstoke, Macmillan.

HMSO (1961) *The Control of Public Expenditure*, Cmnd. 1432, London, HMSO.

HMSO (1973) *Royal Commission on the Constitution 1969–73*, Cmnd. 5460, London, HMSO.

JOHNSON, H. G. (1975) *Crisis '75 . . .?*, London, Institute of Economic Affairs.

MÜLLER-ARMACK, A. (1974) 'Die Anfänge der sozialen Marktwirtschaft', in Lowenthal, R. and Schwarz, H. P. (eds), *Die Zweite Republik*.

TAWNEY, R. H. (1921) *The Acquisitive Society*, London, Bell and Sons.

4 From the paralysis of social democracy to the crisis of the 1970s

C. Leys

4.1 The paralysis of social democracy

From 1961 onwards British politics became dominated once more by the country's economic problems. Britain's share of world exports of manufactures fell persistently (from 15.7 per cent in 1961 to 9.5 per cent in 1978), while foreign manufactures increasingly penetrated the British domestic markets, reaching 25.6 per cent of total domestic sales (nearly 60 per cent, in the case of car sales) by mid-1979. The overall rate of profit (before tax) fell from 14.2 per cent in 1960 to 4.7 per cent in 1978. Investment remained static, falling farther and farther behind the levels of competing economies abroad. By 1978, productivity in manufacturing was little over half that of the German level.

The immediate result was a succession of increasingly severe 'sterling crises'. As the relative decline of exports and growth of imports kept tending to push the current account into deficit, holders of sterling speculated against the pound, reasoning that a devaluation would be needed to close the gap, and hoping to make a profit by forcing the authorities into it. Governments – Conservative until 1964, then Labour – resisted this, by using their reserves of foreign exchange to buy pounds, and by deflating the economy so as to reduce the level of demand for imports. This aggravated the unemployment which was already being caused by the closure of unsuccessful companies. As a result, between 1961 and 1979, manufacturing employment fell by 20 per cent – a loss of 2.1 million jobs. Whole sectors of manufacturing disappeared – from motorcycles (in which Britain in 1950 had led the world) to a large part of the home appliances sector – while others such as shipbuilding, cars and even steel were threatened. Unemployment rose from 0.3 million (1.5 per cent) to 1.4 million (7 per cent) in 1978. Manufacturing output rose only slowly in the 1960s, and hardly rose at all in the 1970s. Inequality was rediscovered, with a vengeance. By the early 1970s it turned out that some 23 per cent of the population were too poor to take a full part in the normal life of the community.[1]

Workers – the unionized rank and file – were not prepared to accept unemployment and downward pressure on wages without a struggle, and thanks to the 'affluent' fifties, when sometimes more job vacancies were recorded than job-seekers, they had become well-placed to resist. In return for sustained production, management, especially in engineering, had conceded a substantial measure of shop-floor influence over the labour process. This influence was channelled through the shop stewards, directly elected by the workers in each 'shop'. As the 1960s progressed, rank and file resistance, enforced through 'unofficial' – i.e. non union-endorsed – strikes, usually lasting less than three days and often only a few hours, came to account for ninety-five per cent of all strikes. Thanks to this, real wages of manual workers still increased on average by 2.5 per cent a year throughout the 1960s, only a little below the 2.7 per cent achieved in the 1950s (Robinson, 1972, Table 9.1, p. 313). Manufacturing companies could not pass all this on in price increases because foreign firms, with superior productivity, were underselling them. As a result, investment fell further and further behind the levels achieved in competing economies. Although governments – most notably the Labour government of 1964–70 – provided subsidies, resulting in some increase in investment (financed, in effect, out of revenues from personal income tax), the results were not impressive.

The failure of successive governments to reverse these trends led to a marked loss of electoral support for the two major parties. In the 1959 election the Labour and Conservative parties between them had taken 93.2 per cent of the vote; by October 1974 their combined share of the vote was down to 75 per cent, or only 55 per cent of the total electorate (see Table 4.1). This reflected more than loss of confidence in the parties' leaderships. The social-democratic values to which even the Conservatives had subscribed during the 1950s were losing some of their authority. The parties themselves, faced with the intractable problem of economic decline, became increasingly polarized. Political currents previously considered 'extreme' – the market-oriented doctrines of the 'new right' and the more radical socialist views of the 'Labour left' – gained ground in the parties outside parliament, and in the case of the Conservatives, captured control

Table 4.1 The decline in the major parties' vote, 1945–1979

	Percentage of votes cast			Labour and Conservative vote as percentage of electorate				
	Labour	Conservatives	Others	Lab	+	Con	=	Total
1945	47.8	39.8	11.8	36.1	+	29.8	=	65.9
1950	46.1	43.5	10.4	39.8	+	37.7	=	77.5
1951	48.8	48.0	3.2	40.2	+	39.6	=	79.8
1955	46.4	49.7	3.9	35.6	+	38.2	=	73.8
1959	43.8	49.4	6.8	34.5	+	38.7	=	73.2
1964	44.1	43.4	12.5	34.0	+	33.4	=	67.4
1966	47.9	41.9	9.7	36.1	+	31.7	=	67.8
1970	43.0	46.4	10.7	31.0	+	33.3	=	64.3
1974 (Feb.)	37.1	37.9	25.0	29.1	+	29.9	=	59.0
1974 (Oct.)	39.2	35.8	25.0	28.7	+	26.2	=	54.9
1979	36.9	43.9	19.2	27.9	+	33.3	=	61.2

inside the parliamentary party as well in 1975. The authoritarian strand in the Conservative Party became more pronounced; the narrowly parliamentary approach of the Labour leadership was increasingly rejected by the party's activists. Outside Northern Ireland there were no outright challenges to constitutional authority comparable to those of 1910–14; but the state increasingly prepared for them.

New aspects

Few people saw the crisis in such a serious light, even by 1981. This was partly because of the time span which separated this crisis from the earlier one, making it hard to recognize it as a recurrence of an old syndrome, and partly because of some novel aspects.

The most obvious of these was that after 1970 the British crisis was compounded by a worldwide accumulation crisis. The reasons for the end of the long post-war boom are complex. The exhaustion of the impulse of technological innovation provoked by the Second World War is usually considered a basic, underlying cause. The advent of Japanese competition in all the most advanced sectors of production also cut into accumulation in the USA and Europe. Spare capacity emerged, and spare investible funds, leading to a strong movement of manufacturing capital towards cheap-labour, anti-union regimes such as Taiwan and Brazil. This aggravated the problem of maintaining growth rates in Europe and the USA, a problem further exacerbated by the oil-price increases after 1973. By the end of the 1970s virtually all the industrialized economies were experiencing reduced growth rates, rising unemployment, inflation and in some cases balance of payments problems as well. What distinguishes the British experience, however, and underlies more clearly than anything else its 'endogenous' nature, is that in Britain the new crisis had already begun in the 1960s – a decade of unparalleled prosperity for the rest of the industrialized world. The worldwide accumulation crisis of the 1970s did not cause the British crisis, it only made it worse.

Another novel aspect of the crisis was the changed nature of manufacturing capital in Britain. It had become extremely centralized, and to a very significant extent internationalized. In 1910 the largest hundred manufacturing companies had accounted for less than 15 per cent of total output. By 1970 they accounted for about 50 per cent, and by 1980, about 60 per cent (Holland, 1975, pp. 49–50).[2] Fifty of these same hundred companies were multinational, and fifty accounted for more than a quarter of Britain's visible exports (op. cit., p. 76). By 1979 American-owned firms alone accounted for 19.5 per cent of Britian's visible exports, and 31 per cent of all British exports were transactions between different branches of single companies – i.e., intra-firm transactions (*British Business*, Table 3). At the same time, British multinational companies owned a disproportionately large share of world assets and made a third of their profits from overseas operations.

As Stuart Holland pointed out, the rise of this 'meso-economic' sector (in-between the 'macro-economic' level of the whole economy and the 'micro-economic' level of the individual firm) rendered obsolete a good deal of conventional wisdom about state economic management. Profit-accounting, transfer pricing and the sheer scale and complexity of the operations of the major companies make them almost impossible to inspect, monitor or police. A large part of the manufacturing sector had become increasingly immune to state efforts to control prices, to regulate the supply of credit, to tax corporate profits or to affect economic growth by exchange rate changes. Much of the failure of successive governments in the 1960s and 1970s to accomplish any of their economic goals was due to more fundamental causes, but some of it was due to the growing difficulty which any government would have experienced in controlling an economy which had increasingly become a mere 'location' in the global division of labour to corporate manufacturing empires – and an increasingly unattractive one.

> There is a crucial contradiction between the fact that Britain ranks first in the European top 500 with 140 firms yet has an economic performance lower than and worse than any of our main European competitors. The reason lies substantially in the extent to which such leading multinationals have written Britain off as the main location for their expansion, and are shunting investment and jobs in modern industry abroad. (Holland, 1975, pp. 77–8)

This affected both Labour and Conservative governments in different ways. Labour governments seeking more control over private-sector investment policies, for example, could find themselves either ultimately impotent in face of corporate control over markets, information and investment funds; or, if they were to make determined efforts to break this control, they could face a crisis of 'business confidence', and a threatened or actual capital flight.[3]

Conservative governments, on the other hand, seeking to strengthen 'market forces', would find that this tended to accelerate the decline of the already too weak *national* (as opposed to multinational) sector of the British economy. Yet, without a national economy, a national party of capital risks the loss of its electoral base. The fact that the Conservative Party's representation in the House of Commons after the 1979 election was overwhelmingly concentrated in constituencies south of the Trent was a painful reminder of this.[4]

Yet – and here was the most striking novelty of the new crisis – the state itself had enormously expanded. In 1910 total state expenditure had been 12.7 per cent of GDP. By 1975 it was 57.9 per cent (including transfer spending). By 1977 the public sector (central and local government and public enterprises employed almost 30 per cent of the labour force.

The expansion of the state, combined with the growth of monopoly in the private sector, accounted for a good deal of the inflation that accompanied the stagnation of output. Since hyper-inflation on Israeli or Chilean lines was judged socially and politically unacceptable, even Labour governments hesitated to try to use the state as an instrument of further economic expansion. The scale of state employment also complicated the problem of wage levels in general. Wage demands in the state sector encountered only the political limits set by governments' will to resist, and by the mid-1970s this will had been weakened. At the same time, the greatly enlarged state seemed no more suited or inclined than it had ever been to initiate and carry through a radical reconstruction of the economy.

Perceptions of the crisis

These new features of the crisis, and the extensive changes that had occurred since the First World War, made it hard for people to recognize it for what it was. As a result, they ran through the gamut of the earlier diagnoses, as if discovering them for the first time: trade union restrictive practices and strikes, amateurism and conservatism in management, technical and scientific backwardness, poor design and poor salesmanship, inadequate scale of production, party competition for votes, excessive overseas investment, an overvalued pound.[5] Some of the diagnoses were new. For instance, the tendency to blame excessive overseas investment, an overvalued pound or the 'stop-go' oscillations of government policy reflected a much greater realization of the conflict of interest between manufacturing and financial or commercial interests than had existed sixty years before. Another new diagnosis was that there were 'too few producers', i.e., too many state employees – a version of the neo-conservative reaction to the growth of the state (Bacon and Eltis, 1976).

By now it should not be necessary to belabour the point that most of these diagnoses are not wrong – on the contrary most of them are essentially correct. For example, a comparative study of British and foreign automobile production by the government's Central Policy Review Staff in 1970 suggested that relative to US and European plants British plants were overmanned. But, it added, 'even when manning levels are virtually identical and the capital equipment, model involved and plant layout are the same, the output of production lines in Britain is about half of that of continental plants'. The report seemed to imply that the fault lay with the workers: 'In other words, with the same power at his elbow and doing the same job as the British worker, a continental car assembly worker normally produces twice as much as his British counterpart' (Central Policy Review Staff, 1970, p. 83). In fact, capital per employee in the British car industry as a whole was much lower than in Europe or the USA, and British plants were also too numerous, and produced too many engine types and a poorly balanced range of models. Another study showed that American-managed firms in Britain were more profitable than equivalent British-managed firms (Dunning, 1966). The truth was that management was less competent *and* – partly because of this – workers worked less efficiently (and perhaps less hard) than elsewhere. No one factor, or a few factors taken in isolation, contain the key to the problem. It can only be understood as the consequence of a total historical process.

By the 1960s the relationship between capital and labour in Britain had been modified in many ways, but not in essentials: on the one hand, a class of capital still deeply attached to many pre-capitalist values, and on the other, an organized working class deeply sceptical of any suggestion that any advantage that they might concede to the employers would actually advance their own long-term interests. What was new in the 1960s was that the workers had acquired the strength to resist any increase in the level of exploitation, when such an increase had finally become essential.

To maintain its existing competitiveness – let alone, improve it – in face of rapidly rising productivity in other countries, big increases in the productivity of British manufacturing were required. This implied massive increases in investment. *The Times*, in 1973, suggested £20 billion. But whatever the figure, the implication was for investment on an unprecedented scale. This in turn implied the need for vast increases in profits. Would the workers be willing to leave these to the shareholders? In any case, part of these sums would have to come from profits on the basis of existing investment levels, i.e., by tax changes in favour of profits.

The conditions which permitted capital in Germany, France or Japan to impose an initially high level of exploitation (i.e., the gap between value added and wages) on the workforce did not exist in Britain – even if British management had had the necessary technical and managerial sophistication. British workers were too well organized, and they were no longer much impressed by the 'work ethic' which had been so assiduously preached to them in the nineteenth century (any more than British management seemed to have been, at least since the turn of the century). As the President of the National Union of Mineworkers, Joe Gormley, put it to the 1979 Labour Party Conference: 'The British people were not made to work' – a sentiment rather unlikely to have been expressed by his opposite number in Germany, the USA or Japan.

On the other hand, the British working class in the 1960s was no more ready to vote for a party seriously committed to an entirely new economic order than it had ever been. Whatever dreams it may once have entertained of building a transformed, egalitarian society – such as the Owenite movement of the 1830s had envisaged, for instance – had long been forgotten. The working-class consciousness which emerged after the defeats of the early nineteenth century was 'corporate', not 'hegemonic': it was consciouness of the distinct interests of the workers as workers – as at most an historic *underclass*. This remained broadly true in the 1960s (see especially Nairn, 1964, 1967). So the contradictions between the need of capital to move to a higher level of exploitation, and the determination of workers to prevent this, presented itself as something to be resolved within the existing political framework defined by the Conservative and Labour parties. It took two decades to discover that this was impossible.

State-led modernization: the Wilson reforms

Harold Wilson, who became Labour leader in 1963, had opposed Gaitskell's efforts to delete Clause 4 from the party's constitution. This maintained his reputation as a man of the left, but his grounds were pragmatic, if not cynical:

> We were being asked to take Genesis out of the bible. You don't have to be a fundamentalist to say that Genesis is a part of the bible. (quoted in Sked and Cook, 1979 p. 207)

Wilson consistently resisted efforts to commit the party to new measures of public ownership. Instead, he laid stress on modernization and technology within the existing 'mixed economy'. Wilson attacked the Conservatives as a party led by aristocratic amateurs, ignorant of the scientific and technological requirements of the modern world, who had presided for 'thirteen wasted years' over an economy whose management cadres were similarly recruited on the basis of class and connections, not merit; without planning, without reform, without keeping up with the times. Instead, he offered a vision of a society run by its men of talent. In a much-quoted speech to the Labour Party Conference in October 1963, after his election as Party leader, he said:

> We are redefining and we are re-stating our socialism in terms of the scientific revolution . . . the Britain that is going to be forged in the white heat of this revolution will be no place for restrictive practices or out-dated methods on either side of industry. (quoted in Butler and Sloman, 1980, p. 253)

The passage illustrates very well the thrust of Wilson's appeal – to 'both sides of industry' against incompetence, not to the working class against capital. Wilson understood that the consensus was endangered by industrial weakness. He offered to do what was necessary to remedy it. He answered the need to reassure people that, after all, 'no one need be defeated in the class war because no war was being fought. Capitalism could provide affluence for the working class while at the same time preserving the gains of the well-to-do' (Bognador and Skidelsky, 1970, p. 10). In the October 1964 election, the Labour Party campaign based on this theme at last secured victory – though with only the barest majority of four seats.

Wilson's analysis of the economic problem was that it was due to a lack of central planning based on a commitment to growth (the French planning system was particularly identified as a model); to production on too small a scale; and to a generally archaic structure of state policy-making and business management, hostile to innovation and closed to lower-class talent. Promising to accomplish more in a hundred days than the Conservatives had done in thirteen years, Wilson quickly set in motion a comprehensive set of reforms. He established a new Department of Economic Affairs, charged with producing a National (five-year) Plan and promoting long-term economic growth, to offset the 'dead hand' of the Treasury, with its traditional preoccupation with short-term policy, balancing the books and maintaining the value of sterling; an Industrial Reorganization Corporation, with substantial funds to subsidize corporate mergers; fiscal policies designed to encourage high levels of investment; and a wide range of institutional reforms designed to modernize the structure of the state.

These included reforms of the civil service, based on the report of a commission of inquiry (the Fulton Commission) which recommended the abolition of the hierarchy of 'classes' into which the policy-making cadre had been divided at the turn of the century, and measures to permit 'specialists' – technically trained officials – to rise into the senior ranks. There were also measures to replace the separate grammar, secondary modern and technical school system of secondary education by all-ability 'comprehensive' high schools; and to break the older universities' status monopoly by sharply increasing the number of degree-granting institutions, including the former Colleges of Advanced Technology (which became universities), the Polytechnics and the Teacher Training Colleges. Parliament was also to be reformed, to give new standing committees oversight of policy-making in government departments; an Ombudsman, rejected by the Macmillan government, was established in 1967; the Official Secrets Act was to be amended, in the interests of more 'open' (and hence more efficient) government; and a major review of local government organization was begun.

The same spirit of innovation was shown in social policy. Besides re-establishing traditional Labour priorities (for instance, by restoring the priority in house-building to one favouring publicly owned housing for rent, over private sector housing for sale) the government introduced a capital gains tax (long since established elsewhere) and a separate corporation tax, and planned for the introduction of income-related pensions based on graduated contributions. All in all, it was a stunning contrast with the era of Churchill and Macmillan. Early in 1966, in spite of the multiple economic difficulties which had been encountered, Wilson called an election, correctly judging that people had been convinced that his government understood the problems facing the country and had an effective formula for tackling them. In that election, in March 1966, Labour's majority (which had fallen from four seats to one through a by-election defeat) was increased to 96.

But the voters were to be disappointed. The economic measures – especially the tax relief and subsidies to industry, and the programme of mergers promoted by the Industrial Reorganization Corporation – did not lead to an increase in productivity relative to Britain's competitors. It is doubtful if these measures – or any measures that did not touch the central relationships between capital and labour – could have achieved much. But they were never really given a chance. To succeed, they needed a climate of expansion. This was the core assumption of the National Plan produced by the new Department of Economic Affairs in September 1965. It assumed a target rate of growth of four per cent per annum, resulting in a

Table 4.2 Output per person-hour in manufacturing, 1963–1970 (1963 = 100)

	1963	1964	1965	1966	1967	1968	1969	1970
Japan	100	111	118	129	151	170	196	223
France	100	107	111	118	124	133	148	157
Germany	100	110	113	116	126	137	144	147
UK	100	106	110	114	118	125	127	131
Canada	100	106	110	114	118	125	129	131
USA	100	104	107	110	112	115	118	122

Source: *National Institute Economic Review*, Statistical Appendices

25 per cent increase in national output between 1964 and 1970. But by the time the Plan was published, the economy was being fiercely deflated in order to prevent a new sterling crisis forcing a devaluation of the pound. In fact the government spent its entire period in office cutting back domestic demand, not expanding it. Output grew by 14 per cent, not 25 per cent; and gross investment grew by 20 per cent, not the 38 per cent forecast in the Plan, so that there was no question of increased productivity relative to other countries from this source (Opie, 1972, pp. 174–5). In fact, British productivity grew 30 per cent between 1963 and 1970, French and German 50 per cent, and Japanese over 100 per cent (Table 4.2).

The immediate reason for this failure was the attempt to maintain the exchange rate of the pound on an industrial base that had already become too weak to support it. When Labour took office in 1964, the exchange rate was still US $2.80, the rate fixed in 1949. But Labour also inherited a current account deficit of £402 million in the balance of payments (the visible trade deficit was £545 million, offset by a surplus of £143 million in 'invisibles' – earnings from shipping, banking, insurance services etc.). If this gap was not closed, a devaluation would be inevitable. Foreign holders of sterling, seeing the new government's first budget (which fulfilled election pledges to improve the level of social security benefits), judged that it would not cut back home demand enough to close the balance of payments gap, and a flight from sterling began.

The US Government urged Wilson not to devalue the pound, fearing that it would force a devaluation of the dollar as well. Wilson, in any case, seems to have thought that the 1949 devaluation had hurt the Labour Party's image as an 'effective' manager of the economy, and was opposed to a further devaluation. In his conviction that bad economic management by the Conservatives was such an important part of the problem, he failed to realize – as did most of his ministers and advisers – the seriousness of the underlying weakness of British manufacturing. There followed a series of piecemeal efforts to defend the pound by borrowing. When this did not work, the government was forced to deflate. Finally, in 1967, it was forced to devalue anyway (from US $2.80 to US $2.40 – a 15 per cent drop); and then, in order to ensure that this was not challenged by further speculation, still further deflation was required.

The result was a disaster. The 'technological revolution', which – if it was to be more than rhetoric – depended on accelerated economic growth, was still-born. Planning, in the words of one of the National Plan's authors, was 'many months dead already, or murdered' by the end of 1966 (Opie, 1972, p. 177). The 'pace-making' Department of Economic Affairs itself was abolished in 1969. A large foreign debt had been incurred in the futile defence of the pound, which had to be repaid before revenues could be applied to the increasingly massive task of economic reconstruction. The other social goals of the government suffered equally. The comprehensivization of schools had to be tackled without building any new schools. The hospital service, starved under the Conservatives – not a single new hospital had been built in their thirteen years in office – continued to be starved.

Most serious of all, from a political point of view, the government set itself to try to save company profitability, and to satisfy its foreign creditors, by curbing wage increases. In the years from 1948 to 1950 the Labour government had secured voluntary wage restraint from the union leadership. Now, expectations were very different, and the unions had less control over their members. After an attempt to rely on voluntary agreement in 1964, legislation was passed in 1965 (partly in response to American pressure) to give the government powers to delay any wage settlements that exceeded a permitted 'norm'. In 1966 the powers were extended to permit the imposition of a general wage-freeze, followed by legal ceilings on all wage increases. Finally, in 1968, seeing that these controls could not be maintained, Wilson proposed legislation on American and Canadian lines, which would, in effect, have outlawed unofficial strikes and compelled the balloting of union members before strikes could be held, on pain of heavy financial penalties against the unions.

Throughout all this the unions, aware that price controls (which had also been instituted) were ineffectual, and that dividends, too, were barely curtailed in practice, grew more and more resistant.[6] In 1969 they finally threatened to withdraw their support from the government if the new proposals (embodied in a White Paper called *In Place of Strife*) were taken any further. Wilson and the minister responsible, Barbara Castle, were forced to retreat. The contradiction between the Labour Party's legitimacy as a representative of the interests of labour, and the Wilson government's attempt to try to save British manufacturing capital, was thus brought into the open.

The attempt to deal with the economic crisis by deflation and wage controls not only cost the Labour Party votes; it also led to a politicization of industrial struggle. Nine per cent more working days were lost in the sixties than in the fifties, though this was nothing compared to what was to follow in the seventies (Table 4.3). The industrial front acquired a new political salience; the Wilson government, as it was drawn deeper and

Table 4.3 Working days lost in strikes, 1951–1980

Year	1951	1952	1953	1954	1955	1956	1957	1958	1959	1960
Million days	1.7	1.8	2.2	2.4	3.8	2.1	8.4	3.5	5.3	3.0
Year	1961	1962	1963	1964	1965	1966	1967	1968	1969	1970
Million days	3.0	5.8	1.8	2.3	2.9	2.4	2.8	4.7	6.8	11.0
Year	1971	1972	1973	1974	1975	1976	1977	1978	1979	1980
Million days	13.6	23.9	7.2	14.7	6.0	3.3	10.1	9.4	29.5	12.0

Source: *Monthly Digest of Statistics*, CSO, London.

deeper into the defence of British capital, found itself more and more frustrated by the unwillingness of the workers to make the sacrifices asked of them. A succession of Councils, Commissions and Boards, appointed (at five-figure salaries) to pronounce on the 'justice' or otherwise of workers' pay claims for sums in the order of £100 or so a year, succeeded only in disposing of any lingering illusion that wages were determined in some 'natural' fashion. In the 1960s the workers lost some of the 'profoundly attractive innocence' which Professor Chapman had found in them only a few years before (Chapman, 1963, p. 56).

The Labour government's eventual subordination of all its other goals to the defence of the capitalist economy led to the emergence of new political forces. The student movement, growing out of the nuclear disarmament campaign and opposition to the government's support for the American war in Vietnam, challenged the whole range of established attitudes, and helped the development of new left-wing organizations, both reformist and revolutionary. Left-wing intellectuals, alienated from the Labour Party, joined more radical groups such as the International Socialists or the International Marxist Group, or the women's movement.

At the other political pole there was the growth of racism. Starting in the mid-1950s, a rapid influx of immigrants from the West Indies, southern Asia and East Africa occurred. By 1970, 1.2 million British people were of 'new Commonwealth and Pakistan' origin. Conservative and Labour leaders allowed themselves to be frightened by racist agitation into competing with each other to demonstrate their readiness to cut down the flow, passing the Commonwealth Immigration Acts of 1962 and 1968. This in turn encouraged the activities of the neo-fascist groups who, in 1966, formed the National Front.

Another development which compounded the crisis was the collapse of authority in Northern Ireland. The system of social, political and economic subordination of the Catholic minority by the Protestant majority in the six counties of Ulster had been connived at for over forty years by Labour as well as Conservative governments. The social-democratic consensus stopped short at the Irish Channel. On the other hand the provisions of the welfare state, which had been gladly adopted by the Unionist government in Belfast (since it was subsidized from Whitehall), had made the Catholics less insecure, and given new educational opportunities to their children. In 1968, partly inspired by the civil rights movement in the USA, the Northern Ireland Civil Rights Association, largely led by educated Catholics, challenged the status quo by demanding equal rights for all, including Catholics. The challenge was met by repression, leading to the intervention of the British army and to a revival of Irish Republican Army activity in the province, inaugurating what quickly became a bitter and intractable new phase in Ireland's two-centuries-old civil and colonial war.

The crisis in Ulster was not a result of the crisis in the economy, but was closely linked to it. Belfast had participated in the earliest stages of the industrial revolution and was now particularly affected by the decline of old staple industries such as shipbuilding and textiles. Unemployment in Northern Ireland was the highest of any region of the United Kingdom, and it affected Catholics most. The Catholic challenge to Protestant domination, especially in the form of discrimination in state employment and housing, reflected this. And the weakness of the British economy precluded any attempt to resolve the problem by large-scale industrial investment programmes.

There were also significant centrifugal tendencies in Scotland and Wales. In England the decline in support for Labour and Conservatives was matched by a revival of support for the Liberals, but in Wales, and especially in Scotland, it was the nationalist parties which chiefly gained. By the late 1970s the nationalist trend was to play a fateful part in breaking up the post-war political order.

Unable to deal with the economic crisis at home, the government also found itself less and less able to act effectively abroad. The most dramatic example of this was its inability to impose its will on Ian Smith and the white settlers in Rhodesia when they made their Unilateral Declaration of Independence in 1965. At that time Labour had a majority of three in the House of Commons, and with no financial leeway Wilson could not have intervened militarily even if he had wished to. Instead, he made the mistake of boasting that economic sanctions would bring down the illegal regime in 'weeks rather than months', while Smith, knowing this boast to be empty, refused the various face-saving compromises which Wilson subsequently offered. Both men, however, underrated the long-run strength of the Zimbabwean liberation movement, which eventually settled the issue by force of arms in 1980.

Wilson's general foreign policy differed little from Macmillan's. In 1968 the decision was finally taken to withdraw all British troops 'east of Suez'. As the timing shows, it was a decision taken on financial grounds, not as an end in itself. And in 1967, Wilson (reversing his position as Macmillan had done earlier) made his own application to join the European Common

Market. This, however, de Gaulle vetoed once again in May 1968, maintaining that Britain was not yet ready to become a member of the European community. In retrospect, it is hard to fault this judgement, especially since Wilson's unswerving support for US policy in Vietnam made it only too clear that Britain's so-called 'special relationship' with the USA had become simply that of a client.

There were redeeming elements in the record of the Wilson years. The laws covering divorce and abortion were liberalized, capital punishment was abolished, and the well-intentioned attempt to promote 'equality of educational esteem' through the comprehensivization of secondary schools was pursued. There was also an expansion of university education (which, exceptionally, was maintained against the general trend of spending cuts). Not everything ended in failure. It was true that unemployment was rising, but for those in employment the end of wage controls and the defeat of the proposed new law to curtail strike action led to a recovery in wages in 1969–70 which substantially made good the relative losses imposed by controls in the previous years. And from the point of view of the City of London, the government's deflationary policies had finally closed the balance of payments' gap.

Labour's defeat in the June 1970 election was, in fact, by no means a forgone conclusion. Shortly before the election the opinion polls suggested that Labour would win. But the gap between the government's economic performance and its promises was too wide. Wilson's rhetoric about harnessing science to socialism had proved too hollow. Labour Party membership had declined precipitously. At the last moment, opinion turned away from the general line of continuity with the past, which Wilson had maintained, and towards the 'new conservatism' propounded by the Conservative leader Edward Heath.

4.2 Into the new crisis

After the Conservative Party's defeat in the 1964 election many party activists and MPs felt that, in effect, Wilson's charge that it was led by an amateur, backward-looking elite contained an uncomfortable element of truth. There was a growing distrust of the party's traditionally upper-class leadership – the 'magic circle', the former Colonial Secretary Iain Macleod called them – including Macmillan himself, and his successor Sir Alec Douglas-Home.[7] It was decided that from now on the leader would be elected by the Conservative MPs. Home stood aside and in the election held in August 1965 the choice fell on Edward Heath.

Heath, like Wilson, had been President of the Board of Trade. He had also been Macmillan's negotiator in the abortive Common Market application from 1961 to 1963, and was very much a 'European' and a 'technocrat'. Like Wilson too, 'Heath's abiding commitment was to the ideology of growth' (Gamble, 1974, p. 91). But where Wilson hoped to achieve modernization through active state intervention, Heath sought it through competition – through reducing state intervention, curbing monopolies, allowing the market to weed out backwardness and reward innovation.

The later sixties also saw a more fundamental right-wing movement than Heath's 'competition policy' gaining ground inside the Conservative Party. Enoch Powell, Heath's 'shadow minister' for health, shared his enthusiasm for the market and for cutting back the state, but went much farther in calling for denationalization, an end to state intervention in industrial disputes, and strict control of the money supply to control inflation. He also combined this with a nationalist campaign against entry into the EEC, and a racist campaign against immigrants, both of which proved popular themes. In 1968 Heath dismissed him from the shadow cabinet for his most notorious speech, a veiled invocation of racial violence ('As I look ahead, I am filled with foreboding. Like the Roman, I seem to see "the River Tiber foaming with much blood"').[8] But the new monetarist, nationalist, racist rejection of the post-war consensus which Powell expressed found a keen response on the authoritarian right wing of the party. These currents converged with Heath's more limited 'competition policy' at a pre-election strategy conference in the Selsdon Park Hotel in Croydon in January 1970 which committed the party to many of the 'new right' policies, including the abolition of universal social security payments and legislation to curtail trade union powers. Wilson commented: 'Selsdon Man is designing a system of society for the ruthless and the pushing, the uncaring . . . his message to the rest is: "you're out on your own"' (Butler and Sloman, 1980, p. 254).

The story of the next decade is the story of how at first Selsdon Man was defeated, because the consensus had not yet been weakened enough, and of how from 1974 to 1979 the consensus was then further eroded in a second unsuccessful attempt by Wilson and his successor, James Callaghan, to rescue Britain's competitive position without challenging the balance of power between capital and labour. Finally, the way was opened for a new, much more radical Conservative attempt to break with the past under the leadership of Margaret Thatcher.

The Heath initiatives, 1970–74

Heath's strategy was straightforward. Having prepared the ground with de Gaulle's successor, Pompidou, he reapplied for admission to the EEC in 1971. Also in 1971, to prevent the inevitable 'sterling crisis' choking off his strategy for economic expansion, he abandoned the fixed exchange-rate and allowed the pound to 'float', thus reducing sterling's role as an international reserve currency, and overcoming one of de Gaulle's former objections to British entry. Britain finally entered the EEC in 1973.

Secondly, he set about dismantling much of the apparatus of state economic intervention created during the Wilson years – the Prices and Incomes Board, the Industrial Reorganisation Corporation, the system of investment grants. Thirdly, the budgets introduced by the Conservative Chancellor, Anthony Barber, during the government's first eighteen months shifted the burden of taxation substantially away from companies and the richer tax payers and onto the working class – to the tune of about £2 billion, or some 12 per cent of total revenue. Combined with a reduction in the subsidy given to council house rents (under the Housing Finance Act 1972) and an increase in the charges made for medical care, the class character of the new fiscal policy was unmistakable. It helped to restore declining company post-tax profits and was supposed to restore incentives to entrepreneurship.

But it also exacerbated the unions' hostility to the fourth main element of the Heath programme, the Industrial Relations Act of 1971. This Act, which came into force in 1972, introduced the North American pattern of legal regulation of industrial conflict by imposing punitive financial sanctions on registered unions whose members took industrial action other than by prescribed procedures. These provided for compulsory 'cooling-off' periods and strike ballots before strikes could be called, and imposed severe penalties for taking industrial action against an employer while an existing contract was in force. Unions were free not to register under the Act, but then they lost their legal immunity from civil actions by employers for breaches of contract. Under the Act, unofficial strikes became either illegal or vulnerable to civil suits; so did 'sympathetic' strikes, the ultimate expression of the solidarity which was the British labour movement's historic source of strength.[9]

The government's idea was that, having altered the balance of power in favour of employers, it should stand aside from industrial relations and let the 'law of supply and demand' determine the level of wages. It therefore began by abruptly terminating the consultative arrangements between Downing Street and Congress House (the TUC headquarters) which had been established since the war. On the other hand, as a major employer, it set itself to resist all wage claims by public sector workers above the level it considered in line with the growth of productivity.

But the labour movement's massive opposition to the Industrial Relations Act became the prime cause of the Heath government's eventual defeat. The Trades Union Congress advised all its member unions not to register under the Act and expelled thirty-two small unions which did so. The militancy displayed against the Act was due partly to the comprehensive nature of the threat – the unions were in no doubt that if the Act prevailed, the balance of advantage would shift decisively to the employers – and partly to the build-up of rank and file confidence, expectations and organizational experience during the previous two decades. Militancy had been increased by the Wilson government's wage controls, rising inflation, and was now intensified by the Heath government's fiscal policies (especially by measures directly affecting workers, such as increased council-house rents, increased charges for school meals and cuts in subventions to areas of high unemployment).

The outcome of this struggle showed that, when the unions and their members were united, they were stronger than the government. In a strike in January and February 1972 – just before the 1971 Industrial Relations Act came into force – the mineworkers forced the government to concede a wage increase three times as big as the Coal Board's 'final' offer. This strike also revealed extensive public sympathy for the miners – a sign of life still left in the 'consensus' which was to cost Heath dearly two years later. Similar confrontations with the railwaymen and the dockers later in 1972 – the latter bringing the country to the verge of a general strike – in effect made the Industrial Relations Act a dead letter within three months of its introduction. A year later, the Director-General of the Confederation of British Industries, Campbell Adamson, publicly condemned the Act as having been responsible for the drastic deterioration in industrial relations which had marked the Heath years.

The strength of the labour movement forced a radical shift in policy. Heath's strategy called for an economic expansion if 'market forces' were to produce the investment boom needed to bring about a radical improvement in productivity. But expansion would be jeopardized if large wage increases led to rapidly rising prices, rather than increased profits and investment. The strikes in the first half of 1972 showed that the Industrial Relations Act was powerless to prevent this. In the summer of 1972, therefore, the TUC leadership was suddenly recalled to Whitehall for discussions on a new voluntary policy of wage restraint. When these discussions failed, the most comprehensive system of legal wage controls yet seen was enacted by parliament in November, 1972. This was a dramatic departure from the philosophy of the market. It was also keenly resented by the unions, contrasting as it did with the spectacular gains awarded to the well-to-do in the Barber budgets of the previous two years.

There now began a dramatic convergence of forces, each indicative of a different side of the contradiction in which the Heath strategy was caught. Internationally, the long boom came to an end in 1970. Competition in world markets for manufactured goods became more intense, and exports harder to sell. 'Hot' money flowed into commodity markets, pushing up commodity prices and causing a sharp increase in Britain's import bill and hence aggravating an inflation already accelerated by expansionary budgets. Retail prices rose on average by 8.4 per cent a year from 1969 to 1973, twice the rate of the preceding four years, adding to the price of exports. The expansion also sucked in imports on an unprecedented scale.

The combined result was a haemorrhage in the balance of payments. The 'visible' balance moved from a surplus of £261 million in 1971 (inherited from Wilson's deflationary policies) to a deficit of £722 million in 1972. This was cushioned by an 'invisibles' surplus of £875 million, to leave a modest overall current surplus. To avoid having to halt the economic expansion needed to defend a fixed exchange rate against speculative selling, the pound had been 'floated'. But in 1973 the visible balance showed a deficit of £2383 million (only half of which was due to the increase in oil prices following the Egypt–Israel War in October), and the overall current balance was just under £1 billion in deficit. Even with a floating exchange rate, there could now be no question of further expansion. That November, an emergency deflationary budget was introduced. The 'dash for freedom' was over.

Meantime the government was chagrined to find that manufacturers failed to respond to its policies by increasing investment. Real manufacturing investment in each of the years of the Heath government stayed more or less constant, at a level slightly below that of the last years of the Wilson government. As Heath complained to the Institute of Directors in 1973:

> The curse of British industry is that it has never anticipated demand. When we came in we were told there weren't sufficient inducements to invest. So we provided the inducements. Then we were told people were scared of balance of payments difficulties leading to stop-go. So we floated the pound. Then we were told of fears of inflation and now we're dealing with that. And still you aren't investing enough. (*The Times*, 8 June 1973)

But companies voted with their profits, and it was not a vote of confidence in the Heath strategy. Between 1970 and 1973 the volume of direct investment abroad tripled.

Even the policy of cutting back the state had to be abandoned. The Conservatives had particularly set their face against using the state to subsidize failing concerns. The 'competition policy' dictated that inefficient companies should be weeded out to make way for efficient ones. But the government's celebrated commitment 'to gear its policies to the great majority of the people, who are not lame ducks' was broken, in 1971, by the decision to salvage Rolls-Royce by nationalizing it. In face of the lack of response by industry, the government also felt obliged to return to a system of investment grants and, in 1972, established an Industrial Development Executive, which bore a striking resemblance to Wilson's Industrial Reorganisation Corporation, abolished in 1970.

Heath's U-turn, back to the essential strategies of the sixties, resulted, ultimately, from the fact that the electorate was not ready to accept the consequences which a consistent application of 'social market doctrine' to British conditions would have entailed – namely, an industrial recession on a scale not witnessed since the 1930s. Heath himself was also unwilling to accept these consequences (as his subsequent attacks on Thatcher's economic policies demonstrated). When confronted by serious political or social costs, his attempt to revert to the 'corporatist' approach of the previous decade (i.e. seeking to secure union compliance in wage controls through their incorporation with business representatives in consultative economic policy machinery) reflected his strictly qualified commitment to the new conservative creed.

The Egypt–Israel War of October 1973 (which led to a doubling, and later quadrupling, of the price of oil) coincided with the start of Stage 3 of the government's wage control programme, which set a ceiling of seven per cent on wage settlements for the coming year. In November the coal-miners, judging that the sudden improvement in the prospects for coal (relative to oil) presented a unique opportunity for them to recover some of the ground in pay which they had lost in relation to other skilled workers since 1946, began an overtime ban to enforce pay claims of between 22 and 46 per cent (depending on the category of worker). Heath responded by declaring a state of emergency under which a variety of measures were taken to conserve coal stocks, culminating at the New Year in a national three-day working week. The TUC nervously sought a compromise, but the miners pressed on and voted for a strike, whereupon Heath called an election for February 1974.

Opinion poll evidence suggested a good deal of public scepticism about the need for this confrontation. What the election result indicated above all was a lack of enthusiasm for both the Conservative and the Labour parties, both of which lost votes, while 6 million votes (19 per cent) went to the Liberals, and 600000 to the Scottish National Party (22 per cent of the Scottish vote). Labour won four more seats than the Conservatives, but had no overall majority. The Liberals, however, declined to keep the Conservatives in office. Heath was obliged to resign and Wilson returned to office as leader of a minority government with Liberal support.

Heath remained leader of the Conservatives for another year. But after losing twenty more seats in the election of October 1974 (called by Wilson in an attempt to secure a parliamentary majority) he paid the penalty by being replaced by Margaret Thatcher, his former Minister of Education, in a leadership contest in February 1975.

Thatcher's victory was seen at the time in largely personal terms – particulary as a revenge by back-benchers offended by Heath's notorious aloofness – as well as an instance of the well-established rule that Tory leaders may not lose more than one election. Heath had lost three, including the election of 1966. But the right wing of the Conservative Party in parliament were also opting for a leader who represented a more aggressive brand of right-wing Conservatism, reflecting more faithfully the prejudices on hanging, race, 'communism in the unions', 'welfare scroungers' and the like, which were entertained by their suburban supporters – and, as Thatcher herself shrewdly understood, by large numbers of workers too. Under the Wilson–Callaghan administrations which followed her election as leader, the remaining credit of the social-democratic consensus dwindled still further, while the Conservative Party was being prepared, under Thatcher's leadership, for a right-wing initiative more doctrinaire, radical and unpredictable in its outcome than anything in the party's previous history. Selsdon Woman was to prove a great deal more deadly than Selsdon Man.

The 'social contract', 1974–79

Wilson, in contrast to Heath, had retained his leadership of the Labour Party after the 1970 defeat without serious challenge. Responding to the industrial militancy of the rank and file of the party and unions, the 1971 Party Conference had adopted a more far-reaching programme than anything it had entertained since 1945, including 'a socialist plan of production, based on public ownership, with minimum compensation, of the commanding heights of the economy' (1971 Labour Party Conference Report). At Wilson's insistence this was later watered-down by the National Executive, although the tone of party statements remained radical. The 1974 manifesto pledged 'a fundamental and irreversible shift in the balance of power and wealth in favour of working people and their families'. Nationalization, however, was promised only for shipbuilding, the aircraft industry and the docks (all ailing sectors). The private sector was otherwise to be brought within the ambit of state-planning, only by means of selective share purchases by a National Enterprise Board, and by 'Planning Agreements' between the state and individual large companies. The party also proposed to introduce a measure of 'industrial democracy' in the largest firms.

Tony Benn, who had become the leading spokesman of the party's left wing, declared at the party's 1972 conference: 'the crisis that we inherit when we come to power will be the occasion for fundamental change and not the excuse for postponing it'. But the party was not converted to this view, and when Wilson took office again in February 1974 it had not come to power. It was a minority government, holding office with Liberal and Nationalist party support. It was also a government confronted with a catastrophic balance-of-payments deficit, inflation accelerating towards 20 per cent and the pent-up frustration of a labour movement more mobilized than ever before – but not, for the most part, any more committed than before to fundamental social and economic change. Wilson, for his part, was as committed as ever to the view that the only realistic goal for Labour was to find an agreed basis for reviving the ailing capitalist economy. The immediate problem was that organized labour was not willing to see profits restored at its expense without any quid pro quo. Heath had deliberately abandoned the institutionalized and regular consultation between the state and the leaderships of organized labour and capital that had been so characteristic of the later fifties and sixties. Wilson now made Labour's special ability to repair the government's relationship with the unions the cornerstone of his policy and of his electoral appeal.

The key phrase in this exercise was the 'social contract', adopted by the party and the TUC to denote the set of understandings between the state, capital and labour on the basis of which the state could look for the labour movement's co-operation with its policies, and which Heath was charged with having destroyed. Wilson undertook to repair the 'social contract' so that the voluntary support of the unions could then be obtained for a new 'incomes policy'.

The immediate necessity was to settle the miner's strike. This was done by accepting the recommendations of the Pay Board, to which Heath had sent the miners' claim before the election, and which gave the miners what they had asked for. The restoration of the 'social contract' was then put in hand. First, trade union rights were restored by a Trade Unions and Industrial Relations Act which repealed the 1971 Industrial Relations Act, and extended the principle of the closed shop, and an Employment Protection Act, aimed at improving job security by tightening up on unfair dismissal and providing compensation paid by the employer for many categories of redundant worker. A commission was also set up (the Bullock Commission) to make recommendations for 'industrial democracy'.

Second, the 'social wage' – collectively consumed services and social security benefits – was to be increased. The 1972 Housing Finance Act which had raised council-house rents was repealed; state pensions and widows' benefits were raised and better indexed against inflation; the tax burden was shifted (slightly) back toward the rich; and price controls were established and prices of some essential foods subsidized. The government later undertook to increase the 'social wage' each year in real terms.

Third, a National Enterprise Board was established to invest public funds in companies in profitable sectors; the nationalization of shipbuilding and aircraft production was embarked upon. 'Planning Agreements' with the largest firms, covering their employment and investment plans, were to be made by the Department of Industry, headed by Benn.

Having outlined this strategy for securing trade union co-operation and state-directed industrial recovery, Wilson called an election in October. The result was equivocal. The Labour vote actually fell slightly, but the Conservative vote fell further, by 1.4 million, and the Liberals also suffered a setback (see Table 4.1). Labour emerged with an overall majority of three seats, too small for a reliable 'working' majority. But in an effort to head off the Scottish National Party's challenge in Scotland (a traditional Labour stronghold) the party had promised to legislate for a Scottish Assembly with devolved powers. The SNP, with 30 per cent of the Scottish vote in October, and 11 MPs, calculated that an Assembly could be used as a stepping-stone towards real independence, and so decided to support the government. The Welsh Nationalists, with three MPs, and the Liberals with 13, also gave qualified support.[10] The government could govern, on this basis – if it could resolve the immediate economic crisis.

By the end of 1974 the rate of inflation was 23 per cent, and over the twelve months from July to July 1975 it rose to more than 26 per cent. Over the same period earnings rose nearly 28 per cent. Meantime the current balance of payments deficit for 1974 was no less than £3.6 billion (on visible trade alone it was £5.2 billion, offset by a surplus of £1.6 billion on invisible trade). The deficit was covered partly by the inflow of funds for investment by foreign companies in the North Sea oilfields, and partly by short-term foreign loans. By May 1975, however, it was clear that a final crisis was not far off. Labour's claim to be able to deliver union co-operation in stabilizing the economy was now to be tested.

The initiative was taken by the one man who had the real authority to do so, Jack Jones, leader of the two million workers in the Transport and General Workers Union. He proposed a voluntary agreement to restrict wage claims in 1975–6 to a flat rate maximum of £6 per week, with no increase in incomes over £8500 per annum – an agreement that would hurt the lowest paid workers least. This was accepted by the government and the TUC and implemented with remarkable fidelity. (To anticipate, it was followed by a further agreement for 1976–7, to limit claims to a maximum increase of 4½ per cent or £4 per week, and in 1977–8, although the unions declined to enter into any further agreement, many of them conformed in practice to the government's wish for a ceiling of 10 per cent. Estimates of the effects of this restraint vary, but it is generally agreed that over the years 1975–7, manual workers as a whole experienced a cut in real income of between 7 and 8 per cent compared with 1974; a loss which was largely made up, however, in 1978.)

On this basis Wilson hoped to get some industrial recovery, and foreign support for interim measures to cover the balance-of-payments deficit. But this was too optimistic. For one thing the world trade recession (after a temporary revival in 1971–3) severely limited the prospect of any recovery of exports. Secondly, the level of public consumption implied in the social contract was higher than foreign creditors thought the economy could afford. Thirdly, there was a general loss of 'business confidence', focused largely on Benn, the left-wing Secretary of State for Industry.

To meet these reservations, the government introduced deflationary measures in November 1974, and began to redistribute the tax burden away from company profits again. In June 1975, taking advantage of a national referendum decision in favour of remaining in the EEC (on somewhat modified terms), Wilson also removed Benn, who had led the campaign for a 'no' vote, from the Department of Industry to the Department of Energy. This spelled the end of any attempt to use the National Enterprise Board or Planning Agreements to extend public ownership or public participation in the economic policy-making of the large-firm ('meso-economic') sector. The only novel elements in Labour's approach to the industrial crisis were thus abandoned in favour of the familiar and self-destructive policy of deflation, just as the National Plan had been abandoned in 1965–6.

In March 1976, Wilson retired, professing himself confident that things were on course for a recovery, and was succeeded as leader and Prime Minister by his Foreign Secretary, James Callaghan. But by this time it was clear that foreign capital was not yet convinced that the balance-of-payments gap would be closed, and a movement out of sterling began which took the value of the pound down from US $2.02 in January 1976 to

US $1.63 in September (it had been US $2.60 at the end of 1971). A devaluation on this scale entailed all sorts of new and intractable problems. To reverse it by a corresponding scale of deflation would, thought Callaghan and the Chancellor of the Exchequer, Denis Healey, court political instability [. . .] The only remaining option – short of abandoning the capitalist system and declaring the whole economy public property, which could not have been further from their thoughts – was to seek a transitional foreign loan. In June 1976 a $5 billion loan was obtained from foreign central banks, but for only six months.

By September, with £1.5 billion of this loan used up, the government accepted the need to seek a longer-term loan from the International Monetary Fund, even though this would inevitably entail drastic deflationary policies;[11] at the same time, the government lost its parliamentary majority as a result of a series of by-elections. From now on, it presided over a programme of ever more severe deflation, sustained in office only by the SNP for the sake of the Scotland Bill, and by the Liberals for the sake of electoral 'credibility' as a party able to influence events – a strategy which eventually led in March 1977 to an official 'pact' between Callaghan and the Liberal leader, David Steel.

From this point onwards, the Callaghan government's policy was almost entirely subordinated to the deflationary goals set by the IMF, although Healey also became convinced of their necessity. By 1978–9 total government spending had risen 11 per cent over the 1973–4 level; but this was largely due to increased spending on debt interest, unemployment pay (the number of people unemployed had risen from 600000 in 1974 to 1.5 million in 1978), and subsidies to employers to maintain employment. Plans to expand provision in other fields were cut back, and in some areas spending was reduced below 1973–4 levels.[12] The 'social wage' also stagnated, increasing by only 0.3 per cent in real terms over the whole period 1974–9. The National Enterprise Board made no acquisitions except to prevent various large enterprises, such as Ferranti and British Leyland, from collapsing with the consequent loss of large numbers of jobs and long-term industrial capacity. The only Planning Agreements concluded were with the Chrysler Corporation, at the time of the government's attempt to induce the company, by a large loan, not to close its Scottish subsidiary in 1975 – and with the National Coal Board! The Bullock Commission's recommendations in 1977 for a system of trade union representation on the boards of directors of all large firms were strenuously opposed by the CBI and later dropped by the government.

As for industrial recovery, it was further away than ever. British exports continued to expand more slowly than the volume of world trade; British productivity continued to rise more slowly than that of France, Germany or Japan. Manufacturing output fell by 6 per cent in 1974–5 and rose by only 4.4 per cent from 1975 to 1979. By the end of the decade 'de-industrialization' had become a large and ominous reality. In Northern Ireland, which had passed under direct rule from Whitehall in 1972, nothing could be done, except, possibly, with massive expenditures, but these were out of the question. Likewise, nothing was done about the scandal of racial discrimination in jobs, housing and in other fields (see Smith, 1977). The only clear accomplishments of these years were, first, that the Labour government approached the end of this decade, like the last, with its inherited balance-of-payments deficit more or less eliminated – partly thanks to the level of deflation (i.e., unemployment and idle plant leading to fewer imports), and partly because of rapidly growing North Sea oil production; and second, that inflation had eventually fallen back to 9½ per cent, little more than its pre-1974 level. The situation had been stabilized – but at the cost of a more or less complete social stasis.

It now fell to the unions, for the third time in a decade, to destroy the fragile (and increasingly opportunistic) political balance. The patience of many workers – especially the lower-paid – was wearing thin. The recovery which had been so often promised in return for their sacrifices seemed more remote than ever. In 1978 the TUC refused Callaghan's request for a fourth year of wage restraint. In September, when all commentators judged that he would be well advised to call an election, he instead called for a new wage ceiling of 5 per cent, a call which was rejected by the Labour Party Conference. Meanwhile the workers at Ford (UK), which had declared profits for 1977 of £246 million, judging (not unreasonably) that most of this would not be invested in Britain but would be remitted to Detroit, demanded a wage increase of 30 per cent. After a strike lasting seventeen weeks, they accepted 19 per cent. The dam now broke in a series of large-scale strikes throughout what also proved to be one of the coldest winters in living memory. The low-paid public sector unions were particularly involved, from ambulance drivers to street-cleaners and school janitors. The snow lay in Regent Street, with no one to clear it away. Rubbish accumulating in normally wholesome districts was not collected. Schools were closed.

While the 'winter of discontent' continued, referenda were held in Scotland and Wales on the proposed devolution of powers from Westminster. Opponents of devolution inside the Labour Party had joined with Conservatives to amend the Scotland Bill to the effect that unless at least 40 per cent of the whole Scottish electorate voting voted 'yes', the government would not be bound to establish a Scottish Assembly. On 1 March 1979 52 per cent of those voting voted 'yes', but they constituted only 33 per cent of the electorate, and Callaghan reasonably judged that this did not warrant implementing the devolution scheme. The SNP members of parliament vented their frustration by deciding to support a motion of no confidence moved by Margaret Thatcher later in March. The Liberals had also abandoned the 'pact' with Labour in 1978 after Labour MPs had voted against the use of proportional representation for elections to the European Parliament (which Liberals had seen as an important precedent for a future change in the British electoral system). So the vote of no confidence was carried against the government and an election was called for May.

Thatcher, aided by a media campaign which suggested mounting middle-class hysteria, attacked the unions and argued, effectively enough, that Labour's claim to be able to secure union wage restraint was empty. The state, she declared, was a rigid, overgrown and parasitic obstacle to economic recovery, not an instrument of prosperity or welfare. She promised to cut income tax as well as state spending and adopted a position on immigration that was seen by some as explicitly racist. The result was a massive swing of 2.2 million votes to the Conservatives (including an 18 per cent swing among skilled manual workers), producing a Conservative majority of 41. The SNP paid the price of their pique, being reduced from 11 MPs to two. In the accelerating development of the crisis, the moment of 'Thatcherism' had arrived.

The new Conservative project of Margaret Thatcher

The failure of the 'social contract' as a basis for economic recovery had finally driven British politics towards a radical realignment. For the first time the leadership of a major party was committed to a project which went to the heart of the relationship between capital and labour. Thatcher had long subscribed to the individualist, anti-state, anti-union, anti-egalitarian views of her party's right wing. Shortly before her election as leader she also adopted the 'social market' and monetarist economic doctrines to which her friend and counsellor Sir Keith Joseph had recently been converted. Unlike the 'competition policy' of Edward Heath, Thatcher's vision meant abandoning, as fast as electoral considerations allowed, the welfare state; effecting the decisive reduction in trade union power from which Heath had drawn back after the failure of his 1971 Industrial Relations Act; and overcoming social and cultural resistance to a new order based on hard work, inequality, and the firm imposition of authority in the workshop and in the streets, by means of 'firm government' and an ideological crusade lasting, if necessary, for a decade or more. Whether realistic or not, the new strategy had a coherent logic. Unlike Heath, its proponents were not only ready to accept the social costs of restoring 'incentives' by creating mass unemployment, but judged that the public could be persuaded to accept them too.

The ideological movement which 'Thatcherism' represented was as important as its economic policies, and perhaps more so. Some observers argued that its long-run significance would be primarily in the extent to which it succeeded in completing the break-up of the amalgam of ideas which composed the post-war social-democratic consensus (Fabian faith in the state, Keynesian commitment to full employment and Liberal commitment to social security); and only secondarily in what it achieved through economic policies in office (notably Hall, 1979, 1980). The campaign to link the pro-market, anti-state doctrines of Thatcherism to popular Conservative themes such as the call for 'law and order' versus 'crime' and 'terrorism', 'the family' versus 'vandalism' or 'permissiveness', 'hard work' versus 'welfare scroungers', and so on – certainly gave it more popular appeal than the Labour left's advocacy of the Alternative Economic Strategy [. . .] which had no such 'populist' dimension.

Moreover, the 'consensus' values which it attacked had already been seriously undermined. The Labour Party could no longer deliver material rewards to the workers when in office; the credibility of the Fabian, full-employment welfare state had been seriously undermined. The state which people encountered as school parents or state employees, or when they were retired, unemployed or sick, often seemed patronizing, bureaucratic and mean, rather than an instrument of the popular will. The working class itself had been undergoing some profound changes, too [. . .] The 'common style of proletarian life' of the 1930s and '40s, with which the welfare state had been so intimately linked, had begun to break up. For both these reasons commitment to the 'welfare state' was no longer 'second nature', as it had been for the previous generation. It was no longer unthinkable for workers to be hostile to the state; it was even possible for Thatcher to win an election on a platform explicitly *attacking* equality.

But in the short run the internal contradictions of Thatcherism as a strategy of economic management and reconstruction seemed liable to offset whatever ideological appeal it might possess. It is hard to compress into a short formula the policies of the Thatcher government from 1979 to 1981, since they aimed at a comprehensive re-ordering of government priorities, public attitudes and the political and industrial balance of power. Their common source of inspiration was 'neo-liberalism' – replacing the welfare state by the incentives of the market far more systematically and comprehensively than anything attempted by Heath in the early 1970s. At least three major themes are discernible – 'monetarism', 'supply-side economics' and what may be called 'class-war politics'. 'Monetarism' refers to the idea that the principal economic task of the state should be to keep the growth in the supply of money in line with the growth of output. This done, inflation must eventually disappear. In particular, if workers demand, and receive, wage increases larger than the increases in output they produce, their employers will be unable to finance this by borrowing, and workers will be laid off until wage settlements are in line with productivity. 'Supply-side economics' refers to the view that the obstacles to growth do not lie with limited demand, as Keynesian thinking was supposed to assume, but in factors inhibiting the supply of goods – such as too large a public sector 'crowding out' the private sector (by creating shortages of labour or capital, or by taxing away the incentive to make profits) or trade unions' restrictive practices. 'Class-war politics' (not, of course, a term used by the supporters of Thatcherism) refers to the redistribution of class power in a wide variety of spheres, from industrial relations to education and health services.

These ideas converged in specific policies, especially in public-spending cuts, which were intended (a) to reduce the money supply by reducing state borrowing (the Public Sector Borrowing Requirements, or PSBR); (b) to reduce the share of the state and increase the share of the private sector in total spending; and (c) generally to reduce the 'social wage' – collective consumption – which was more important to wage-workers than to the middle classes.

The main measures implemented in the years 1979 to 1981 were:

1 *Public spending cuts* Thatcher sought cuts of £8 billion, or roughly 10 per cent, in total government spending over three years. £7 billions' worth of cuts (except in defence spending, which was supposed to rise by 3 per cent per annum in real terms) had been imposed by early 1981. The cuts fell on road-building, house-building, and nationalized industry investment of all kinds. They also fell on recurrent expenditure and were meant to lead to reductions in central and local government employment as well as employment in the nationalized industries. Nationalized industries were instructed to 'break even' within two years.

2 *'Privatization'* Forty-nine per cent of the government's shares of British Petroleum were sold, and a majority of the shares in Cable and Wireless; plans were announced for selling minority share-holdings in British Airways, and in the British National Oil Corporation. The National Enterprise Board with its collection of former 'lame ducks' was run down as far as possible; nationalized industries were instructed to sell off various assets, such as the urban real estate owned, for example, by British Rail on or near its main-line stations. Council-house tenants were given the right to buy their houses at a 30 per cent discount on the 1980 market price, thus fulfilling the Conservative aim of a 'property-owning democracy'.

3 *Money supply* The money supply was set to rise at well below the current rate of inflation by cutting the PSBR and raising the Minimum Lending Rate to the unprecedented level of 17 per cent from November 1979 to June 1980.

4 *Fiscal policy* The June 1979 budget of Sir Geoffrey Howe cut income tax, as promised in the election campaign, but sharply increased the Value Added Tax (indirect taxation). The resulting overall tax reduction was large for those in the top income brackets, but negligible for those in the lowest.

5 *Industrial relations* The Employment Act of 1980 banned 'flying pickets' (the importation of union pickets from other work-sites) and sympathetic strikes, and restricted 'secondary action' and the closed shop. The government dropped all consultation with the TUC and (with one exception) made a great show of refusing to be drawn – at least not openly – into industrial disputes. The days when 'both sides' in major disputes expected to be summoned to discussions at 10 Downing Street were over.

6 *Social policies* 'Comprehensivization' of the remaining grammar and secondary modern schools was halted. Funds were provided to local authorities to pay for selected pupils to attend private schools. Private

medical care was encouraged. Charges for services under the National Health Service were increased. Police and military pay was dramatically raised.

The most immediate results of Thatcherism in practice were a spectacular deflation, combined with a sharp *increase* in the rate of monetary inflation (from 11 per cent in May 1979 to 22 per cent in the second quarter of 1980), a sharp *increase* in the growth of the money supply, a *growth* of the state's share of GDP, and even a *rise* in the level of taxation. These results – the precise opposite of what Thatcher had promised – flowed from three main contradictions in the programme: the contradictions inherent in monetarism as a strategy of deflation, the contradictions of market doctrine, and the contradiction between the government's commitment to neo-liberalism and its attachment to privilege.

The fundamental contradiction of monetarism lay in its only partially-acknowledged aim of reducing trade union power by means of a level of deflation which would drastically increase unemployment. This was dictated by the discouraging example of Heath's experience in 1972–4, when he tried to curb union power by comprehensive legislation. But coming on the heels of three years of expenditure cuts by the Labour Chancellor, Healey, and in the midst of a world depression, the result was a national slump. Officially recorded unemployment rose from 1.6 million (over 6 per cent) in 1979 to nearly 3 million (12 per cent) by December 1981, almost a million more than the government had predicted a year earlier. (In fact, even the official figure was about a million less than the real total, ignoring, as it did, those, mainly women, who were available for work but did not register as unemployed; the true rate of unemployment was 16 per cent.)[13]

Unemployment on this scale meant a large drop in home demand, declining profits and a record level of bankruptcies. GDP fell by 5 per cent between May 1979 and December 1981. Manufacturing output fell 15 per cent in 1980 alone. Like all its predecessors, the government talked constantly about the recovery to come in a year or two, but even its warmest sympathizers found this hard to envisage.[14] As output contracted, government spending on unemployment rose, with the result that the state's share of GDP was 3 per cent higher in 1981 than it had been in 1978–9, with a parallel surge in the growth of the money supply. By 1981 the burden of financing unemployment had reached the point where the prospect of tax cuts, which had been a major part of the Conservative election campaign in 1979, was dwindling.[15] Inflation had also been increased, first by a big shift to indirect taxation and then by the price increases imposed by the nationalized industries as a result of the government's anti-subsidy policy.[16] The problem was that a deflation sufficient to achieve the government's *political* goals (in relation to the unions) severely damaged the economy's remaining productive potential, as well as leading to other consequences which flatly contradicted the beliefs of monetarism.

There were two main contradictions in 'market doctrine'. In the first place, the economy was not a system of perfect competition, so that 'market forces' did not produce the results theoretically ascribed to them. This was immediately noticeable in the public sector, where spending cuts led to reduced services, but not to greatly reduced staff. It was also obvious that small business could not play the regenerative role in manufacturing which Thatcherite theory assigned to it; it tended to be the large corporations which could both weather deflation on this scale and develop market-leading innovations.

Secondly, there was a serious contradiction between the Thatcher government's dependence on a *national* economic regeneration, and the *international* nature of the market to which it looked for the forces to bring about efficiency. For instance, international market forces in the production of cars pointed to a drastic contraction of British production, beginning with the elimination of British Leyland, the only significant British-owned producer remaining of those that had been taken over by the state as 'lame ducks' under the Wilson government in 1975. Faced with its imminent collapse, the government found itself agreeing to very large additional state funding as a lesser evil than that of allowing a workforce estimated at up to 700000 (including suppliers, dealers etc.) to be added to the social security bill.

The contradiction between neo-liberalism and the government's attachment to privilege was revealed in its lack of interest in a radical reform of the state and 'civil society' – the private social and economic framework of British life. The notorious inefficiencies of British life, from the secretive and ineffectual system of state economic policy-making to the archaic systems of taxation, banking and law, the insanely slow and costly system of real-estate conveyance, and an educational system as spectacularly inadequate in its day as it had been in 1900 – such spheres were not objects of Mrs Thatcher's concern.[17] She distrusted the civil service, the universities and the BBC for their past attachment to the social-democratic consensus, but her 'populism' stopped short of a radical assault on the structures on which the establishment's power rested, perhaps because she and the middle class were too attached to them.

Some of these contradictions converged in a policy crisis in November 1980, when some limited U-turns were executed. A £4 billion commitment was made to preserving the state-owned steel industry from extinction, and a £1.1 billion commitment to British Leyland. These measures were followed in February 1981 by a dramatic government retreat in face of a threatened mineworkers' strike. The issue here was a proposal to accelerate the National Coal Board's programme of pit closures, primarily in order to cut back coal production which, thanks to the big drop in demand for energy resulting from deflation, was leading to the accumulation of costly excess stocks. The National Union of Mineworkers threatened to strike. The government agreed to abandon the accelerated closure programme and to find an unspecified sum (at least £70 million) for the National Coal Board to cover its losses on excess production. Meantime, frustrated by the scale of public sector pay increases in 1979–80, the government announced a ceiling of 6 per cent on public sector pay increases, to be enforced through 'cash limits', for 1980–1 – in other words, public sector wage controls.

The rest of 1981 saw no relief from the government's policy failures, but no change of basic policy either, apart from a modest reduction of interest rates. The level of strikes had fallen to the lowest point since 1976, which was not unconnected with the fact that unemployment, close to four million and still rising, was costing the unions a loss of some 10000 members every week. The balance of payments was also stronger than ever, thanks to the degree of deflation and the contribution of North Sea oil output. Manufacturing productivity had risen, but largely due to the closure of marginal plants and to lay-offs. In fact, it seemed that the rise was no greater than in earlier recessions, while manufacturing investment was down by a quarter (below the rate of replacement). Thus, government claims that a radical transformation was in progress rested almost wholly on the view that reduced manning and improved work practices induced by deflation would continue into reflation and *then* be matched by large investments (Kellner, 1982, pp. 38–46). But even the most optimistic of the serious forecasting models expected only minimal growth over the next four years, and a further increase in unemployment.[18] The government blamed the world recession but most indicators were worse for Britain than for other industrial countries.[19] There was no doubt that the deflation caused by monetarist policies – the maintenance of a high exchange rate, high interest rates and a drastic reduction in the 'true' level of government borrowing (i.e., borrowing other than that required to pay for the extra unemployment created) – had made matters substantially worse. Government spokesmen still talked of a future recovery on a 'leaner, fitter' industrial base, but few commentators were convinced.

Yet – it was doubtful how many people cared. The most remarkable feature of the situation at the end of 1981 was that, in spite of real unemployment of 16 per cent (20 per cent or more in many cities), in spite of real cuts in personal incomes for the majority of those still in work (due partly to wage settlements below the rate of inflation and partly to increased taxation of all but the richest), and in spite of the growing conviction, even among commentators who had been attracted to monetarism, that the government's policies had, if anything, made industrial recovery less rather than more likely, the 'neo-conservative' mood remained strong. In 1979 Thatcher had campaigned strongly on the themes of opposition to the welfare state, support for private rather than collective consumption, competition and inequality. Research by the Institute for Economic Affairs (a right-wing 'think tank') had shown that these ideas to be quite popular among former Labour voters, especially skilled manual workers, and it was indeed this group who swung most strongly to the Conservatives. Two-and-a-half years later there was little sign that these social attitudes had changed.

Moreover the Conservatives' electoral prospects were by no means hopeless. This was partly thanks to divisions within the Labour Party, and the formation of the SDP which drew support from Labour as well as from Conservatives in the opinion polls. But these developments themselves were due to the crisis. The Conservatives had proved that savage deflation, on the scale of the 1930s, no longer carried an automatic electoral penalty as had formerly been believed. The 'moderates' in the Conservative leadership who argued in the autumn of 1981 that the level of deflation being inflicted could destroy the party had not yet been shown – in any obvious way – to be correct. That the new Conservative project contained the germs of an industrial renaissance seemed improbable. But it was not out of the question that it foreshadowed a durable change in the mode of defence of the capitalist social and political order in Britain.

Notes

1 An even larger proportion were poor, or on the 'margin' of poverty, by the state's own poverty-line criteria.

2 Holland cites a forecast that by 1985 the proportion would be 66 per cent.

3 A well-publicized threat of a capital flight was that of Pilkingtons, the glass manufacturers, after the October 1974 elections. Private investment abroad during the years 1975–78 inclusive was equal to 31 per cent of gross investment in Britain by industrial and commercial companies.

4 The Conservatives won only 75 (32 per cent) of the seats in northern England and Scotland, the lowest share in any general election won by the Conservatives since 1951; conversely they won 186 (85 per cent) of the 219 seats in England south of the Midlands, excluding London (see Butler and Sloman, 1980, p. 213).

5 A list of the sources for these views in the sixties and seventies would be very long. Early examples are Thomas (ed.) (1959), Chapman (1963), Shanks (1961) and Nicholson (1967).

6 On price controls see Panitch, 1976, pp. 129, 160 and 210; on dividend controls see pp. 114, 140 and 154.

7 Home became Prime Minister and leader of the party in 1963 on the basis of advice tendered to the Queen by Macmillan (when he resigned from ill-health) after informal consultations within the party leadership.

8 Andrew Gamble (1974, p. 121) notes that Powell received 105000 letters of congratulations within a few days of this speech.

9 Sympathetic strikes had been banned by the Trades Disputes Act of 1927 passed by the Conservative government after the General Strike in the previous year. Repealing the 1927 Act had been one of the first acts of the Attlee government in 1946.

10 The offer extended to Wales too, although Welsh opinion was much less strongly nationalist.

11 On the operation of the IMF see Payer (1974).

12 See Glyn and Harrison (1980, p. 121) for an analysis of the figures.

13 The evidence is summarized by Kellner (1982, pp. 26–33); see also Field (1982). The Manpower Services Commission broadly accepted the arguments: see *The Times*, 27 January 1982.

14 See, for example, *The Economist*, 4 April 1981, pp. 47–52; or the leading article in *The Times*, 27 January 1982.

15 In March 1980 the Treasury had forecast scope for tax cuts of £2.9 billion in 1982–3 and £4.1 billion in 1983–4. In March 1981 these forecasts had fallen to £1 billion and £2 billion respectively – less than the personal tax *increases* of 1980 and 1981. The March 1982 budget for 1982–3 arguably did not reduce taxation at all, but redistributed it from employers to employees.

16 In the six months ending in March 1981 the prices of food, clothing and household goods rose by only 2 per cent; the prices of coal, electricity, gas etc. rose 27 per cent (W. Eltis in *The Sunday Times*, 8 March 1981). By the end of 1981, however, the rate of inflation was still higher than it had been in May 1979.

17 At a time when the Danish government sought to ensure mass competence in the use of electronic calculators by issuing them free to every school child, and the Japanese government's long-term aim was to give every member of the population higher education, in Britain only 30 per cent of manual workers had any vocational qualifications (compared with 60 per cent in Germany); only 13 per cent of the age-group were in higher education (compared with 19 per cent in Germany and 30 per cent in Japan); and nearly one adult in three could not divide 65 by 5 (results of a survey carried out for the Cockcroft Committee on the teaching of mathematics, reported in *The Times*, 27 January 1982). Meantime the Thatcher government was reducing by 20000 (8 per cent) the number of students to be admitted to university from 1982–3.

18 That is, not counting Professor Minford's 'Liverpool' model. The next most optimistic was that of the London Business School; see *The Times*, 14 March 1982.

19 There was also a very large increase in the outflow of funds into investment abroad – a net flow of £8 billion in the eighteen months from January 1980 to June 1981.

References

BACON, R. and ELTIS, W. (1976) *Britain's Economic Problem: Too Few Producers*, London and Basingstoke, Macmillan

BECKERMAN, W. (ed.) *The Labour Government's Economic Record*, London, Duckworth.

BOGNADOR, V. and SKIDELSKY, R. (1970) *The Age of Affluence*, London and Basingstoke, Macmillan.

BUTLER, D. and SLOMAN, A. (1980) *British Political Facts 1900–1979*, London and Basingstoke, Macmillan.

BRITISH BUSINESS (1981) 'Ninety-four firms account for half Britain's exports', 3 July.

CENTRAL POLICY REVIEW STAFF (1970) *The Future of the British Car Industry*, London, HMSO.

CHAPMAN, B. (1963) *British Government*, London, George Allen and Unwin,

DUNNING, J. H. (1966) 'US subsidiaries in Britain and their UK competitors', *Business Ratios*, No. 1, Autumn.

FIELD, F. (1982) 'The missing half million', *The Times*, 28 January.

GAMBLE, A. (1974) *The Conservative Nation*, London, Routledge and Kegan Paul.

GLYN, A. and HARRISON, J. (1980) *The British Economic Disaster*, London, Pluto Press.

HALL, S. (1979) 'The great moving right show', *Marxism Today*, January.

HALL, S. (1980) 'Thatcherism – a new stage?', *Marxism Today*, February.

HOLLAND, S. (1975) *The Socialist Challenge*, London, Quartet Books.

KELLNER, P. (1982) *Slump '82*, London, NS Report 6.

NAIRN, T. (1964) 'The English working class', *New Left Review*, No. 24.

NAIRN, T. (1967) 'The nature of the Labour Party', in Anderson, P. and Blackburn R. (eds), *Towards Socialism*, London, Fontana.

NICHOLSON, M. (1967) *The System*, London, Hodder and Stoughton.

OPIE, R. (1972) 'Economic planning and growth', in Beckerman, W. (ed.).

PANITCH, L. (1976) *Social Democracy and Industrial Militancy*, Cambridge, Cambridge University Press.

PAYER, C. (1974) *The Debt Trap*, Harmondsworth, Penguin Books.

ROBINSON, D. (1972) 'Labour market policies', in Beckerman, W. (ed.).

SHANKS, M. (1961) *The Stagnant Society*, Harmondsworth, Penguin Books.

SKED, A. and COOK, C. (1979) *Post-war Britain*, Harmondsworth, Penguin Books.

SMITH, D. J. (1977) *Racial Disadvantage in Britain*, Harmondsworth, Penguin Books.

THOMAS, H. (ed.) (1963) *The Establishment*, London, Anthony Blond.

TOWNSEND, P. (1979) *Poverty in the United Kingdom*, Harmondsworth, Penguin Books.

5 Devolution without consensus: the experience of Northern Ireland

Liam O'Dowd

5.1 Devolution in Northern Ireland: political and historical framework

Devolved government in Northern Ireland was a by-product of the long drawn out struggle for Irish independence. Its establishment in 1921 marked the UK's first, and so far only, example of legislative devolution. In many respects, Northern Ireland was an unintended and undesired outcome of the triangular struggle involving the British government, the unionist and nationalist movements in Ireland.

Irish nationalists had sought an all-Ireland state with a large measure of autonomy from Westminster. Their alliance with the Liberals in Britain had eventually led to the passage of Home Rule legislation through the British parliament. This legislation, which was due to come into effect in mid-1914, was to give limited devolved powers to an all-Ireland parliament located in Dublin.

Irish unionists in alliance with the British Conservative Party and other elements of the British economic and military establishment bitterly opposed Home Rule. The core of opposition was located in Protestant Ulster among the descendants of the seventeenth century English and Scottish colonists brought to the province by the English government. The aim of the Ulster plantation was to subdue the last stronghold of Gaelic resistance to the English conquest of Ireland.

From the mid-nineteenth century onwards, however, a resurgent popular Catholicism throughout Ireland and a sustained nationalist agitation for self-government had laid the basis for Irish independence. Unable to prevent the secession of the rest of Ireland from the UK, one million Ulster Protestants settled reluctantly for the exclusion of the six north-eastern counties from the Home Rule settlement. They mobilized and armed over 100000 men in the Ulster Volunteer Force in 1912–13 to resist Home Rule by force if necessary. Their capacity to mobilize support from the Conservative Party and within the officer class of the British army posed a major challenge to the authority of the British parliament. In the event, the outbreak of the First World War led to the postponement of Home Rule. A major constitutional crisis, bordering on civil war, had been averted.

By the end of the war, however, the balance of forces had shifted. The 1916 Easter Rebellion in Dublin led to the displacement of the Irish Home

Rule Party by more militant nationalists under the banner of Sinn Fein. In the 1918 general election, Sinn Fein won an overall majority of Irish seats and set up an alternative parliament in Dublin: Dail Eireann. Between 1919 and 1921 the IRA, as the military arm of the Dail, waged a guerrilla war largely outside the north-east of Ireland.

The 1920 Government of Ireland Act provided for two separate parliaments in Northern and Southern Ireland, both subordinate to Westminster. While this act was never to be implemented in the south, it came to form the basis of Northern Ireland's constitution. Under the terms of the Anglo-Irish treaty negotiations in 1921, the British government agreed that the whole of Ireland should become a self-governing dominion but the Northern government was allowed to opt out retaining its powers under the 1920 Act. This it duly did. The existing boundaries of Northern Ireland were not confirmed until 1925 following the report of a controversial Boundary Commission.

The setting up of two new political units in Ireland was the result of a mixture of coercion and compromise. The northern statelet was born against a background of sectarian assassination and intimidation in Belfast. In the south, the Anglo-Irish Treaty provoked an intense year-long civil war which resulted in victory for the pro-Treaty faction. Subsequently, the party system in both parts of Ireland was to be largely determined by struggles around the 1920/21 settlement.

The main aims of both Ulster unionists and Irish nationalists were compromised. The unionists had failed to maintain the integrity of the Union; the nationalists were left with a truncated state. The six-county area represented the maximum area which unionists could control militarily and within which they were assured of a permanent electoral majority. While they had not sought a developed government from the outset, they quickly came to see it as a means of preserving their place with the UK. Here, Ulster unionists have always differed from Scottish and Welsh devolutionists who have sought self-government as a means of distancing themselves from British sovereignty. In the south, nationalists had their own state at last which could be presented as a stepping-stone to complete independence. They had failed, however, to establish an all-Ireland republic.

The policy of the British government had partially succeeded. Although its envisaged Home Rule parliament for the whole of Ireland within the Empire had not materialized, the 1921 settlement relegated the potentially explosive Irish question to the margins of British politics. The Irish settlement had a stabilizing impact on the British parliamentary system. The withdrawal of Irish nationalist MPs from Westminster speeded the demise of the Liberal Party as a major force. British politics henceforth developed a two-party system where the complicating features of peripheral nationalism and pressures for secession were greatly reduced. In Northern Ireland, however, while a surface stability was established after 1925, the seeds of future conflict had been sown.

For one large group the Partition settlement had little to recommend it. Northern nationalists found themselves enclosed and politically powerless within the six-county area. The very existence of Northern Ireland was a permanent reminder of their defeat and their subordinate status. Although constituting a large minority (one third) of the province's population they had no prospect of challenging the one-party domination of the Ulster Unionists. They were unwilling to accept the legitimacy of a state which had been imposed upon them.

Branded as disloyal, they were to suffer discrimination in the administration of justice, in housing, employment and local government. They were politically isolated as the British government consistently pursued a policy of non-interference in the internal workings of the Unionist administration. Periodic attempts by the Southern government to raise the plight of Northern nationalists were rejected by the British. Within Northern Ireland itself, nationalists were hopelessly divided among constitutional nationalists, militant republicans and several varieties of labourism. Indeed, it was the Catholic church, rather than the various political groupings, which typically represented Northern nationalists in their dealings with the unionist state.

In contrast, the close identification of the Unionist Party with the Northern Ireland state cemented the Protestant class alliance. The support of the substantial Protestant working class for a party led by large land-owners, businessmen and professionals remained relatively solid in the face of common enemies within and without the province. The Orange Order, to which the vast majority of unionist politicians belonged, allowed for the channelling of patronage through various levels of the Protestant class hierarchy. This was further facilitated by the total control of the state apparatus by the Unionist Party for fifty years after Partition.

It was not until the outbreak of the current conflict that Ireland was to become, once more, an issue in Westminster politics. The Civil Rights Movement, composed mainly (but not entirely) of Northern Catholics, succeeded in the 1960s in mobilizing British and international support for reform in Northern Ireland. Inured to compromise by fifty years of unchallenged supremacy, the Unionist government now faced both internal pressure from the civil rights protesters and external pressure from a British government increasingly embarrassed about the internal affairs of Northern Ireland. The monolithic Ulster Unionist Party began to splinter as divisions appeared in the Protestant class alliance over how to deal with rising nationalist disaffection and pressures to restructure the state in Northern Ireland.

By the late 1960s, however, the Irish Question had lost much of its historical capacity to disrupt the British parliamentary politics. An overall bi-partisan policy on Northern Ireland emerged in Westminster between the Conservative and Labour parties which has proved remarkably resilient on the broad issues. It has involved commitment to suppressing armed opposition to the state, to respecting the right of the majority in Northern

Ireland to remain in (or secede from) the UK and to a range of reform measures within the province. Since 1972 British government policy has been directed at some form of power-sharing or consensus government within the province. Above all it has been committed to containing the conflict within the six-county boundary.

Clearly, then, the history of devolution in Northern Ireland was not the outcome of a peaceful process of negotiation, legislation and consensus. The regional administration was viewed differently by the three main parties to the Irish conflict. Unionists saw it as a means of preventing their incorporation in a predominantly Catholic, all-Ireland republic. For Irish nationalists, particularly those in the North, the new regional government was illegitimate – a negation of the right of the Irish people as a whole to self-determination. The British government initially saw devolution as a prelude to some form of eventual Irish unity under the aegis of the British Empire or Commonwealth. Nevertheless, it was content to support a Unionist administration for fifty years as it provided stability and kept the 'Irish Question' off the domestic agenda of British politics.

5.2 Institutionalizing internal division

In Ireland, however, Partition was to consolidate division rather than encourage unification. One of its major effects was to further institutionalize the identification of religion and nationality. An overwhelmingly Catholic state was created in the south and a Protestant dominated state in the north. Not only did the border create an international division within the island of Ireland, it sharpened the divisions within the new unit of Northern Ireland. Here the boundaries which defined the mosaic of Catholic and Protestant territories now took on a new political significance. Every major political issue such as employment, housing, law and order, and the location of industry became reducible to one of loyalty or disloyalty to the state.

The political and cultural divisions within Northern Ireland and between north and south were underpinned by economic divisions. In the course of the nineteenth century, the gap between the north-east and the rest of Ireland had widened. Belfast became the only major centre of industrial capitalism in Ireland. Its shipbuilding, engineering and linen industries linked it with the north of England and Scotland. The craft industries in the rest of Ireland were destroyed by free trade and the rise of factory production, leaving most of Ireland heavily dependent on a relatively stagnant agriculture. In Northern Ireland large-scale employers were overwhelmingly Protestant and unionist as were the workers in the more skilled jobs. Catholics were more dependent on agriculture, casual labour and poorly paid jobs for women in manufacturing and services.

Not only was there a north–south economic division within Ireland, there was an east–west division within Northern Ireland itself. The east of the province was heavily Protestant and unionist and contained the bulk of economic activity and industrial employment. Belfast and its environs dominated its hinterland to such a degree that Northern Ireland was almost a city-state. The west and south of the province was more sparsely populated and had many local Catholic nationalist majorities. Economically poorer, these areas were marked by high unemployment and out-migration.

Devolution, therefore, seemed to rest on mutually reinforcing divisions at the economic, political and cultural levels. The central weakness of Northern Ireland remained, however. As a separate political unit, it was built around an ethnic–national division which precluded consensus on the boundaries or existence of the state itself.

5.3 The framework of regional administration

The Government of Ireland Act (1920) inserted a regional administration between the Imperial parliament and local government. Whatever the 1.5 million citizens of the new statelet lacked it was scarcely political institutions (see Figure 5.1)! Prior to the reshaping of the political and administrative system in the early 1970s, Northern Ireland had over seventy local authorities of varying power and size. On top of this, it had a regional civil service, a House of Commons and a Senate, replete with all the trappings of Westminster parliamentary procedure. In addition, the province sent 12 MPs to the Westminster parliament. These political and administrative structures reflected and often served to deepen the economic, political and cultural divisions which pervaded the province.

The powers of the new regional government were heavily influenced by the attitudes of the other two tiers. Local government, which stemmed from the Local Government (Ireland) Act (1898), remained largely unchanged until the restructuring of local government in the 1970s. Northern Ireland thus inherited a pattern of county councils, county boroughs, urban and rural district councils comparable to those established in 1888 and 1894 in England and Wales. The major difference was that in Northern Ireland (as in the whole of Ireland under the Union) policing and education were predominantly the responsibility of central rather than local government (Buckland, 1979, pp. 37–8).

The 1920 Act underlined the supreme power of the British parliament and established a division between responsibilities transferred to the Stormont government and those reserved to Westminster. At the outset, the new Northern Ireland government seemed to have a large measure of

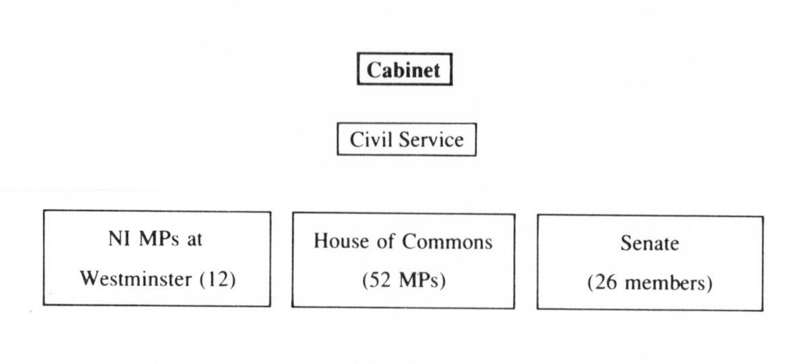

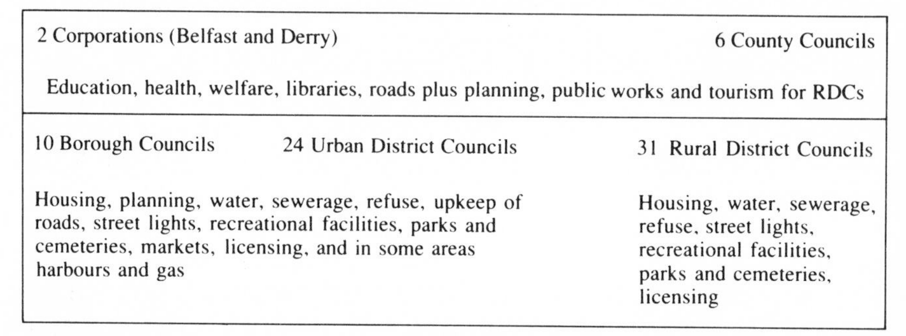

Figure 5.1 Regional and local government in Northern Ireland, 1920–72
Source: Birrell and Murie, 1980, p. 157.

autonomy with its own parliament, civil service and internal security forces. It had wider powers than the old devolved administrative system which had operated from Dublin Castle for the whole of Ireland since 1801. The parliament had power to 'make laws for the peace, order and good government of the area subject to certain specific exceptions, reservations and restrictions'. It could not legislate on issues such as the Crown and Succession, peace and war, defence and foreign affairs, citizenship, postal services, the Supreme Court, or on reserved taxation such as income tax, surtax, profits tax or capital levy (Elliott and Wilford, 1987, pp. 288–9).

The Partition settlement established Northern Ireland as a self-financing region with no provision for grants from central government or central control over its expenditure. The province also had to pay an Imperial contribution to defray the costs of national defence and foreign affairs. While the status of the Northern Ireland government appeared to be closer to the federal rather than the devolved model (Birrell and Murie, 1980, pp. 28–9), in practice both legislative and financial autonomy were either left underdeveloped or were severely circumscribed by the relationship with Britain.

The Legislature

One historian of the inter-war period has observed that the Northern parliament was a cipher and whatever autonomy the Stormont system had resided in its Cabinet and civil service (Buckland, 1979, p. 9). There were several reasons for the irrelevance of the local parliament. Firstly, despite its careful copying of Westminster procedure, it had neither a competitive party system based on liberal democracy nor an effective social democratic party. Parliamentary elections were invariably plebiscites on Partition involving sectarian head-counts. Given the sectarian geography of Northern Ireland this led to a large number of uncontested seats. Between 1929 and 1969, 46 per cent of all seats were uncontested in Stormont general elections. This lack of competitiveness extended to both local government and Westminster elections (O'Dowd, 1980, pp. 10–12).[1] The overwhelming dominance of the Ulster Unionist Party which always held between 32 and 40 of the 52 Stormont seats meant that the opposition could be ignored. The largest opposition group, the nationalists, who did not fully participate in parliament until the 1950s, did not become the official opposition until 1965.

Ironically, while there was a huge political divide between unionists and nationalists over Partition, both parties were conservative on socio-economic issues. Various labourist groupings, including the Northern Ireland Labour Party had a small number of members elected but they never seriously challenged unionist dominance even in industrial Belfast. Parliamentary debate was less concerned with socio-economic issues than with raising of constituents' problems and rehearsing the rights and wrongs of Partition. The parliament was very much a part-time affair, sitting for an average of 45 days in the 1930s, 60–65 days in the 1950s and 86–88 days between 1965 and 1971 (Birrell and Murie, 1980, p. 65).

Financing of devolved government

The financial autonomy of the Northern Ireland government proved to be more apparent than real for several reasons. Firstly, about 80 per cent of Northern Ireland's income derived from revenue raised by Westminster (Buckland, 1979, p. 81). The regional government controlled only minor taxes such as death duties and motor taxation, while rates, the other main source of revenue was controlled by local government. Northern Ireland's share of revenue was allocated on the basis of tax yield in the province, rather than on a population basis. The regional government did have formal control over about 80 per cent of total expenditure, although within limits laid down by the Treasury (Lawrence, 1965, pp. 80, 190–1). In addition, in the inter-war years there was a loose commitment to parity of services with the rest of the UK.

For the first twenty years of its existence the financial basis of the Stormont regime was precarious. Tax yield in Northern Ireland was lower than in the rest of the UK as the province's main industries contracted. The recession of the 1920s and 1930s was felt even more sharply in Northern Ireland where unemployment reached almost 30 per cent of insured industrial workers compared to 13 per cent for Britain as a whole (Buckland, 1979, p. 53). This created a major crisis over the funding of unemployment insurance. There was much behind the scenes wrangling between the Treasury on the one hand and the Unionist Cabinet and civil service on the other hand. The latter were in the main extremely conservative and committed like the national government to a balanced budget. Locally, the business, land-owning and professional interests which dominated the Unionist Party also favoured derating policies. All this left little scope in inter-war Northern Ireland for innovative government policies. Instead, government at local and regional level was more concerned with keeping rates low and minimizing entitlements to unemployment insurance and benefit.[2]

Areas of autonomy

Given the nature of the Northern Ireland Parliament and the limits on financial autonomy, it is tempting to write off the whole devolution experiment in Northern Ireland as inconsequential. This would be misleading, however, as the Unionist Party used the 1920 settlement to considerable effect in a number of key areas to consolidate its power. The unionists' most active use of devolved power reflected the violent origins of the statelet, the presence of a large disaffected minority, and their perceived need to strengthen the Union.

The areas most influenced by devolution included law and order, public administration and manipulation of the electoral system. Among the more notable features of the 1920 Act was that it devolved responsibility for state coercion to the regional government. In practice, this meant that the local security forces came under the direct control of the Stormont Ministry for Home Affairs.[3]

A Civil Authorities (Special Powers) Act allowed the Minister to make any regulation thought necessary for the 'maintenance of order' without even having to consult Stormont. These measures included arrest without charge or warrant, internment without trial, flogging, execution, destruction of buildings, requisitioning of land or property and the prohibition of organizations, meetings and publications (Tomlinson, 1980b, p. 179). Law and order was therefore firmly under the control of the Unionist Cabinet. The judiciary and the police force were overwhelmingly Protestant. Both were supplemented by a completely Protestant part-time paramilitary force: the Ulster Special Constabulary (B-Specials).

The policing and legal system constituted the most powerful expression of unionist authority. In practice it was used to pre-empt and counteract any challenge to the existence of the state from the nationalist minority especially republicans.[4] Its effects were far-reaching, however. Law and order never appeared as a separate (apolitical) issue apart from the ordinary business of governing as in liberal and social democratic systems. As far as nationalists were concerned, the police, B-Specials and judiciary could not be easily seen as acting in the 'public interest'. Far from being seen as 'above politics', the system was a constant reminder to nationalists of the coercive nature of communal relations and of the identification of the state with one political party and one community. To unionists the security apparatus was there to police a potentially rebellious and disloyal population who wished to subvert the state.

The whole area of public administration was also firmly under unionist control. The civil service, a major feature of the Stormont system, was overwhelmingly Protestant. The Orange Order campaigned continuously against Catholic infiltration of the civil service and government ministers took its representations seriously.[5]

Likewise discrimination against Catholics in local government appointments fitted in to the general pattern of exclusion. Unlike the Dublin government, Stormont did not seek to reshape, centralize and bureaucratize the functions of local government. Instead, it sought to ensure that the large number of inherited authorities functioned to consolidate unionist domination. Gerrymandering of ward boundaries was practised in some councils in the west of province, notably in Derry. Here, nationalists were denied control even of local council areas where they were in a majority. This deepened their sense of alienation from Northern Ireland as an entity which they felt had been created to construct a permanent Protestant majority.

The local government franchise was further restricted in 1946, going against the trend of democratization in Britain. The fixing of ward boundaries, the denial of the vote to the propertyless and the multiple business vote contrived to disenfranchise large numbers of Catholics and many Protestant working-class voters also. (The demand for 'one man, one vote' was to be one of the most powerful slogans of the Civil Rights Movement in the late 1960s.) Unionists controlled all the major local authorities until the reform of local government in the early 1970s. Indeed, only one (rural district) council ever changed hands between Unionists and Nationalists up to 1967 – a testimony to the 'frozen' pattern of local representation (Birrell and Murie, 1980, p. 163).[6]

Local councils were slow to build houses, especially in the inter-war period and there was considerable discrimination in housing allocation at local level so as not to upset the electoral arithmetic in specific areas. Job discrimination was also evident especially in marginal areas (Whyte, 1983).

Remarkably, although it had the power to do so, the British government, refused to interfere with the Unionist government's implementation of devolved powers in controversial areas. Part of the reason was the relative quiescence of anti-unionist opposition and the government's intention not to get embroiled in Irish politics. All this was to change with the eruption of protest in the late 1960s.

5.4 Undermining the 1920–21 settlement: the impact of the welfare state

The Civil Rights protests and the ensuing conflict was only the final stage in a long-term process which was subtly changing the relationship of Stormont to Westminster while altering the internal politics and administration of Northern Ireland. This process can be dated to the Second World War but it became more apparent with the extension of the welfare state system to Northern Ireland in the post-war years. A tension was generated between the more universalistic application of welfare measures and the more particularistic and discriminatory practices of the Stormont government.

The post-war welfare state measures were implemented by Stormont although Unionist MPs had voted against their introduction in Westminster. With an eye to retaining Protestant working-class support, the Northern prime minister welcomed the welfare state as a benefit of the Union, thereby guaranteeing 'parity in social services' with 'our kinsmen across the water' (cited in O'Dowd, 1980, p. 17).[7] In the short run, the welfare state reforms seemed to consolidate Northern Ireland's place within the UK. The Northern Ireland Labour Party adopted a pro-Union stance and attracted some Protestant and Catholic working-class support in Belfast. A renewed border campaign by the IRA between 1956 and 1962 failed miserably for want of support from Northern Catholics. The economic crisis in the south in the 1950s also seemed to be making Irish re-unification a less attractive goal for the Northern minority.

The long-term effects of the welfare state reforms were destabilizing, however. Two broad areas were affected. Firstly, the relationship between the Catholic community and Stormont widened considerably and in the process the Protestant monopoly of state power became more incongruous. Secondly, the structures of regional and local government and the ideology of the Unionist Party itself were ill-equipped to perform the more interventionist role demanded in the new political climate. The transition from 'protecting the Union' to constructing policies for modernizing Northern Ireland was problematic, especially at a time in which the central pillars of the local economy were crumbling. It not only created intercommunal tensions, it also exposed clashes of interest within the class alliance on which unionism was built.

From the outset, the post-war reforms affected areas of contention between Stormont and the Catholic community: education, health, housing and social security. There was much controversy within the Unionist Party over the increased state grants eventually made to voluntary schools controlled by the Catholic church (Birrell and Murie, 1980, p. 238). By the 1960s there was a noticeable growth in Catholic university entrants. Education and health services for Catholics, hitherto heavily influenced by the Catholic church, now became more dependent on state funding. New and more universalistic provisions reduced the discretionary role of the Stormont government in administering social security benefit – a role which had generated considerable class and sectarian conflict in the 1930s (McCullagh, 1986; Munck and Rolston, 1987). Stormont established the NI Housing Trust with a remit to build and allocate housing relatively free of Unionist Party and local authority control. It concentrated its building programme in the Protestant environs of Belfast to service the new multinational firms beginning to locate there.[8]

In effect, the Stormont administration was becoming increasingly the agent of the central British state in certain areas (O'Dowd, 1980, pp. 17–18). This in turn threatened the identification of the Unionist Party with the state. The development of health, education and social security services benefited both Catholic and Protestant working classes. There were misgivings among some unionists that free social services would increase Catholic numbers, raising the old spectre of being 'out-bred' and voted out of the UK. On the other hand, some moderate civil servants and academics welcomed the changes, some even suggesting that it might be advantageous to remove the semblance of self-government altogether (Isles and Cuthbert, 1955, p. 166; Lawrence, 1965).

Yet the contradictions hidden just below the surface began to emerge in the late 1950s and 1960s. The legal system, local government and discriminatory electoral practices were left unreformed. Even more important, however, the weakness of the Northern Ireland economy was now thrown into relief. The war had reduced unemployment to its lowest ever level (3.8 per cent in 1944) as local industries expanded as part of the war-effort. Thereafter, however, shipbuilding, engineering, linen and agriculture began to contract, shedding labour on a large scale. Unemployment rates at between three and five times the UK average persisted even though Britain was coming close to full employment.

By the beginning of the 1960s, huge lay-offs in the shipbuilding and aircraft industries began to affect even Protestant skilled workers. Unemployment in Catholic areas remained much higher than in Protestant areas despite Catholics' proclivity to emigrate which was three times that of Protestants (Barritt and Carter, 1972, pp. 105–8). The Unionist government was slow to react. Its deep conservatism and commitment to *laissez-faire* policies was complemented by its reluctance to see regional government as a policy innovator.

Long-standing Catholic grievances were now supplemented by a growing dissatisfaction within the unionist community. The NI Labour Party began to attract Protestant working-class support in Belfast in response to the government failure to combat large-scale redundancies. Some civil servants and younger members of the Unionist cabinet were pushing for a more active development policy (Oliver, 1978). From a unionist point of view, the difficulty was in reconciling modernization with the continuation of unionist domination.

Modernization was not just a response to internal factors, however. By the 1960s the international restructuring of manufacturing was in full swing. Traditional manufacturing regions like Northern Ireland were particularly affected. Multinational firms and competition from newly industrializing countries were undermining industries like linen, shipbuilding and engineering. By the early 1960s Britain was moving into an active phase of regional policy aimed at attracting new forms of manufacturing to declining peripheral areas. Service and state employment was also growing at the expense of employment in agriculture and manufacturing.

Constraints on public expenditure were also being eased. In the 1960s, Stormont civil servants had begun to operate an 'expenditure-based system' free from the notional idea of a balanced Northern Ireland budget. This made it possible for the civil service to make a case for particular developments to the Treasury. Between 1946 and 1963 overall revenue doubled and expenditure (largely administered by Stormont) increased sevenfold (Lawrence, 1965, p. 80).

The combination of internal and external pressures was pushing the regional government into a role it was reluctant and ill-equipped to perform. The decentralized structure of administration, especially in local government, inhibited development initiatives. Politically, the Unionist government was ill-fitted to mobilizing consent behind a series of more interventionist policies. A nascent civil rights movement was giving warning of growing Catholic disenchantment with elements of the Northern state. The government's own supporters, not only opposed Catholic demands, they also feared encroachment by the central state on the traditional unionist preserve of local government. The Protestant working class perceived its traditional skilled employment to be vulnerable and was impatient with the persisting gap between wages and unemployment in Northern Ireland and Britain.

The initiatives eventually taken by Stormont inevitably increased the potential for conflict. A physical plan for the Belfast region and a subsequent economic plan for the province sought to facilitate and order the incoming multinational firms. Following British precedent, growth centres were designated, greenfield industrial sites and housing estates to serve them were built. Railways were closed and considerable expenditure on roads initiated. A new university for Coleraine and two new towns, Craigavon and Antrim/Ballymena, were planned (for account see O'Dowd, 1985).

The rhetoric of regional planning, however, was quickly decoded in the context of Northern Ireland politics. There was much controversy over the location of the new towns, the new university and the growth centres. As these were all located in predominantly Protestant areas, nationalist politicians alleged that Stormont was trying to further entrench unionist privilege. Plans to reform local government to make it a more appropriate vehicle for development were opposed by local Unionist associations. There were also tensions within unionism at local level between traditionalists who supported the paternalism of the Orange Order and those who advocated a more active role for the state. Both sides, however, wished to preserve the Unionist Party's domination (Caul, 1988).

5.5 Conflict, reform and direct rule

It was against this background, therefore, that civil rights protesters and counter-protesters led by Ian Paisley took to the streets. Unlike previous anti-unionist movements, the Civil Rights Movement did not make Partition the central question. Instead, they demanded British standards of democracy in Northern Ireland: one man, one vote; the abolition of the B-Specials and the Special Powers' Act; and an end to discrimination in housing and jobs. Non-violent protest was met by a violent response from the police and the Paisleyites on the streets. As the international media poured into Northern Ireland, and the conflict on the streets was projected on television screens all over the world, the province quickly changed from being a political backwater of the UK to being a major international troublespot.

Initially, the British government sought to persuade the Stormont government to introduce reforms. Divisions began to appear in the Unionist Party between supporters of the prime minister, Terence O'Neill, who favoured limited reform and those who demanded suppression of the civil rights protests. As the police and B-Specials clashed with demonstrators, the relationship of the Catholic community with the local security forces deteriorated. Approximately 60000 people were forced to move house in Belfast (80 per cent of them Catholic) as inter-communal violence developed (Darby and Morris, 1974). Faced with the large-scale breakdown of law and order, the British government reluctantly committed the British Army to keep the peace. The B-Specials had been replaced with the Ulster Defence Regiment in 1970 and a series of reforms introduced in policing. Stormont still controlled internal security, however, and its introduction of internment without trial in 1971 led to a major increase in violence and mass Catholic disaffection. Significantly, Stormont was suspended and direct rule from Westminster introduced when security powers were removed from local politicians.

The thrust of British government intervention, from the outset, was to remove controversial areas of housing, electoral reform and law and order from the arena of party politics. (See Figure 5.2 for the post-1972 structure.) The Northern Ireland Housing Executive was established in 1971 charged with allocating public housing on a points system throughout Northern Ireland. The old local government system was replaced with a new single tier of twenty-six district councils, elected under the proportional representation system, and was now responsible for only minor environmental and recreational services. Four health and social services boards and five education and library boards were also set up. Local

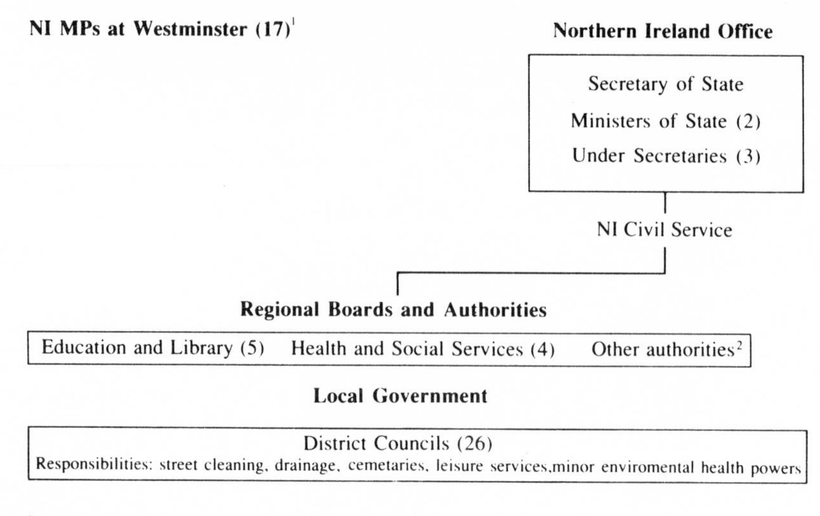

Figure 5.2 The government of Northern Ireland under direct rule

councils had nominees on both the Housing Executive and the new Boards but they were in a minority in each case. The new bodies were dominated by ministerial appointees often representing professional, business and voluntary group interests. Planning, roads and sewerage became the responsibility of the Department of the Environment, while electricity and fire services were centralized in regional authorities.

The search for new political frameworks

The new local government arrangements all pre-supposed the existence of an elected regional tier at Stormont. Since 1972 there have been four attempts to create such a tier which would be widely acceptable to both communities and which would recognize Northern Ireland's special relationship with the Irish Republic. Each proved abortive (see Table 5.1). In November 1985, following Anglo-Irish negotiations in process since 1980, the Anglo-Irish Agreement was signed. The Irish Republic guaranteed the right of the majority in Northern Ireland to decide their constitutional affiliation. In return the Republic was guaranteed a formal consultative role with respect to Northern Ireland. Both governments pledged co-operation in combating terrorism, in economic development and making the Northern security forces more acceptable to the Catholic community. The scope of the Agreement was to be reduced once Northern Ireland political parties (excluding Sinn Fein) could agree on a devolved partnership government. The Agreement is operated via a small Anglo-Irish secretariat in Belfast and regular meetings between British and Irish

Table 5.1 Attempts to find an agreed structure for devolution since 1945

1974	Power-sharing Executive and NI Assembly Council of Ireland (Brought down after five months by Loyalist General Strike)
1975–6	Elected Consultative Convention (Fails to find cross-communal agreement: majority report shelved by British government)
1980–81	Unsuccessful negotiations between Secretary of State (Atkins) and local parties
1982–6	Rolling Devolution: NI Assembly (Boycotted by nationalists and republicans; no executive powers were devolved; its main function was in scrutinizing direct rule administration; ended by British government in 1986)
1980–85	Anglo-Irish Negotiations and New Ireland forum (1984) (Outcome: Anglo-Irish Agreement: Conference and Secretariat – rejected by Loyalists and Sinn Fein; provision for devolved government if cross-communal agreement emerges)

government ministers (see McCullagh and O'Dowd, 1986; Benyon, 1986; Teague, 1987).

It is hard to assess the concrete effects of the Agreement. It continues to be opposed by Sinn Fein and all shades of unionist opinion. Subsequent to the Agreement there was widespread unionist protest and local councils under unionist control were frequently adjourned in protest. The IRA campaign has not diminished and unionists refuse to discuss devolved government while the Agreement is in place. Nevertheless, the Agreement provides an internationally recognized framework which allows both governments to co-operate in dealing with Northern Ireland. It underlines again the contingent place of Northern Ireland within the UK by giving the Irish government the formal right to be consulted on the administration of Northern Ireland.

Administration under direct rule

Whatever about the 'high politics' of finding an agreed form of government for the province, direct rule has begun to find an established niche within the complex governmental system of the UK. Three major interrelated factors continue to shape its evolution: first, the thrust towards more centralized and bureaucratic administration fuelled by a high level of public spending; secondly, the persistence of the violent struggle over the future of Northern Ireland; and, thirdly, the radical restructuring of the local economy, notably the collapse of manufacturing industry, the growth of service sector and the rapid rise in unemployment since the mid-1970s.

The growth of local bureaucracy and professionalized service delivery has been a direct result of government attempts to improve the impartiality of local administration. Inevitably this has meant the growing importance of the Northern Ireland Office and the local civil service and the relegation of the elected representatives of both communities. This has been combined with a dramatic rise in the level of public expenditure and public sector employment in Northern Ireland. Whereas public expenditure per capita in Northern Ireland was only 88 per cent of the English level in 1960, it was 3 per cent higher in 1969 and 41 per cent higher in 1978 (Northern Ireland Economic Council, 1984, pp. 4–5). This differential, which has been roughly maintained since, widened rapidly between 1972 and 1979. Although growth in public spending has slowed since, the Conservative spending cuts have had much less effect in Northern Ireland than in other regions of the UK. Since 1972, discretionary public spending in the province has not been constrained by local tax income. By 1983 only 54 per cent of government expenditure in Northern Ireland was being financed by tax revenue from the province (Canning *et al.*, 1987, pp. 223–5).

Unemployment doubled from 1974 to 1979 and again between 1979 and 1982 leaving the province with a rate which is still double the UK average. Northern Ireland is now a state-dependent economy with 42 per cent of all employees directly employed by the state and a private sector heavily subsidized by the state (O'Dowd, 1986).[9] The decisions of the direct rule administration are now obviously crucial to local economic prospects.

The nature of administration continues to be influenced also by the persisting IRA campaign and the more spasmodic violence of Protestant paramilitaries. Since its inception one of the great weaknesses of devolution in Northern Ireland has been the identification of one community with the maintenance of law and order. Despite the reforms of the early 1970s, the continuation of the conflict has intensified divisions over local security. While Unionist politicians call for more draconian security measures to defeat the IRA, nationalists and republicans complain about non-jury courts, 'shoot-to-kill' policies, supergrass trials and the attempts of successive administrations to criminalize the 'troubles'. Since 1974, there has been a major expansion of the RUC and the Ulster Defence Regiment. Both have been recruited overwhelmingly from the Protestant community and have become frequent targets for assassination by the IRA.

The communal divisions over policing and security are the sharpest manifestation of the lack of consensus which has always been associated with devolved government in Northern Ireland. The Anglo-Irish Agreement is the latest attempt to provide a framework for overcoming this critical problem but shows little signs of alleviating it in the short run. The issue is posed most starkly in Catholic working class areas where the republican movement is strong. Here, whatever the intentions of policy-makers, the implementation of security policies is likely to deepen polarization and alienation. On the other hand, among unionists, attacks on local security forces are seen as an attack on the Protestant community itself, particularly in rural isolated communities where many Protestants are connected with the police or the UDR.

Direct rule has brought about greater equity in public sector employment practices, in housing, local government and electoral practices. It has failed in three critical areas, however. Firstly, the violence continues at a high level although it has been generally contained within Northern Ireland.[10] Secondly, the British government has failed to realize its goal of restoring devolved government to the province in a manner acceptable to elected representatives in both communities. The third failure is a more qualified one. British policy has failed to generate the structural conditions necessary for equality of employment opportunity between both communities. Catholic male unemployment, for example, still remains over two and a half times that for Protestants, roughly the same margin as in 1971. It may be, of course, that this inequality demonstrates the limits of state policy committed to managing capitalism in a peripheral region. Although the state is the major economic actor in the province and has restructured local administration to offset discrimination, it has failed to alleviate major internal disparities and inequalities within and between both communities.[11]

5.6 Conclusions

Northern Ireland has been a part of the British state for well over three hundred years. It is a reminder of the historical connection between religion, ethnicity and nationality in British history and the role of coercion in establishing national boundaries in the British Isles and elsewhere.

Yet, since 1920, Ireland, and Northern Ireland in particular, has been largely defined out of discussions about the restructuring of the British state. Devolution in the province was part of the more general insulation or quarantining of nationality questions from mainstream British politics. The post-war welfare state reforms, the current conflict and direct rule since 1972 have threatened this insulation and provoked new strategies of distancing Northern Ireland from British politics.

The instability of Northern Ireland devolved government within a British context results from the inability to compartmentalize two sets of issues. The first has to do with ethnic/national loyalty, the boundaries of the state and the monopolization of force within these boundaries. The second concerns the 'normal' politics of state restructuring which includes changing economic and social policies which arise from a particular balance of power between classes and other interest groups. Under the Stormont regime, the dominance of one party and community ensured the fusion of both sets of issues in the interests of maintaining both unionist domination and the position of the state within the UK.

While direct rule has cast the British government in a more detached role with respect to communal division than that occupied by the old Unionist Party, the interrelationship of law and order, nationality, socio-economic policy and administration remains striking. The British response has been to centralize and bureaucratize while legally extending the powers of the security forces and the judiciary. By British standards, the Secretary of State has sweeping powers. As Elliott and Wilford (1987, p. 295) observe, civil policy and military administration are combined in the thrice-weekly meeting of British ministers, senior civil servants and the heads of the security forces presided over by the Secretary of State. Administrative reforms to induce greater impartiality in local administration as well as a measure of cross-communal support for the state have had to be imposed against the wishes of the unionist parties. One of the costs has been the lack of accountability of administration in Northern Ireland to local elected representatives. The paramilitary campaign and the policy of 'Ulsterizing' security threatens continually to identify law and order with the unionist community.

The impact of the welfare state reforms in the 1950s and 1960s starkly underlines the problems of devolved government in Northern Ireland and the nature of its relationship with Britain. While these reforms have been commonly portrayed as establishing a 'post-war political consensus' in Britain, in Northern Ireland they helped to lay the basis for mass protest and the current conflict. They did lead ultimately to a radical restructuring of the regional state including its security apparatus. By the late 1970s, however, when social provision in Northern Ireland had largely caught up with the rest of the UK, its legitimizing power was greatly weakened by the political and military conflict which had accompanied the changes.

It is doubtful if Northern Ireland holds many lessons for other devolution movements in the UK. Devolution in the province has differed historically from other regional movements which have sought to restructure the UK state. Unlike Welsh and Scottish nationalists and others who have advocated less radical devolution in Ulster, unionists did not have a political programme which they hoped devolution would advance. Their's was a movement to maintain the status quo. Accordingly, there was little potential for overt conflict between Stormont and Westminster on economic and social policy, once Westminster had underpinned Stormont's control of security.

The significance of Northern Ireland is perhaps wider than the devolution issue. It remains a testimony to the persistence and disruptive potential of ethnic-national divisions within the UK and other multinational states. It demonstrates the difficulty of establishing a liberal or social democratic consensus where the legitimacy of the state itself and its territorial extent is at issue. Significantly, it also provides a ready-made model for managing dissent from ethnic, racial and other minority communities in Britain and in other advanced industrial countries.

Notes

1 Inter-party competition was reduced when the Unionist government abolished proportional representation for local elections in 1922 and for provincial elections in 1929. Since PR was restored in 1973 for all Northern Ireland elections, it is clear

that its main effect has been to increase electoral competition within the two communities rather than between them.

2 Several historians of the inter-war period have held that Northern Ireland achieved parity with the rest of the UK with respect to unemployment benefit. McCullagh (1986, pp. 313–16) argues, however, that parity existed at the level of legislation only. There were major differences in the way it was implemented in Northern Ireland due to the class and sectarian biases of an administration faced with mass unemployment. In the late 1920s and early 1930s there was considerable social unrest in Belfast among both Protestant and Catholic workers protesting against the denial of outdoor relief to the unemployed (for an account of this period, see Munck and Rolston, 1987). The failure to match legislative parity with Britain with parity of implementation is one of the recurring themes of devolved government generally in Northern Ireland.

3 Miller (1978, p. 128) argues that it was not the 1920 Act which made Northern Ireland a state, rather it was the local unionist control over security. Wright (1982, p. 156), although he does not see Northern Ireland as a fully fledged state, suggests that the only significant powers of the Stormont government were the 'regulation of the national conflict'. The Ulster Volunteer Force which had been mobilized against Home Rule had been incorporated en bloc into the British Army in the First World War. There it suffered massive casualties. Between 1920 and 1927, however, it was resurrected, re-armed and incorporated into the B-Specials and the RUC. This was done with the connivance and explicit support of British officials despite the expressed misgivings of a minority (Farrell, 1983). Bew *et al.* (1979) see the final shape and composition of the new security forces as a response by the ruling unionist clique to the demands of its grassroots supporters, allowing them to mobilize and control them simultaneously.

4 Special Powers, while on the statute book continuously, were activated against nationalists and republicans in 1921–22, 1938–39 and 1956–62 in response to attacks on the state. The NI Special Powers Act was replaced by the Northern Ireland (Emergency Provisions) Act, 1973 and the Prevention of Terrorism Act in Britain (see Hillyard, 1983).

5 Buckland (1979, pp. 20–9) points out that in 1943 none of the top 55 posts in the Northern Ireland civil service and only 37 of the 634 administrative and technical posts were held by Catholics. Little changed until the 1970s. Greatly increased Catholic participation in the civil service (especially in the lower grades) is one of the most concrete effects of changed recruitment practices under direct rule (Fair Employment Agency, 1983).

6 The political accountability of local councils was limited. Birrell and Murie (1980, pp. 163–4) report that in the 1967 local elections only 66 of the 496 seats on rural district councils were contested. Their survey of pre-1973 councillors revealed that 25 per cent had never fought an election.

7 Birrell and Murie (1980, p. 295) note that, even in the 1960s, the Stormont government was reluctant to pursue parity of standards and make up leeway with Great Britain in housing, education, health, the environment and personal social services. Instead, Stormont concentrated on aids to enterprise, the economy, law and order and physical infrastructure (see also O'Dowd, 1985). Canning *et al.* (1987, pp. 224–5) note that it was only in the 1970s, under direct rule, that public expenditure began to be related to social need using British standards.

8 There was tension between the NI Housing Trust and local councils where the house-building by the former threatened local electoral arithmetic. Slum clearance by the Trust in Derry and Belfast was inhibited by the use of planning powers by both Corporations. The Trust had two advantages: its building did not put pressure on the rates and its allocation procedures were not as subject to sectarian

discrimination as those of the local councils (Tomlinson, 1980a).

9 Rowthorn (1987, p. 118) uses the analogy of the workhouse to describe Northern Ireland's economy 'where most of the inmates are engaged and servicing or controlling each other'. He sees the province as unable to survive in its present form without massive external support. Canning *et al.* (1987, p. 225) suggest that the Northern Ireland 'troubles' may have resulted in a net gain in employment. Although the conflict brought about a greater than expected decline in manufacturing jobs, it generated a greater than expected increase in public sector employment. The reasoning here is that direct rule is a product of the 'troubles' and without it public spending would be still constrained by local tax income and a notional balanced budget.

10 Some idea of the scale of the violent death rate in Northern Ireland can be adduced by extrapolating the proportionate figures to Great Britain. Northern Ireland deaths as a result of the 'troubles' between 1969 and 1984 would have a British equivalent of 86 000. The corresponding figures for extrapolating the Protestant and Catholic death rates would be 66300 and 133600 respectively. If arrests without charge in Northern Ireland were extrapolated to Britain for the same period, they would amount to 1.8 million (Roche, 1984).

11 Without the massive expansion in public service employment, especially in health and education, the Protestant-Catholic unemployment differential might have actually widened (O'Dowd, 1987, p. 206).

References

BARRITT, D. and CARTER, C. F. (1972) *The Northern Ireland Problem: A Study in Group Relations*, London, Oxford University Press.

BENYON, J. (1986) 'The Anglo-Irish Agreement', *Social Studies Review*, Vol. 1, No. 4.

BEW, P., GIBBON, P. and PATTERSON, H. (1979) *The State in Northern Ireland*, Manchester, Manchester University Press.

BIRRELL, D. and MURIE, A. (1980) *Policy and Government in Northern Ireland: Lessons of Devolution*, Dublin, Gill and Macmillan.

BUCKLAND, P. (1979) *The Factory of Grievances: Devolved Government in Northern Ireland, 1921–39*, Dublin, Gill and Macmillan.

CANNING, D., MOORE, B. and RHODES, J. (1987) 'Economic growth in Northern Ireland: problems and prospects', in Teague, P. (ed.).

CAUL, L. (1988) *State Management of Newtownabbey, 1950–83*, unpublished PhD thesis, Queen's University, Belfast.

CLANCY, P., DRUDY, S., LYNCH, K. and O'DOWD, L. (eds) (1986) *Ireland: A Sociological Profile*, Dublin, Institute of Public Administration.

DARBY, J. and MORRIS, G. (1974) *Intimidation in Housing*, Belfast, Northern Ireland Community Relations Commission.

ELLIOTT, S. and WILFORD, R. (1987) 'Administration', in Buchanan, R. H. and Walker, B. M. (eds), *Province, City and People: Belfast and its Region*, Belfast, Greystone Books.

FAIR EMPLOYMENT AGENCY (NORTHERN IRELAND) (1983) *Report of an Investigation by the Fair Employment Agency for Northern Ireland into the Non-Industrial Civil Service*, Belfast, Fair Employment Agency.

FARRELL, M. (1983) *Arming the Protestants*, London, Pluto Press.

HILLYARD, P. A. R. (1983) 'Law and order', in Darby, J. (ed.), *Northern Ireland: The Background to the Conflict*, Belfast, Appletree Press.

ISLES, K. S. and CUTHBERT, N. (1955) 'Economic policy', in Wilson, T. (ed.), *Ulster under Home Rule*, London, Oxford University Press.

LAWRENCE, R. J. (1965) *The Government of Northern Ireland*, Oxford, Clarendon Press.

McCULLAGH, M. (1986) 'The social construction of unemployment in Northern Ireland', in Clancy, P. *et al.* (eds).

McCULLAGH, M. and O'DOWD, L. (1986) 'Northern Ireland: the search for a solution', *Social Studies Review*, Vol. 1, No. 4.

MILLER, D. W. (1978) *Queen's Rebels*, Dublin, Gill and Macmillan.

MUNCK, R. and ROLSTON, B. (1987) *Belfast in the Thirties: An Oral History*, Belfast, Blackstaff Press.

NORTHERN IRELAND ECONOMIC COUNCIL (1984) *Public Expenditure Priorities: Overall Review*, Report 42, Belfast, Northern Ireland Economic Council.

O'DOWD, L. (1980) 'Shaping and reshaping the Orange State: an introductory analysis', in O'Dowd, L. *et al.*

O'DOWD, L. (1985) 'The crisis of the regional strategy: ideology and the state in Northern Ireland', in Rees, G. *et al.* (eds), *Political Action and Social Identity: Class, Locality and Culture*, London and Basingstoke, Macmillan.

O'DOWD, L. (1986) 'Beyond industrial society', in Clancy, P. *et al.* (eds).

O'DOWD, L. (1987) 'Trends and potential of the service sector in Northern Ireland', in Teague, P. (ed.).

O'DOWD, L., ROLSTON, B. and TOMLINSON, M. (1980) *Northern Ireland: Between Civil Rights and Civil War*, London, Conference of Socialist Economists.

OLIVER, J. (1978) *Working at Stormont*, Dublin, Institute of Public Administration.

ROCHE, D. (1984) 'The political consequences of a changing pattern of violence', *Fortnight*, No. 207, September.

ROWTHORN, B. (1987) 'Northern Ireland: an economy in crisis', in Teague, P. (ed.).

TEAGUE, P. (ed.) (1987) *Beyond the Rhetoric: Politics, the Economy and Social Policy in Northern Ireland*, London, Lawrence and Wishart.

TOMLINSON, M. (1980a) 'Housing, the state and the politics of segregation', in O'Dowd, L. *et al.*

TOMLINSON, M. (1980b) 'Reforming repression', in O'Dowd, L. *et al.*

WALSH, D. (1983) *The Use and Abuse of Emergency Legislation in Northern Ireland*, London, The Cobden Trust.

WHYTE, J. H. (1983) 'How much discrimination was there under the unionist regime, 1921–68?', in Gallagher, T. and O'Connell, J. (eds), *Contemporary Irish Studies*, Manchester, Manchester University Press.

WRIGHT, F. (1982) 'The Ulster spectrum', in Carlton, D. and Schaerf, C. (eds), *Contemporary Terror Studies in Sub-State Violence*, London and Basingstoke, Macmillan.

Section III Restructuring and the state

Introduction

If the 1970s were dominated by discussions of crisis, that crisis seems to have been moving towards some resolution in the 1980s. In Section II some of the key features of political crisis were related to the development of the social-democratic state after 1945, and its inability to deal with the pressures of relative economic decline. It might, therefore, be expected that in moving away from crisis the British state, too, will be taking on new forms. The post-war British state has been described as a Keynesian welfare state, because of its involvement in the management of the economy and in the provision of welfare support, which symbolized its role as guarantor and institutional expression of an unspoken agreement between the different classes of British society. The chapters in this Section consider ways in which the state has been and is being restructured, looking in particular at the relationship between state and economy as well as changes in the structure of central–local government relations. British local government has been an important part of the post-war welfare state, both as a mechanism of service delivery and as a channel for political legitimation, so any restructuring of that state is also likely to be reflected in the relations between central and local government.

In Chapter 6 Helm looks at the rise and fall of state intervention after the war with the help of a thoughtful survey of theoretical debates about state–economy relations. He stresses the importance of moving beyond debates between those who equate the market with 'perfect competition' and those who challenge the validity of such approaches because the assumptions of 'perfect competition' can rarely (possibly never) be met in practice. He points to rather different arguments against state involvement which arise from what he calls 'Austrian' theories, before going on to argue that the debate between market and state cannot be settled on technical grounds, but is actually one about values – in other words, for him it is a political issue, to be decided on political grounds, albeit with the help of adequate technical advice. He contrasts the views of market pessimists, such as Keynes, with those of the market optimists, as represented in the policies of the Thatcher government and considers various forms of both market and government failure in economic decision-making. But the central point of his argument is that there is no single 'correct' level of state intervention – where the line between state and economy is drawn depends on value judgements and he suggests some ways in which the consequences of these judgements can be translated into different policies.

Helm's arguments are largely conducted in terms of debates drawn from the field of academic economics. They tend to deal in rather broad categories which assume a relatively uniform geographical space and to accept the ground rules of the capitalist economy, which are questioned in some of the earlier chapters. Lovering and Boddy in Chapter 7 analyse the spatial impact of defence spending which in principle is decided – at national level at least – separately from economic policy and from any consideration of regional policy. Yet the forms taken by defence spending in practice actually help to determine the direction of technological development, since a great deal of research is actually funded through defence budgets rather than any specifically earmarked for research. And it also helps to determine the regional pattern of growth, reinforcing development in those areas where it is already concentrated without any open debate over the value of such a concentration.

Chapter 8 consists of an extract from the *London Industrial Strategy* which was produced by the Greater London Council and published in 1985, a year before the Council's abolition. It challenged the orthodoxies of traditional economic policy from two points of view. First it suggests not only that the market provides an unhelpful and negative guide to economic decision-making but also that an alternative approach based on 'popular planning' is more appropriate. And, secondly, it stresses the importance of locally based economic initiatives when traditional economic policies have always been developed from the top down. The extract indicates some of the ways in which the Council tried to achieve its aims, and the gap between ambitions and achievement is probably apparent even here. But it should be remembered that the Council was abolished before having the chance to develop them further, and some of the broader arguments remain important, even if the GLC was not able to implement the policies which might be expected to follow from them.

The GLC was probably not abolished because of the impact of its economic policies, although it must have been embarrassing for central government to see a local council presenting such a radically alternative approach on its very doorstep. In Chapter 9 Rhodes looks back over the experience of central–local relations since 1945. His analysis stresses the way in which sub-national government expanded as part of the growth of the welfare state and he emphasizes the organizational and structural reasons for its growth, tending to minimize the significance of territorial, and particularly 'local', politics, at least in the growth phase. He focuses on what he calls functional politics which links national and local officials (and politicians) through policy networks based on specialist functional areas, such as education, social services and housing. These networks, he argues, have been a key source of political initiative and power, making it difficult to develop an overall (corporate) set of policies at either national or local level. Rhodes acknowledges that territorial politics have increased in importance as the 1970s progressed, because they provided a focus for political opposition to the pressures from above. Since the 1970s saw increased economic constraints on the welfare state, it was effectively through local government that opposition developed, to the extent that in some cases it became difficult for the policy networks to remain intact. They were also being increasingly placed under pressure because some central government departments were given the responsibility of managing budgets as well as developing and managing spending programmes. Within the central–local government systems the Department of the Environment effectively took on the Treasury role.

But Rhodes remains sceptical about the coherence and direction of change. If this is restructuring, it is crab-like and rather uncertain, since he suggests that the result is a 'mess' rather than a new form of organization. Both Helm and the Greater London Council in their different ways would be more confident about the identification of structural change. Helm largely accepts the political claims of 'Thatcherism' to have made a break with the post-war political consensus while the GLC claims that economic changes have opened up the possibility of new forms of economic intervention.

Allan Cochrane

6 The economic borders of the state

Dieter Helm

6.1 Introduction

[. . .] The [economic] borders have shifted markedly in the twentieth century. Governments, throughout the industrialized world, have extended their activities from the provision of minimal basic services – such as the maintenance of the value of the currency, defence, and law and order – to a much more comprehensive role in allocating resources, in providing education, health and social security, and in macroeconomic management. In addition, a new feature of twentieth century government has been the conscious attempt to alleviate poverty and redistribute income. This expansion has involved the development and use of a wide variety of policy instruments, and a vast expansion in the scale of public expenditure and taxation.

This transformation did not take place as a smooth and steady progression. The role of the state expanded markedly during the two World Wars. Governments, forced to attain maximum output from their limited resources, were not prepared to leave production to the private market and indeed, during the Second World War, planned the mobilization of resources in great detail with considerable success. After the Second World War, a new consensus emerged based on the 'mixed economy' with considerable government intervention both at the macroeconomic and microeconomic levels. In the UK the foundations for the post-war economic order were laid with the Beveridge Report (1942), the Education Act (1944), the Employment White Paper (1944) and the subsequent setting up of the welfare state and the nationalization of major sections of industry.

In broad terms, this consensus remained intact so long as economic growth continued to finance the demands on welfare services and the public sector. While it lasted, there was a tendency for politicians to compete as managerial teams, committed, in the 1950s and 1960s, to the achievement of ever more ambitious goals for output, employment and welfare. The principles on which this consensus was based were not seriously challenged at the intellectual level until the revival of monetarist theory and the political philosophy of the 'new right' in the early 1970s. Since then, the question of the proper role of the state has been one of the most contentious issues on the political agenda.

In Britain the change in government in 1979 produced the first serious and sustained political challenge to the foundations of the mixed economy. The Medium Term Financial Strategy (introduced in 1980) redefined the role of macroeconomic policy, assigning it largely to the reduction of inflation. The Conservative government also embarked upon a *laissez-faire* policy towards the private sector and, with the general ambition of 'making markets work better' sought to reduce governmental interference and intervention. Department of Trade and Industry programmes of regional and industrial aid were radically reduced (and the then Secretary of State wondered whether the department itself might 'wither away'). Labour market monopoly was attacked in an attempt to liberalize its working, so that wages might adjust 'naturally' to restore full employment. Incomes policies, the traditional response to wage inflation in the consensus years, were abandoned. In theory at least, the goals of full employment and growth were to be achieved by free markets and microeconomic flexibility, whilst control of the money supply would ensure low inflation. (In practice, however, the macroeconomic and microeconomic aspects have increasingly become mixed up, as the privatization programme has been geared to maximizing sales value in order to curtail the Public Sector Borrowing Requirement (PSBR) at the expense of efficient resource allocation.)

Though the details of these policies are of immediate concern, this assessment attempts to look behind the practical aspects at the fundamental principles which provide a rationale for state intervention. For the relationship between these policies and the economic theory of the market upon which they are based is nowhere straightforward. The economist, faced with the diversity of practical policy questions and the complexity of their effects, can contribute to this debate in a number of ways. Some of the questions which arise are instrumental ones – what options are there available to pursue a specified objective? Is present policy the best means available? These kinds of question relate to such matters as whether particular taxes are well-fitted to raising revenue, or are progressive or regressive; whether privatized firms are likely to be more efficient than nationalized ones [. . .]

The answers that economists can provide to these questions are necessarily incomplete. In part, this is because the data economists have available are itself typically incomplete and unreliable. But, in addition, theory requires simplifications which necessarily involve divergence from the actual world. Model-failure is inevitable. Yet despite these difficulties, the kinds of disputes which arise with instrumental questions are ones which can be tackled in a rational manner and progress can be made. We now know, for example, more about the role and methods by which competition operates, about the transmission from money to economic activity and so on.

But although some of the evaluational questions about the economic role of the state are instrumental, others are more elusive. These are questions about ends, goals and values. It is less clear here what the economist can contribute. On the one hand, the economist cannot say that one value judgement is superior to another. But, on the other, such judgements cannot be avoided. An ordering of objectives must be made. Faced with this dilemma, the economist can, where a number of objectives are being pursued, at least indicate where there is or is not consistency and can further examine what the consequences in terms of practical policy might be of pursuing them. Recent developments in welfare economics have gone a considerable way to open up this discussion beyond the narrow traditional Paretian grounds.

This assessment examines the economic arguments at both the instrumental and value judgement levels. It attempts to identify the various rationales proposed for the market allocation of resources and for state intervention. It looks at the ways in which the fundamental economic theories of markets and planning have affected the growth of the economic borders of the state in the twentieth century and, in the light of this analysis, reassesses the instrumental case for government intervention and the values upon which it is based. The arguments are focused on market and government failure and the case for liberty and social justice. The role and design of macroeconomic policy [are] largely neglected here, except in so far as [they] relate to the underlying principles of economic organization.

The structure is as follows. Section 6.2 looks at the arguments 'behind' the current policy debate to bring out the theoretical case which economists have put forward for and against the market. Section 6.3 then turns from this abstract discussion to see what impact these theoretical arguments have had on the economic expansion of the state in the twentieth century. Section 6.4 reassesses the instrumental and value questions and suggests an alternative way forward, while section 6.5 presents the major conclusions.

6.2 The rationale for state intervention and the market philosophy

There has been a tendency in academic economics to focus on ever-narrower technical modelling and to shy away from grander questions such as the rationale for the market system. Increasingly this field has been left to political theorists and politicians. Yet economics has much to contribute to this debate and has in fact, provided the core arguments for the expansion and now contraction of state activity. 'The ideas of economists and political philosophers, both when they are right and when they are wrong, are', as Keynes (1936, p. 383) noted, 'more powerful than is commonly understood. . . . Practical men, who believe themselves to be quite exempt from any intellectual influences, are usually the slaves of some defunct economist.'

The central question to which economists have given different answers since Adam Smith is whether or not the competitive market system, left to its own devices, free of government interference, will produce superior results in terms of efficiency and social justice, than alternative systems of economic organization. It is this claim which again dominates the political and economic policy agenda in the UK and many other countries.

It is a claim about both means and ends. The market system is argued to be the best *instrumental* method for attaining certain predetermined fundamental goals. Thus the argument for a policy of *laissez-faire* rests upon two necessary conditions – the merits of the ultimate goals and the instrumental efficiency of the market in attaining them. The debate about ends is one which market theorists have not avoided. Indeed it is here that the political philosophy of the 'new right' and economic theory have come together. The defenders of the market are typically neo-liberals, rejecting the paternalism of the state (from the right and the left) and stressing the importance of liberty for the individual. These writers favour the competitive market system because, compared to alternative economic systems, it is argued to generate greater individual liberty through voluntary consumer choice.

At the instrumental level, the proponents of the market divide between those who optimistically claim great virtue for the market and those with less exacting views. The former group see the market as generating the maximum wealth and the the maximum freedom, while the latter rest their case on the weaker and less exacting argument that the market – while not perfect – is better than the available alternatives such as state intervention.

Any economic system ultimately relies for its justification upon the effects it has on welfare. The different theories of the market make different assumptions about human behaviour – about what motivates people and how they react to incentives. They can be divided into those which view competition as an incentive system bringing out the best in individuals and those for which competition acts as a necessary discipline on the tendency to idleness and the exploitation of monopoly profit. Thus the market can be seen either as a positive system of incentives or 'carrots' to encourage the development of talents, skills and abilities of individuals, or as a negative 'stick' to force people to be efficient.

Unfortunately for defenders of the market system, the models which they employ at the instrumental level and the goals or values advanced at the deeper level can also point in the opposite direction. The neo-classical model typically employed in defending markets relates to decentralization of production and exchange – a perfect market or a perfect planner will both produce optimal results. And, in terms of values, the appeal to liberalism can also point in the direction of intervention. But this is to anticipate the reassessment in section 6.4 below. We first examine the traditional arguments.

Economists have typically focused on the efficiency gains from competition and we shall follow this tradition by first examining the instrumental efficiency of the market. This approach requires both a positive theory demonstrating the merits of the market and, in addition, a negative theory about the defects of state intervention. We then turn to the debate about values which lies behind the market defence.

Instrumental arguments and the economic efficiency of markets

The somewhat counter-intuitive notion that the pursuit of self-interest unimpeded by government interference might be superior in efficiency terms to co-operative behaviour is a legacy of Adam Smith's 'invisible hand' doctrine. Yet, as Jacob Viner has pointed out (1960, p. 65): 'The classical exponents of *laissez-faire* always qualified their enthusiasm for the free market by the condition that it should be a competitive market'. The defence of the market rested then on the consequences of its competitive nature. Yet in the literature, there are two quite distinct broad accounts of the operation of competitive forces and hence two defences of market solutions generally. These are, first, the static neo-classical economic model (in tradition of Walras and Jevons) and, second, that of the Austrian tradition, which has focused on the dynamics of competition (in the tradition of Menger, Mises, Hayek and Schumpeter). The former is the paradigm used most generally in mainstream economic theory and relies on the model of perfect competition. The latter relies on the superiority of the price mechanism as a means of co-ordination compared to government planning where uncertainty is pervasive. Both rely on value judgements, but again these (as we shall see) differ strongly. We have, therefore, three levels of analysis in the theory of markets – perfect competition, co-ordination and the value judgements.

Perfect competition

The traditional argument for *laissez-faire* is constructed by examining how a decentralized market system, unimpeded by distortions, would function. That competitive form is then shown to be compatible with an apparently acceptable and uncontroversial welfare judgement and hence demonstrated to be ideal.

A perfectly decentralized economy operates in markets where there are a large number of consumers maximizing their utility and producers maximizing profits. Everything is owned and the property rights are clearly defined. In each and every market, the product is homogeneous, there are no barriers to entry, returns to scale are constant and relevant information is generally available and free of charge. Each firm has no market power and hence is a price-taker rather than a price-maker. In such an economy, firms maximize profits where price is equal to marginal cost. Any deviation from this would lead to loss of market as new entrants came into the market and consumers turned elsewhere for their goods and services. Thus firms earn just sufficient profit to make it worth their while staying in the industry. There are no super-normal or monopoly profits.

The next step in the market defence is to show that a perfectly competitive economy, where these conditions are met, is one which would be desirable. This is demonstrated by invoking the seemingly harmless welfare criterion of Pareto optimality. A state of the world is Pareto optimal if there are no possible changes which could be made which would make at least one person better off without making at least one other person worse off. The first fundamental theorem of welfare economics demonstrates that a perfectly competitive economy is Pareto optimal.[1]

Apart from the immediate difficulties with the correspondence of the model with the real economy (to which we will return below), this economy lacks anyone to set the prices (since all are assumed to be price-takers). Thus a further assumption is invoked – that there exists an 'auctioneer' or co-ordinator who sets and adjusts prices.[2] This auctioneer is assumed costless. But since the co-ordination is costless, it could equally well be carried out by a planner and hence, a perfect allocation of resources could be achieved either through the market, driven by the price mechanism, or by a planned economy with quantities chosen by planners. There is nothing in this result which suggests that prices are better than quantities in co-ordination, precisely because the information is costless.

Thus the neo-classical model of perfect competition as the paradigm of an efficient economy relies upon a series of claims – that the economy approximates the assumptions of perfect competition, that it is costlessly co-ordinated and that the achievement of a Pareto optimal state is worthy of merit. Using this same model, however, it is also possible to produce an analysis of the reasons for state intervention, by examining the extent to which the assumptions of perfect competition are not met.

The perfect competition model is a model of an ideal economy. It shows what an economy would have to look like if it were to generate the most efficient outcome. To the extent that markets in practice deviate from these assumptions, they can be deemed to 'fail'. The model of perfect competition can then be used 'backwards' to identify cases of market failure.[3] These then serve as necessary conditions for state intervention in the economy. Such cases are not, however, sufficient. The reason for this is obvious. The economy which exists today is complex and it is highly unlikely that there are any unique, simple and perfect solutions to its failures. In intervening in the market, governments also make mistakes and hence the extent of 'government failure' must be balanced against 'market failure'. It is by no means clear that the latter is less severe than the former. In practice, market optimists have (as we shall see in section 6.3) tended to focus on the negative aspects of government failure, while market pessimists have stressed market failure.

Market failure arises in a number of ways and it will prove useful to consider the major sources at this stage. There are a number of approaches, including classification into demand, supply and market structure. In practice, however, market failure is rarely pure and this should be borne in mind in roughly following this classification. We begin then on the demand side, with consumer preferences. The demand for goods and services in an economy ultimately rests on the preferences of individual consumers. In conventional neo-classical theory, these consumer preferences are assumed to be consistent and complete. Given a choice between any two alternatives, the consumer can rank these in order. Furthermore, given a set of alternatives, consumers will choose consistently. However, it is clear that in practice consumers often lack the relevant information to yield a complete ordering of all alternatives and hence preferences are often partial and incomplete. In addition, there is considerable evidence to suggest the existence of at least local inconsistency and the influence of non-rational factors on choice (see Kahneman, Slovic and Tversky, 1983).

Where these weaknesses arise, the state may be able to provide better information about the opportunities available to individuals so that choices may be improved. Alternatively, the state may act instead of consumers in a paternalistic fashion – by trying to alter or replace preferences. The most important examples of this sort of state paternalism are in health care, education and social security – in smoking, school milk and compulsory education. This sort of preference failure can in addition lead to the imposition of compulsory insurance provision and the development of social insurance as the basis of welfare provision. The position is even more complex where one person chooses for another, without the state being directly involved. There is, for example, a tension between the 'rights' of the parents to choose freely the appropriate education for children, and the 'rights' of the child. Should the state intervene here? Many people would argue that the state here does have a duty to intervene, though this view would not be shared by the 'new right'.

In addition to direct preference failures and issues about adjudication between different people's preferences, the market system might fail because insufficient incentives exist for individuals to reveal their true preferences. Public goods constitute such a case. A public good exists where the marginal cost of consumption of another individual is zero and there is no possibility of exclusion from consumption. For example, it costs society almost nothing more to defend one additional person than it costs for the other fifty or so million and it cannot defend the others without also defending the one. The demand failure that arises is in determining how much of a public good to produce. Since the additional cost to myself of the production of an extra unit of a public good is very close to zero, the incentive is to demand increasingly greater provision. There is, therefore, no straightforward market mechanism for revealing the 'true' demand for public goods. Further, since the costs cannot be easily recouped (because of non-excludability) there is little or no incentive for the market to provide these goods.

The provision of public goods can be met either by the state choosing an appropriate level (and hence replacing individual choice) and financing the expenditure by taxation, or by the formation of 'clubs' whose members consume the good, paying an entry or membership fee. In the former case, the problem for the state is to choose the optimal level of provision. In the latter case, the club internalizes the public good, yet is unlikely to set the membership fee at the 'correct' marginal cost. (Sandler and Tschirhart (1980) provide an accessible survey of the theory of clubs.)

Supply failures arise when the private costs of production do not coincide with those of society and where there are economies of scale. In both of these cases, the assumptions of the perfect competition model are violated and the market will not produce at the optimal price/output combination. Social costs arise either because the social value of production is undervalued by the market, in areas like employment and the arts, or because private firms evade paying for the consequences of their actions in the production of externalities. Pollution is the obvious example in the latter case. Where externalities arise (and they tend to be pervasive), there are a number of solutions available to deal with them. Each involves an attempt to incorporate the costs of the externality into the firm's decision-making. The first method is the classic Pigou/Meade tax/subsidy technique. The level of externality is estimated and a tax or subsidy is imposed on the firm to adjust costs to their true social level. Second, firms may internalize externalities by merging. Third, the sufferers from the effects of the externality may be able to take legal action against the firm, provided that the ownership of the right not to suffer from the external effect is well-defined (see Coase, 1960). Where it is not, the state may intervene to rectify this weakness.

Supply failures may also arise in the presence of substantial scale economies, though the impact of these typically comes about through the resulting industrial concentration. In the traditional analysis, as market structure tends towards monopoly, price increasingly diverges from marginal cost and output falls. At the extreme is 'natural monopoly' where scale economies are so great that there can be only one firm in the industry. This analysis derives from the standard structure-conduct-performance paradigm in analysing industrial markets. It neglects the competitive practice which typifies many oligopolistic markets.[4] However, the fact that oligopolies can be competitive does not detract from the general problem of monopoly. Indeed, the static analysis tends to neglect the social costs of anti-competitive practices which firms employ to gain market power and hence a host of additional problems.

Co-ordination and the Austrian theory

The perfect competition paradigm is clearly a weak basis for defending the market system. Its conditions are rarely if ever met and in practice the various types of market failure pervade the economy. Far from being a basis for defending the market, it is much better suited as a basis for state intervention. Hence, market pessimists have pursued this framework as a guide to intervention.

But because perfect competition may be an inappropriate model upon which to base the argument for *laissez-faire*, it does not follow that there are no other alternative defences. As noted above, the possibility of 'government failure' typically serves this purpose. It is within this context that the Austrian model of competition has been exploited by market optimists.

The Austrian model rests on imperfect competition and in particular on imperfect information. For Hayek, the principal modern exponent of the Austrian view,[5] 'the argument in favour of competition does not rest on the conditions that would exist if it were perfect' (1948, p. 104). Indeed, perfect competition is for Hayek a state in which competition has ceased, when the market has reached its ideal equilibrium. The competitive process takes place out of equilibrium, in a world of uncertainty and imperfection. Innovations arise and are tested in the market-place. The incentive to engage in research and development, to develop new products, is the possibility of profit. The larger existing profits, the greater the attraction of entry.

On this view, the attraction of the market system and of competition is not, however, limited to research, development and market entry. The market system is co-ordinated by the price mechanism. Each individual in society need only know the relative prices of all the goods and services in the economy. Given that information and each individual's knowledge of his or her own preferences and resources, the pursuit of their own self-interest will lead people to place demands on the economy and to supply goods and labour. The price system allocates the resources to best satisfy conflicting demands. By rises and falls in the price of goods relative to each other, it signals to individuals changing degrees of scarcity and resource costs, which enables gluts and shortages to be eliminated.

This property of the price system has one great advantage. It is informationally undemanding. Each individual need only know his or her own preferences and the relative prices of goods and services available to them. Each firm need only know its costs and, again, the relative prices. By contrast the state planner, if he or she is to replace the markets, must know much more. While in the price system each individual need only understand his or her own predicament, the planner must try to comprehend that of all. This differential in information requirements and the impossibility of 'socialist calculation' was for Mises and Hayek a central argument for the market.

The above argument is permissive. With the relevant information provided by the price mechanism, individuals *can* make efficient choices. They *do* in fact do so because of the enforcement powers of the market. The market selects out winners by their profit achievement and eliminates the inefficient loss-makers. This process of competition is indeed often argued to be analogous to the way in which the environment acts in the theory of evolution and natural selection. Inefficiency is weeded out by the forces of competition rather like ill-adapted mutations are in biological models.[6] Competition enforces efficiency by negatively eliminating inefficiency. As Keynes put it:

> The parallelism between economic *laissez-faire* and Darwinism . . . is very

> close indeed. Just as Darwin invoked sexual love, acting through sexual selection, as an adjutant to natural selection by competition, to direct evolution along lines which should be desirable as well as effective, so the individualist invokes love of money, acting through the pursuit of profit, as an adjutant to natural selection, to bring about the production on the greatest possible scale of what is most strongly desired as measured by exchange value. (1926, cw xi, p. 284)

Competition then acts to eliminate inefficiency. But where cost conditions vary, market power may arise. Yet here again competition is seen as a panacea. Where monopoly profits arise, rivals are attracted and their entry into the market drives down prices. Thus competition protects consumers. It is this argument which the modern advocates of privatization have appealed to. As Beesley and Littlechild put it:

> Competition is the most important mechanism for maximising consumer benefits and for limiting monopoly power. Its essence is rivalry and freedom to enter a market. What counts is the existence of competitive threats, from potential as well as existing competitors. (1983, p. 5)

The mechanisms of enforcement depend on constraints arising in the capital market (such as take-overs and bankruptcies), in managerial competition and in the product market. Competition is an external constraint. As long as it exists, at least potentially, the firm is forced to act in the interest of consumers.[7] Provided that entry is relatively cheap, monopoly need not lead to exploitation, since competitive selection will undermine excessive prices. Such a view of competition, therefore, combines the virtues of the price system in circumstances in which information is imperfect with the self-regulating constraint of potential entry. Though the outcome of the market would not be perfect, it would be superior to an attempt by government to replace it.

In analysing government failure, Hayek (1944), in *The Road to Serfdom*, and Popper (1945), in *The Open Society and its Enemies*, advanced an additional argument purporting to demonstrate that state planners would inevitably worsen the welfare of the society if they attempted to replace markets. Since the social world, and in particular the economy, is extremely complex, planners and social scientists can only have limited understanding of it. Because of this complexity, unintended consequences of planning decisions inevitably arise. These would themselves tend to create further difficulties, being (they assumed) largely negative in effect. Hence well intentioned planners were likely to accidentally lower welfare. The road to hell – the road of planning – is thus paved with good intentions. The alternative to the 'open society' is the 'serfdom' of socialism.

This particular argument is problematic. For, as Sen (1983) has pointed out, the observation that policies and actions may have unintended consequences is hardly startling. It is the assumption that these will tend to be perverse which drives Hayek's and Popper's theory and that assumption has no direct justification. Many unintended consequences will, of course, be irrelevant. Others will be beneficial. There is no justification for the assumption of perversity.

But even if some interventions by planners did have unfortunate consequences, the comparison with what the price system achieves is somewhat misleading. Recall that, because of market imperfections, transactions typically take place at the 'wrong' prices. Now, unfortunately for Hayek, just as the price system can be very helpful in conveying the right information, this transmission property applies to all information contained in prices, and not just that of 'correct' prices. Hence, should prices be distorted, as they inevitably are by monopoly, externalities and other characteristics of market failure, Hayek's supposed advantages in information transmission become disadvantageous in an imperfect economy. The decisive property of informational economy is advantageous if the prices are right, but quite the opposite in a distorted economy.

Thus, the case for the market system as opposed to planning based upon government failure cannot be carried as a general rule. Rather, like the market failure approach, a case by case procedure must be adopted. Economic theory does not lead to a general presumption either for or against the market system.

Market co-ordination and macroeconomic failures

We have seen that co-ordinating the economy in the neo-classical theory relies on a costless auctioneer and in the Austrian approach is carried out by the price mechanism. There remains, however, the further complication of co-ordinating the *macroeconomic* activity in an economy. Neither of the above approaches adequately copes with this difficulty. The reason why these approaches cannot cope with macroeconomic problems is that for them, strictly, there are no macro-phenomena. The economy is characterized by individual tastes, by technology and by firms. 'Macro' aggregates are simply the sum of their constituent parts. Statements about these must be translated into statements relating to individuals.

Unfortunately, this simplistic view does not stand up to close scrutiny. First, the macro outcomes of individual actions can often be quite contrary to the individuals' aims and intentions (see Schelling, 1978). Second, voluntary co-operation without government intervention is frequently not enough; in many cases the co-operative solution to problems fails because of strategic considerations, which have been well represented in the so-called Prisoners' Dilemma and subsequent developments in games theory.[8] Co-operative solutions are, in this scenario, superior to the pursuit of narrow self-interest, but each party to the potential solution has an incentive to encourage the others to engage in co-operative acts, while themselves exploiting the situation. Oil producers may, for example, all agree to cut back output to increase profitability for all, but if everyone else cuts back and you don't, the rewards to yourself (but not the others) are much greater. Opportunities to 'free-ride' on others are considerable and it can be governments who are best placed to enforce co-operation. Third, the aggregate of individual preferences may not yield a consistent democratic social ordering of alternatives, unless undesirable and strong assumptions are placed upon the derivation of the social welfare function. The aims and objectives of society are not, contrary to Hayekian individualism, a simple function of those of individuals.[9]

Finally, and here Keynes' contribution is of great import, the private sector does not always produce a stable level of output and employment. It is liable to booms and slumps and can get stuck in inferior equilibrium positions from which only the state, by guiding and manipulating its policy stance, can rescue it. Capitalism is an imperfect system which may need careful guidance and control to save it from itself. This last co-ordinating role gives a rationale for macroeconomic policy, while leaving open the question of its design. The debates on macroeconomic policy (for example, between the Keynesian and Monetarist camps) will not be discussed here, except in so far as they bear upon the overall case for intervention of *laissez-faire*.

The liberal defence of markets: arguments about values

So far in this section the instrumental case for the market and competition in generating economic efficiency has been set out and a number of objections have been raised. However, even if the market were a good mechanism for creating wealth and allocating resources, ultimately the defenders of the market rest their case on a further requirement – that economic freedom and hence the free-market economy is a necessary condition for political freedom. (See, for example Friedman (1962) and Friedman and Friedman (1980).) We now explore this claimed relationship between economic efficiency and freedom and show that it rests on a particular narrow concept of freedom. Further, having identified that concept, we note that the two are not necessarily consistent.

The arguments for the market in the Hayekian tradition ultimately derive from the central neo-liberal tenet of individualism. The liberty of the individual always dominates the efficiency of the economy. Happily for them, the defenders of *laissez-faire* thought they had discovered both a system which guaranteed efficiency *and* the maximum of liberty. However, should any conflict arise, the latter would always dominate the former in liberal thinking. It is the individual upon whom ultimate moral worth is placed and society is nothing more than the sum or aggregation of the individuals who comprise it. Society is the slave of its individual components. Governments whose role is not restricted by rules and constitutions will inevitably try to impose the preferences and interests of particular groups of individuals upon others.[10] To be free means to be free from interference, to have the maximum domain of choice within which an individual can do as he or she chooses. The role of government is to impose the rule of law to prevent unjustified interference of some individuals upon others, but at the same time to minimize its own interference. It is a restraining negative role, rather than an activist one.

Though the primacy of liberty is ultimately a value judgement, its consistency with efficiency is one which modern social choice and welfare theorists have addressed analytically. One of the earliest and most famous attempts to reconcile them was Adam Smith's, who tried to demonstrate the natural harmony of liberty and the market. He claimed that:

> All systems either of preference or restraint, therefore, being thus completely taken away, the obvious and simple system of natural liberty establishes itself of its own accord. Every man, as long as he does not violate the laws of justice, is left perfectly free to pursue his own interest in his own way, and to bring both his industry and capital into competition with those of any other man, or order of men. The sovereign is completely discharged from a duty, in attempting to perform which he must always be exposed to innumerable delusions, and for the proper performance of which no human wisdom or knowledge could even be sufficient; the duty of superintending the industry of private people and of directing it towards the employments most suitable to the interest of the society. (Smith, 1776 (1976, p. 687))

Hence liberty meant the absence of constraints and since governments constrained the market when they interfered and the market was voluntary to its participants, economic freedom from government interference could not but enhance political freedom, Indeed, Smith is quite precise on the exact duties of government. He goes on to state these as follows:

> According to the system of natural liberty, the Sovereign has only three duties to attend to . . . first, the duty of protecting the society from violence and invasion of other independent societies; secondly, the duty of protecting, as far as possible, every member of society from the injustices or oppression of every other member of it, or the duty of establishing an exact administration of justice; and thirdly, the duty of erecting and maintaining certain publick works and certain publick institutions, which it can never be for the interest of any individual, or small number of individuals, to erect and maintain.

Such an automatic harmony of interests and such a weak domain for government cannot, however, be taken for granted. One of the central difficulties in neo-liberal thought which has not been fully explored is that the market is itself a social institution. It cannot be accounted for by individual elements; rather it is, as we saw above, the co-ordinator of individuals. Hence the need for rules by which social institutions, like markets, are to function. The price mechanism may bring individuals into balance in trading between goods and preferences, but this is only possible if some individuals do not exert undue influence and power over others. *Laissez-faire* cannot be anarchic; it must be strictly confined by rules. The market thus must maintain neutrality between individuals and must be free from governmental interference. Hence social institutions must have rules, or constitutions, and the society as a whole must have an agreed code of conduct which meets the liberal criterion of fairness. These rules then define the role of government and the limits of competition.

The problem then is how to frame these rules. What is to be a 'fair' code of conduct? What is a 'fair' competition? It is on this question that the *laissez-faire* advocates of the market turn to the liberal theorists of the state. For much of liberal political theory – in the tradition of Hume, Locke and Mill – has been concerned with justifying the rules of a constitution, by reference to the choices of individuals. The modern liberal theory, as developed most notably by Nozick (1974) on the right and Rawls (1971) on the left, seeks to justify the principles of a social arrangement, by asking what individuals would choose if they were abstracted from society. In particular, for Rawls, the choice is based on what they would choose if they were ignorant of the place in society they might come to occupy once it had been set in motion. The liberal rules for the framing of the role of government, the limits of *laissez-faire* and 'natural' competitive forces are those that idealized individuals would choose. Thus the central tenet of individualism is preserved and made the guiding arbiter of the structure of the state and its legal arrangements.

Though ultimately this is the foundation of the neo-liberal case, it is not at all clear that the market solution is the best preserver of individual liberty, nor that individuals would select such a constitution. For the market system to maximize the degree of freedom, there must be no conflict with Pareto optimal efficiency. Unfortunately, it has been demonstrated by Sen (1970) that to hold both Paretianism and liberalism simultaneously can be inconsistent. This result arises because the Paretian concept is applicable to the degree of preference satisfaction with unrestricted domain. However the requirements of liberty restrict the domain of preferences that individuals may exercise to prevent interference in one person's choice by others. Hence one person could be made better off without harming others in the utility sense, but at the same time, exercise choices which the liberal would find objectionable. Satisfying preferences may conflict with the restriction of the domain of choice. As Sen concludes, 'while the Pareto criterion has been thought to be an expression of individual liberty, it appears that in choices involving more than two alternatives it can have consequences that are, in fact, deeply illiberal'.

But even if liberty and efficiency were consistent, there is no guarantee that the resulting income distribution would meet the requirements of social justice. Since much of the expansion of the economic role of the state has been in redistribution and that redistribution has reduced the 'natural' efficiency of the market system, the critique of state intervention also relies on an argument about the importance of distributional considerations in social welfare. A more positive concept of freedom, which included a degree of equality, would undermine the case against government intervention. This will be discussed in greater detail in section 6.4 below.

6.3 Theory and policy in the growth of the state

We have seen in the previous section that the arguments for and against market solutions to economic organization are complex and typically combine both instrumental and welfare arguments. Politicians who use economic arguments when considering state intervention tend to draw on them to support their prior value judgements. But because this use is inevitably selective and because these arguments do not necessarily mesh well together, the outcome can be other than might be expected.[11] This section looks at the growth of the state in practice, comparing the arguments used with those discussed at a theoretical level in the previous section.

The role of the state prior to the First World War was largely that of the 'nightwatchman'. The state guaranteed property rights, provided for defence, kept law and order on the streets and maintained the value of the currency. Redistribution of income was largely left to charity and revenue raising was restricted, in the main, to customs and excise, monopoly and commodity taxation. The state was thus largely restricted to the three roles allocated to it by Adam Smith.

The First World War required economic mobilization to a degree not previously experienced by Western countries and led to an expansion of the economic role of the state in production, labour mobilization and taxation. Though the state tried to withdraw after the First World War and return to the pre-war world of the gold standard, the inter-war period witnessed the development of social assistance in response to unemployment, involvement in labour relations and a tendency towards greater emphasis on corporatist solutions (see Middlemas, 1979, esp. Chs 5–8).

The 1930s debate

The intellectual debate of the 1930s, with the growth of Keynesian economics and socialist planning theory, was in part a response to the growing 'crisis of capitalism' and the growth of fascism and communism. While textbook classical theory suggested that markets were either in equilibrium or tending towards it, the reality of collapse in Europe and the United States of capital and labour markets pointed elsewhere. The theoretical responses were diverse. At one extreme, both classical and Austrian theorists redefined their theories of the market and pointed to 'distortions' (such as unions, the concentration of capital and government intervention) as the source of depression. At the other, theorists of the left explored alternative economic arrangements where markets were replaced by planners. Ironically both sets of theorists could and did appeal to the perfect competition paradigm as their starting point. The free market theorists looked to the removal of market distortions; the left identified the market failures associated with monopoly, cartels and the absence of proper accounting for social costs and attempted through planned solutions to increase the accountability of industry to public needs.

A third, and largely new, strand argued that macroeconomic failure could occur – that there were co-ordination problems at the macro-level regardless of what happened at the micro-level. Thus aggregate demand could be deficient, even if labour and capital were competitively supplied and paid their marginal products. This Keynesian approach recognized that the economic system was not necessarily self-correcting. But it could be saved from collapse by a little guidance and support from the state. The government should inject demand into the economy when there were signs of slack and recession, but restrain demand when inflation threatened. This did not involve interfering directly in markets, but rather providing the right macroeconomic framework.

For somewhat distinct reasons, pressure for a more concerted effort by the state to redistribute the rewards generated by the market intensified after the First and then again after the Second World War. Though it had been on both liberal and socialist agendas in the nineteenth century, the wars had a socially levelling effect and led to much greater expectations of social justice in their aftermaths. The liberals and the socialists did, however, have distinct approaches to the question of social justice and these were well established by the time that Beveridge laid down the principles for the post-war welfare state.[12]

Neither the neo-classical nor the Austrian paradigms gave satisfactory justifications in terms of social justice as to why the distribution of income generated by the market should be socially and politically acceptable. The debate about the proper redistributional policy to adopt was partly one about means and partly one about ends. On the one hand, social insurance was advocated as a method of overcoming the accidents which might befall individuals – such as sickness, unemployment, maternity and so on. On the other, direct redistribution was advocated by those who identified the 'causes' of poverty as beyond individual control. In other words, the social insurers saw poverty as the consequence of market failure (the insurance market and preference failure), whereas the redistributionalists saw it as a separate issue, regardless of the perfection of the market. Perfect markets do not, on this latter view, produce just distributions of income. It was, as we shall see, the liberal approach – that of the social insurance principle – which dominated the design of the welfare state, whereas the redistributional approach dominated taxation design.

The three pillars of the post-war consensus

The welfare state

The design of the welfare state was loosely based on a number of theories which had been developed in the inter-war years. At a fundamental level, the concept of a 'welfare state' represented a political and moral concept, invented to stand as a central war aim to be counterposed against Hitler's 'warfare state' (Marwick, 1982). From the wartime experience of co-operation between parties in planning almost every aspect of social and economic life, emerged the consensus around a new social partnership between capital, labour, the state and the market.

But the moral and political commitment lacked an instrumental basis – the practical aspects of implementing this vision were less clearly spelt out. In reality, many of the important caveats of the economic theory were ignored and a series of *ad hoc* measures employed. Thus market failure arising from monopoly and collusion was 'solved' by nationalization, without due attention to 'government failure' and hence little careful attention to the form of controls. Similarly the insurance and redistributive aspects of welfare were conveniently merged.

The Beveridge system relied upon social insurance and universal benefits. Though its origins go back to the early social insurance legislation of Lloyd George's 'People's Budget' in 1909, the first major steps during the Second World War were taken by the Coalition Administration. The Butler Education Act laid down the principle of equal access to education for all and the Beveridge inspired 1944 White Paper extended the macroeconomic commitments of government, and set the scene for the extension of the provision of social insurance. That in turn was based upon the new assumption that the state was both capable of and had a positive duty to generate full employment. The Beveridge system had a number of key features which were taken over by the Attlee government and since these remain to a greater or lesser extent the dominant characteristics today, it is worth reminding ourselves of these (see Dilnot, Kay and Morris (1984), Ch. 1 and Creedy and Disney (1985)). First, Beveridge considered that poverty was an absolute concept – being poor related to absolute levels of food, clothing, health care and so on. As the economy grew and expanded, it would therefore tend to disappear. Second, poverty was caused by 'accidents' and could, therefore, be insured against. But since people tended, for a variety of reasons, to under-provide for these contingencies, an element of compulsion was required to ensure that nobody fell below a certain minimum standard of living. This provided the rationale for state intervention to correct for what was referred to in section 6.2 above as a preference failure. Benefits were then paid to those upon whom such 'social accidents' as unemployment or sickness fell. The Beveridge system did not purport to deal with inequality and thus the 'means-tested' entitlement to benefits was inappropriate.

Beveridge's approach also rejected a general income basis for benefits. These were to be in kind. Poverty related directly to the absolute levels of certain defined goods for which a minimum of consumption was required to enjoy a basic standard of living. Hence, under Beveridge, 'experts' (in practice civil servants and politicians) would select and provide these basic goods on behalf of individuals, rather than give them cash to exercise their choices in the market. State paternalism was justified by preference failures. Now, in practice, some basic goods – like health and education – were best provided free of charge and on demand, rather than engage in complex insurance administration. Others, such as unemployment benefits, were more directly related to premiums paid.

The Beveridge scheme did not however work out as its inventor had imagined. The reasons were partly practical – the reality of the post-war UK economy – and partly theoretical. First, Britain had emerged from the Second World War as a virtually bankrupt economy. The war had been essentially debt-financed, and this accumulation could be repaid in one of the following ways – by higher taxation, by export-led growth, by debtors 'aiding' their clients, or by cuts in expenditure. Britain, unlike its defeated European and Japanese rivals, continued to aspire to world power status and hence could not rapidly run down its military and diplomatic services. Its capital stock was much depleted by the war effort, and Marshall Aid was insufficient to offset this, and less generous than that received by other European countries. World markets outside the US were not expected to expand with the rapidity which was actually experienced. The consequence was a continuation of war-time austerity, with rationing, and controls holding back domestic demand to enhance the current account of the balance of payments. Many of the more expensive aspects of the new welfare state had thus to be trimmed, of which the introduction of prescription charges in 1948 was but one example.[13]

The second was the growing realization that poverty could be the result not only of social accident, but also of more fundamental social and economic factors. The consensus of the post-war period took a much more relativistic view of poverty, and the development of Supplementary Benefit as both means-tested and income-based was a significant departure from the Beveridge ideal.

Private and public ownership

If the design and introduction of the welfare state derived from a confusing mixture of principles and practical reality, the nationalization of industry and the emergence of national planning was even more complex. Like privatization much later, the rationale for nationalization owed much to political principle and political expediency. The politics were then bolstered by appeal to economic arguments.

The economic rationale of nationalization was complex. At one level, the socialist concept of a planned economy required that the 'commanding heights' be under state control. This was both a macro- and microeconomic argument. It was macroeconomic to the extent that nationalized industries were seen, under the auspices of national planning, as instruments for economic management, and it was microeconomic in as far as planning was considered superior to the market allocation of resources. But, in addition to these general arguments, there were more industry-specific reasons, associated with monopoly, social costs and cross-subsidization. Finally the desire for workers to control and participate in their work-places also played a part, especially when these arguments coincided with powerful union interests as, for example, in the mines. The mix of arguments led to a neglect of the price mechanism in economic planning under the Labour administration. As Cairncross summarizes the position:

> It corresponded to a fundamental cleavage between two approaches to economic planning: a socialist, egalitarian, approach which saw planning as a purely organisational activity akin to the planning that goes on within a productive enterprise, an army or, for that matter, a political party; and a liberal, Keynesian, approach which saw planning as a corrective to the operation of market forces and dwelt particularly on the need for a level of effective demand adequate to maintain full employment. (1985, p. 308)

Thus little consideration was given to pricing, and the catch-all 'break-even' financial objective left 'social' non-profit maximizing activities (such as rural railways, and employment) to be set at levels dictated by Boards, and met by cross-subsidization.[14] Yet, despite the rather ill-defined form of control, the state sector of industry set up in the 1940s remained largely intact until the 1980s (with the exception of steel which has been pushed back and forward from government ownership to the private sector). Successive governments (especially those of Wilson (1964–70) and Heath (1970–74)) added further companies as they fell into bankruptcy. 'Lame ducks' like British Leyland and Rolls-Royce fell into this category.

Co-ordination and the macroeconomic role of the state

In addition to the welfare state, attending to the relief of poverty, and nationalization, as an aid to planning and the solution of monopoly problems, the third major pillar of the post-war period was the new macroeconomic role of government in co-ordinating the economy to maintain a high level of employment, whilst restraining inflationary pressure. The 1944 Employment White Paper is significant in that it took on the commitment to tackle what had been the major problems of the inter-war years. To fulfil this objective, there were essentially two possible types of policy – on the one hand, demand management and, on the other, planning to ensure that the outcome of micro-behaviour would aggregate to produce an acceptable macro-level of employment.

Demand management was the Keynesian solution; planning was that of the socialist theorists. Though the conventional wisdom had it that the former was the chosen instrument, that was true much more of the period after 1951 than of the Attlee government. The Attlee government saw employment less in terms of overall fiscal stance, and more in terms of the extent of planned intervention. Though not averse to deficit financing, full-employment was to be achieved by positive (micro) public works, not general spending. Furthermore, the immediate post-war chronic balance-of-payments position, and the desire to maintain sterling's artificially high level against the dollar, were hardly conducive to Keynesian expansion.

Planning for the Labour government was to be a mix between short- and long-term plans, as well as special cases. Though there were different views and emphasis, the Crippsian approach was perhaps the most cohesive. As he saw it, the 'basic' industries were to have long-term plans, 'economic budgets' were required for macro-aggregates such as the national income and expenditure aggregates, and manpower and 'special' measures would deal with problems such as the external position, capital investment and fuels (Economic Survey for 1947; see Cairncross (1985), pp. 305–7).

With the increased provision of welfare benefits and a state production sector, these three pillars of post-war economic organization remained intact – as indeed they did throughout western Europe – throughout the 1950s and 1960s. The challenge that was finally presented came as the perceived costs began to rise to unacceptable levels. At the microeconomic level, the continued financial burdern imposed by the nationalized industries and the provision of social benefits required increased rates and levels of taxation. More generally, the onset of inflation, continued external payments problems and the impact of oil price shocks, led to a questioning of the underlying validity of the mixed economy. These developments in turn led to the re-opening of the intellectual questions raised in the first part of this assessment – had the expanded economic borders of the state brought benefit, or had they caused inflation and 'crowding out' of more effective private sector activity? The intellectual challenge of monetarism and of the philosophy of the 'new right' translated into a radical political redirection of policy after the 1979 Conservative election victory.

The challenge of Thatcherism

The Thatcher government since 1979 has pursued fundamentally different policies in each of the major areas of economic policy to their post-war predecessors. Rather than expand the economic borders of the state to meet greater social and economic pressures, it has explicitly attempted to curtail the role of the state in the economy, in an attempt to enhance the freedom of the individual and to encourage the growth of 'the enterprise culture'. The basis of this redirection has been an explicit appeal to a mix of Austrian and neo-classical market theories, and to libertarian values. In this section, the major policy changes will be briefly reviewed, and related to the underlying philosophy.

The cornerstone of the Conservative administration's macroeconomics was the Medium Term Financial Strategy (MTFS) introduced in 1980. The essence of the MTFS was a set of targets for the PSBR and £M3[15] which the government pre-committed itself to achieve. Its intention was to bind the government to its targets and to signal commitment, and hence gain credibility in financial markets. The philosophy which lay behind it was monetarist. Though monetarism has many interpretations, the Thatcher variant had a number of easily identified broad features. These can be summarized by two simple propositions – that the market system functions so as to generate full employment 'naturally' if left to its own devices; and that money is the main (or sole) determinant of the price level.[16] Monetary growth was in the MTFS directly linked to the PSBR, and since increases in taxes were deemed to have undesirable effects, reduced public expenditure was the chosen route to implement the policy.

The emphasis on reducing public expenditure to meet its macroeconomic objectives tied in well with a more general dislike of the growth of the absolute size of government in the post-war period. Aside from the more overtly political motives, government activity was deemed to be less efficient than that undertaken by the private sector. The state sector failed to reward risk-taking and enterprise, and lacked the discipline of the marketplace to punish inefficiency. Furthermore, government borrowing 'crowded out' private sector activity, and the necessary taxation to finance it reduced the returns to innovation and enterprise, as well as the incentive to work.

The economic rationale for this pessimistic view of government economic activity was variously supported by three conflicting arguments – that private markets were 'competitive', and hence produced socially optimal results; that 'market failure' was less significant than 'government failure', and, finally, in an Austrian vein, that monopoly profits were transitory, and longer-run competition would eliminate them. Thus each of the approaches to defending the market identified in section 6.2 above were, when convenient, appealed to. Those who believed in pragmatism could agree with those ideologically committed to the market in cases such as Jaguar Cars, Amersham International and Cable and Wireless, but would have greater reservations where market failure was more apparent in such cases as British Gas and the Water Authorities.

The privatization programme, which constituted a major part of the microeconomic attempt 'to make markets work better', came a little later. It was a much broader policy than asset sales (see Kay and Thompson (1986) and Yarrow (1986)), involving a host of measures including the withdrawal of industrial aid, deregulation and franchising. The policy followed a number of phases, as did the emphasis on its intellectual justification. At first the state withdrew aid and subsidies, radically pruning industrial policy as traditionally conceived. If the market 'naturally' achieved an efficient equilibrium, the state could not better it, and indeed might make matters worse by preventing the discipline of the market from being imposed. The next step was to increase competition in the state sector. Deregulation of buses, the Oil and Gas (Enterprise) Act 1982 and the Energy Act in 1983 were the major legislative achievements of this phase, encouraging entry by the private sector and relaxing state monopolies.

The next phase concentrated on ownership, and the transfer of public assets to the private sector. Whilst this transfer of assets to the private sector was initially viewed as a method to enhance efficiency by increasing the intensity of competition and its long-term success was to be judged (Moore, 1983) 'by the extent to which it maximizes competition', it was soon apparent that asset sales, considered as 'negative public expenditure', provided a method of financing tax cuts, whilst remaining within the boundaries of the MTFS. In addition, there were a number of other variants of the new competition policy. These included the contracting out of services traditionally performed by state organizations (such as dustbin collection and health service laundry) as well as more ambitious franchising arrangements.

The new market philosophy was also apparent in the labour market, and the attack on 'monopoly' as a source of market failure was nowhere more apparent than in this area. The cause of unemployment lay not in the stance of macroeconomic policy, nor in the absence of the traditional method of restraining wages via incomes policy, but rather in the labour market's uncompetitive characteristics. Indeed both of the traditional policies were now deemed to be self-defeating. The labour market displayed rigidities, and 'a more flexible labour market is the key to increased competitiveness and thus to lower unemployment (Economic Progress Report, 1986, p. 1).

In the competitive model of the labour market, equilibrium is attained where the wage is equal to the marginal revenue product of labour. Unemployment arises because of deviations of the world from that model. These deviations are caused by market failure, and in the labour market the most notable was identified as that of monopoly power from the supply side, and hence legislation was introduced 'to reduce the monopoly power of trade unions, and to make union executives more responsive to the wishes of their members. The aim has been to create a climate in which realistic pay bargaining and acceptance of flexible working practices become the norm (EPR, op. cit.).

A number of interesting points arise from this model. First, the traditional microeconomic model of the labour market does not rule out the manipulation of labour demand to enhance employment. Thus if supply-side policies are solely used, the reason must lie in the undesirable macroeconomic consequences of demand stimulation for rejecting this method of coping with employment. Second, the rhetoric of union reform has not always lent itself to either the reduction of monopoly power or wages. Making unions accountable to their members does not reduce bargaining power necessarily; indeed it might enhance it.[17]

The policies pursued by the Thatcher administration rely on both value judgements and instrumental theories. It would thus be a mistake to perceive the policies merely in an economic framework, concerned with efficiency. Rather the economic policy derives from an ideology which has a reasonably well-defined set of fundamental principles. It is from these principles that the new emphasis on private market solutions arises. The philosophy of Thatcherism is remarkably close to that of the Hayekian brand of liberalism, outlined in section 6.2 above. The starting-point is individualism. People realize their potential as individuals, and not primarily as social beings. That implies that individuals are the best judges of their own welfare, that they have given (exogenous) preferences. The impact of the state is to constrain these choices, and hence the less government interference, the better. Unfortunately, a society without government tends towards anarchy because property rights and personal liberty cannot be guaranteed. Ownership requires protection from attempts to encroach upon it. A framework of law and order is required to prevent some individuals from interfering with others' property. Taxation does interfere with property, and hence it is justified only to the extent that it prevents greater loss of property from others. Defence is the external variant of protection of property rights. Liberty and economic freedom are thus equated with the ability to enjoy property and to exercise consumer choice with the minimum of government interference. Law and order and defence spending enhance liberty; taxation (except where it aids law and order and defence) reduces it.

The prevention of encroachment upon property rights should not, however, be interpreted narrowly. Individuals may unjustifiably exploit others in a variety of physical and non-physical ways. One such way is by monopoly. Monopoly power and exploitation can in theory arise in both the capital and labour markets, but it is the latter case which has, as we have seen above, received most attention. The former is 'solved' by arguing that monopoly capital exploitation is only transitory, and indeed may be a spur to competition. This is a variant of the Austrian approach to economics, which is quite different from the conventional market failure neo-classical approach used in the labour market case.

Consider now how the major features of the Thatcher administration's view of the state conform to these principles. Control of the currency, and protection of its value, defends the value of people's savings. Privatization reintroduces specified property rights and spreads share ownership. Tackling labour monopoly through trade union reform reduces exploitation. The sale of council houses gives people property rights. The encouragement of the private provision of health insurance and education increases individual choice and responsibility rather than reliance on the state. The reduction of taxation reduces the state's infringement of individuals' right to enjoy their income. Pay increases for the army and police, as well as greater expenditure on resources for them, enhances the power to curtail physical interference with individuals' liberty.

But, as with the setting up of the pillars of the post-war period, theory and practice do not always meet, especially in the political sphere. For despite the apparent consistency and coherence of the theory behind the general policy approach, the programme has frequently resorted to *ad hoc* pragmatism. Furthermore, as with the 1945 Labour government, economic theory has not been sacrosanct. Rather it has often been plagiarized to meet political necessity. The result is frequently a mish-mash of ideas, influences and values. But what Thatcherism has done is to reopen the debate about these fundamental principles of the organization of production, the distribution of income and individual liberty. In returning to the principles of *laissez-faire*, the debate has once more been couched in terms of the market versus planning, and market versus government failure. In the next section, we look for other alternatives.

6.4 Weighing up the arguments

The economic borders of the state are not matters that economists can decide without reference to value judgements. To that extent, as Beckerman has persuasively argued (1986), there will never be unanimous agreement on where the boundaries lie.

However, the economist can analyse the relative merits of alternative policies for the achievement of preset goals, and can further analyse the foundations of economic policies by pointing out to which goals these ultimately relate. Thus in weighing up the relative merits of the arguments about the economic borders of the state, we must conduct the analysis at a variety of levels. These include the goals of economic policy, and the instrumental policies designed to achieve them.

The argument so far

Section 6.2 of this assessment considered the arguments for and against market solutions to economic organization. It was there shown that the two major defences of the market – the neo-classical and the Austrian – are quite distinct. The traditional neo-classical case rested on perfect competition and Pareto optimality conditions. However, markets quite generally fail to meet the requirements of perfect competition. Furthermore the fundamental Pareto welfare judgement rests on efficiency alone, without due attention to distribution and liberty. It is individualistically based upon utility, and hence rules out a number of other morally relevant sources of information in adjudicating between alternative economic options. The Austrian case for the market, as best represented by Hayek, ultimately rests on a libertarian value judgement, combined with an instrumental analysis of competition based on information costs and uncertainty. Thus section 6.2 demonstrated, first, that the case for the market depends on an instrumental theory of how the market works and, second, a deeper set of fundamental principles based on value judgements. It showed why the two instrumental theories typically employed are open to objection, and a number of reasons why the value judgements of both approaches are questionable.

Section 6.3 of this assessment related this theoretical debate to the practical policies which have defined and redefined the role of the state in the UK economy. The Attlee government's expansion of the economic borders of the state was based on a view of market failure, on the co-ordination role of the state through planning and on the redistributive functions and powers of the state. The Thatcher period has seen an emphasis on the merits of competition, on the informational problems associated with state planning and on a macroeconomic conception of currency maintenance. The reasons behind this new conservatism about the capabilities of the state rest on a different view of how competition works and a different emphasis on the relative merits of the fundamental goals when the inevitable conflicts between them arise. The neo-liberal emphasis on the rights of the individual against state interference, the merits of private property as opposed to state ownership, and the emphasis on markets rather than planning, all derive ultimately from this framework.

The consequences of this is that it is futile to question the present economic policy framework solely at the instrumental level, without analysing the merits of the underlying value judgements and hence of neo-liberalism. In this section of the paper, the objectives and instruments of economic organization will be reassessed. It is argued that an alternative vision of liberalism provides an integration of liberty with equality, and can form an alternative way of defining the economic borders of the state. For while many policies raise difficulties at the level of the objectives, there remains a series of instrumental questions concerning the design and assignment of policy about which much can be said and considerable progress made. Let us start, then, by reconsidering the instrumental efficiency of the market system.

Reassessing the efficiency of markets

That markets fail to meet the stringent optimality conditions of perfect competition is both obvious and crucial. For it follows that there will always be a *prima facie* case for government intervention for efficiency reasons. Such a condition is not, however, sufficient, and the case for intervention at the microeconomic level must always be balanced against its costs. Just as markets are rarely, if ever, perfect resource allocators, so too governments are rarely, if ever, perfect planners. The argument must inevitably be a pragmatic one – is 'market failure' more serious than 'government failure' in the provision of particular goods and services? Despite the Hayekian attempt to show that government failure must always exceed market failure, there can be no general rule concerning the preference for or against market or government solutions so long as the neo-classical theory is the instrumental basis of the argument.

Market failure arises in a number of different ways – in public goods, externalities and monopolies most noticeably. Where such cases do arise, there are a number of alternative policies available. Broadly, these can be classified into those which seek to *replace* the market by state provision and planning, and those which aim to make markets work better. In the former case, the government takes direct responsibility; in the latter it changes the rules of the game, by regulation and taxation most noticeably, and perhaps acts as referee. Thus governments have a variety of policies available, ranging from nationalization to the use of quasi-government bodies, such as the Monopolies Commission and the Office of Fair Trading.

Government failure also has many facets. At its most direct it involves corruption, bribery and deliberate misallocation of resources. Though some on the new right claim that this is likely to be endemic, it is not usually central to the critique of government. Rather, the critics point to the organization behaviour of bureaucracies, to the lack of market discipline and accountability and to problems of information management. The public service is open to persuasion and manipulation by interest groups which may 'capture' the administrators. These problems of control influence the extent to which intervention is justified at all, and the structure and form that intervention takes.

What a number of case studies have shown is that the question of the extent to which competition can be enhanced (the degree to which markets can be made to work better) or government intervention increased (by replacing markets) to provide for greater efficiency is a complex one, and varies considerably between sectors of the economy. The adoption of a general competition/privatization policy to deal with market and government failure relies ultimately on the assumption that this complexity of different cases is irrelevant, and hence denies this central result. To that extent, such blanket policies are straightforwardly wrong. Ultimately the methods by which competition and the market work are not simple; often they can be surprising and perverse. Thus simplistic advocacy of '*competition*' will not itself solve for market failure. Careful attention to entry conditions, the market power of dominant firms, the availability of information, and so on, can critically alter the impact of competitive forces.

But because competition cannot necessarily solve for market failure, its presence is nevertheless often generally advantageous. Indeed *competition*, rather than *ownership*, is more likely to enhance efficiency. The privatization programme makes the fundamental error of confusing these two. Ownership transfers without competition have left the market failure in telecommunications at least as serious as prior to privatization, and arguably worse. The case of gas is also likely to follow this dismal path (see Hammond, Helm and Thompson, 1985).

In both the nationalization and the privatization of major firms and industries in the UK, the political argument tended has to gloss over the importance of complexity. Economic arguments were employed either for or against the market without due regard to the caveats, assumptions and restrictions which necessarily surround economic models. This process is nowhere better observed than in the economics of Thatcherism. In the early period (1979–1983) the emphasis was on liberalization and competition. Thus simple market models (based on both neo-classical and Austrian economics) were marshalled to justify, for example, the abolition of statutory monopoly (the Oil and Gas (Enterprise) Act 1982, and the Energy Act 1983) and the appraisal of state monopoly by the Monopolies and Merger Commission (the Competition Act 1980). As macroeconomic constraints began to bind, political factors influenced the shift towards ownership transfers, and economic arguments were marshalled to show how the capital markets enforce efficiency, as well as the virtues of wider share ownership. Most political positions can be bolstered by appeal to economic theory, but the disregard of the assumptions behind the models, and the selection of theory according to the support for a prior political position are lamentable.

Not all the problems of applying economic theory to policy design arise from disregard of assumptions and caveats, however. Another source of difficulty arises because the objectives selected by politicians have over-determined policy. Especially since the Second World War, governments have assumed ever greater commitments – to generate full employment, alleviate poverty, increase growth, reduce inflation, and so on. If the government assumes a multiplicity of objectives which leads to conflicts and inconsistencies, a coherent interventionist policy cannot be devised, unless the trade-offs between the objectives are pre-determined.

One of the major political failures of the post-war period has been the attempt by governments to achieve too much – to engage in a competition of promises for ever greater economic and social achievements. While the desire to attain efficiency in production, a fair distribution of income *and* to minimize interference by the state in individual's lives are laudable, the conflicts between them and the failure on the part of governments to deliver is sadly inevitable.

Two examples will illustrate this. The first is the design of the tax system. As John Kay argues (1986, pp. 1–2), taxation is required to raise revenue, to redistribute income and to meet the requirements of social justice. Many of these functions it shares with the social security system with which it overlaps. But, a tax system cannot be both *simple* and fair, if these objectives conflict. The laudable desire of virtually every post-war government to reform the tax (and indeed the social security) system has foundered on the problem of their political inability to relinquish cherished objectives. The second example is privatization policy. It has become (as we saw above in section 6.3) embroiled in the conflict of economic objectives – competition, ownership, PSBR [levels], tax cuts and wider share ownership. Multiple objectives thus cause inconsistency where they conflict. In as much as recent policy has attempted to reduce the commitments made by the state, and to reduce people's expectations of what the state can provide, this problem has been somewhat alleviated. But while the reduction of commitment may reduce problems of consistency, it very much matters which objectives are dropped. And that brings us back to the question of values.

Reassessing the value judgements

The market philosophers rest their case on its efficiency and ability to generate the maximum freedom. That freedom is ultimately the ability of individuals to freely exercise their choices without undue interference. But the type of society that individuals typically might choose to live in may not be one in which distributive issues are neglected. Indeed the growth of the role of the state has been in part a response to a greater demand for social justice and hence the alleviation of poverty and the reduction of inequalities.

The value judgements which provide the rationale for the state include a positive as well as a negative concept of freedom (using Isaiah Berlin's (1958) classic distinction) which has far greater interventionist implications. Rather than focus on individuals as abstracted out of society, to be protected from encroachment and limitation on their actions, positive freedom looks towards enhancing the capacity to enjoy a reasonable standard of living. (See Dasgupta (1986) and Sen (1984).)

If the focus moves towards positive freedom then the question arises as to which goods and services best contribute to giving individuals the capacity to enjoy that minimum standard. Certain basic social goods – such as health, education, nourishment and employment – would typically attain widespread inclusion. Thus, to attain a certain level of positive freedom, the state would need to provide these goods universally.

Perhaps, unsurprisingly, this provision turns out to be quite close to what the welfare state set out to provide. However, as we saw above, in three crucial respects this deviated from the Beveridge system. These goods were not provided as 'social insurance' against accidents; they were provided in monetary compensation as well as in kind; and they were not absolutely defined. The definition of basic social goods and the levels required to maintain a minimum standard of living may vary considerably between societies and within societies over time. It is a matter of relativities, and hence includes redistribution as well as the relief of poverty.

This argument is not, however, necessarily paternalistic, though it could be consistent with such a position. The choice of the basic primary social goods can be made through the political process, rather than via state selection. Nevertheless, in reality paternalism is regularly employed, given the practical difficulties of using the political system to ascertain detailed information about preferences and the theoretical problems referred to above in constructing a social welfare function.

The consensus years of the post-war [era] were largely founded upon a basic agreement about the fundamental value judgements. Once the welfare state was established, and key industries nationalized, the major political parties concentrated on competition at the instrumental level. Each party sought to present itself to the electorate as better managers of the economy. True, there were differences of emphasis, between equality and liberty for example. But these were largely cosmetic in the battle for the centre ground of politics.

This broad agreement about the goals of policy lasted as long as economic growth continued. But with creeping inflation in the 1960s, devaluation in 1967, the drift up in unemployment and the oil shocks of the 1970s, it broke apart. Thatcherism in the 1980s was based upon a return to fundamentals. The goals of policy were questioned, and the state retreated from intervention and paternalism. The debate about the ends of economic organization was reopened. All this was to the good. The consensus over goals was in fact one which could only survive while there was enough growth to meet expectations – to provide for increased prosperity and redistribution, to finance the losses of the nationalized industries and to pay for the welfare state. But what occurred was not symmetrical amongst either political parties or academics. The right redefined their ideology and their political machinery, and shifted away from the instrumental to the domain of values. The left on the other hand continued to emphasize its managerial skills at running the economy. While freedom of choice and the retraction of the state from interference in the lives of individuals became the justification of policy for parties of the right, the left continued to carefully 'cost' their economic proposals and to debate exactly how fast unemployment could be reduced.

That may now be coming to an end, at least at the intellectual level. The concept of liberty, we have seen, which underlies the philosophy of the new right is a negative one, which stands in opposition to that of equality. The new liberalism which underlies the positive approach to freedom – the capabilities and capacities of individuals required to be able to enjoy a reasonable standard of living – can be set against the negative approach. That in itself is not new, though neither are the central arguments of the new right. Modern welfare economists have, however, added much in redefining the scope and limits of this position.

The more difficult step, which would be innovative, is to translate the concept of positive freedom into a practical and coherent set of policies. That attempt involves not so much a further round of debate on the merits of interventionism, but rather the attempt to answer the question of what the state should provide as the minimum conditions for guaranteeing individuals the capacity to enjoy a reasonable standard of living. The answer to that question, on this approach, lies in an identification of the basic goods and services which individuals need. In that sense it requires a return to Beveridge. But it is not necessarily consistent with the principle of social insurance. In a sense the current debates on health and education reflect these arguments. The motives for state provision of these basic goods relate less to market failure and efficiency, and more to social justice. Though the argument does at times get bogged down in discussions of whether this provision should be by the private or public sector, by and large it is about the level of provision and the access to it.

6.5 Conclusion

Economic theory does not furnish an answer to the question as to where the economic borders of the state ought to lie. In part, this is because economic theory is an imperfect corpus of knowledge. But the major reason is that there is no 'right' answer to the question. It all depends on value judgements.

Nevertheless, there are a number of aspects of the question on which economics can inform, which refer to the instrumental efficiency of markets and the consistency between market based solutions and underlying fundamental principles. It is worth restating them here. First, economic theory does not provide any evidence to support a general preference *either* for markets *or* for planning. Markets always fail in some degree and so do governments. The relevant question to ask is not whether they fail, but where, when and by how much they fail. Similarly, given a particular potential intervention by government, the questions should be how much information do administrators and civil servants have, how likely are they to be 'captured' by vested interests and how good are the instruments of intervention available? Pointing out the complexity of market and government failure does not lend itself easily to simple political platforms, but it does underline the desirability of a pragmatic approach to defining the economic borders of the state.

These efficiency reasons for intervention arise not only in microeconomic examples, but also at the macroeconomic level. Economies do not seem to 'naturally' adjust to equilibrium and the persistence of unemployment throughout the industrialized world well illustrates this. A major economic role of government is, therefore, in co-ordinating the actions of individuals to achieve greater efficiency. Governments can bring parties together and encourage desirable outcomes in ways in which individuals cannot.

Pragmatism in state intervention in industry and a macroeconomic role for the state in co-ordinating individual behaviour were two central pillars of the post-war consensus. The third was the commitment by government to guarantee a minimum standard of living for the poor via the welfare state. The system set up in the 1940s set the task of government as the provision of basic primary goods – such as health and education – to provide for that minimum. It deviated from Beveridge's concept of social insurance insofar as it rapidly took on a more relativistic view of poverty and hence involved (with the tax system) a redistributional aspect. Economic theory suggests that poverty has very few of the relevant characteristics of an insurance problem and hence social insurance is not the appropriate way to achieve social justice.

Before turning to social justice, however, it is worth restating the conclusions reached on the relationship between the theory of the market and certain value judgements to which its defenders have appealed. Economic theory clearly suggests that the requirements of economic efficiency, as represented by Pareto optimality, and those of liberty can be inconsistent. It is, therefore, not true, contrary to conventional belief, that the market necessarily always maximizes liberty. The light that economic theory does, if properly employed, throw on the question of the economic borders of the state is thus often negatively directed. It shows what cannot be claimed. It shows that general rules favouring the market or state intervention are inferior to pragmatic approaches and it shows that liberal values and market based economic organization may be inconsistent.

Political arguments about economic policy tend to start with ideology and progress to a search for an economic rationale. Economic theory does, however, have a greater role to play than as fodder for political argument. Ideologies do not simply emerge. Indeed economic theory has provided many of the arguments that have influenced both the form ideologies have taken and their political acceptability. One of its most abiding influences has been to enhance the appeal of neo-liberalism by (mistakenly) emphasizing the compatibility of freedom and the market, thus neatly side-stepping the problem of distribution. The rewards which individuals get arise, in traditional neo-classical theory, not from any 'rights' or entitlements that they might have, but as returns to their ownership of factors of production – their own labour and any capital that they might have. On all the really interesting distributional questions, however, neo-classical theory is silent. This state of affairs has meant that one of the major pillars of the post-war consensus – the welfare state – has been without an economic rationale. Indeed, worse than that, it often seemed to be inconsistent with received theory. Providing goods rather than money, it is argued, undermines freedom of choice and income-based supplements reduce work incentives. Thus the welfare state weakens the very market forces which will maximize economic efficiency.

This critique of the welfare state results from a confusion about means and ends. For the above arguments reduce the question of the design of the welfare state to one of means, conveniently forgetting that the principles upon which it is based (distributive justice and positive freedom) conflict directly with those underlying the appeal to markets as conducive to the freedom of the individual. Neo-liberalism and distributive social justice are conflicting moral sets of principles. To reduce the question of the rationale of the welfare state to the instrumental level begs the fundamental value judgements. The appropriate policy must depend upon the value judgements. The 'new' welfare economics, referred to above and which Dasgupta's (1986) article addresses, is based on alternative value judgements. These are what the debate on the distributive role of the state are about and to discuss policy solely in terms of economic efficiency and market failure is incorrect.

Recent government policy has re-opened these debates by challenging the pillars of the post-war consensus. The policies which have been introduced – the MTFS, privatization and labour market reform – represent an attempt to return to a *laissez-faire* economy, with the state retreating towards a nightwatchman's role. The residual role of the state to which such position leads is the protection of property, law and order, defence and maintenance of the value of the currency. To the extent that this approach derives from old-fashioned defences of the market, the Thatcherites provide a good example of Keynes' dictum. They are 'the slaves of some defunct economist'. The new welfare economics, on the other hand, points towards a positive set of criteria to provide a rationale for the welfare state and intervention as mechanisms for the achievement not of neo-liberal values, but rather of social justice.

Notes

1 The Pareto principle is discussed more comprehensively by Beckerman (1986). See also Sen (1975) for a discussion of this theorem and its converse.

2 The alternative approach is to assume that co-ordination takes place through bargaining, where property rights are perfectly defined and the legal system is costless in enforcing them. See, for example, Coase (1960).

3 The classic article setting out this approach is by Bator (1958).

4 For an overview and analysis of the modern industrial theory of oligopoly and monopoly, the reader is referred to the issue of the *Oxford Review of Economic Policy* devoted to the topic (Autumn 1985) and especially to the articles by Mayer and Vickers.

5 The presentation here closely follows Hayek's arguments. This is largely for ease of exposition and many of the important differences between Mises and Hayek in particular have been suppressed. See Mises (1920), Lange and Taylor (1938) and Dobb (1969) for more detail.

6 See Helm (1984) for an analysis of this relationship between evolutionary theory and individual and firm selection.

7 This reliance on potential competition has been much exploited in the recent literature on 'contestable markets'. See on this Baumol (1982) and Shepherd (1984).

8 An introduction to Games Theory is provided by Bacharach (1976). See Vickers (1985) for a non-technical discussion of applications to oligopoly theory.

9 This result is presented in social choice literature as Arrow's General Possibility Theorem. It demonstrates that even if we assume weak Paretianism, unrestricted domain and independence of irrelevant alternatives, a non-dictatorial social welfare function cannot be defined if there are at least three individuals and three social states. See Arrow (1961) and Sen (1971) for expositions, and Sen (1979) for an accessible account of why this result arises.

10 This approach is rooted in the liberal tradition, from Locke and especially Mill (1859) onwards. Hayek's *The Constitution of Liberty* (1960) is the classic modern treatise on this brand of constitutionalism. Economists in the 'new right' tradition who have followed in this direction include most notably Buchanan and Tullock (1962) and Tullock (1976).

11 This theme is developed in Allsopp and Helm (1985).

12 See Clarke (1978) and Freedom (1978) for analyses of the origins and developments of the splits between the new liberals and social democrats in the late nineteenth and early twentieth centuries.

13 See Morgan (1985) for an account of the politics of the period, and Cairncross (1985) for the economics.

14 For a detailed account of the intentions and consequences of the organizational structures, see Chester (1975).

15 £M3 is one definition of the money supply comprising all notes and coins as well as all current and deposit accounts and all deposits in the UK banking sector held by UK citizens.

16 The best 'official' exposition of the intellectual basis of the MTFS is given in Lawson's Mais Lecture (1984). For a critical assessment of the MTFS, see Allsopp (1985). A wider survey and critique of the first stages of the Thatcher government's economic policy is to be found in Buiter and Miller (1984).

17 The Summer 1985 issue of the *Oxford Review of Economic Policy* was devoted to unemployment, and the reader is referred in particular to the article by Mayhew for a more detailed appraisal of recent government policy in the labour market.

References

ALLSOPP, C. J. (1985) 'Monetary and fiscal policy in the 1980s', *Oxford Review of Economic Policy*, Vol. 1, pp. 1–20.

ALLSOPP, C. J. and HELM, D. R. (1985) 'The political economy of public policy', *Times Literary Supplement*, December.

ARROW, K. J. (1961) *Social Choice and Individual Values*, New York, Wiley (second edition, 1963).

BACHARACH, M. (1976) *Economics and the Theory of Games*, London and Basingstoke, Macmillan.

BATOR, F. M. (1958) 'The anatomy of market failure', *Quarterly Journal of Economics*, No. 72, pp. 351–71.

BAUMOL, W. J. (1982) 'Contestable markets: an uprising in the theory of industry structure', *American Economic Review*, Vol. 72, pp. 1–15.

BECKERMAN, W. (1986) 'How large a public sector?', *Oxford Review of Economic Policy*, Vol. 2, No. 2, pp. 7–24.

BEESLEY, M. and LITTLECHILD, S. (1983) 'Privatisation: principles, problems and priorities', *Lloyds Bank Review*, Vol. 149, pp. 1–20.

BERLIN, I. (1958) *Two Concepts of Liberty*, Inaugural lecture, Oxford, Clarendon Press.

BEVERIDGE, W. H. (1942) *Social Insurance and Allied Services*, Cmnd 5404, London, HMSO.

BUCHANAN, J. M. and TULLOCK, G. (1962) *The Calculus of Consent*, Ann Arbor, MI, University of Michigan Press.

BUITER, W. H. and MILLER, M. H. (1984) *Changing the Rules: The Economic Consequences of the Thatcher Regime*, Brookings Papers on Economic Activity.

CAIRNCROSS, A. (1985) *Years of Recovery: British Economic Policy 1945–51*, London, Methuen.

CHESTER, N. (1975) *The Nationalisation of Industry*, London, HMSO.

CLARKE, P. (1978) *Liberals and Social Democrats*, Cambridge, Cambridge University Press.

COASE, R. H. (1960) 'The problem of social cost', *Journal of Law and Economics*.

CREEDY, J. and DISNEY, R. (1985) *Social Insurance in Transition*, London, Oxford University Press.

DASGAPTA, P. (1986) 'Positive freedom, markets and the welfare state', *Oxford Review of Economic Policy*, Vol. 2, No. 2, pp. 25–36.

DOBB, M. (1969) *Welfare Economics and the Economics of Socialism*, Cambridge, Cambridge University Press.

DILNOT, A., KAY, J. and MORRIS, N. (1984) *The Reform of Social Security*, London, Oxford University Press.

ECONOMIC PROGRESS REPORT (1986) 'A Flexible Labour Market', No. 182.

FREEDOM, M. (1978) *The New Liberalism*, London, Oxford University Press.

FRIEDMAN, M. (1962) *Capitalism and Freedom*, Chicago, University of Chicago Press.

FRIEDMAN, M. and FRIEDMAN, R. (1980) *Free to Choose*, London, Secker and Warburg.

HAMMOND, E., HELM, D. R. and THOMPSON, D. (1985) 'British Gas: options for privatisation', *Fiscal Studies*, Vol. 6, pp. 1–20.

HAMMOND, E., HELM, D. R. and THOMPSON, D. (1986) 'Competition in electricity supply: has the Energy Act failed?', *Fiscal Studies*, Vol. 7, pp. 11–33.

HAYEK, F. v. (1944) *The Road to Serfdom*, Chicago, University of Chicago Press.

HAYEK, F. v. (1948) *Individualism and Economic Order*, Chicago, University of Chicago Press.

HAYEK, F. v. (1960) *The Constitution of Liberty*, Chicago, University of Chicago Press.

HELM, D. R. (1984) *Enforced Maximisation: Competition, Evolution and Selection*, unpublished DPhil, University of Oxford.

KAHNEMAN, D., SLOVIC, P. and TVERSKY, A. (1983) *Judgement Under Uncertainty: Heuristicss and Biases*, Cambridge, Cambridge University Press.

KAY, J. (1986) 'The rationale of taxation', *Oxford Review of Economic Policy*, Vol. 2, No. 2, pp. 1–6.

KAY, J. and THOMPSON, D. (1986) 'Privatisation: a policy in search of a rationale', *Economic Journal*, Vol. 96, pp. 18–32.

KEYNES, J. M. (1926) 'The end of *laissez-faire*', reprinted in *Essays in Persuasion*, c.w. xi, London and Basingstoke, Macmillan.

KEYNES, J. M. (1936) *The General Theory of Employment, Interest and Money*, London and Basingstoke, Macmillan.

LANGE, O. and TAYLOR, F. M. (1938) *On the Economic Theory of Socialism*, Minneapolis, Minn., The University of Minnesota Press.

LAWSON, N. (1984) *The British Experiment: The Mais Lecture*, London, HM Treasury.

MARWICK, A. (1982) *British Society Since 1945*, Harmondsworth, Penguin Books.

MAYER, C. P. (1985) 'Recent developments in industrial economics and their implications for policy', *Oxford Review of Economic Policy*, Vol. 1, pp. 1–24.

MAYHEW, K. (1985) 'Reforming the labour market', *Oxford Review of Economic Policy*, Vol. 1, pp. 60–79.

MIDDLEMAS, K. (1979) *Politics in Industrial Society: The Experience of the British System Since 1911*, London, Andre Deutsch.

MILL, J. S. (1859) *On Liberty* (in *Utilitarianism, Liberty, Representative Government*, London, Everyman, 1972).

MISES, L. v. (1920) *Die Wirtschaftsrechnung in Sozialistischen Gemeinwesen*, Archiv für Sozialwissenschaften und Sozialpolitik, 47. Reprinted in Hayek, F. v. (ed.) (1922) *Collectivist Economic Planning*.

MOORE, J. (1983) Speech by John Moore, MP, at the Annual Conference of City of London Stockbrokers, 1 November,

MORGAN, K. (1985) *Labour in Power*, London, Oxford University Press.

NOZICK, R. (1974) *Anarchy, the State and Utopia*, Oxford, Basil Blackwell.

POPPER, K. P. (1945) *The Open Society and its Enemies* (fourth revised edition, 1962; London, Routledge and Kegan Paul).

RAWLS, J. (1971) *A Theory of Justice*, London, Oxford University Press.

SANDLER, T. and TSCHIRHART, J. T. (1980) 'The economic theory of clubs', *Journal of Economic Literature*, Vol. 18, pp. 1481–521.

SCHELLING, T. C. (1978) *Micromotives and Macrobehaviour*, New York, Norton.

SEN, A. K. (1970) 'The impossibility of a Paretian liberal', *Journal of Political Economy*, Vol. 78, pp. 152–7.

SEN, A. K. (1971) *Collective Choice and Social Welfare*, San Francisco, Holden-Day. (Reprinted 1979, North-Holland.)

SEN, A. K. (1975) 'The concept of efficiency', in Parkin, M. and Nobay, A. R. (eds), *Current Economic Problems: Conference Proceedings*, Cambridge, Cambridge University Press.

SEN, A. K. (1979) 'Personal utilities and public judgements', *Economic Journal*, Vol. 89, pp. 537–58.

SEN, A. K. (1983) 'The profit motive', *Lloyds Bank Review*, No. 147, pp. 1–20.

SEN, A. K. (1984) 'The living standard', in Collard, D. A., Dimsdale, N. H., Gilbert, C. L., Helm, D., Scott, M. FG. and Sen, A. K. (eds) (1985), *Economic Theory and Hicksian Themes*, London, Oxford University Press.

SHEPHERD, W. (1984) 'Contestability vs. competition', *American Economic Review*, Vol. 74, pp. 572–87.

SMITH, A. (1776) *An Inquiry into the Nature and Causes of the Wealth of Nations* (Republished 1976, London, Oxford University Press).

TULLOCK, G. (1976) *The Vote Motive*, Hobart Paperback 9, London, Institute of Economic Affairs.

VICKERS, J. (1985) 'Strategic competition among the few', *Oxford Review of Economic Policy*, Vol. 1, pp. 39–62.

VINER, J. (1960) 'On the intellectual history of *laissez-faire*', *Journal of Law and Economics*, Vol. 3, pp. 45–69.

YARROW, G. (1986) 'Privatisation in theory and practice', *Economic Policy*, Vol. 2, pp. 324–77.

7 The geography of the military industry in Britain

John Lovering and Martin Boddy

World military spending is currently around $1.7 million a minute. Over the last twenty-five years world military spending has grown more than world output, implying that the world's civilian output has shrunk (Sivard, 1986, p. 6). Military spending is a key factor in the development of certain kinds of industry, particularly high-technology industry (Kaldor, 1981; Gansler, 1982).

In this context, it is to be expected that military expenditure might have a significant geographical impact within the major defence equipment producing countries. In the US, for example, it has been suggested that the growth of defence spending in the 1980s has given rise to a 'military remapping' of the US, involving a shift of activity towards the 'defence perimeter' (Markusen and Bloch, 1985). Castells suggests that the changing geography of the US industry reflects the shift from a 'welfare' to a 'warfare' state (Castells, 1985). In the UK, where Ministry of Defence procurement is now [1988] running at almost one million pounds an hour, studies have pointed to its uneven regional impact (Short, 1981; Dunne and Smith, 1984; Simmie and James, 1986). Case studies have shown that the presence of major defence industries has been an important factor in the historical prosperity of some localities. Some major manufacturing centres in the north and on the coast have been based on military industry (Law, 1983) and the existence of a major defence complex has been a factor differentiating the Bristol area from south Wales, for example (Lovering, 1985; Boddy and Lovering, 1986). Defence spending appears to have played a role in the relative prosperity of southern England in the 1980s, and the growth of the 'western crescent' or 'M4 sunbelt' (Hall *et al.*, 1987; Boddy, Lovering and Bassett, 1986).

In this chapter we present some new data on military industrial activity at the regional level. Our primary source is procurement statistics provided in correspondence by the Ministry of Defence. This information has been made available through channels such as parliamentary questions. The data coverage, however, is limited and we stress at the outset that this paper does not provide a definitive or comprehensive review of the geographical dimensions of defence spending. Nevertheless it is possible to paint a broad-brush picture of the regional distribution of defence industry and changes through time. The results show that military activities are connected with wider spatial changes in the 1980s. We consider some possible explanations for this relationship in the conclusion.

7.1 Defence industries in a deindustrializing economy

During the Second World War Britain was more highly militarized than any other advanced capitalist country (Barnett, 1986). After the war most factories converted to civil products, but military work remained an important and largely separate activity within manufacturing. It also cornered a disproportionate share of national research and development (Council for Science and Society, 1986). This pattern became entrenched through succeeding cycles of defence spending. Real defence spending increased abruptly in 1950, with the formation of NATO and the outbreak of the Korean War, and returned to a path of gradual decline from 1952. From 1959 it again increased, and continued to do so, with only two brief pauses, until the mid-1980s. By 1983 Britain ranked 22nd out of 142 countries in terms of per capita GNP, but 12th in terms of public military expenditure per capita (Sivard, 1986, p. 36). It is a relatively highly militarized economy. UK government defence spending is set to decline by 6 per cent in real terms over 1986–9, and this is spurring intense efforts to expand into export markets.

Table 7.1 summarizes the major phases of expansion and contraction of real defence spending. The growth of defence spending since the 1960s has contrasted with the 'deindustrialization' of civil activity (Blackaby, 1979). Since 1979 a major rearmament programme has been juxtaposed against a sharp decline, followed by virtual stagnation, in total manufacturing output (Coutts, Godley, Rowthorn and Ward, 1986, p. 4).

Table 7.1 Major cycles in UK defence spending (% change in real spending)

Expansion phase			Contraction phase		
Years	Net growth	Annual growth	Years	Net decline	Annual decline
1950–52	56	28	1952–9	−16	−2
1959–67	17	2	1967–9	−12	−6
1969–76	20	3	1976–8	−4	−2
1978–85	30	4			

Sources: *Statement on the Defence Estimates* (various years)

7.2 The industrial impact of defence spending

The Ministry of Defence estimates that some three-fifths of the employment generated by defence procurement falls within manufacturing industry. In 1985 sales of military equipment to the MoD alone (that is, leaving aside exports) accounted for 45 per cent of the output of the aerospace

Table 7.2 Employment in UK industry generated by defence spending (000s)

	1963	1978	1984	1985
Attributable to:				
Ministry of Defence—direct	492	319	310	285
—indirect	379	263	240	230
Total MoD	871	582	550	515
UK defence exports—direct	55	69	70	60
—indirect	40	62	50	50
Total exports	95	131	120	110
Total employment generated by defence	966	713	670	625

Source: Pite, 1980; MoD

industry, 65 per cent of that of the ordnance industry, 30 per cent of the shipbuilding industry, and 15 per cent of the output of the electronics industry. These aggregates conceal sub-sectors and companies within which the degree of defence dependence is very much higher. Although some 45 000 companies contract to the MoD, only 50 regularly receive over £5 million, and only eight firms receive over £100 million. The British defence industries therefore consist of a fairly small group of companies in a limited range of industrial sectors.

The Ministry of Defence periodically makes available estimates of the employment generated by procurement spending. Early estimates were generated by applying a measure of productivity for each industry to the value of payments made (Pite, 1980). The MoD has since refined its methods, and attempts where possible to base employment estimates on the performance of the major defence companies. However, these estimates inevitably involve some simplification. Since productivity in defence production has often been lower than in civil work (Levitt, 1985), official statistics should perhaps be regarded as minimal estimates of defence-induced employment. It would be unwise to place too much weight on the absolute values, but these estimates provide a useful impression, especially of the broad changes over time (Table 7.2).

The defence sector shed about a quarter of a million jobs between 1963 and 1978, twice the rate of job loss experienced in manufacturing as a whole. But in the early 1980s the relationship was inverted; between 1978 and 1984 employment induced by defence spending fell at one third of the rate of decline in manufacturing as a whole (Table 7.3). Despite a marked increase in the proportion of UK defence spending allocated to equipment and related items (Table 7.4), employment in the defence industries has fallen. This suggests that the defence sector is now characterized by 'jobless growth', which reflects its increasing high-technology bias. The rapid

Table 7.3
Employment in defence sector, all manufacturing, and working population

	1963	1978	1984	1963–78	1978–84
Absolute numbers					
Employees in employment	22600	22900	21000	+1%	−8%
(a) Employees in manufacturing	7800	6900	5100	−12%	−26%
(b) Employment generated by defence spending	96	713	670	−28%	−6%

Sources:
Pite, 1980: *Employment Gazette* and *Economic Trends* (various issues); MoD

Table 7.4 Increase in Ministry of Defence spending by defence budget headings, 1978–85

	1985 Index (1978 = 100)
Total defence spending	252
Spending on personnel	198
Spending on equipment	306
– sea equipment	322
– land equipment	268
– air equipment	344
– other	184

Sources:
HMSO, 1986, 1982, Table 2.1

rearmament of the early 1980s together with the expectation of expanding export markets, provided defence companies with the immediate financial resources and the longer-term motivation for a radical restructuring. This has been reflected in major reorganizations of corporate structures, management styles, product strategies and production processes. These have been accompanied partly by a diversification into civil markets, partly by consolidation of specialist military activities, especially in the electronics and aerospace industries, and by selective job loss and 'jobless growth'. These in turn have had geographical effects.

7.3 Geographical dimensions

Defence procurement impacts unevenly across the regions. The MoD estimates regional impacts on the basis of the location of companies

Table 7.5 Regional distribution of MoD procurement spending (%)

	1977/8	1983/4	1985/6
North	6	2	3
Yorkshire and Humberside	2	2	2
East Midlands	7	5	4
East Anglia	4	3	3
South East	42	54	49
South West	15	11	12
West Midlands	7	4	4
North West	8	11	14
Wales	1	1	2
Scotland	7	6	6
Northern Ireland	1	1	1
United Kingdom	100	100	100

Sources: Short, 1981; MoD

receiving contracts. Table 7.5 presents regional data for three years. These provide a rough picture of the relative importance of defence spending on industry across the regions and of changes over time.

A number of reservations should be noted. First, the MoD's estimates are based on a sample of contracts generated by its main billing computer. This computer does not cover all payments and the sample accounted for about 90 per cent of contracts in 1978 and 80 per cent in 1985. It is probable that this method biases the results towards the South East, as some companies bill the MoD through their London offices. Secondly, there appear to be wide year-upon-year variations in the shares going to the regions, especially those which receive relatively small amounts. The estimates given for these regions in Table 7.5 may therefore be a poor guide to the longer-term average. Thirdly, they take no account of the location of subcontractors. There is some evidence to suggest that major subcontractors on major defence projects tend to be located in the same set of favoured regions as their main contractors, indeed many are divisions of the prime contractors (Law, 1983; Breheny, 1987; Southwood, 1985). This would imply that the distribution across regions may be even more biased towards the dominant regions than shown in Table 7.5.

Three regions – the South East, South West and North West – accounted for two-thirds of all spending in 1978. By the mid-1980s this had risen to three-quarters, the South East increasing its already large share of defence spending to half the total. The North West has increased its share to second place, just overtaking the South West which has nevertheless retained a high share.

Defence-generated employment

The value of MoD payments in to each region may be used to generate regional employment estimates, on the assumption that employment is proportional to contracts received. This method was used by Dunne and Smith (1984) and is adopted here, but it should be noted that it involves further simplifying assumptions. Employment per unit of MoD spending varies widely from industry to industry and a proper regional estimate should be weighted to take account of this. However, appropriate weightings will not be available until the MoD publishes its own regional estimates. In Table 7.6 defence-induced employment is allocated across each UK region in proportion to Ministry of Defence procurement spending. The impact of defence spending on manufacturing industry is particularly important (Kaldor, Sharp and Walker, 1986). Table 7.7 presents an estimate of the regional impact on manufacturing, on the assumption that direct employment induced by MoD spending, and export-induced employment, correspond to manufacturing activity. Table 7.7 should be regarded only as a very rough indication of the relative defence orientation of manufacturing employment in the regions.

These tables suggest that the regions with the greatest concentrations of defence spending and consequent industrial employment are also the most dependent on defence. Procurement appears to account for one in twenty jobs in the South West, one in twenty-three in the South East and one in twenty-seven in the North West. The employment impact of defence contracts is much lower in all other regions. The manufacturing sector in these three regions appears to be heavily dependent on defence, with the proportions rising in the South West and South East to one manufacturing job in nine, and one in fourteen in the North West.

These estimates suggest that the influence of the defence spending in the most defence-dependent regions has been appreciable. The South West, which was the most defence-dependent region in the 1970s, has remained so. Defence demands have become particularly influential in the South East, although they were already disproportionately so in the 1970s. The same is true, at a more modest level, for the North West, which has become a major 'peripheral' concentration of defence industries. In terms of manufacturing industry alone, the South West remains heavily dependent, although it may now be rivalled in this by the South East (Table 7.7).

As noted earlier, over 100000 jobs are generated by military exports. This work is unevenly distributed between companies and thence locations. It has been assumed so far that export-induced employment follows the same regional pattern as MoD spending. In fact this is unlikely to be the case. Many of the plants specializing in defence exports within the aerospace and electronics industries are based in the South East, South West and North West, and some in Scotland. In some cases increased exports have compensated for the decline in MoD-induced employment. The South West, which contains some major aerospace exporters, is a

Table 7.6 Estimated regional distribution of employment generated by MoD procurement spending and exports

	Employment induced by procurement		Defence-induced defence employment as % of all employment	
	1978	1985	1978	1985
North	43	19	3.5	1.8
Yorkshire and Humberside	16	13	0.8	0.7
East Midlands	50	25	3.7	1.8
East Anglia	28	19	4.1	2.7
South East	299	306	4.1	4.2
South West	107	75	6.8	4.8
West Midlands	50	25	2.3	1.3
North West	56	87	2.1	3.7
Wales	7	13	0.7	1.3
Scotland	50	37	2.4	1.4
Northern Ireland	7	6	1.4	1.3
United Kingdom	713	625	3.1	2.9

Table 7.7 Estimated regional distribution of manufacturing employment on defence, 1977 and 1985

	Defence-induced employment in manufacturing		% of regional manufacturing employment	
	1978	1985	1978	1985
North	23	10	5.6	3.6
Yorkshire and Humberside	8	7	1.1	1.3
East Midlands	27	14	4.5	2.8
East Anglia	16	10	7.7	5.7
South East	163	169	8.8	10.9
South West	58	41	13.6	11.2
West Midlands	27	14	2.7	2.0
North West	31	48	3.1	7.1
Wales	4	7	1.2	3.3
Scotland	27	21	4.5	4.7
Northern Ireland	4	3	2.8	3.4
United Kingdom	388	344	5.3	6.2

leading case in point. It seems likely therefore that exports may reinforce the bias of defence activities towards the dominant military-industrial regions.

Defence spending and regional assistance

The regional imbalance in defence procurement and the importance of this to employment and economic activity in each region is evident from these figures. It is salutary to contrast the scale and pattern of MoD industrial expenditure with that of formal regional assistance. Spending on regional assistance, compared with defence procurement, has declined since the mid-1970s (Table 7.8).

Table 7.8 UK Regional assistance compared with regional procurement spending (current prices)

1974/5	1975/6	1976/7	1977/8	1978/9	1979/80	1980/1	1982/3	1983/4
Regional Assistance:*								
274	450	497	489	571	463	650	1062	738
Procurement expenditure:								
1302	1792	2138	2565	2984	3640	4885	6297	6939
Regional assistance as % of procurement:								
21	25	23	19	19	13	13	17	11

* Regional development grants plus selective assistance, including Northern Ireland

Sources: *Regional Trends* (various issues); *Statement on the Defence Estimates* (various years)

Table 7.9 Expenditure on defence procurement and regional assistance by region, 1977/8 and 1983/4

	Regional assistance		Change	Procurement spending		Change	Change in combined total
	1977/8	1983/4	'78–'84	1977/8	1983/4	'78–'84	'78–'84
North	144	92	−36%	154	139	−10%	−22%
Yorkshire and Humberside	27	36	+33%	51	139	+173%	+124%
East Midlands	2	18	+800%	180	346	+92%	+100%
East Anglia	—	—	—	103	208	+102	+102%
South East	—	—	—	1077	3747	+248%	+248%
South West	8	12	+50%	385	763	+98%	+97%
West Midlands	—	—	—	180	278	+54%	+54%
North West	60	137	+128%	205	763	+272%	+240%
Wales	80	114	+43%	25	69	+176%	+74%
Scotland	117	222	+90%	180	416	+131%	+115%
Northern Ireland	50	108	+116%	25	69	+176%	+136%

Sources: *Regional Trends*; MoD

Between 1978 and 1984 (the most recent year for which data are available for both series), defence procurement rose by 114 per cent in current prices. Over the same period regional assistance rose by only 29 per cent. The relatively rapid growth of procurement, especially in those regions which were already the most defence oriented, has intensified the bias of public expenditure under these two headings in favour of the more advantaged regions. The less buoyant regions have continued to receive most in terms of regional assistance, but little by way of MoD expenditure (Table 7.9). The main exceptions are Scotland and the North West, each of which has received relatively high levels of regional assistance and even larger volumes of MoD procurement. Regional and procurement expenditure have both increased markedly in the North West. Meanwhile Wales, the North, and Yorkshire and Humberside, the other main targets for regional assistance, have received only minor increases in industrial defence spending. The North has suffered a decline in both regional and military expenditure. But the absolute increase in procurement spending in the South East (£2670 million) towers above the increases, and indeed the absolute value, of regional and defence spending in every other region. (Note that these figures take no account of military exports which, as suggested earlier, possibly favour the southern regions and the North West.)

7.4 Discussion

The development of British industry in the 1980s has been profoundly influenced by the juxtaposition of deindustrialization and a major rearmament programme (Kaldor, Sharp and Walker, 1986). The evidence presented here suggests that this has had major geographical effects, which have yet to be sufficiently appreciated. Put bluntly, the much-discussed widening of the 'gap' between 'north and south' in the 1980s is related to the remilitarization of the British economy. The areas which are economically buoyant, the 'M4 corridor', the 'outer south east arc' and the emergent 'M11 corridor', are those which have benefited disproportionately from military spending. But it would be an oversimplication to suggest that the military impact consists simply of a bias towards the South East, as is sometimes implied (Wray, 1987). For the defence industries are also prominent along a western axis, in the form of military aerospace, electronics and nuclear specialists in the South West and North West. To a more modest extent they are also important in Scotland, mainly in the electronics sector in the Scottish central valley.

The shifts in the regional distribution of defence-induced activity in the 1980s show a centripetal tendency, consolidating the 'core' military-industrial regions of the South, the West and Scotland. (This impression is confirmed by further analysis and case studies at the sub-regional level, see for example Hall *et al.* (1987), Boddy and Lovering (1986), Lovering (1985).) This retrenchment towards the core regions contrasts with the move towards a 'periphery' reported for the US (Markusen and Bloch, 1985; Lovering, 1987).

At first sight, the association between military industry and regional prosperity might suggest that defence spending has been, in effect, a sort of 'hidden' regional policy. As a regional policy it is certainly remarkable since in simple quantitative terms it greatly outweighs formal regional spending, and contradicts it geographically. However, it would be foolish to draw policy conclusions from this. In the absence of a theoretical explanation of the relationship between defence spending and regional development it is not possible to say whether the regional distribution of military spending in the 1980s has been a cause or an effect of wider regional economic change.

There are as yet no comprehensive studies of decision-making in defence industries, and at the present stage of research, the true relationship must remain a matter of informed speculation. In the space available here we can only outline the arguments for and against different conceptions of this relationship. This can be done by contrasting the implications of different scenarios.

Defence industries as autonomous sources of regional change

In this scenario, the regional distribution of defence-industrial activities is an influence on wider regional development. Defence industries are channels through which exogenous (politically determined) demand and supply influences are projected into the regions. For this to be the case military demands must be translated exclusively into demand for a set of given 'defence industries', whose location is fixed. Defence industries are largely unaffected by other sectors in their host regions. Empirically, the problem with this model is that it probably overstates the corporate, technological and geographical rigidity of the defence sector. Certainly, some large concentrations of defence industrial activity are virtually immobile, as a result of the inherited distribution of built capital, and trained labour (for example, see Boddy and Lovering, 1986). And it seems that these sites will remain important – it has been claimed that aerospace is the only major manufacturing sector where the UK will continue to play a leading international role (Munchau, 1987, p. 26). However, although the major companies in the defence sector have been there for two or more decades, there is some evidence of increasing entry and exit at the margin of the sector (*Statement of Defence Estimates 1987*, p. 45). Meanwhile, the major established companies are undergoing radical upheavals. The rising technological intensity of military equipment means that the major contractors are facing new requirements, especially of skilled labour and production equipment. Whether these can be met on their inherited sites depends on the location of those sites and the strategies companies adopt for acquiring scarce labour.

Defence industries as reflecting regional change

In the alternative scenario, the location of defence industries follows the fortunes of the regions. For this to be completely the case defence companies would have to be like any other kind of company, with similar locational behaviour. If defence companies are expanding or moving into the semi-rural areas in the south and west this would be because that is where they can most profitably find the labour and premises they need. The growing defence bias of the south would then be an effect rather than a cause of its general relative good fortune. Empirically, the problem with this scenario is that it probably overstates the commonalities between military and civil industry. As suggested earlier, some major sectors of the defence industry still have distinctive requirements of built capital (for example, large airfields or shipyards) and need distinctive combinations of skilled labour. There is also some evidence of an institutional basis for a distinctive locational pattern; some companies need to have ready access to decision-makers amongst military or government customers (Hall *et al.*, 1987). The access points are concentrated in the south. (However, there is little indication that this factor has influenced the recent shifts in the location of military industry.)

These considerations suggest that it is likely that the defence industries contain some sectors which exert a direct causal influence on regional economic change, and others which are more dependent on regional change. In some sectors the cost of major relocation would be prohibitive, and markets can still be found for existing activities. The sites are likely to correspond to the first scenario above (for instance, aerospace, marine, and tank building activity in the South West, North West and North East). In other cases the priority is increasingly on scarce labour which is often recruited externally (for instance, scientists and engineers with transferable skills). For these establishments a location in the preferred southern regions may be something between an advantage and a requirement. These cases are likely to correspond to the second scenario; examples would include new sites open by long-established defence companies like British Aerospace and Plessey in Bracknell, Plymouth and Yeovil.

It should be born in mind, however, that even in these cases, where defence companies appear to be responding 'passively' to given regional circumstances, defence spending may still play a causal role, albeit indirectly. For at the macroeconomic level military demand is a major influence on the scarcity of certain categories of skilled labour. It is estimated that one-third of qualified scientists and engineers in the UK are employed on defence work (Kaldor, Sharp and Walker, 1986, p. 39; CSS, 1986). As a result, military activity exerts a major influence on the market power, and thus the spatial distribution, of key groups of labour. In short, through direct and indirect channels, it appears that military-industrial activity has played an important role in shaping the pattern of regional development in Britain in the 1980s.

References

BARNETT, C. (1986) *The Audit of War*, London and Basingstoke, Macmillan.

BLACKABY, F. (ed.) (1979) *Deindustrialisation*, London, Heinemann/NIESR.

BODDY, M. and LOVERING, J. (1986) 'High technology industry in the Bristol sub-region: the aerospace/defence nexus', *Regional Studies*, Vol. 20, pp. 217–32.

BODDY, M., LOVERING, J. and BASSETT, K. (1986) *Sunbelt City? A Study of Employment Change in Britain's M4 Growth Corridor*, Oxford, Clarendon Press.

BREHENY, M. (ed.) (1987) *Defence Expenditure and Regional Development*, London, Mansell.

CASTELLS, M. (1985) 'High technology, economic restructuring, and the urban-regional process in the United States', in Castells, M. (ed.), 'High technology, space and society', *Urban Affairs Annual Review* 28, pp. 11–40.

COUNCIL FOR SCIENCE AND SOCIETY (1986) *UK Military R&D*, Oxford, CSS.

COUTTS, K. J., GODLEY, W., ROWTHORN, R. and WARD, T. S. (1986) *The British Economy: Recent History and Medium Term Prospects, A Cambridge Bulletin on the Thatcher Experiment*, Cambridge, Faculty of Economics, University of Cambridge.

DUNNE, J. P. and SMITH, R. P. (1984) 'The economic consequences of reduced UK military expenditure', *Cambridge Journal of Economics*, Vol. 8, pp. 297–310.

GANSLER, J. S. (1982) *The Defence Industry*, Cambridge, Mass., MIT Press.

HALL, P., BREHENY, M., McQUAID, R. and HART, D. (1987) *Western Sunrise: The Genesis and Growth of Britain's Major High Tech Corridor*, London, George Allen and Unwin.

KALDOR, M. (1981) *The Baroque Arsenal*, London, Andre Deutsch.

KALDOR, M., SHARP, M. and WALKER, W. (1986) 'Industrial competitiveness and Britain's defence', *Lloyds Bank Review*, No. 162, pp. 31–49.

LAW, C. M. (1983) 'The defence sector in British regional development', *Geoforum*, Vol. 14, pp. 169–84.

LEVITT, M. S. (1985) 'The economics of defence spending', *National Institute of Economic and Social Research, Discussion Paper* 92.

LOVERING, J. (1985) 'Regional intervention, defence industries, and the structuring of space in Britain, the case of Bristol and south Wales', *Environment and Planning D*, Vol. 3, pp. 85–107.

LOVERING, J. (1987) 'Islands of prosperity: the spatial impact of high-technology defence industry in Britain', in Breheny, M. (ed.).

MARKUSEN, A. R. and BLOCH, R. (1985) 'Defensive cities: military spending, high technology and human settlements', in Castells, M. (ed.), 'High technology, space and society', *Urban Affairs Annual Review* 28, pp. 106–20.

MUNCHAU, W. (1987) 'A day of reckoning', *Financial Weekly*, 23 July.

PITE, C. (1980) 'Employment and defence', *Statistical News*, CSO, November, 51.15–51.19.

SHORT, J. (1981) 'Defence spending in the UK regions', *Regional Studies*, Vol. 15, pp. 101–10.

SIMMIE, J. and JAMES, N. (1986) 'The money map of defence', *New Society*, 31 January, pp. 17–18.

SIVARD, R. L. (1986) *World Military and Social Expenditures 1986*, Washington, DC, World Priorities Inc.

SOUTHWOOD, P. (1985) 'The UK defence industry', *Peace Research Reports 8*, School of Peace Studies, University of Bradford.

WRAY, I. (1987) 'Defence and the great divide', *Guardian*, 21 April 1987.

Official publications

CMND 9763–I, *Statement on the Defence Estimates 1986*, Volumes 1 and 2 (HMSO).

CMND 8951–II, *Statement on the Defence Estimates 1983*, Volume 2 (HMSO).

CMND 101–1, *Statement on the Defence Estimates 1987*, Volume 1 (HMSO).

CM 9702–I, *The Government's Expenditure Plans 1986–87 to 1988–89*, Volume I (HMSO).

8 Alternative forms of state intervention: the London Industrial Strategy

Greater London Council

8.1 Productive intervention in practice: popular planning

1.158 A central task for the *London Industrial Strategy* is to increase social control over the process of restructuring. By and large, the immediate power to restructure has been in the hands of private companies and public sector managers. Trade unions have had to concentrate on defensive campaigns. In the nationalized industries industrial restructuring has been extensive but it has largely been dominated by commercial criteria. In the large public corporations, managers are usually recruited from the private sector and are neither encouraged nor inclined to involve workers and consumers in reorganizing public enterprise. The battle that the Greater London Council (GLC) had in bringing London Transport under control exhibits the difficulties faced by any strategy of 'restructuring for labour'.

1.159 One of these is that commitment by politicians and planners to alternative strategies is not enough. They lack the range of knowledge that is necessary to survive, let alone transform, the complex commercial world of marketing, technology and finance. It becomes necessary to depend on managers and experts who, in general, are unsympathetic to alternative forms of restructuring and economic control. How can this be changed?

1.160 The development of an alternative investment institution is a necessary first step, staffed with people who understand the practices of management, and the principles of the alternative. This is the purpose of the Greater London Enterprise Board (GLEB). But our experience has shown that new public investment institutions like GLEB are not enough. They and the political authorities to which they are accountable need the power and the knowledge of both trade union and community organizations if they are to carry out restructuring for labour. Without them, the GLC with its limited resources, and a handful of GLEB managers, will be quite isolated and forced back into a dependence on traditional managers. They will end up against all their good intentions, restructuring for capital.

1.161 The manifesto embodied that understanding, and in doing so reflected the new directions in trade union action that had grown in the 1970s. As industrial restructuring gathered pace from the late 1960s, trade unions developed fresh forms of action. Between 1969 and 1972 there were over 100 occupations against redundancies in the north east alone. In the traditional but declining industrial conurbations, for instance Merseyside, Tyneside and the West Midlands, shop stewards, trades councils and various trade union resource centres tried to develop a more strategic, less reactive trade unionism in defence of their communities. In London, the Lucas Aerospace stewards in west London played a central part in developing an alternative corporate plan with which to resist management's redundancy plans. In east London the fight to save the upper docks took a more offensive form as the 1970s progressed. In the public sector there were many hospital occupations in the late 1970s, and both NUPE and the NCU (previously POEU) have taken up and adapted themes developed in an industrial context – early warning through investigating employers, alternative plans and public enquiries – as a focus of campaigning. These have emphasized the involvement of users and the community.

1.162 These new kinds of trade union and community initiatives have come up against limitations through lack of political support. For groups in London the GLC's industrial strategy has provided the opportunity to achieve this support and the resources and platform it entails. On the other hand for GLEB and GLC the new developments in trade unionism have provided a vital, albeit precarious, base within production.

1.163 It is a new development in economic strategy for a local authority, or indeed any state body within the UK, to base its industrial policies on support for the initiatives and organizations of labour. The only other move in this direction was the drastically foreshortened attempts of Tony Benn and others of the Department of Industry in 1974–5. Normally the resources and the powers to plan have remained at the centre within the state or shared with management. Worker or community involvement has taken on a secondary consultative form commenting on plans drawn up within the public authority. Popular planning by contrast involves sharing power, empowering those without official power. The end-result on many occasions, for instance the People's Plans in Docklands and Coin Street, the campaigns against hospital closures, and the alternative plan at Ramparts Engineering, is an alliance around policies worked out together. Such alliances allow more power than either the GLC or the trade union and community groups would have on their own.

1.164 These alliances have taken a variety of forms. The Industry and Employment Branch has financed a network of trade union resource centres based in 20 different areas and different sectors of London. The Industrial Development Unit has been set up to work with trade unionists to anticipate management's redundancy plans and prepare strategies for resistance and alternatives. The Popular Planning Unit has provided support for trade unionists especially in the public sector. The unit has worked closely with shop stewards in multinationals seeking to establish international links. Trade unions have been involved in the conferences, public inquiries, hearings and working groups which are reflected in much of [*The London Industrial Strategy*]. There has been a close working relationship with the South East Region of the TUC. GLEB, whose chair is a noted London trade unionist, has developed enterprise planning through a support team drawn largely from the trade unions. There has been a programme of work around the use of GLC purchasing power (contracts compliance) and also trade union discussions fighting discrimination against black people within the workplace and within trade unions – discrimination which has often served to weaken the trade union movement.

1.165 This work has taken place against the background of recession. Industrial decline has seriously reduced the numbers and political weight of shopfloor organization in manufacturing. Large sections of workers in London are in unorganized workplaces or, if formally recognized, are not actively organized. In many areas the destruction of industry has gone so far that, in Docklands, for instance, people's livelihoods depend not on the future of the factories – there are none left – but on the future of the land itself.

1.166 For these reasons the original tools we inherited – enterprise planning, early warning, popular planning – have had to be modified. Enterprise planning has often been concerned not with extending the scope of collective bargaining but with establishing a framework for collective bargaining in the first place. Work on early warning has rarely been about anticipating crises. More usually it has been about bringing together the power of the GLC and GLEB with that of the trade unions to save something out of a crisis. The idea of alternative plans has been taken forward most in the public sector where sections of the trade union movement have been able to maintain a strength to mount positive campaigns and bargaining positions, rather than in the manufacturing sector where it first began.

1.167 In spite of these difficulties, the steps that have been taken both by the trade unions and the GLC, have been of importance in developing the ideas and perspectives that are reflected in [*The London Industrial Strategy*] and in the *London Labour Plan* [published in 1986].

1.168 A second perspective of the manifesto was the importance of linking users and local communities with trade unions in the making and practice of strategy. The significance of this has been brought home in the public sector campaigns against the cuts. Unions in Direct Labour Organization (DLO) and tenants organizations, for example, have often been in conflict with each other. The same divisions existed on London Transport (LT), or among caretakers and tenants on council estates. There have been notable achievements in overcoming these divisions in the past few years. The campaign against STOLport [the City of London Airport] was one instance. The Hayes hospital occupation another. There has been slow but significant progress on some estates with tenants' groups working out compromises with local DLO organizations. There has been some coming together of transport workers and users in the campaign against the government takeover of LT. Where these links have taken place it has greatly strengthened the campaign for maintaining and improving jobs and services.

1.169 A number of the public sector chapters [in *The London Industrial Strategy*] raise and reflect these problems. But it is important for a number of private sectors as well. The movement for the conversion of the arms industry to peaceful purposes is one example, the food industry another. In terms of employment GLEB has concentrated on meat products, wholefood and ethnic minority food. On the user side, the GLC has funded a Food Commission to work for the improvement of food products, while the Inner London Education Authority (ILEA) has adopted a new food policy for the school meals service.

1.170 Another way in which the interests of people as workers and users have been linked is through industrial area initiatives – in the King's Cross area, in the Hackney Road, in the Royal [Docks], in south Docklands, and west London. Here sites have been developed which provide local housing and local work opportunities together (this is the aim behind the Coin Street and the Courage developments on the south side of the river, and in the Battlebridge Basin area in King's Cross). In other places, the area offices support community enterprises, and provide premises and services for local industries which use local skills.

1.171 There are two basic points underlying this part of the GLC strategy. First, no alternative plan for an industry can be developed adequately without the central involvement of workers and users in that industry. Second, any strategy must not only address the question of alternatives. It must also take account of how such alternatives can be brought about. It must deal with the question of power as well as direction.

8.2 Boundaries and incursions

1.172 The struggle between the economics of capital and the economics of labour has taken place within each of the three main sectors of the London economy. It has also taken place over the boundaries between them and their relations one with the other. At the present time, the government is attempting to reduce the public economy, pushing labour back into the home and colonizing areas of public production by private capital.

1.173 A strategy for socially useful production would aim to reverse this movement. Its first task is to re-assert social control over the public economy itself, and having done that to use this base to strengthen those forces that are arguing for an economics of labour in the private economy. There are a number of ways this can be done:

- by extending direct labour to produce goods and services required by public bodies and their employees;
- removing restrictions on public producers which prevent them from selling in the private market. In the public market, direct labour organizations should be assessed against private competitors employing workers on parallel wages and conditions to those of public sector workers;
- the planned consolidation of the public economy to extend the public sector market for direct labour production and increasing the bargaining power of public sector bodies with the external market. In 1979 public corporations alone spent £12500 million on goods and services from the private sector. At the moment there is severe fragmentation in the public sector. Different public authorities run their own laundries, canteens, maintenance departments, purchasing organizations, with no reference to others. Why should not the GLC Supplies Department purchase as full a range of products for the National Health Service as the London County Council did when it organized most of London's hospitals through the 1930s and 1940s?;
- purchases from the private sector should be restricted to firms on an approved list who adhere to a code designed to maintain fair wages and equal opportunities on a par with requirements prevailing in the public sector;
- taking back into social control those public enterprises and services which have been sold off to the private sector, particularly the transport and telecommunications networks;
- insisting on public ownership of technological innovations funded by the state;
- ensuring that any public funds advanced to the private sector carry with them a share in the equity of the receiving firms. This is particularly important in the case of interventionary rescues;
- selected interventions in key parts of industrial sectors to ensure a programme of effective restructuring.

1.174 Much of the discussion of British industrial policy has centred on institutions: public ownership, a national investment bank, a national enterprise board, and so on. From the perspective of alternative production all these are necessary but they mean little if not geared to a strategy. How would Unilever be different if they were taken under public control? What would restructuring for labour mean in that instance? What is the key point of control in the food industry – research and development, the supply of materials, food processing plants, marketing or retailing? Which is the relevant public instrument will depend on the strategy to be pursued.

There is no point in extending public power for its own sake, particularly if that power is not organized to support trade unions and users in developing alternative strategies in the industry.

1.175 There is one more general point about the public sector which relates to employment. There is currently little prospect of a return to full employment though the expansion of private sector jobs. The attack on the public economy has reduced employment and the provision of necessary services. Its expansion could improve both. The basic principle of the public economy is to employ labour to meet specific needs. The barrier to providing work for all who want it in the public sector has faced one overriding barrier: that it would have to be financed from taxation and thus in part from withdrawal of funds from the private economy. According to Keynesianism, the return to full employment would expand national output so that the funds would effectively generate themselves. We have seen that there are limits to this. Nevertheless, if new jobs were provided both to expand services and to contribute to the productive restructuring of both private and public economics, the inflationary effect would be reduced. We should remember that two-thirds of the increase in service sector jobs in western Europe in the post-war years have been in the public sector.

1.176 In summary, an interventionist strategy based on production has the following main features:

- an emphasis on long-term strategic production planning of industries;
- a concern that restructuring in all sectors of the economy should be carried out in the interests of those who work in the industry and use its products;
- a commitment to the development and application of human-centred technology;
- a strategic concern with improving the conditions and hours of work in the domestic economy, and with improved means of integrating domestic work with other parts of the economy in order to improve the living and working conditions of women;
- a priority to extending social control over the public economy through increasing political, trade union and user control;
- a commitment to popular involvement in all aspects of strategic policy-making (popular planning) and in the operation of enterprises (enterprise planning).

8.3 Local and national

1.177 In both the monetarist and Keynesian strategies there is little room for local government in the development and implementation of economic strategy. For monetarists, the main task of local councils is to reduce their interference with the market and, where they do intervene, ensure that this intervention removes barriers to the market. In the property market, they argue that councils should put surplus sites on the market and that planning restrictions should be eased. Enterprise Zones are an example of the monetarist strategy of restoring employment through reducing controls.

1.178 The most important monetarist employment policy for local government is the cutting of rates. The Confederation of British Industry (CBI) has for long said that it is the rates which are cutting employment in London and have used this as their principal argument for supporting proposals for the abolition of the GLC.

1.179 Recent research undertaken for the Department of the Environment has now effectively undercut this argument by showing that there is no evident relationship between the levels of rates and employment. This is confirmed by the GLC's own research, which suggests that the main effect of a rate rise is to reduce property prices. In the short run small firms may have to bear the cost of this increase until their next rent review, but even if they do go out of business, new firms will start or old firms expand to take up the gap in the market. For these sectors are predominantly local. In the case of larger firms with national and international markets, rates are a trivial portion of total cost and are not cited as significant in the large firm surveys that have been conducted.

1.180 The argument can be extended to support the proposition that financing employment through rates is likely to expand overall employment in London. If rates are lowered, property prices rise and with them the rents received by property owners. Some of this increased rental income might be spent locally – on the consumption of services or on local investment. But there is likely to be a high leakage out of the local economy, both through consumption on imported goods and on investment outflows. The same sum if held by the local authority through a rate increase would be largely spent locally. A local council's propensity to import or transfer funds out of London is almost certainly less than that of the owners of property and the recipients of rent.

1.181 Part of the evidence for the inverse relationship of rents and rates has come from the Enterprise Zones. The rate exemptions in the Zones have meant that property prices and thus rents have risen within the Zones, so that much of the incentive for new development has been lost. Certainly the Isle of Dogs Enterprise Zone has created few jobs in its initial years of operation, apart from the impact arising from the large public investment in its infrastructure.

1.182 The urban property market is inherently imperfect. Reductions in rates or the offer of other incentives attached to land (such as are found in the Enterprise Zones and Freeports) merely serve to increase land prices and provide windfall gains for property owners.

1.183 This is the basis of the case against monetarist policy on the land market. But there is a more general point. The reliance on the market by local authorities cannot be expected to expand employment, since London's present unemployment is the result not of the market working imperfectly, but of it working too well.

1.184 Keynesians too have given little place to local councils in broader economic strategy. For them the problems of London require national reflation rather than local intervention. Local councils have only marginal significance. They should step in where local markets fail – in the training of labour for example, or the provision of small industrial premises, business advice or economic information. Again, as with the monetarists, the emphasis is placed on getting the market to work, and, as with the monetarists, the weakness of the strategy at a local level is that it has been the market that has been the bearer of London's recession.

1.185 With an interventionist approach to production, however, local authorities have an important place in national strategy. They are in a position to support changes in the domestic economy and to consolidate their own public economies. They can extend the influence of their public economies, through municipalization and the use of purchasing power and pension funds, and intervene in the private economy through direct investment. Furthermore, if strategies and institutions are to be built from below then local councils form one of the principal building blocks.

1.186 It has been in part the economic initiatives taken by local authorities over the last four years that have focused interest on the production-led approach. The emphasis has varied. Sheffield has sought to extend direct labour production to provide goods previously bought from the open market. They have also emphasized the improvement of the working conditions of women, at home and in wage work, and on extending democratic control within the public sector. Lancashire has developed through their Enterprise Board an industrial complex centred on the fishing industry in Fleetwood. The West Midlands have concentrated on measures to provide long-term funds to medium and large firms, linked into a restructuring plan for key segments of the engineering industry. Leeds have developed a substantial programme of co-operative development and training. In London the GLC and, now, Hackney and Haringey have set up Enterprise Boards and have been pursuing similar policies. In each case these councils have refused to remain on the sidelines, offering a grant here, running an advertisement campaign there. They have entered directly into production and, in doing so, have shown the potential and the difficulties of this approach in practice.

1.187 What emerges from these experiences is that the local and the national are not alternatives, with local councils extending municipal production while the national government takes care of reflation. Rather, in case after case, it has been clear how local initiatives need the power and scope of national government to be fully effective. With multinationals, for example, alternative strategies can be developed by the unions working in conjunction with relevant local authorities. But it needs the power of a central government to bargain with Ford over its location of investment and its access to both national and public sector markets. With cable, energy, software, food, airports and the docks, national policies are immediately called for as the result of the studies of these sectors in London. In some cases it is a question of finance, in others one of tariff policy or national regulations. But beyond this in almost every private sector we have studied, the extension of social control for the purposes of restructuring requires intervention at the national level.

1.188 These studies indicate that a national public investment body is needed with the powers, the staff and the funds to control the commanding heights of the main sectors of the economy. In one sector it will be a strong social presence in distribution. In another it might be in research and development. In a third, the best approach will be the take-over of a leading firm that integrates different parts of the sector. In each case a strategy of public intervention will need an understanding of the structure and direction of the industry, in order to identify the key points for social control.

1.189 We would see a national production board standing in a federal relation to local enterprise boards, providing a forum for the co-ordination of local municipal initiatives and a framework for linking national and local interventions in the same sector. The same would be true of the development of sector strategy, for if a national production board is to avoid a discredited planning from above, it must build on the work that emerges from below. Learning from the experiences of GLEB it would be important to devise appropriate forms of democratic control based on parliamentary accountability, a strong trade union input and a federal relation to local and regional enterprise boards. It would provide a framework for linking national and local interventions in the same sector. It would develop sector strategy in a way that built on plans put forward by trade union organizations and local authorities. It would be part of a newly constituted Ministry of Industry. It would co-ordinate sectoral policy and implementation, linking with unions, local councils and a co-ordinated public sector.

1.190 Traditionally local government has been seen as performing tasks delegated to it by national government. But the approach of popular planning suggests a different model, one that starts from the local and ends with a role for the national by virtue of its power over law, tax, money and the foreign exchanges.

1.191 Work towards this has already begun. Local authorities who have been concerned with the clothing industry are meeting to develop their local strategies into a national one. There have been similar meetings on food, and on a number of multinational firms who dominate particular sectors. These discussions need to be extended, so that over the next three years a set of national sector strategies emerge from municipal, trade union and user initiatives. The studies presented [in *The London Industrial Strategy*] are intended as a first contribution to this process. Each needs extending and deepening. Others need to be worked on [. . .]

A prospect for London

1.192 What does all this imply for employment in London? The 1981 Labour Party manifesto foresaw a GLC employment programme which built up to a level of 10 000 jobs a year by 1985. If we add to the 2300 GLEB jobs, the 5000 construction jobs financed through the GLC and GLEB industrial property programme and the 2600 training places funded by the Training Board, we see that this target had been effectively reached by the beginning of 1985. This is quite apart from the 600 jobs in childcare and the jobs in the voluntary sector funded through the GLC's grants programme, particularly in the cultural industries.

1.193 [The chapters of *The London Industrial Strategy*] cover only a section of the sectors of London's market economy, yet they suggest that a further 14 000 jobs could be saved or created by GLEB and the GLC within existing budget over the next four years, on the basis of known projects and firms. This excludes the many projects that come to GLEB from other sectors. Indeed GLEB currently has before it three times as many project proposals as it can fund. If adequate funds were available we would foresee GLEB creating 24 000 jobs over the next four years through direct investment and loans.

1.194 In GLEB's existing investment, the 2300 jobs are expected to increase to 3500 over the next two years as firms carry out planned expansion. This is a job expansion ratio of 50 per cent. There will be further job multiplier effects as the result of increased demand by those employed on GLEB projects, and the demand for machinery and inputs by the enterprises themselves. These would not necessarily increase the jobs in London. Some would be supplied from other parts of the country or from abroad. One of the important reasons for extending the *London Industrial Strategy* would be to ensure that such indirect expansion effects did serve to strengthen further the London economy, and the economies of other depressed areas. In this context, we estimate that each GLEB job could generate another half a job through these indirect effects. Adding this to the direct job expansion plans of GLEB supported enterprises means that we can expect the target of 24 000 direct GLEB jobs to lead to 48 000 permanent jobs in London over the next four years.

1.195 This is a measure of the scope for a policy of active local intervention in the market economy, and also of its limitation. A new

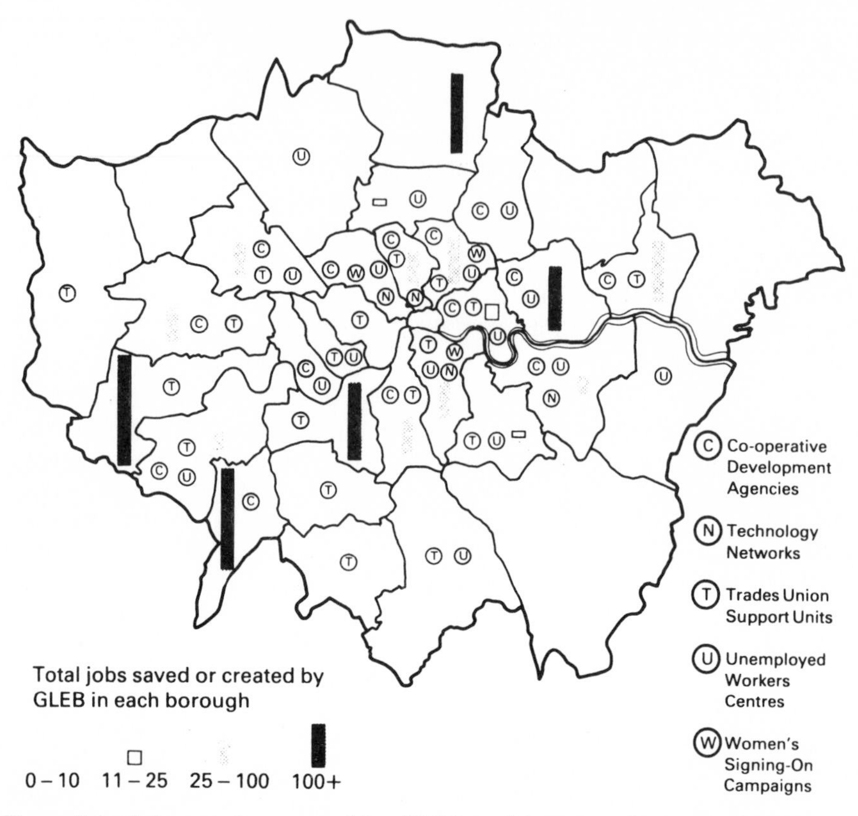

Figure 8.1 Jobs saved or created by GLEB and location of agencies funded by GLEB and the GLC

national industrial strategy is required to ensure that the direct and indirect employment creation from local initiatives is secure, and to extend further the process.

1.196 Registered unemployment is currently [1985] 400000, and still rising. The GLC, even with an expanded budget and in conjunction with a network of Borough Enterprise Boards, could not expect to provide the bulk of the jobs that are needed. Within the market sectors [. . .], new government policies on cable, the cultural industries, software and the motor industry could be expected to save or create 37000 jobs in London. A national strategy for the food, furniture, clothing, instrument engineering, and printing industries could significantly add to the job targets drawn from GLEB's own plans. The policy on the conversion of the defence industries, particularly in relation to the government funding of military technology, would have a major impact on the long-term prospects of London non-military production. Merely diverting a third of military expenditure to alternative public sector programmes would create 100000 jobs in London.

1.197 In the public economy, a nationally financed infrastructure programme and new policies on energy, telecommunications, public transport, airports and the docks, could save or create 97000 jobs in London. This would be much larger were it not for the shortage of skill resulting from the run-down of training over the past five years. The health care programme outlined here involves the creation of 50000 jobs. We also estimate that an adequate childcare programme would involve the creation of 6000 jobs, bringing the public sector targets to 153000 jobs by the end of the decade. Added to the 37000 extra jobs in the private sector resulting from national government policies, we can see that changes in government policy in the limited number of sectors we have studied, could save or create 190000 jobs, rising to some 300000 when we allow for expansion and multiplier effects. If the approach we have outlined here was extended to a comprehensive national industrial policy and if the interests which stand in the path of progressive restructuring could be confronted with the same vigour that the present government has shown in defending them, then we believe that there is a prospect of providing jobs for all those who want them. More than that, there is a chance too of taking a major step in that much deeper transformation of what is produced in London, how and for whom.

9 'A squalid and politically corrupt process?' Intergovernmental relations in the post-war period

R. A. W. Rhodes

9.1 Introduction

It is only to be expected that opposition front-bench MPs will search for the *mot juste* to impugn the motives of the government of the day. However, Jack Straw's judgement (*Hansard*, 25 February, 1985) that Conservative policy on local government was 'squalid' would evoke sympathy beyond his Labour Party colleagues. The feeling that 'all is not as it should be' is prevalent. One does not have to search far to find condemnations of government policy as ill-conceived, prognostications about the demise of local government, or expressions of concern about excessive centralization. Indisputably, Conservative governments since 1979 have had dramatic effects on local government. The central questions are what has changed and why?

The answer to the first question seems straightforward: the government has sought to control both the income and the expenditure of individual local authorities. In the past, governments sought to control their contribution to local expenditure. Since 1979, the rules of the game have been changed unilaterally and the government has not only reduced its grant to local government but it has set ceilings to the expenditure of individual local authorities; withdrawn grant at a penalty rate from 'overspenders'; stipulated the maximum rate that can be levied by the high spenders; and abolished the worst overspenders, namely the GLC and the metropolitan county councils. The description 'control' seems a mild appellation for these changes.

Paradoxically, in spite of an ever-better-stocked armoury, the government has experienced some difficulty in achieving its stated objectives. Although capital expenditure has fallen sharply, local current expenditure has continued to rise in real terms. There have also been a number of unintended consequences with 'cuts' in local government serving only to increase expenditure elsewhere in the public sector. Unilateral central action has fostered recalcitrance by, and conflict with, local authorities. With increasing frequency, the two levels of government have resorted to the courts to regulate their conflicts. Some major policies have scarcely got off the ground: priviatization, in the relatively mild guises of charging and contracting out, has been widely 'considered' but introduced sporadically not to say sparsely. There can be no clearer evidence of the government's difficulties, than the continuous modification of the grant system and the never-ending stream of legislation. Consequently, 'instability' rivals 'control', for first place on the list of consequences arising from Conservative policy.[1]

The second question of why central–local relation has changed also seems to have a fairly obvious answer. A Conservative government committed to social market liberalism confronted an economy suffering from high inflation, high unemployment, declining productive capacity and a lack of international competitiveness. A reduction in the role of the state and, more especially, in public expenditure was a central component of their strategy for economic revival. Consequently, local expenditure had to be contained and reduced. Control is, therefore, a product of economic decline and of Conservative ideology. But this explanation is incomplete. It explains why the Conservatives sought control. It does not explain why they experienced so much difficulty in gaining that control. Elsewhere I have argued that the institutionalization of service interests in policy communities has been a source of inertia but this explanation is only one step in the right direction (see Rhodes, 1985). Nor can any account of of central–local relations restricted to the post-1979 period provide it because the roots of the problem lie in the evolution of British government throughout the post-war era. Moreover, analysis must extend beyond central–local relations to encompass sub-national government (SNG) in its entirety because a central characteristic of British government since 1945 has been the development of differentiated or fragmented service delivery systems: the centre has had 'hands-off' controls over a multi-form institutional structure. The objective of this chapter is to provide a sketch of developments in SNG in the post-war period and explain why Conservative policy since 1979 has had manifold unintended consequences.

The argument proceeds in three stages. First, some of the concepts to be used in examining the development of SNG are defined and the major processes of change are identified. Second, a synoptic or broad-sweep history of SNG in the post-war period is provided. Finally, the causes and consequences of Conservative policy are re-examined and I suggest a different, if equally pessimistic, interpretation of recent events: namely that, from the standpoint of local self-government, central policy on SNG has always been 'a squalid and politically corrupt process'.

9.2 Concepts and processes

Given that 'SNG' is yet another addition to the 'alphabet soup' of British government acronyms it would be as well to define it. Figure 9.1 presents a summary of the descriptive terminology to be employed.

Territorial representation refers to the representation of ethnic-territorial units (i.e. Scotland, Wales and Northern Ireland) at the centre and the

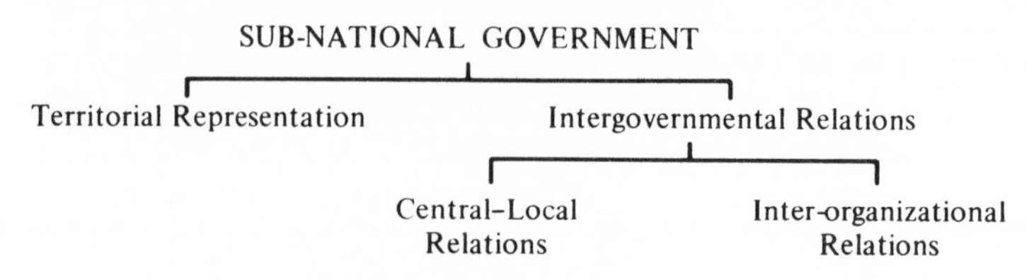

Figure 9.1 The scope of sub-national government

activities of territorially based political organizations. *Intergovernmental relations* (IGR) refers to the relations between central political institutions and all forms of governmental organizations beyond the centre. It is subdivided into *central–local relations* or the links between central departments and local authorities and *inter-organizational relations* which encompasses all other types of sub-national government (i.e. nationalized industries, the National Health Service, the 'regional' organization of central departments and non-departmental public bodies). In short, SNG refers to that arena of political activity concerned with the relations between central political institutions in the capital city and those sub-national political organizations and governmental bodies within the accepted boundaries of the state:[2] a broad definition which immediately makes it clear that British SNG is complex and not limited to local government. The importance of this extension will become obvious from the discussion in section 9.3.

In order to analyse the transformations in SNG, it is necessary to distinguish clearly between the macro, meso and micro-levels of analysis. At the macro-level, the politics of SNG have become part and parcel of the politics of Westminster and Whitehall and, without providing a comprehensive account of changes in British government, it is necessary to explore the *national government environment* or central government institutions and their socio-economic environment as they impact on SNG.[3] At the meso-level, it is necessary to look for regularities in the relationships between the range of sub-national bodies. The concept of *policy networks*, or complexes of organizations connected to each other by resource dependencies and distinguished from other complexes by breaks in the structure of resource dependencies, is a useful tool for ordering the profusion of links. Finally, at the micro-level, it is necessary to explore the behaviour of particular *actors*, be they individuals or organizations. Their behaviour is not simply a product of their environment: they can shape that environment to greater or lesser degrees.

In a relatively short article, it will not be possible either to describe all species of SNG or to explore all three levels of analysis. The emphasis falls on the national government environment and on policy networks in general and, to be more specific, on the processes of change within the national government environment and their (reciprocal) effects on policy networks. For present purposes, six processes are of key importance: instability of the external support system, decline of the mixed economy, increasing functional differentiation (coupled with professionalization) within the welfare state, the oscillating conflicts between functional and territorial politics, political differentiation and change *and* continuity within the British political tradition (most notably in the territorial operating code of central elites). Each process is introduced *seriatim*: their interrelationships are described in the next section.[4]

The external support system

Bulpitt, from whom this phrase is taken, argues not only that 'any centre will attempt to minimize the impact of external forces on domestic politics' but that the British centre has been unable to maintain a stable external support system (Bulpitt, 1983, pp. 59, 137, 167). Thus, by the 1970s, Britain had lost much of its capacity for independent military action (e.g. Suez); its old alliances had weakened in effectiveness (e.g. the Commonwealth, the 'special relationship' with the USA); and sovereignty was qualified by membership of international organizations (e.g. EEC, NATO) and by dependence on the international economy (e.g. IMF, OPEC). Britain was an 'open polity', vulnerable economically and politically to external forces. Nowhere was this more evident than in the management of the economy.

The decline of the mixed economy

As the era of 'stop-go' gave way to 'stagflation', the decline of the British economy became an inescapable fact. Domestic economic weakness was exacerbated by an unstable external support system, giving rise to 'de-industrialization' or the lack of 'an efficient manufacturing sector . . . which, currently as well as potentially, not only satisfies the demands of consumers at home but is also able to sell enough of its products abroad to pay for the nation's requirements' (Singh, 1977, p. 128). The economic problem – 'the British disease' – was variously compounded of an aged and ageing industrial base, a declining productive (especially manufacturing) capacity, a lack of international competitiveness, high inflation, high unemployment, an unreformed pay bargaining structure, a large and expanding public sector and, in consequence of some combination of these factors, a low growth rate. Side-stepping the thorny question of the relative importance of these factors, the fact of economic decline had the effect of translating the 'problems' of SNG into an epiphenomenon of national economic management. The centre has 'off-loaded to the periphery'; that is, it has sought to resolve its economic problems initially by modernizing the institutions of SNG to make them more efficient and subsequently by directly regulating their expenditure. The sheer size of SNG as a proportion of public expenditure (and employment) made it vulnerable to retrenchment.

Differentiation, professionalization and the welfare state

SNG is large because it was the prime vehicle for building the welfare state up to the 1970s. Central departments are, for the most part, non-executant agencies: they depend on SNG for the implementation of policy. This simple fact has had three important consequences. First, it created interdependence in the form of vertical, function-specific links between centre and locality. Second, the expansion of the welfare functions of SNG was not matched by an expansion of its resources. Grants-in-aid financed the expansion and, with the onset of economic decline, the centre had to hand the means for regulating SNG expenditure. It could cut grant, confident that SNG lacked adequate resources of its own.[5] Finally, local government was not the sole beneficiary of the expansion. The post-war years were the era of 'ad-hocracy' as numerous specialized, even uni-functional, invariably non-elected public bodies were created (for example, New Town Corporations, Manpower Services Commission, National Health Service). With the increasing size of government and the ever broader range of its interventions, functional differentiation became the order of the day: growth by elaboration and specialization.

Allied to the process of differentiation is that of professionalization. The specialists in the several policy areas became institutionalized in the structure of government. The professions became key actors in the function-specific policy networks. Dependence on expertise fostered functional differentiation and the employment (even creation) of professions which, in turn, accelerated the fragmentation (and complexity) of government.

In short, policy-making in British government became characterized by professional-bureaucratic complexes based on specific functions: a series of vertical coalitions or policy networks in which central dependence on SNG for the implementation of policy was complemented by SNG's dependence on the centre for financial resources. Fragmentation between functions within the centre went hand in hand with centralization within policy networks. In Luhmann's provocative phrase, there was no one centre but the 'centreless society': the differentiated polity with multiple centres (Luhmann, 1982, pp. xv, 353–5).

Functional versus territorial politics

The emergence of policy networks with the growth of the welfare state could be interpreted as the triumph of functional over territorial politics. Thus, channels of communication between centre and locality were not based on territorial representation but on professional-bureaucratic contacts within policy networks. The politics of service provision, of a centrally dispensed territorial justice, rivalled the politics of place; uniform standards challenged local variety. But the pre-eminence of functional politics created tensions. As Sharpe (1979, p. 20) argues, the decentralist trends in western Europe are a political reaction against the integration imposed by the centralizing policy networks. Nor is the tension between functional and territorial politics visible only in ethnic nationalism and the devolution debate. On a smaller scale, it is re-enacted within local authorities in the tension between local needs and best professional practice and within the policy networks between the technocratic and topocratic professions.[6] It became most apparent with the politicization of SNG during the 1970s.

For the bulk of the post-war period, central and local political elites were insulated from each other. Local parties were poorly organized and, in many local authorities, virtually non-existent: dominated by 'a culture of apolitisme'. The 'dual polity' prevailed wherein the centre sought to distance itself from SNG and 'Low Politics' (e.g. public health) in order to enhance its autonomy in matters of 'High Politics' (e.g. foreign policy).[7] However, the modernization of local government in 1974 politicized local authorities. Nor was this trend evidence of the nationalization of local parties. They may wear national labels but, as events since 1979 demonstrate, that is no guarantee of compliance. If recalcitrance has been a feature of local Labour Parties, it has not been unique to them and many Conservative-controlled councils have foresworn reticence for an overtly critical stance towards the national party's policy. The search for control by the Thatcher governments has provided a considerable shot in the arm to territorial politics. The perceived effect of control was the erosion of local services. The consequent protests, the search for redress against functional politics, provide yet one more illustration of the oscillating relationship between territorial and functional politics. If the latter has been pre-eminent for the bulk of the post-war period, the former has never been extinguished and its persistent flickerings serve as a reminder that questions of territorial structure lie at the heart of the modern nation state.

Political differentiation

The fluctuating fortunes of territorial representation are one manifestation of a wider phenomenon: increased political differentiation. Class may remain the basis of British politics but it is not unchallenged. Language and culture, nationalism, religion and race have all become increasingly salient bases of political allegiance. Partisan de-alignment characterized British politics; that is, electoral allegiance to the two main parties declined, votes were decreasingly cast on class lines, turn-out declined and the electorate became more volatile.[8]

To complicate the picture further, new bases of political differentiation emerged: the policy networks generated sectoral cleavages within localities. In brief, services provided by policy networks created client groups with a vested interest in maintaining those services. These clients can be mobilized to resist threatened reductions in expenditure or to highlight gaps in service provision. For example, the protests of middle-class parents at both the reduction in places at universities and the increasing cost of such education has been a constraint on attempts to restrain expenditure on higher education. Conversely, sectoral support for the compulsory sale of council houses has facilitated government action to the discomfort of Labour opposition. Policy networks can determine the framework within which any debate about their services takes place and can shape local political fragmentation which both cuts across traditional class allegiances, creating alliances based on mutual dependence on government services, and also reinforces the advantages of privileged groups, providing additional points of access.[9]

Continuity within the British political tradition

Without denying that there have been some significant changes, stable elements within the British political tradition have nonetheless limited the capacity of the centre to respond to the changes touched upon above. Two features of this tradition can be mentioned only in passing. First, Britain is a unitary state wherein 'the power to delegate or revoke delegated power remains in the hands of the central authority' (Rose, 1982, p. 50). Parliamentary sovereignty is the cardinal feature of British politics. Second, the two-party system concerned pre-eminently with functional politics serves to integrate the constituent territorial units of the UK. The main concern of this section is with the ideology of central elites. The very phrase suggests that the main topic to be discussed is the shift from Butskellism to monetarism and social-market liberalism under Margaret Thatcher's governments. This shift is important but has been widely noted (see, for example, Plant, 1983, pp. 7–29) and will not be elaborated upon here. In marked contrast, two other features of central elite ideology have been unwisely ignored: the reassertion of executive authority and the centre's territorial operating code.

A central feature of social-market liberalism is its belief in the 'minimalist state'. However, the attempt to bring it into being has provided the clearest assertion for more than a decade of the centre's belief in its right to govern. With the ever-increasing functional differentiation of British government, there has been an ever more fraught tension between the tradition that 'leaders know best' and the centre's dependence on SNG for the delivery of services. If control strategies are adopted, then governments have to confront unintended consequences, recalcitrance, instability and confusion. If compliance is sought, then governments have to confront 'slippage' or the adaptation of policies in the process of implementation. And yet it is precisely such slippage which provides the incentive for unilateral action. This tension has plagued all governments in the post-war period – it induces ministerial schizophrenia.[10]

With the introduction of controls to create the minimalist state, the centre abandoned its traditional 'territorial operating code'. This phrase refers to the 'rules of "statecraft" employed over time by political elites' and the code had taken the form of the 'dual polity' in which the centre was insulated from localities which were allowed considerable operational autonomy. In its place, Bulpitt detects a populist code: the by-passing of intermediate institutions such as local government in favour of direct links with citizens (Bulpitt, 1983, pp. 68, 165–7, 235–6; 1982, p. 168). Perhaps more significantly, the government has foresaken central autonomy to pursue 'High Politics' for a command, or a bureaucratic-hierarchy, model of domestic intervention. Repeated interventions to exact control at the level of the individual local authority bespeak not of populism but of the foreman and the shop-floor. Such a code may be congruent with the exercise of executive authority but it is faulty, representing a failure to appreciate the complexity of the differentiated polity.

These remarks on the processes of change within the national government environment are introductory. The value of such a focus can only be established by surveying the evolution of SNG in the post-war period.

9.3 The development of SNG

Four phases in the development of SNG can be identified. 1945–61 was the era of growth in welfare expenditure, grant consolidation and quiescent territorial politics. 1961–74 was the era of institutional modernization, intergovernmental bargaining and territorial protest. 1974–79 was an era of economic decline in the UK, in which local elites were incorporated into central decision processes and territorial problems were factorized. 1979–83 was the era of sustained economic recession, repeated central interventions to control sub-national institutions (and expenditure) and a centralization of territorial politics.

1945–61: growth, consolidation and quiescence

Strictly speaking, the years 1945–51 should be treated as the era of post-war reconstruction and the subsequent decade as one of growth. Any such division on economic grounds masks, however, other substantial continuities; with the benefit of hindsight the era is significant for what did not happen. Nationalist parties were conspicuous only for their electoral weakness. The seeds of civil unrest in Northern Ireland were being sown by the Unionists but the crop had yet to be reaped. Conflict between central and local government was spasmodic and had a certain novelty value. If any concern was expressed it focused on the loss of functions by local government and the growing dependence of local authorities on central grant, the perennial cry of centralization yet again rent the air. Nonetheless the era has a number of features of considerable significance.

First, the period was one of low unemployment, low inflation and relatively high growth rates. This economic surplus provided the means, whilst the central elite ideology provided the motive, to create the welfare state and local government was to be the prime vehicle for the delivery of its services. Central departments in Britain were and have remained non-executant units of government. They have 'hands-off' control of such major services as housing, education and health and welfare. Thus, if the period 1961–74 was to see the rate of growth accelerate, this period sees the foundations being dug for that development.

The second major development was the increasing use by government of *ad hoc* agencies, or non-departmental bodies. The best known of these agencies is, of course, the National Health Service but the period also saw the removal of public utilities from local government and the creation of the nationalized industries (such as gas, electricity).

Third, the period saw the increasing prominence of professionals not as powerful interest groups lobbying government but as part of the structure of government: they became institutionalized. The long-established professions in local government emerged to prominence in the 1950s. This period saw the accountants, lawyers, engineers and public health inspectors consolidate their position and the arrival of such 'newcomers' as teachers, social workers and planners. For the most part, career advancement was solely within the public sector and professional work organization and the departments of local government were identical. The expansion of the welfare state went hand in hand with the extension of professional influence and the emergence of functional politics.[11]

Fourth, central funding of local services was 'consolidated'. During the 1930s some 30 per cent of central funding was in the form of general grants: that is, monies were *not* assigned to specific services. By 1961 this figure had risen to 68 per cent. And yet one would expect the central departments with responsibilities for particular services to resist such an erosion of their influence – and indeed the (then) Ministry of Education did oppose such consolidation in 1929. Central resistance to block or general grants evaporated in this period because 'other constraints on local government emerged in Britain alongside the growth in the grant system, so that specific grants became less necessary in the influencing of local service delivery'. These constraints include the development of the legal framework of services; the vertical coalition of professionals in central and local government with shared values about (and responses to) service delivery; and finally the creation of vested interests by the specific grant so that producers and consumers support service expenditure.[12]

Finally, the period is distinguished by '*apolitisme*'. There are a number of strands to this argument. First, partly colonization of sub-national politics was incomplete and, for example, the numerous *ad hoc* agencies were subject to otiose forms of accountability. Second, a substantial proportion of local councils were controlled by 'Independents' not the political parties. Third, the incursion of party politics into local government was resented and resisted – after all 'there's only one way to build a road'. Fourth, even when the parties did control local authorities, this control could be purely nominal with little or no impact over and beyond the election. Decision-making was the preserve of committee chairmen and chief officers. Above all, IGR were characterized by professional-bureaucratic brokerage and the relative weakness of political linkages between centre and periphery (Bulpitt, 1983, pp. 146–55).

In the light of subsequent developments, this was the era when that (cliché'd) dog did not bark. Scottish interests were accommodated by both the growth of expenditure and the gradual expansion of the functions of the Scottish Office (Kellas, 1975, pp. 31–40). The same central strategy of accommodation through economic and administrative growth was applied to local authorities and the Northern Ireland Office, the only exception being Wales. To a significant degree, sub-national and central interests were united in the development of the welfare state and the pursuit of economic growth. The consolidation of functional politics was founded on consensus and quiescence *and* served the interests of the centre.

1961–74: modernization, intergovernmental bargaining and territorial protest

'The white heat of the technological revolution' did not herald the modernization of the British economy – that lies with the Macmillan–Maudling experiment with planned growth from 1961 – but it provides the era with one of its more potent symbols. Along with the introduction of national planning, regional planning and a new budgetary process came a more interventionist style of government and extensive reform of the machinery of government at every level. Britain was to be modernized.

And yet consultation and bargaining was the normal style of intergovernmental relations. For most of the period local service spending was buoyant. Central governments of both parties kept an eye out for the electorally damaging implications of any slippage by local government in areas of key importance. For example, road construction, slum clearance and rehousing were the major public conerns for most of the 1950s and 1960s, as was the reorganization of secondary schooling from the mid-1960s until the mid-1970s. A whole series of expectations about reasonably consensual dealings between Whitehall and local councils were embodied in the concept of 'partnership'. Ministers often went out of their way to choose modes of implementing policy that maximized voluntary local authority co-operation.

The bargaining phase lasted throughout the Heath government's period of office, despite some selective attempts by the Conservatives to develop more stringent controls over council policies. The government forced through changes in council housing finances against strong resistance (including the attempt by the Labour council at Clay Cross in 1972 to refuse implementation of the rent increases imposed). But elsewhere the government was cautious. Sales of council housing were successfully obstructed by many Labour councils. And although a full-scale re-organization of local authorities was put through against much opposition from councils destined to lose many of their powers, the Conservative government adopted a two-tier system which both protected party interests and was more popular with existing councillors and officers than previous proposals for unitary authorities. Moreover, having decided on the principles of reform, the government was prepared to bargain over such 'details' as the allocation of the planning function. Nowhere is evidence of bargaining clearer than in the determination of the level and allocation of central grant. Through their national representative organizations, local authorities were able to gain small but significant changes in the total and rate of growth of central grant. For local government, therefore, the period witnesses both centrally initiated reform and consultation.

Modernization intensified conflict between national and sub-national units of government. Central intervention provoked confrontations in the fields of education and housing. But given the scale of institutional change, the increase was modest. In part, protest was limited by the pre-existing structure of intergovernmental relations (IGR). Local access to national political elites was relatively weak whereas professional actors were key advocates of the reform (Rhodes, 1985, Ch. 6). Perhaps most important, the centre 'factorized' the problem of reform. Thus, there were separate reorganizations of local government in Scotland, England and Wales, London and Northern Ireland: of particular functions (such as water, health); and of the centre's decentralized arms (for example, regional economic planning councils, Welsh Office). At no time was the reform of IGR comprehensively reviewed and key aspects of the system were ignored altogether (for instance, finance). The central strategy of factorizing encouraged a fragmented response and dampened the level of protest.

If this period saw the continued fragmentation of functional politics, it also saw major conflicts in the arena of territorial representation. In the late 1960s, the introduction of direct rule in Northern Ireland and the rise of Scottish and Welsh nationalism represented a far greater threat to the consensus which had governed territorial politics in Britain.

Explanation of the rise of nationalism abound. The factors which caused the resurgent electoral performance of the SNP include: the decline of the UK economy, loss of confidence in British government, institutional weakness, the relatively greater economic decline of the regions, cultural differences, nationalist feeling, and specific issues or grievances – for example, North Sea oil, membership of the EEC. There is corresponding disagreement on the importance of these factors.

Nationalism is not a phenomenon of the 1960s and early 1970s. It is a persistent feature of the British political landscape reinforced by separate educational, legal, religious and governmental systems. Nor can such popular expressions of nationalism as a separate international football team, a national flag and a national anthem be omitted from this list of distinctive characteristics. Although it is a long-standing phenomenon, the strength of Welsh and Scottish nationalism can be overstated. As Rose has pointed out, 'By fighting elections, Nationalists register the weakness of their support in their own nation' (Rose, 1982, p. 88). The 'problem' to be explained is *not*, therefore, the rise of nationalism but why the centre in this period took the challenge so seriously. In other words, the issue to be explored is the constraints upon and the weakness of central government. In addition, the increasing salience of nationalism cannot be divorced from the increasing salience of other social and political cleavages. The combined effects of central weakness and political differentiation were to become marked from 1974 onwards.

Above all, the prominence of nationalism in this period should not obscure the substantial continuities in IGR. The policy networks remained paramount in the expansion of welfare state services; the centre remained politically insulated from local elites; and in Urwin's phrases 'tolerance and indifference'; 'the concern to accommodate demands within the prevailing structure'; and 'an *ad hoc* attempt to resolve a specific complaint or demand' continued to characterize central attitudes and actions (Urwin, 1982, p. 68).

The key feature of intergovernmental relations in this period is instability not crisis. Economic pressures were mounting, the central strategy of institutional modernization was bearing no obvious fruit and the incidence of conflict and protest was increasing. The onset of economic decline was to alter the picture markedly.

To this point, the narrative has merely suggested explanations for the changes in SNG between 1945 and 1974. It is now necessary to provide an explicit explanation of the development of SNG in this period. Figure 9.2 provides such a summary. It begins with the assumptions of a stable external support system, economic growth and a central elite ideology based on the mixed economy welfare state. The consequent expansion of the welfare state led to increased functional differentiation and the institutionalization of the professions. The resulting policy networks lie at the heart of a system of functional politics which marginalized local political elites and supported the dual polity. This duality was further supported by both an external support system which still afforded central elites a role in High Politics and a two-party system based on functional economic interests which subsumed other social cleavages to class and which failed to colonize the localities. In sum, functional politics came to dominate territorial politics.

However, there were stresses and strains within the system of functional politics. Economic growth and the subsequent occupational restructuring fostered class de-alignment. Traditional social cleavages re-emerged – for example, nationalism – and functional politics generated sectoral cleavages. Moreover, Union had established a unitary state with multiform institutions and the expansion of the welfare state had further fragmented service delivery systems. This complex of organizations became the locus

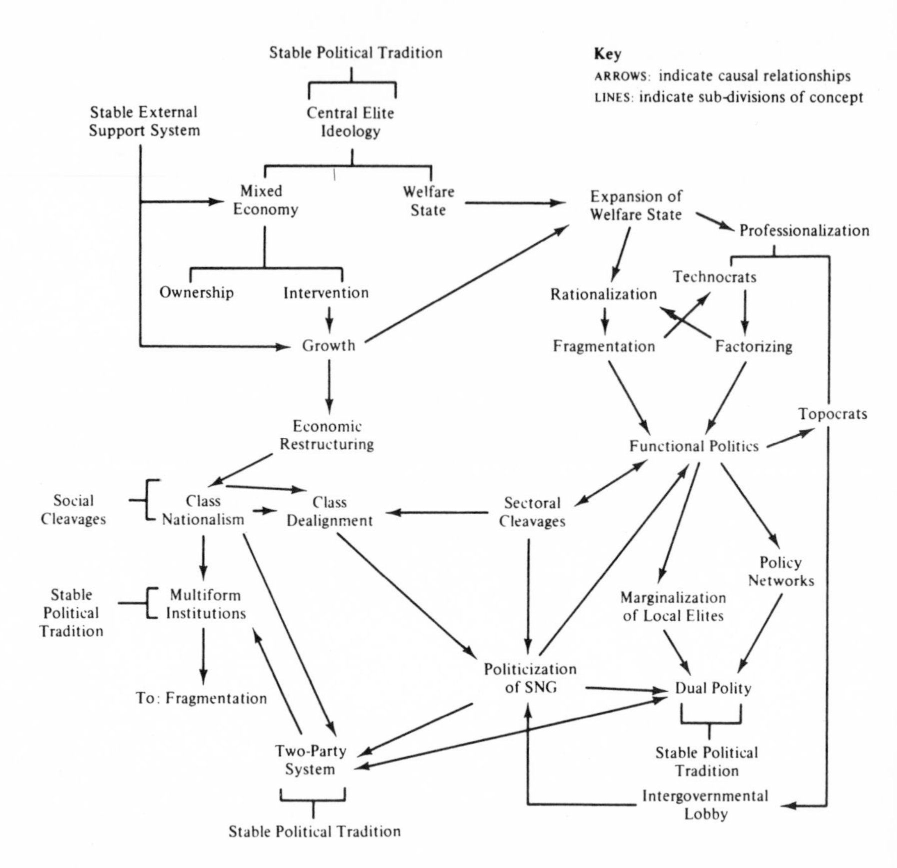

Figure 9.2 A summary explanation of the politicization of sub-national government

within which the conflicts of a social structure characterized by multiple cleavages were played out. Economic growth and functional politics did not herald the homogeneous society but increased the degree of social and political differentiation. Functional politics fostered a territorial reaction.

It is important to remember that the politicization of local government began in an area of relative stability and prosperity. With deepening economic decline, an increasingly unstable external support system and a shift in central elite ideology, there was a quantum leap in politicization. In addition, the problem-solving capacity of the system began to experience ever-intensifying difficulties. The rational planning experiment, whether in the guise of the public expenditure survey (PES) or of local corporate planning, was substantially abandoned and the compromises fostered by economic growth and incremental service expansion were now denied to the centre. If the centre's (in)ability to solve problems remained unchanged, the opportunities to avoid solutions by moving money were shrinking rapidly.

1974–9: economic decline, incorporation and territorial factorizing

Three factors are particularly important for understanding developments in this period. First, the economic decline of the UK was accelerated by the escalation of world commodity prices, most notably in oil prices. Confronted by massive inflation, the government had to seek a substantial loan from the IMF which required drastic cuts in public expenditure. Second, the reorganization of local government stimulated the spread of party politics and the virtual demise of the 'Independent'. The consequent politicization of local politics was to spread to intergovernmental relations. Third, the 1974 election produced a minority Labour government and a consequent imperative to negotiate with minority parties to preserve a parliamentary majority. This conjunction of external economic disruption and political fragility called forth central strategies of incorporation for English local authorities and factorizing for nationalist political demands.

There is clear evidence that the Labour government did not make a sustained effort to introduce a kind of top-level, overall corporatism into its dealings with local government. Their essential innovation was to try to incorporate the powerful local authority associations (and their joint bodies) into a sort of 'social contract' about local government spending. For the first time, Whitehall set up a forum in which to discuss the long-run future of local spending with the local authority associations. This Consultative Council on Local Government Finance (CCLGF) was remarkable also in bringing the Treasury, ministers and local authority representatives into face-to-face contact for the first time, and in explicitly integrating the planning of local spending into the Public Expenditure Survey system. The government's hope was that by involving the local authority associations in policy-making affecting local government it would be able to persuade them of the 'realities' of the economic situation, and thus enlist them as allies in the battle to keep down the growth of local spending. In the Treasury's view, the objective of the CCLGF was 'effective control' and, if it was not achieved, 'other measures would have to be considered' (HMSO, 1976, p. 327).

How effective the CCLGF was in meeting this aim is difficult to say. Many of its members argue that it was successful in getting the local authority associations to persuade their members to behave with restraint. But, of course, there were other forces working in the same direction: for example, cash limits on central grants to local authorities and the swing in mid-term local elections to Conservative-controlled authorities committed to expenditure restraint. Whatever else it accomplished, however, the Council did help to shift influence within local government away from service-orientated councillors and officers (for example, the education policy community) and towards local politicians and finance directors more concerned with 'corporate planning', increased efficiency and financial soundness. In effect, the Council was a Whitehall attempt to build up the influence of the national community of local government, in order that it would be better able to control the rest of the local government system in return for consultation and a direct voice in future planning.[13]

The important of aggregating interests was matched only by the difficulty of the task. The range of sub-national bodies had reached substantial proportions, far in excess of the government's capacity to manage them. Bowen (under-)estimates the cumulative increase in non-departmental bodies alone at 64 per cent between 1949 and 1975 and the Pliatzky Report (which excluded the NHS and the nationalized industries) estimated that there were 2117 such bodies in 1979 (Bowen, 1978, p. 1; HMSO, 1980, p. 5). The centre regularly experienced difficulty in imposing its policy preferences on these non-elected species of SNG.[14]

The threat from nationalist politics produced an almost incoherent response from the centre. The elections of 1974 produced a minority Labour government, dependent upon third parties (including the SNP) for its stay in office. These elections provided clear evidence of 'partisan de-alignment' as the proportion of votes cast for third parties rose, not only in the periphery, but also in England. To remain in office, the Labour government required the support of the Liberals and the SNP, both of which supported devolution.

As if minority party status was an insufficiently daunting problem it was compounded by the parlous state of the British economy which saw the end of economic growth and denied the government the compromises, so typical of functional politics, of marginal improvements in service provision. Both inflation and unemployment rates rose, and 'cuts' in public expenditure came to be seen as necessary. Between 1976 and 1979, the Labour government introduced a species of monetarism, the Conservative opposition was taking a decisive step towards social-market liberalism, and the belief in salvation through institutional modernization was collapsing on its transparent failures. Whether these shifts are seen as a loss of confidence in government or the loss of confidence by governing elites, the period was one of re-assessment and search for new directions. Moreover, the government was now denied the usual escape route of adventures in High Politics. Britain's role in the world had contracted immeasurably and the country was vulnerable to externally generated instability. Attention upon domestic economic ills was not easily distracted and the Labour government did not have its 'Falklands' to rescue its public esteem. Devolution was, therefore, a policy bred of central weakness rather than nationalist strength. Certainly the policy was much disliked by both ministers and civil servants. The legislation bears all the hallmarks of antagonistic reluctance, being both internally inconsistent and ambiguous (often at the same time).

The first point to note is that the problem of nationalist politics was factorized. Separate policies were pursued in Scotland, Wales and Northern Ireland. Moreover, there was a policy (of sorts) for England. 'Organic change' or the redistribution of functions between the different types of local authority, three years after a major reorganization was first mooted in a devolution White Paper and preoccupied the Secretary of State for the Environment in the period 1977–9. There was still no grand design for the reform of territorial politics, just a series of *ad hoc* responses.

Second, at no stage was the doctrine of the supremacy of Parliament under challenge. Throughout, the centre insisted, for example, on the retention of all powers of economic management. However, it is probably a mistake to suggest that constitutional issues were at stake. Political survival was the key consideration for a minority party government; the centre was to concede as little as possible commensurate with the Labour Party retaining power.

Third, although the growth of central intervention took a very poor second place to the devolution debate at the time, the changes in the form of that intervention were particularly significant. The definition of the centre's responsibility for economic management had stressed aggregate control. For local government, this responsibility encompassed the level of central grant to local government. From 1975 to 1976 this responsibility was unilaterally redefined. Local *expenditure* (not grant) was explicitly included in PES, the anticipated level of expenditure for individual local services was identified and general guidance on the level of rate increases was proffered. In other words, central government was intervening to regulate local expenditure. It had not been so targeted before. Hereafter, the control was to become more specific.

And as ever, finally, there was the sorry plight of Northern Ireland. Direct rule via the Northern Ireland Office prevailed. Public expenditure was increased to offset economic decay. But the most striking facts are the continued insulation of Northern Ireland from mainland politics and the growing indifference of Westminster to maintaining the Union. Governing without a consensus and the failure of the several attempts to find a substitute for direct rule have bred 'contingent commitment' (Rose, 1982, p. 218). Whatever else Northern Ireland may illustrate, it highlights the *ad hoc* and variegated strategies of the centre in managing SNG.

Ostensibly a period of dramatic transformations, the years 1974–9 reaffirmed the resilience of the Union. If anything, nationalist politics were weaker in 1979 than at any time in the past decade. But there had been important changes. If the new forms of centre interventions in IGR were not newsworthy, they had the potential for transforming the system. That potential was soon to be realized.

1979–85: economic recession, control and centralization

If one single theme permeates this period, it is the search by central government for more effective instruments of control (not influence) over the expenditure of local government. The consultation so distinctive of the mid-seventies has been replaced by direction and confrontation. The government's policy was to make *local* income and expenditure conform with *national* decisions.

The achievements of the new system can be described, at best, as mixed. Between 1979/80 and 1982/3 under the Conservatives total expenditure rose as a proportion of GDP and central government's expenditure increased sharply. The big spenders were not for the most part local government services and some local services – for example, housing – declined dramatically. The Conservatives cut substantially the centre's contribution to local services – the proportion of net current local expenditure financed by grant fell from 61 per cent to 56 per cent. Local government manpower fell by 4 per cent in the same period. Most dramatically, local capital expenditure was subject to stringent regulation and was reduced by some 40 per cent in real terms from an already severely reduced base. And yet, in spite of the 'cuts', local current expenditure *increased* between March 1979 and March 1983 by 9 per cent in real terms. Even attempts to 'cull the herd' of non-departmental bodies were conspicuously ineffective, involving some 240 bodies and a mere £11.6 million. The savings actually made were more than off-set by the expansion of other non-departmental bodies – for example, the Manpower Services Commission.

In short, as with the previous Labour government, the bulk of the 'cuts' fell on local government, on selected services and on capital expenditure while, ironically, the Conservatives presided over both an increase in total public expenditure and local current expenditure.

Strategies towards Scotland, Wales and Northern Ireland in this period are variations on the same theme. Scotland can be seen as the 'test-bed' for English legislation. Most of the grant innovations were introduced in Scotland first and, since 1981, the Secretary of State for Scotland has been able to reduce the grant to an individual local authority if he thinks its expenditure is 'excessive': a power subsequently available to the Secretary of State for the Environment. In Northern Ireland, grant to local authorities actually rose as the centre pursued a strategy of 'more of the same', that is, proposing (unacceptable) alternatives to direct rule, using public expenditure to fight economic decay and insulating mainland politics from the problem. In Wales, a Welsh Consultative Council on Local Government Finance was introduced to implement the new grant system. Revealingly this innovation had initially been proposed as part of the Labour government's devolution package. It now reappeared as a means for control, *not* devolution. *Both* cases provide a wonderfully clear example of the centre factorizing problems and using institutional reforms to solve its own problems.

With the increasingly apparent failure of successive governments to manage the mixed economy successfully, the post-war consensus on Keynesian demand management, intervention, ownership and the welfare state began to founder in this period. In its place, the 'new right', concerned with the money supply, the PSBR and the minimal state, emphasized reductions in public expenditure and the contraction of the welfare state. This 'resources squeeze' intensified competition between policy networks determined to preserve their turf. Clients were mobilized and direct contact with local political elites was established. The 'hands-off' character of the Dual Polity was replaced by a directive territorial operating code. Nowhere was this change more obvious than in the changes to the system for distributing grant to local authorities but it is also evident in the efforts to reduce the number of quangos and in the investment and pricing controls over the nationalized industries. But direction was a high cost strategy. At first, the centre had channelled its political contacts through an intermediate tier of representation based on the national community of local government. Increasingly, this channel was replaced by face-to-face contact between ministers and individual (or small groups of) local authorities. Directive strategies provoked recalcitrance and non-compliance and, reluctantly, ministers were dragged into conflict with the 'overspending' local authorities: conflict which spilt over, ever more commonly, into litigation (Loughlin, 1985). The costs in time and even loss of political face were mounting. To make matters worse, the policy was failing. The planned cuts in total public expenditure did not materialize. The new central elite ideology had not countered economic decline with a reduction in the size of the public sector but it had intensified the politicization of SNG and generated a policy mess wherein nobody achieved their objectives.

Moreover, the changes in SNG began to exert an increasing influence on the national government environment. Thus, expenditure controls fell largely on local capital expenditure and, in effect, off-loaded public sector cuts onto the private sector – for example, the construction industry. This simply contributed to the de-industrialization of the British economy. Government action was intensifying economic decline which, in turn, increased the pressure on the welfare state, most notably social security payments to the unemployed. Coupled with the difficulties of making cuts because of both the capacity of some integrated policy networks to resist the pressure for reduced expenditure and increasingly strident protest from client groups, welfare state expenditures continued to rise. This increase threatened the government's monetary targets; intensified the search for means to control public expenditure; and generated yet more recalcitrance in SNG – thus the downward spiral continued. The resultant policy mess casts doubt on the efficacy of the ideology of central elites and thereby further contributes to partisan conflicts and the politicization of SNG.

This summary explanation of changes in SNG is bald in the extreme. In one short article, many of the necessary caveats and modifications to the foregoing model have to be omitted and reserved for another occasion. More positively, there is a major advantage to a skeletal presentation: it is by its nature argumentative, challenging accepted accounts of SNG. The final section draws out the implications of the foregoing analysis for understanding both Conservative policy and the future of local government.

9.4 Conclusions

The post-war period may not provide ten commandments for the management of SNG but it is possible to adduce ten lessons which are central to any understanding of developments.

First, changes in SNG in the post-war period were not caused by any one process – for example, economic decline – or any simple combination of processes – for example, economic decline and the resurgence of ideology. To understand the contradictory results of Conservative policy, it is necessary to explore the tension between executive authority and differentiation; between economic decline and the institutionalization of interests (most notably professions) in the structure of government (that is, in policy networks); and between territorial and functional interests.

Second, the roots of current problems lie in earlier periods and are not solely the product of Conservative policy. The use of local government as the vehicle for delivering the welfare state and the predeliction of 'ad-hocracy' created the differentiated polity with its range of disaggregated service delivery systems. And with differentiation came the professionalization of policy systems and the presumption that territorial justice required national or uniform standards. Fragmentation at the centre came to co-exist with centralization within the policy networks.

Third, national economic management problems have dominated the practice and reform of intergovernmental relations. Local expenditure decisions were increasingly determined by central government's public expenditure survey system and the attendant Cabinet decisions throughout the 1970s. Many of the rapid changes in the expenditure targets of local authorities can be attributed directly to the decline of the British economy. It is clear that intergovernmental relations have become inextricably entwined with economic management whether the government of the day is Labour or Conservative.

Fourth, the relationship between central and sub-national governments is one of 'asymmetric' interdependence. IGR operate in a system characterized by a strong executive tradition and can be no more divorced from the effects of the larger system than any other facet of British politics. But equally, the combination of disaggregated service delivery systems and the 'hands-off' tradition of central departments has fostered complex patterns of interdependence. Central to any understanding of central–local relations is the recurrent tension between the interdependence of centre and locality on the one hand and authoritative decision-making by central government on the other: a tension which the Conservative government of 1979–83 was no nearer to resolving than any of its predecessors.

Fifth, the resurgence of party ideology is crucial to understanding the *form* of the response to economic decline. If both major parties have sought to control local expenditure, only the Conservative Party, with its social-market policies, has sought to privatize parts of the public sector. Party ideology has been the grit in the well-oiled machinery of the policy networks, challenging not only the assumption of inevitable incremental growth but also existing policies and values.

Sixth, and in spite of protestations and (ostensibly) policies to the contrary, confusion and ambiguity have remained pre-eminent characteristics of intergovernmental relations over the past decade. It would require saint-like charity to describe the ever-changing grant system as stable, consistent or predictable. Underlying the twists and turns of central policy is the simple fact that central government has many interests. Intervention may serve the interests of the Treasury and even the DoE but not so for other spending departments. Some policy networks have fought a rear-guard action of consequence. The Treasury has had to confront the unwelcome fact of life that the alliance of professions and spending departments in policy networks has generated substantial inertia. Policy has had to confront the conservatism of vested interests lodged in the actual structure of government. The pervasive influence of the professions has paralleled the fragmentation of service delivery systems and constrained the centre's ability to redirect policy.

Seventh, the paradox of British government is that the tradition of 'leaders know best' co-exists with weakness at the centre; which 'is struggled against manfully by the Treasury, CSD, Cabinet Office, and CPRS. But it is a debility all the same'. The debility is government by a committee in which 'most committeemen are also the chief executives of their own departmental empires'; 'Everyone knows they serve themselves by serving their department' (Heclo and Wildavsky, 1974, pp. 369, 371). And the chief executive and his empire are embedded in a network which is not only a constraint but also a source of support in the 'manful' struggles against the central capability. Policy co-ordination is confronted and confounded not simply by a determined minister but by the structure of the centre with its diversity of interests enshrined in discreet networks.

Eighth, government action threatens the long standing insulation of national and local political elites. The politicization of local government has proceeded apace and the government's determination to control individual local authorities has brought ministers into face-to-face conflict with local leaders. Perhaps the most significant feature of the refusal of Liverpool City Council to make a legal budget was the *bargaining* between the Secretary of State and local leaders. Rate-capping is, potentially, a catalyst to such interaction between national and local elites. And this politicization also demonstrates that IGR are no longer government and politics 'beyond Whitehall' but are part and parcel of the politics of Whitehall. These changes are probably the most important ones in the British system of IGR during the 1980s and their full weight remains to be felt.

Ninth, the problem of managing SNG continued to be factorized with separate innovations and/or expenditure policies for Scotland, Wales and Northern Ireland. And the corollary of factorizing is the insulation of Westminster and Whitehall from SNG. If separateness can be interpreted as reinforcing national or regional identities, in the UK context it also facilitated central control. If regional demands were accommodated, that accommodation perpetuated central dominance. And yet the conflict between territorial and functional politics continued to be played out in SNG and the centre's territorial operating code, the 'dual polity', displayed manifest signs of obsolesence.

Finally, the demise of the dual polity with the onset of intervention led to the adoption of a command operating code at variance with the differentiated polity. Not only did the centre lack the capacity to control SNG but its reliance of bureaucratic strategies multiplied unintended consequences and accelerated the politicization of SNG. This faulty operating code may have its roots in the centre's 'culture of disdain'[15] but it is more plausibly a product of the dual polity – in which the two levels of government were insulated from each other – and of central fragmentation – in which the policy networks are insulated from each other. When structure imposes blinkers, cultural explanations are embellishment and detail. The command code represents a failure to comprehend that British government is differentiated and disaggregated: the unitary state is a multi-form maze of interdependence. To operate a code at variance with this reality is to build failure into the initial policy design.

In short, any understanding of developments in SNG has to be rooted in an analysis of the range of sub-national organizations and the evolution of their relationships with the national government environment. From this perspective it is possible to explain not only why the Conservatives sought control but also why their search experienced so many problems. Developments over the past decade suggest that, when control is the preferred strategy, the outcome will be unintended consequences, recalcitrance, uncertainty, ambiguity and confusion. To a considerable degree, the government has been and remains a prisoner of the interests it seeks to regulate for those interests are part of the structure of government. And in seeking to escape, government actions have politicized SNG and further intensified the problem of control. The economic context imposes constraints, it may even generate imperatives for action, but it does not dictate the form of action. Political traditions and choices determine courses of actions even if, once chosen, they constrain future options. The history of SNG is compounded of multiple contradictions – economic, political and organizational. Mono-causal explanations, whether propounded by politician or academic, are doomed to inadequacy.

Forsaking the literal meaning of this chapter's title and interpreting the phrase as an indictment of the selfish pursuit of narrow partisan interests, the history of intergovernmental relations in Britain throughout the post-war period is a story of central selfishness. If interventions have not been corrupt, they have served the centre's political interests whether the example is the construction of the welfare state, the modernization of SNG or the containment of public expenditure. If central actors have not been literally squalid, the results of their actions have been a mess through their failure to comprehend the differentiated nature of the system. Whatever one's views on the merits of local self-government, it is clear that it has not been the pre-eminent or even a major value to be sustained by central action. Indeed, a counter-presumption prevails wherein national action is seen as essential to territorial justice. To equate the centre with redistribution and uniform standards and SNG with inequality is to undermine the validity of local self-government.[16] If the arguments of this chapter contain only a kernel of truth, nonetheless the prospects for local government are bleak because the challenges and problems it confronts are not the product of a particular set of economic conditions or of a particular political ideology but of trends throughout the post-war period. The cry on the wind is for the reform of local government but, if the objective is to preserve local self-government, the need is to reform the centre for there lies the heart of the problem.

Notes

1 For a detailed appraisal of Conservative policy see Rhodes (1984), pp. 311–33.

2 This definition is modified from Bulpitt (1983), p. 1.

3 This definition is modified from Stewart (1982), pp. 11–12, 65–8.

4 This article draws upon Rhodes (1988) Chapter 2, which provides a full exposition of the three levels of analysis.

5 This point is taken from Sharpe (1981), p. 6.

6 The term 'technocratic profession' refers to programme or functional specialists. The topocratic professions – from *topos* meaning place and *kratos* meaning authority – cover the range of functions and speak for their areas. See Beer (1978), pp. 9–21.

7 Although the point cannot be developed here, the discussion of central elites and central autonomy benefits if a distinction is drawn between political and bureaucratic elites.

8 For a useful introduction see Crewe (1983).

9 For a more detailed discussion see Dunleavy (1980), pp. 42–55, 70–86.

10 The description originated with Anthony Crosland and was cited in Kogan (1971), p. 171.

11 On the growth of professional influence see Brand (1974), Page (1985) and Dunleavy (1982).

12 The figures and quotations in this paragraph are from Page (1981), pp. 19–24.

13 This subsection and the previous one draw upon Dunleavy and Rhodes (1983), pp. 123–6.

14 See, for example, the essays in Hogwood and Keating (eds) (1982).

15 As argued, for example, in Greenwood (1982), p. 72.

16 This point is from Sharpe (1985).

References

BEER, S. H. (1978) 'Federalism, nationalism and democracy in America', *American Political Science Review*, Vol. 72, pp. 9–21.

BENSON, J. K. (1982) 'Networks and policy sectors: a framework for extending interorganizational analysis', in Rodgers, D. and Whitten, D. (eds), *Interorganizational Co-ordination*, Ames, Iowa, Iowa State University Press.

BOWEN, G. (1978) *Survey of Fringe Bodies*, London, CSD.

BRAND, J. A. (1974) *Local Government Reform in England*, London, Croom Helm.

BULPITT, J. G. (1982) 'Conservatism, unionism and the problem of territorial management', in Madgwick, P. and Rose, P. (eds), *The Territorial Dimension in United Kingdom Politics*, London and Basingstoke, Macmillan.

BULPITT, J. G. (1983) *Territory and Power in the United Kingdom*, Manchester, Manchester University Press.

CREWE, I. (1983) 'The electorate: partisan dealignment ten years on', *West European Politics*, Vol. 6, pp. 183–215.

DRUCKER, H. M., DUNLEAVY, P., GAMBLE, A. and PEELE, G. (eds) (1983) *Developments in British Politics*, London and Basingstoke, Macmillan.

DUNLEAVY, P. (1980) *Urban Political Analysis*, London and Basingstoke, Macmillan.

DUNLEAVY, P. (1982) 'Quasi-governmental sector professionalism', in Barker, A. (ed.), *Quangos in Britain*, London and Basingstoke, Macmillan, pp. 181–205.

DUNLEAVY, P. and RHODES, R. A. W. (1983) 'Beyond Whitehall', in Drucker, H. M. *et al.* (eds).

GREENWOOD, R. (1982) 'Pressure from Whitehall', in Rose, R. and Page, E. (eds), *Fiscal Stress in the Cities*, Cambridge, Cambridge University Press.

HECLO, H. and WILDAVSKY, A. (1974) *The Private Government of Public Money*, London and Basingstoke, Macmillan.

HMSO (1976) Committee of Inquiry into Local Government Finance (Layfield), Appendix 1, *Evidence by Government Departments*, London, HMSO.

HMSO (1980) *Report on Non-departmental Public Bodies* (Pliatzky), London, HMSO.

HOGWOOD, B. and KEATING, M. (eds) (1982) *Regional Government in England*, Oxford, Clarendon Press.

KELLAS, J. G. (1975) *The Scottish Political System*, Cambridge, Cambridge University Press.

KOGAN, M. (1971) *The Politics of Education*, Harmondsworth, Penguin Books.

LOUGHLIN, M. (1985) 'The restructuring of central–local government legal relations', *Local Government Studies*, Vol. 11, No. 6, pp. 59–74.

LUHMANN, N. (1982) *The Differentiation of Society*, New York, Columbia University Press.

PAGE, E. (1981) 'Grant consolidation and the development of intergovernmental relations in the United States and the United Kingdom', *Politics*, Vol. 1, No. 1, pp. 19–24.

PAGE, E. (1985) 'State development and local government', paper to Thirteenth World Congress of the International Political Science Association, 15–20 July.

PLANT, R. (1983) 'The resurgence of ideology', in Drucker, H. M. *et al.* (eds) pp. 7–29.

RHODES, R. A. W. (1984) 'Continuity and change in British central–local relations: the "Conservative threat" 1979–83', *British Journal of Political Science*, Vol. 14, pp. 311–33.

RHODES, R. A. W. (1985) *The National World of Local Government*, London, George Allen and Unwin.

RHODES, R. A. W. (1988) *Beyond Westminster and Whitehall: The Sub-national Government of Britain*, London, George Allen and Unwin.

ROSE, R. (1982) *Understanding the United Kingdom*, London, Longman.

SHARPE, L. J. (1979) 'Decentralist trends in western democracies: a first appraisal', in Sharpe, L. J. (ed.), *Decentralist Trends in western Democracies*, London, Sage.

SHARPE, L. J. (1981) 'Is there a fiscal crisis in western European local government? A first appraisal', in Sharpe, L. J. (ed.), *The Local Fiscal Crisis in Western Europe*, London, Sage.

SHARPE, L. J. (1985) 'Territoriality and the European state system', paper to the SSRC Joint Committee on Western Europe, March.

SINGH, A. (1977) 'UK industry and world economy: a case of de-industrialization?' *Cambridge Journal of Economics*, Vol. 1.

STEWART, J. D. (1982) *Local Government: The Conditions of Local Choice*, London, George Allen and Unwin.

URWIN, D. W. (1982) 'Territorial structures and political developments in the United Kingdom', in Rokkan, S. and Urwin, D. W. (eds), *The Politics of Territorial Identity*, London, Sage.

Section IV Locality and politics

Introduction

The previous chapter presents and analyses local government as part of a national system. Local government is largely explained in terms of functional divisions within the welfare state. The emphasis is on political relationships within and between policy networks, and Rhodes explains the increasing importance of territorial politics in the late 1970s in terms of the failure of those networks and not the positive vitality of local politics. In this Section the emphasis is shifted and a stress is placed on the importance of locality. Locally distinct forms of politics are identified and explored as part of a process of uneven development, which links economic, social and political phenomena.

The most effective way into these debates is through the development of the case studies rooted in particular localities. But all of the chapters in this Section are more than simple case studies. It is not enough to attempt to list all the features which make a place (and its politics) identifiable; it is also necessary to place it in the context of wider processes with which it interacts and itself in turn helps to shape. So the case studies which follow are self-consciously developed within a context of national and international change. They are not free-standing and independent of that context. In another sense, too, they are more than merely explorations of the unique, because they utilize recognizably wider categories – such as class and gender – and develop them in their particular cases. Only by doing so, it is implied, can they be given life, but there is no suggestion that a whole new set of theoretical tools is required to look at each case.

Chapter 10 sets out to explain the decay of the tradition of 'red Clydeside', while Chapter 11 focuses on the break-up of a conservative tradition in Lancaster in the 1970s. Both of them, therefore, investigate the particular balances of social and political forces in the localities which they are studying. Each is concerned to explore the process of structural change over a longer period, dating back to the 1920s in one case and the turn of the century in another. Each concludes at a time when long-standing local arrangements were under threat from national and local pressures.

Glasgow's 'red' reputation at the start of the 1920s reflected the power and politicization of the Clyde Workers' Committee through which workers in most of the city's engineering and munitions plants were represented during the 1914–18 war, and whose political statements reflected a sort of revolutionary syndicalism influenced by Marxist ideas. The Committee did not restrict itself to workplace activities and its most notable success probably arose from its involvement in 1915 with a major rent strike led by working-class women which forced the Lloyd George government into the speedy introduction of rent controls. Several of the leading figures in the committee were to be founder members of the Communist Party of Great Britain. After the war, the election of a group of left-wing (Labour and

Independent Labour Party) MPs, including David Kirkwood, James Maxton, Emmanuel Shinwell and John Wheatley, seemed to provide confirmation of Clydeside's 'redness'.

In fact, the tradition of 'red' Clydeside, at least as a revolutionary centre, was probably always exaggerated. Despite a series of major conflicts with the government which resulted in the deportation and imprisonment of leading shop stewards and others for a time, the Committee's main task was always to negotiate for the workers it represented. There were no lengthy strikes for political or other reasons, partly because practical concessions were made by government and employers, which tends to support the conclusion that the disputes were more centred on those issues rather than the threat of revolution. But, however exaggerated, there clearly was a strong left-wing tradition, strong enough at any rate to encourage contemporary and retrospective exaggeration. Savage sets out to explain why this radicalism has faded in local politics since the 1920s.

In the 1970s and early 1980s the councils in Strathclyde played little part in the political battles between local and central government, in contrast not only to a number of English authorities (such as Sheffield, Liverpool and others) but also to other Scottish councils, such as Edinburgh and Stirling. He explains this in terms of the role which the Glasgow Labour Party developed in order to retain the political dominance which it had initially won with the help of locally based collective action. This, he suggests, was a rather uncertain long-term foundation of electoral support, since it related to other political and social traditions as well. Labour in Glasgow was only one expression of working-class politics among many. Some of the bases of collective action declined alongside economic and industrial decay, but through its housing policies the Labour Party itself also helped to undermine the possibility of such action. According to Savage, the Labour Party came to rely on passive support generated through the delivery of services, which discouraged the development of any radical initiatives because of the party's dependence on access to and control of the 'local state'.

Savage's assessment of Glasgow's political history stresses the role of the Labour Party in developing a strategy for retaining power. He refers to other factors in society and economy, but his main emphasis is on that strategy as a key factor in reducing the potential for collective action. In some ways, Savage's chapter raises important questions without quite settling them.[1] The specific social and economic context remains elusive, to the extent that, for example, there is little discussion of divisions (including sectarian divisions) within the local working class. Nor does he make much reference to the strategies of other political parties superseded by Labour (or still competing with it), which makes it difficult to judge whether Labour's electoral success was somehow inevitable and, if so, for what reasons. Nevertheless, the strength of his analysis lies in its local explanation of local politics. Despite the shared labels of political parties at local level, he shows how their political practice often differs significantly.

The discussion of a changing political environment in Lancaster undertaken by Mark-Lawson and Warde in Chapter 11 takes a rather broader view than Savage. Of course, the context is different, too, but the very concept of 'local political environment' which is developed suggests a slightly different theoretical emphasis with less stress on the strategy of a locally dominant political party and more on the context within which parties operate as well as influence: 'It implies a notion of incremental change, of one element affecting another . . . the environment structures the agenda for all political actors, setting the agenda for interaction between all parties' (Mark-Lawson and Warde, 1987, p. 5).

The aim of the chapter is to explore first why Lancaster's politics until the 1960s were substantially more conservative (and Conservative) than would have been expected on the basis of the town's class composition and, secondly, to explain the ways in which this conservative political environment has been eroded since the mid-1960s. Mark-Lawson and Warde stress the complexity of the process and the importance of interaction between different elements. The initial basis for political conservatism is largely explained by the dominance of a limited number of large employers and the dependence of the local workforce on them. Local authority politics until the 1960s was dominated by an anti-Labourism or anti-socialism, rather than an ideological commitment to Conservatism, which was reflected in the continued high proportion of Independents on the Council.

The changes which began in the mid-1960s reflected the beginning of industrial restructuring, as the big local employers ceased to be local as a result of amalgamation and take-over, and new sources of employment arrived. The growth of white-collar (and public sector) employment seems to have gone alongside a growth in support for Labour. There were also major conflicts over housing in the 1960s, particularly, but not only, focused on rent levels, which Mark-Lawson and Warde argue gave Labour the main opportunity to break the local conservative hegemony. The same period also saw an increase in trade union militancy (in part reflecting national trends) and a growth of 'social movements', particularly the women's movement, which seems to have had an initial base in the University but spread outwards at various times. All of these factors represented challenges to the existing conservative political environment. In contrast to the implications of Savage's arguments, here, even if a general direction of change can be identified, the stress is placed on the complexity of interrelations between these various factors.

After 1974 (when the chapter ends) the nationally inspired reorganization of local government both encouraged the break-up of past traditions and helped to channel local political conflict into different directions. The new boundaries created by the merger of Morecambe and Lancaster into a new District Council helped to mask Labour's electoral dominance in the old Lancaster Borough and encouraged the development of cross-class spatial coalitions as there was competition between the two main towns over the distribution of council-controlled resources.

The focus of this chapter, like the previous one, is on *local* politics. Although reference is made to external constraints and pressures, they are considered important only insofar as they influence the local political environment, whose individuality is a starting-point for the analysis. As in the previous one, too, a particular emphasis is placed on the politics of service provision as a focus for political differentiation. In different ways in the different places, housing issues (rather than those centred on the workplace) appear to have provided a major focus for political identification, and to have encouraged a growth of support for Labour. Since the late 1970s, housing has continued to be an important area of political controversy, but as Savage points out it is by no means so clear that Labour has been the beneficiary of these more recent conflicts.

It is in this context that the arguments developed by Blunkett and Jackson in Chapter 12 have to be understood. They want to identify areas of political activity in which new coalitions of support for Labour can be constructed at a time when the bases for some of the older ones seem to have been undermined. In this chapter the main emphasis is on the development of local economic policies in Sheffield, and, as Chapter 8 suggests for the GLC, similar attempts were being made by some other Labour authorities. An important part of the argument is about the creation of jobs and the nature of the jobs being created, but underlying it is an alternative vision of local government, which may be relevant beyond those councils which are controlled by Labour. This is a call for councils to be at the centre of a set of initiatives, linking different groups – including employers as well as workers – to generate growth in a way which is acceptable to all of those involved. It is a call for local government to take the lead in generating effective partnerships capable of drawing forth inventiveness from the public and private sectors, management as well as workforce, community as well as workplace.

The focus of the argument suggests an ambition which goes beyond the politics of service provision identified by Savage and Mark-Lawson and Warde. It may also be one which is more appropriate to a period in which the resources available for services are likely to be limited unless support can be mobilized from outside the local government system. All three of the chapters in this Section suggest that local political organizations can themselves play a major part in determining what is possible at local level, even if they generally have to operate within fairly tight constraints.

Allan Cochrane

Note 1 In this context it is important to note that Savage's chapter is part of a (previously unpublished) report of work in progress. For this reason many of his arguments should be seen as tentative and partial.

Reference MARK-LAWSON, J. and WARDE, A. (1987) *Industrial Restructuring and the Transformation of a Local Political Environment: a Case Study of Lancaster*, Lancaster Regionalism Group, Working Paper 33 (extracts printed as Chapter 11 in this volume).

10 Whatever happened to red Clydeside?

Mike Savage

10.1 The undermining of 'red Clydeside', 1920–1960

In Scotland the Labour movement drew initially on a rich associational life of diverse mutualist associations (Smith, 1980). These organizations provided powerful means of co-operative provision, stretching from Friendly Societies (notably the Foresters, Rechabites and Shepherds), the Co-operative Movement (45 000 members in the early twentieth century), the Temperance Movement and craft unions, especially in the engineering and shipyard trades (Smith, 1980; Reid, 1980). These organizations drew their strength from the disproportionately large numbers of independent craft workers, and from the peculiar character of working-class neighbourhoods, where community provision and co-operation were encouraged by the way in which washing and other forms of domestic labour could not be carried out in individual households, but needed to be done in public. Whilst in many areas the early Labour Party relied on trade union contacts, in Glasgow the ILP emerged on the backs of ward committees and Tenants Associations (Melling, 1983, especially Ch. 4). The 'heroic' interpretation of Glasgow's politics often overlooks the extent to which the strength of these mutalist currents tended to neglect the role of the state in providing services and amenities (Fraser, 1985). Only in the context of war was this changed, where state intervention in the shipbuilding and engineering industries forced the craft workers to recognize the significance of state directed campaigns to secure improvements in working conditions (Reid, 1985). Similarly the major Rent Strike and demands for state housing did not represent a fully fledged demand for widespread state intervention, but were testimony to the fact that the provision of large amounts of good quality housing was outside the capability of mutualist organizations, however well organized. In the context of wartime state interventions mutualist associations, combined with effective political action by the ILP, generated a radical moment, on the back of which the Labour Party developed a major electoral presence. In 1922 the majority of Glasgow MPs were Labour, and a host of local authorities around Clydeside fell under Labour control in the 1920s, though Glasgow Corporation itself, the biggest prize, was not won until 1933 (McLean, 1983).

The problem, however, was that the Labour Party had developed a strong influence on the local state without actually being supported by groups with particularly strong demands of the state, especially outside housing. Mutualist associations had specific concerns over the state (the Co-op over proposals to charge income tax on the 'divi' for instance), but no general concern to use the state (local or national) to dramatically improve conditions. The development of long-term unemployment from the 1920s, again an issue which the Friendly Societies and Trade Unions' own benefit funds could not cope with, kept them interested in politics, especially over the issue of unemployment relief. Nonetheless, as Gallacher (1982) shows for the Vale of Leven, the most marked characteristic of developments of the inter-war years was the growth of mutualist self-provisioning wherever possible, with street committees, Co-op functions, socials and the like, Hence, the danger was that once the specific issues were met, their support for the Labour Party might weaken. This would leave the Labour Party without secure sources of support and might weaken their electoral position. Of utmost consequence to the development of politics in Clydeside was the fact that the local Labour Party took the option of anchoring itself within the local state in order to compensate for its weaknesses outside it.

There were several reasons for this. Firstly, especially until the local government reforms of 1930, it was rather easy to take secure control of important local authorities, especially in the smaller industrial settlements. Unlike England, the poor relief was handled by parish councils, which if they only covered small industrial villages could easily be taken over, as happened in the Vale of Leven (Gallacher, 1982). Similarly the peculiarly Scottish institutions of Ward Committees, which were elected by ward residents under universal suffrage, and which were given a small public grant, could provide a valuable springboard for more important elections (Melling, 1983, p. 41; Brennan, 1959, Ch. 6).

Secondly, the Labour Party was not the only party which claimed to be the party of the working class. In Clydeside, alone of all British conurbations, it suffered real challenges from both the Communist Party and the Independent Labour Party (especially after 1932 when the national ILP disaffiliated from the Labour Party, but the parties had been distinct even before this). And, further, the links between these two parties and the various autonomous mutualist associations were rather stronger than the Labour Party could muster. The CP drew much of its strength from the skilled workers of the engineering industry, and from the unemployed, whilst the ILP retained its close links with tenants groups and neighbourhood organizations (Melling, 1983; Gallacher, 1982). The main advantage of the Labour Party itself was its position in local government, rather than in the popular associations outside it. It owed this to the power of the Catholic machine to deliver large numbers of loyal voters in return for vague commitment to Irish independence. The partial 'solution' of this question from the 1920s, however, even put this source of support in doubt.

This same feature made it difficult to use the strategy of developing a party led and directed by the popular organizations. This strategy was adopted in many parts of northern England where the limited prospect of secure local authority control, and the power of non-Labour organizations in the neighbourhoods, forced Labour to intervene to build up support. In Preston, for instance, the party increasingly based itself on its Labour Clubs, which became the centres of organization and local social life, at least for a period in the later 1920s, and developed its own social life including Labour choirs, rambling clubs, sports leagues, debating societies and the like (Savage, 1987). Yet the pre-existing hold of the ILP and churches in Glasgow made this strategy most difficult to implement, and the ward organization and neighbourhood presence of the party was to remain shadowy, and in places almost non-existent (see Minkin and Seyd, 1979).

The Glasgow Labour Party was hence inclined to use the state as a means of support. Only a few other local Labour Parties in Britain could do the same thing. Clydeside had high levels of Labour voting, allowing Labour access to the local state. In many places, such as Preston, Labour never won control of the council in the inter-war years and hence was forced to carry on relying upon popular capacities for collective action (Savage, 1987). In others Labour was the only working-class party and felt less need to separate itself from other left-wing parties. The Glasgow experience was, however, replicated in south Wales, where mutualist forms of collective action also persisted, as did a strong Communist presence. As a result the Labour Party here also looked to the local state.

Yet there are various ways in which the local state can be used by a political party. One of these is to develop a patronage machine. Shefter (1977) argues that patronage normally develops where a party is 'internally mobilized' (that is, it develops within an existing regime where there is access to rewards), and where there are no strong bureaucratic, civil service statutes preventing patronage. In this period both of these conditions applied. The Labour Party, by gaining access to local authority control had potential rewards. Equally, while there were certain well-established bureaucratic procedures in local government, these did not apply in two key areas. Firstly, until the 1940s local authorities had considerable discretion over recruitment of workers. This extended as far as the police force, where in cities and County Boroughs the Watch Committee could select police officers (HLG 51/956). In the inter-war years several local authorities used their powers to ask all applicants if they were members of trade unions (HLG 51/957), and there is good evidence that Labour-controlled authorities were able to pay higher wages to their workers.

Yet no fully fledged patronage machine developed in Glasgow, nor indeed elsewhere in Britain outside Northern Ireland and, to a lesser extent, Liverpool (Savage, 1985). The reason lies mainly through the problem of electoral reliability. Only in a few places is control of a local authority secure enough to use it firmly to develop machinery which will benefit the ruling party. The danger, of course, is that it will fall and be taken over by rivals. This is a particular problem with attempts to develop 'patronage' machines on the North American model (Shefter, 1977) where patronage may fall into the hands of the opposition. In the US it tended to develop alongside ethnic identification where voting patterns were fairly predictable and this was less of a problem. Further, in the US, the greater autonomy of local government, and the weak purchase of national party politics for local politics meant that it was unlikely for local parties to get voted out through dissatisfaction with central government policy, a process which was always common in Britain, and ensured that, however effective patronage could be at the local level, there was always the danger that national trends would see the local party lose office. In fact the only known cases of jobbery in Britain were in areas of total party hegemony (HLG 51/110). This was especially so in south Wales, where nepotism or jobbery was reported in eight local authorities. This apparently reached a peak in Merthyr Tydfil where 'it is freely stated by responsible people that about forty of (Cllr Jones') relatives are employed by the Council'. Nonetheless, it was rare for more than the odd individual to be involved in such allegations, and the sort of patronage developed in the US, where several thousand jobs could be handed out by the party machine, was unknown.

The Labour Party did not develop a patronage machine to establish itself. So how did it retain its local political dominance? A variety of processes served to undermine the previously potent capacities for collective action, which as we have seen helped bring Labour to power, but which were independent of it.

Some of these changes were related to structural changes in the local economy. Economic change in the shipbuilding industry made it more difficult to mobilize workers. Although there was little evidence of direct deskilling of skilled workers which might have weakened the capacities of the craft workers (McGoldrick, 1982), the trade unions were severely weakened by the 1922 engineering lock-out. Furthermore, the craft system of working had always relied on the tolerance of foremen. Rarely had unions been strong enough to unilaterally enforce apprenticeship ratios on to employers. Rather they relied on the trade loyalties of the foremen to respect them, and they would also take on the children or acquaintances of existing workers, so allowing craft control to be perpetuated. Attempts by employers to undermine the foremen's trade loyalty never proved entirely successful, but they did have a considerable impact in the immediate post-war period, when large numbers of foremen joined the employer-approved Foreman's Mutual Benefit Society (Melling, 1980; Burgess, 1986). Hence the erosion of older patterns of craft control, reduced the potential for unrest, and this was amplified by the fact that employment prospects in the shipyards were increasingly linked to naval demands, so leading to a clientistic workforce dependent on central government contracts (Dickson, 1980).

Militancy in the workplace hence declined considerably, and did not upset Labour dominance. The situation in housing was more complex, however, for here the Labour Party was part of an administration which contributed to the erosion of neighbourhood capacities for collective action. Here the local state actively presided over a process of individuating the population, and in this the local Labour Party, if not always conscious supporters, were heavily implicated.

The best account of the changes taking place in Glasgow's social life remains that of Brennan, who surveyed the housing policy of Glasgow between 1918 and the mid-1950s. He found that neighbourhood cohesiveness had declined, both in the new council estates and in the old inner-city areas, under the aegis of a Labour Party administration. There were several dimensions to this. The council had prioritized the need for houses above all else, and hence the newer estates such as Pollock were deprived of virtually all social facilities. They had very few shops, no neighbourhood halls or meeting places, no public houses, no cinemas and very few schools (at least until after the Second World War). The building of houses rather than tenements undermined the older solidarity arising out of everyday interaction and sharing of domestic labour. In short, the capacities for collective action were massively eroded. Similarly, in Govan, an inner urban area, it was apparent that the Labour Party, still electorally dominant in the area, had lost its neighbourhood base. Brennan noted that very few Labour Party leaders were active in any other associations in the area. 'One does not come across any evidence of a strong body of Socialist Thought outside of the organization of the Labour Party itself' (Brennan, 1959, p. 126). Finally, in the proposed redevelopment of the Gorbals, much of the plan seemed preoccupied simply with reducing the social amenities of the area. The population was to be reduced by two-thirds (from 26000 to 10000), but the number of planned shops was to drop from 444 to 57 and the number of pubs from 46 to 9 (Brennan, 1959, p. 61).

Another major effect of Labour Council policy was to increase social segregation within the working class. As Melling emphasizes, pre-First World War housing had relatively low levels of social segregation, largely because the insecurity of the shipbuilding industry made skilled workers reluctant to over-commit themselves by moving to expensive rented housing (Melling, 1983, Ch. 2). Yet the introduction of mass council housing massively increased social segregation. This was because the new houses fell into three types. 'Ordinary' houses were designed for respectable working-class residents, but 'rehousing' houses were cheap houses built for people who could afford nothing else, while intermediate houses fell between the two. Housing inspectors would visit potential tenants to assess which category they fell into, both in terms of the rent they could pay and the type of 'standards' of household care they exhibited, and would then decide to which sort of house they should be allocated (Brennan, 1959, pp. 171–2). This sort of segregation did not begin when the Labour Party took control in 1933 (Mooney, 1983, pp. 19–23), but it was not challenged by them afterwards. Hence, the growth of municipal housing went along with increased segregation within the working class between 'respectable' and 'non-respectable' tenants. One issue which remains unclear is the extent to which a Labour Party based patronage machine developed over housing allocation. In Glasgow there was no formal points scheme for public housing until 1979, and in 1976 there was a major scandal over a councillor using his influence to secure housing. Whether this was the norm or the exception remains uncertain, but it indicates how the Labour Party might use its position to individuate residents, by making individual contacts with key individuals so important.

The central question is how Glasgow council decided upon a policy of mass dispersion of the population to peripheral estates which underlay the dramatic erosion of neighbourhood solidarity. Why did they attempt to undermine the very features of cohesive working-class solidarity upon which they were originally based? As Brennan makes clear, the answer was not simply that there was no alternative. The Bruce Plan, first developed in the late 1940s, proposed massive redevelopment of existing central urban sites to improve housing conditions, but without needing any major reduction in housing density (Brennan, 1959, pp. 26–7), but it was opposed by the Labour Group. Equally the Labour Group opposed Abercrombie's Green Belt and New Town proposals ensconced in the 'Clyde Valley Regional Plan' of 1946, which proposed massive decentralization of the population, not to suburbs but to freshly created New Towns, where, incidentally, there would be rather more social facilities than had been provided on the council estates.

In fact the policy which the Labour Party adopted was contradictory. Their main policy was the need for low-density housing, with separate entrances and gardens. Yet they wanted this to take place inside Glasgow's boundaries, not through New Town development. Hence the lack of space within Glasgow meant that the council had a contradictory policy of low-density housing redevelopment, but without space for adequate building. What seems to have been important was the alliance between the local Labour Party and certain local professional planners, an alliance facilitated by the way in which the Labour Party became reliant on the state for its structural support. Local government planners were in the inter-war years slowly hankering after professional status, yet this needed some form of 'objective' knowledge about which they could claim to be expert. This problem was compounded by the inherent fragmentation of local authority workers, employed by a number of spatially disparate bodies. The profession came to define its tasks, however, by reference to a number of key statistical indicators which could provide the pretence of objective knowledge. Some of these were medical details, already collected in massive numbers and published in Medical Officers of Health Reports, which allowed detailed inter-authority comparisons of birth and death rates, types of disease etc. (Melling, 1983, pp. 17–18 on the Glasgow situation). This was combined with detailed housing statistics, and the professional planners' problem increasingly became defined as the need to improve health by reducing densities. In this quest everything could be sacrificed. It was this which explains the lack of concern over social facilities on the newer estates and the obsession with house-building at low density.

The Labour Party hence presided over a council whose action helped undermine the capacity for working-class action. Although there is very little evidence that housing conditions had been improved, by the 1940s working-class action over housing had died away (cf Butt, 1979, p. 165: 'From the housing situation between the wars, one would not have expected that Red Clydeside would have adopted a paler shade by 1939, and if there was a revolutionary moment in George Square in 1919 there was no need for it to pass away.') The passive Labour voting of consumers reliant on state services, particularly in housing, persisted.

This Labour hegemony was not unchallenged, and throughout the post-war period there were signs that it would crack. The immediate post-war revival of shipbuilding – Glasgow's Indian summer – created a new militancy among the old craft workers, and there were a number of major apprentices' strikes, culminating in 1960 when 33 500 apprentices, led by the CP, struck throughout Scotland for higher pay (Dickson, 1980). The famous Upper Clyde Shipbuilders work-in of 1971 was also testimony to this new unrest, but the Labour Party was not an active force in it.

Perhaps more serious than this, however, was the dramatic loss of electoral support in the late 1960s and early 1970s, mostly to the SNP. This had a severe shock effect on the Labour Party, especially the loss of the formerly rock-solid Labour seat of Glasgow Govan in the 1973 by-election. Much of this SNP support was concentrated in the New Towns and among the skilled manual working class (Dickson, 1980; McLean, 1970). This testified to a new problem facing the Labour Party. Its political grip on the Glasgow area had been secured by the continued passive dependence of local citizens on the local state and its governing party. There was, however, a slowly growing group of people who were less reliant on the local state, especially for transport, if not so much for housing. This new semi-affluent working class, with some access to the means of 'privatized consumption', were in a better position to vote for other parties. To them a paternalist Labour regime was becoming at best an irrelevance and at worst an imposition. At the same time as these people were supporting the SNP, a number of more deprived public tenants were recovering their voice and there was a string of rent strikes in this period (Gallacher, 1982). For many years as public housing was being developed there was a high residential turnover, but increasingly a static population was becoming settled (Barlow and Savage, 1987) and the capacities for collective action once again increasing.

Ultimately, the Labour Party was able to win over these voters again. In the context of dramatic economic recession it became clear to the affluent workers that their relative prosperity depended on employment, and

Labour seemed the party best placed to secure this at the national level. But the pattern of historical development of the Labour Party was to have major ramifications on its contemporary policy options.

10.2 Contemporary politics in Glasgow

There are a number of specific features of local authority policy in the Strathclyde area which need emphasizing. Firstly, local authorities have not defied central government legislation attacking local government finances or autonomy, in the way shown by Liverpool and several London boroughs, and closer to home by Stirling and Edinburgh. This is despite the fact that government restrictions have been more marked in Scotland than in England, and indeed Scotland was the test bed for rate-capping (Duncan and Goodwin, 1988, Ch. 5; Scott, 1986). Yet in 1984–85, when the government severely cut back the rate fund contribution, all the Strathclyde authorities agreed (albeit reluctantly) to increase council house rents to make up the shortfall rather than follow Edinburgh's policy of non-compliance (Scott, 1986).

Secondly, over the past decade there has been a widespread disenchantment with 'local authority paternalism' and a number of authorities have pioneered various decentralization measures. These have been prompted particularly by Strathclyde Regional Council in their attempt to develop an 'area approach' where resources are concentrated in particularly deprived areas, and seventy-five areas of Priority Treatment defined, and here Urban Programme funds were made available and extra teachers deployed (Young, nd; Young, 1983). In housing administration decentralization has not been as well publicized as in parts of England (for example, Seabrook, 1984) but has been very extensive. In Strathkelvin, for instance, the district has been split into five Area Teams, each with control over estate management in their area, and in Glasgow there are now sixteen semi-autonomous officer units.

Thirdly, there has been a willingness to compensate for loss of central government funds by working with the private sector in housebuilding (Barlow and Savage, 1987). Glasgow DC in particular has encouraged housebuilders to build 'under licence', allowing the council certain rights over nominating the new occupiers of rehabilitated buildings. Initially, the private sector was most reluctant to get involved, but this has changed under the inspiration of the Glasgow Eastern Area Renewal Project which has rehabilitated many central Glasgow properties for owner-occupation. Furthermore, there has been strong encouragement for housing co-ops and housing associations. In many respects the sorts of housing policies pursued could be heralded as examples of radical Thatcherism had they been introduced in England. Certainly, its housing policy seems no different from that of Wandsworth, for example.

Finally, local authorities in Strathclyde (particularly Glasgow DC) have developed new forms of economic policy, geared to attracting service employment and encouraging 'gentrification'. Whereas in many areas (particularly in the US) capitalist interests (particularly real estate and local capital) have been to the fore in encouraging such processes, and although there is good evidence that such trends do not assist working-class residents very much, the Labour Party has been a leading force (though supported also by central agencies such as the Scottish Development Agency). The most notable examples of this are in the attempt to develop owner-occupation in the city, to develop tourism and recreational facilities (though as one Labour councillor observed 'probably somewhere else in Scotland will lose out as we benefit'). The most notable example of this is the money spent on the Scottish Exhibition Centre by Glasgow DC (Lever and Mather, 1986). There has been no attempt to develop a radical strategy on manufacturing despite the fact that the creation of the SDA in 1975 severely restricted the formal powers of local authorities to attract inward investment. Yet these authorities still do what they can do to obtain branch plants, but there is still no concern even with whether such plants are unionized. One of the main conerns of several DCs remains the 'advantages' which the New Town Development Corporations have in inducing companies to locate, and the role of the SDA.

Now I want to argue that these three types of local policy are best explained in terms of the development of Labour politics in the Strathclyde region. The central feature of the Labour movement is its dependence on the institutions and structures of an extremely pervasive local state. This distinguished it from other areas where the Labour Party's control has never been secure enough to allow this. Liverpool is a classic example, for here Labour never won control until 1955, and has never become a dominant party. As a result the Liverpool Labour Party always maintained its autonomy from the local authority and was ready to use it as a pawn in its opposition to central government policy. This could not occur in Glasgow, however, where any attempt to defy central government which might run the risk of leading to direct government intervention could only threaten the entire basis of the Labour movement. More than this, in recent years the Liverpool Labour Party became dominated by public sector trade unions (Parkinson, 1985). These unions were acutely aware of the fact that central government policy had important ramifications for their membership, and hence were more willing to fight it. At the same time any attempt to defy central government to the point of making Liverpool 'ungovernable' threatened the jobs of local authority workers. Indeed it was for this reason that in the end the trade unions deserted the Militant leadership of the Labour Party and hastened the collapse of opposition to the government.

The situation in Scotland was very different. Here the Labour Party was more concerned to ensure the legal autonomy and viability of local government than the interests of those working for it. This is one reason why it had been able to push through its decentralization measures with reasonable efficiency and without much fuss. Indeed Strathclyde Regional Council had to overcome opposition from teaching unions in its new 'under-five' initiative. The situation in Sheffield also bears comparison. Here, unlike in Glasgow, the engineering and steel industries remained buoyant until the later 1970s, and enabled the trade unions in these sectors to remain active and dominant in the local Labour Party. After the sudden collapse of these sectors in the late '70s, the Labour Party became actively involved in developing local authority economic policy, but it was still geared to the task of regenerating manufacturing industry (Goodwin, 1986). The local authority and its policies were only a means to this end, and it could be sacrificed if needs be. In Strathclyde the continued existence of a (semi) autonomous local state was the end-goal of the Labour Party: this meant that at the end of the day they could not risk central government intervention to undermine it.

The problem, of course, was that if the Labour administration in Scotland was to preside over large public expenditure cuts the voters might take a hard opinion of them. The passive Labour support cultivated by the Labour Party would have been under threat. In this context the decentralization strategies offered some sort of solution. It is very difficult to be anything other than cynical about these policies. In some cases they were designed to give tenants a say in where the cuts were to be made. Thus in Strathkelvin DC's modernization programme tenants were to be told that there were insufficient funds for comprehensive modernization, but could decide which specific piece of modernization they wanted first (such as window replacement, external painting etc.). So long as public funds remained plentiful the Town Council decided where the extra was to go, but as soon as they began to dry up then the decisions as to where the cuts would go was devolved to the tenants.

Strathclyde RC's 'area approach' is in some respects even worse. Here different local areas are often invited to bid against each other for (limited) funds, such as the 'under-five' initiative where local groups had to compete for £3 million funds. This seems a little like the 'divide and rule' strategy used before. But there are more positive elements to decentralization. Until the last decade the local authorities had not needed any more positive support from its population than the periodic voting in of the Labour Party. The attack on local government from Whitehall has, however, made leading councillors realize that they need to encourage popular political mobilization as one means of opposing new legislation, and the critique of the 'town hall syndrome' is one aspect of this.

Finally, however, is the concern with developing service employment and getting 'yuppies' to live in the city, largely through private sector involvement in housebuilding, and wherever possible in employment initiatives. In part this reflects the long-term decline of manufacturing and the realization that manufacturing has gone for good – a perception still alien to party activists in Sheffield or London who still remember the not-so-distant days of jobs a plenty. It also testifies to the lack of concern with its trade union base. Since the unions had become peripheral to the Labour Party it was a matter of little concern to get employment only from those employers likely to have unionized workforces. Significant also was the rates question. At a period of decline in central government revenue the need to develop a large rateable base above all else seemed very important, and more expensive housing was one way of obtaining this. The concern was more with shoring up the finances of the local state than in improving the prospects for its traditional supporters, as might have been the case elsewhere.

10.3 Conclusion

The Strathclyde Labour movement has policies which are both spatially and temporally specific. They have none of the radical features of the early 'red Clyde' period, nor have they been receptive to any of the new initiatives developed by contemporary Labour local authorities elsewhere. It is not enough to explain this simply in terms of the contemporary patterns of social relations in the area, but as I have indicated it is the historical trajectory of the specific place that is of key importance: a Labour Party catapulted to power but without firmly rooted bases of support was forced to use the local state as its axis of power, and in so doing helped undermine the various patterns of collective endeavour which initially placed it there.

It is this dynamic nature of local politics which needs to be emphasized. Local political parties are not the passive reflection of their environment. They are not the simple embodiment of 'traditions' or of 'local political cultures'. To see them in such terms makes it very difficult to see how anything can actually change: a key problem with Johnston's generally interesting attempt to examine local politics. Radicalism, as Offe and Wiesenthal (1980) have argued, is an inherently unstable quantity always threatening to dissolve itself.

We can now turn to our [central] question. What explains why some areas can see 'persistent' radicalism and others 'declining'? The critical determinant here is the strategy of the local party itself, and the way it can manage the tension between the local state and the local environment. The position of parties in the local state gives them a measure of autonomy from their immediate local social environment, but they continue to need some measures of popular support. In the Glasgow case the Labour Party used their influence in the local state to undermine the collective capacities which might threaten their rule and relied on the votes of passive urban consumers to keep them in power. Yet not all parties adopt such a strategy. In some cases control of the local state is never well enough assured for the local party to burn its bridges with its outside constituents. Some capacities for collective action, particularly those based in the workplace, cannot be very powerfully influenced by local authority action and so may remain active and influential: the Sheffield trade union movement may be an example of this.

There is, however, a further point. If a political party exists in a state of tension between its constituents and the local state, the local state also exists in tension with the central state. Whether a local authority takes a confrontational approach or not depends on how a local party establishes itself locally. If its strength lies in collective organizations outside the local state it is more likely to see the local state as a tool to be used in a wider struggle. If it lies in the local state itself (as in Glasgow), it cannot endanger the legal legitimacy of its existence by outright defiance, but is forced to carry out legitimation exercises to persuade local electors that it is not responsible for cuts.

Acknowledgements

This research was carried out as part of the ESRC programme on 'Economic Restructuring, Social Change and the Locality'. I have drawn on other people's work, especially James Barlow. Much of the information in the latter part of the paper has been gathered from interviews with local councillors and officials. Further details from me.

Note

This paper was written as a discussion paper and has not been revised for publication. This partly explains the schematic character of some of the arguments.

References

BARLOW, J. and SAVAGE, M. (1987) *The Relationship between the Housing and Labour Market: The Case of Central Scotland*, University of Sussex Working Paper in Urban and Regional Studies.

BRENNAN, T. (1959) *Reshaping a City*, Glasgow, Grant.

BURGESS, K. (1986) 'Authority relations and the division of labour in British industry: with special reference to Clydeside c1860–1930', *Social History*, Vol. II, No. 2.

BUTT, J. (1979) 'Working-class housing in Glasgow, 1900–1939', in MacDougall, I. (ed.), *Essays in Scottish Labour History*, Edinburgh, Donald.

DICKSON, T. (ed.) (1982) *Capital and Class in Scotland*, Edinburgh, John Donald.

DUNCAN, S. and GOODWIN, M. (1985) 'The local state and local economic policy: why the fuss?', *Policy and Politics*, Vol. 13, No. 3.

DUNCAN, S. and GOODWIN, M. (1988) *The Local State and Uneven Development: The Local Government Crisis in Britain*, Cambridge, Polity Press.

FRASER, H. (1985) paper in Gordon, G. (ed.), *Perspectives on the Scottish City, 1831–1981*, Oxford, Pergamon.

GALLAGHER, R. (1982) 'The Vale of Leven: change in working-class organization and action', in Dickson, T. (ed.).

GOODWIN, M. (1986) *Locality and Local State: Sheffield's Economic Policy*, University of Sussex Working Paper in Urban and Regional Studies, No. 52.

LEVER, W. and MATHER, C. (1986) *The City in Transition*, Oxford, Clarendon Press.

McGOLDRICK, J. (1982) 'Crisis and the division of labour: Clydeside shipbuilding in the inter-war years', in Dickson, T. (ed.).

McLEAN, I. (1970) 'The rise and fall of the Scottish National Party', *Political Studies*, Vol. XVIII, No. 3, pp. 357–72.

McLEAN, I. (1983) *The Legend of Red Clydeside*, Edinburgh, John Donald.

MELLING, J. (1980) '"Non-commissioned officers": British employers and their supervisory workers 1880–1920', *Social History*, Vol. 5, No. 2, pp. 183–221.

MELLING, J. (1983) *Rent Strikes: People's Struggles for Housing in West Scotland 1890–1916*, Edinburgh, Polygon.

MINKIN, L. and SEYD, P. (1979) 'The Labour Party and its members', *New Society*, 27 September.

MOONEY, G. (1983) *The State, Housing and the Reserve Army of Labour*, Centre for Urban and Regional Research, University of Glasgow, Discussion Paper No. 11.

OFFE, C. and WIESENTHAL, H. (1980) 'Two logics of collective action: theoretical notes on social class and organizational form', pp. 67–115, in Zeitlin, M. (ed.), *Political Power and Social Theory*, Greenwich, CT, Jai Press.

PARKINSON, M. (1985) *Liverpool on the Brink*, Hermitage, Berks, Policy Journals.

REID, A. (1980) *Shipbuilding and the Division of Labour: 1880–1920, with special reference to Clydeside*, unpublished PhD thesis, University of Cambridge.

REID, A. (1985) 'Dilution, trade unionism and the state in Britain during the First World War', in Tolliday, S. and Zeitlin, J. (eds), *Shop Floor Bargaining and the State*, Cambridge, Cambridge University Press.

SAVAGE, M. (1985) 'Ethnic divisions in the labour market and working class politics', paper presented at ESRC Symposium on Segregation in Employment, University of Lancaster.

SAVAGE, M. (1987) *The Dynamics of Working Class Politics: the Labour Movement in Preston, 1890–1940*, Cambridge, Cambridge University Press.

SHEFTER, M. (1977) 'Party and patronage: Germany, England and Italy', *Politics and Society*, Vol. 7, No. 4, pp. 403–51.

SCOTT, D. (1986) 'Local v. central government: the spending conflict', *Scottish Government Yearbook*, Edinburgh, Unit for the Study of Government in Scotland.

SEABROOK, J. (1984) *The Idea of Neighbourhood*, London, Pluto.

SMITH, J. (1980) *Commonsense Thought and Working-class Consciousness: Some Aspects of the Labour Movement in Glasgow and Liverpool in the Early Years of this Century*, unpublished PhD thesis, University of Edinburgh.

YOUNG, R. (1983) 'A little local inequality', in Brown, G. and Cook, R. (eds), *Scotland: The Real Divide*, Edinburgh, Mainstream.

YOUNG, R. (nd) 'Social strategy in Strathclyde: where now?', mimeo.

11 The changing political environment of Lancaster

J. Mark-Lawson and A. Warde

11.1 The making of a Conservative environment

Lancaster was a medium-sized city [of] 51 000 in 1951, the most northerly in Lancashire, surrounded by a very extensive rural hinterland [. . .] It was an established commercial and service centre in the eighteenth century when it was a port for the Atlantic trade, but this declined thereafter. It was comparatively late to industrialize: its principal industry, oilcloth manufacture (primarily linoleum), expanded only after 1880. The production of artificial fibres became important in the inter-war years, and by the mid-twentieth century these two industries provided about 20 per cent of local employment and over half of manufacturing jobs. The 1951 Census shows the relatively unskilled nature of the labour process in these, and other, local industries, recording 36 per cent of the population in social classes IV and V, a considerably greater proportion than average. (In their analysis of the 157 British towns with a population of over 50 000 in 1951, Moser and Scott (1961) showed that only seventeen towns had a higher proportion than Lancaster of classes IV and V. Among the towns with a lower proportion were found the likes of Gateshead, Sunderland and Rotherham.)

It is in the light of the class composition of the town that its political character appears distinctive. Only once between 1923 and 1987 did it return any but a Conservative MP. Piepe *et al.* (1969), using aggregate data analysis to isolate places which deviated from the class-party model of voting, showed that in 1955 the Conservatives took 11 per cent more of the vote than would have been predicted on the basis of the class composition of the city, making it the most deviant, pro-Conservative constituency in Britain. Lancaster also appeared conservative in many other respects. There was virtually no industrial conflict in the town before the late 1960s and Labour institutions were weakly developed.

The development of social, industrial and political conservatism among the electors of Lancaster was a complex process. Politics in the city in the twentieth century have passed through four distinct phases. First, the years to 1911 saw a nascent socialist movement mount an unsuccessful challenge to a rather idiosyncratic Liberalism sponsored by the town's principal employer, Lord Ashton. Second, from 1911 until 1935 the labour movement scarcely stirred in the context of a non-partisan, almost apolitical, climate that served to entrench the established system of dominance and social order. Third, between 1935 and the 1960s partisan electoral politics developed, though Labour support remained at unexpectedly low levels and industrial conflict continued to be conspicuous by its absence. Fourth, from the mid-1960s to the present, the local political environment has been transformed by the severe erosion of Conservative support, the growth of more combative workplace politics and the extension of sympathies for 'new' social movements.

The origin of the local political environment of conservatism was a decisive political victory for the local employers at the end of the first phase in 1911. (This account relies heavily on Todd (1976).) An initial attempt at the organization of labour in the early 1890s petered out in 1896. Renewed efforts in 1905 revived a local Independent Labour Party (ILP) and the Trades Council who co-operated fitfully to provide labour representation locally. The largest employer in the town, James Williamson II (elevated to Lord Ashton in 1895), made a determined effort to extinguish the challenge of labour. For the previous thirty years city politics had been fronted by the big employers with a somewhat eccentric Liberalism, sponsored by Ashton, generally in the ascendant (Pelling, 1967; Clarke, 1971). The local employers were powerful. They were high-profile benefactors to civic and welfare projects: between them they built the Town Hall, extended hospital buildings, provided technical and adult education, built swimming pools, endowed a park etc. Moreover, after a large carriage and wagon works, externally owned, closed down in 1909, they were the town's principal employers.

Resistance was limited. The only organized workers in the local linoleum industry were a small minority of craftsmen in the Amalgamated Society of Engineers and they subscribed to the Liberalism of the employers. General labourers' unions were prohibited by the main employers. Trade union backing for socialist or labourist parties came from railwaymen, woodworkers and engineers outside linoleum. However, without the support of the factory proletariat in linoleum, labour politics would necessarily be feeble.

Battle lines were drawn up over the political mobilization of linoleum operatives. Ashton, a suspicious, secretive and autocratic man, was easily upset by socialist criticism of his activities. For instance, a rather mild article in the *Co-operative News* in 1909 which said that Williamsons paid low wages and that unionization would therefore benefit the workers, was transformed into a major local incident regarding the good reputation of his lordship. The climax of four years of irritation came with the local elections of 1911. In the Skerton Ward of the town, where many of his employees lived, the most prominent militant in the ILP, Patrick Wall, a railwayman, secured the same number of votes as a candidate publicly supported by Ashton. Ashton reacted strongly. He dismissed known supporters of the ILP at his works. He posted notices at the works saying that he was no longer prepared to consider a prospective advance in wages. He announced an intention to cease retaining workers during trade recessions. And he engineered splits within the Trades Council and the ILP. (For a full account see Todd (1976).) His victory was enormous and decisive. Organized opposition crumbled. But, ironically, Ashton himself immediately withdrew from any involvement in politics or civic affairs in Lancaster, taking his charity elsewhere as a final response to the 'ingratitude' of Lancastrians.

This defeat of Labour was followed by twenty-five years of immobilization. The Labour Party made a very poor showing in General Elections and, more significantly, scarcely contested local elections. The local council was controlled by Independents and was petit-bourgeois in social composition. Its policies were directed towards infrastructural building projects and its expenditure on social welfare measures was niggardly (see Mark-Lawson *et al.*, 1985).

The basis of working-class quiescence in this and the subsequent period was the development of a political hegemony founded on and sustained by the economic dependence of labour. Lancaster was a dominated labour market: in 1921 about 35 per cent of the employed population were engaged in linoleum production, the vast majority either at Williamsons or Storeys [. . .] It was also a relatively isolated, self-contained labour market, the nearest large towns, Preston and Kendal, [being] each twenty miles distant. These conditions increased the power of employers in the local labour market and restricted the opportunities available to people seeking work. The employers took great advantage of these circumstances adopting various collaborative practices among which were the prohibition of general unions, agreement on wage levels and the operation of exclusive internal labour markets [. . .]

With respect to trades unions, a successful 'divide and rule' strategy was adopted. Both Williamsons and Storeys recognized the same craft unions and paid the regional wage rates for such jobs. But unskilled workers remained non-unionized until the 1960s, though not for want of attempts to recruit on behalf of general unions. Throughout the first half of the twentieth century labour movement speakers regularly visited the town, expressed dismay at the levels of unionization and exhorted Lancaster workers to organize. But nothing happened, largely because Williamsons and Storeys needed to do little more than announce that they would not employ members of such unions. The new firms producing artificial fibres that located in the town in the inter-war years – partly because of the docile workforce – were happy to co-operate in maintaining that united front against labourers' unions.

Employers also colluded over wages. There is solid evidence, in the form of letters passed between Williamsons and Storeys, of collaboration over wage levels right through to the 1970s. Union rates were paid to craft workers, and regular consultation between managements of all the large manufacturing firms fixed wage rates for the non-skilled. There was thus no wage competition for labour, and consequently not only were wages low but there was no real incentive for workers to shift around between firms. These inter-firm agreements were certainly facilitated because the labour market was both dominated and self-contained.

The most effective mechanism of all in maintaining the dependence of workers was the operation of internal labour markets at Williamsons and Storeys. Internal labour markets are not very well understood. So far as their effects on industrial politics are concerned the worker responses produced can easily be confused with the deference frequently attributed to workers in paternalist enterprises. In Lancaster, especially, where there were relatively few alternative opportunities for unskilled workers, the internal labour markets of the two main employers rendered the workforce heavily dependent. Investigation into the organization of Storeys shows that it was very rare for a worker aged 18 or over to be taken on by the firm. Only 13 per cent of new workers taken on between 1925 and 1937 were [over] 18, and the majority of those had actually been employed previously by the firm. Thus, there was effectively a single port of entry for labourers; the resulting job-for-life meant that industrial indiscipline was a potentially extremely costly individual risk, because obtaining a job elsewhere in the area would be virtually impossible. Various devices were used to maintain the exclusivity of the internal labour market, including collaboration between the two employers. One entry in a register of leavers from Storeys gave the reason for the dismissal of a certain Vincent Landor as: 'Discharged. We found he had worked for J(ames) W(illiamson) and S(on) and had not left properly (they complained)' (Storeys' Leavers' Book, 1897–1907). In many respects the mechanism of the internal labour market is a more powerful reason for industrial quiescence that the more transparent and shocking aspects of Ashton's practices of surveillance and coercion. The cost of industrial or political resistance was frequently too great.

The economic power of the big firms vis-à-vis the local workforce was thus very considerable. Obedience or migration was the basic choice for the factory workers. This situation was reflected in industrial politics. There were scarcely any strikes, and none of much size or duration in any of the Lancaster factories between 1900 and 1967. The General Strike obtained support locally only from railwaymen and woodworkers. The extensive introduction of scientific management techniques in the early 1930s raised but one half-day stoppage. Industrial action in the 1950s was confined to public servants of various sorts; local engineers even refused to take part in national engineering disputes. Capital was well in control in the sphere of industrial relations.

Hegemony was reinforced by another important set of practices, those concerned with the provision of services which might be considered as reproducing labour power. This is a vital but often much neglected sphere in which employers, and the employment relation, are actually frequently implicated [. . .] Much of Lancaster's welfare provision was in the voluntary sector throughout the first half of the century. The civic benevolence of the large employers was especially important in the early years of the century, giving them yet another source of power, not to mention legitimacy, within the town. Their involvement, plus a fairly well-developed set of voluntary (though not mutualist) institutions, effectively precluded local state intervention. The local authority provided very little, comparatively much less than many other local authorities (see Mark-Lawson *et al.*, 1985). This situation meant that service provision was not a political issue. The established local voluntary system effectively precluded political mobilization on the issues of urban politics, another prop to the system of local hegemony and political inaction. It was, however, in this sphere that Labour finally was sparked into action, for it was welfare issues, especially housing, which provided the raison d'être for Labour organization and representation after 1935.

A particular form of labour politics grew out of these conditions of dependence. The politics of the inter-war period were largely non-partisan: the bulk of councillors were Independents who formed an anti-socialist front once Labour began to make an impact in the late 1930s. After the war it was with regret that many local Independents began to campaign under the auspices of the Conservative Party, but there were still Independents standing for the local council who were unopposed by Conservatives as late as 1969. It is this apparently apolitical local political environment, which appears almost antithetical to forms of *party* politics, that indicates the conservatism of the town. As Pugh observed:

> Ultimately, Conservatism has proved comparatively elusive because . . . its real strength often lies in silence. The historian is therefore less likely to be able to depict Conservatism satisfactorily either as a doctrine or as a party programme, but is obliged to look into the informal underlying conservatism which reveals itself in ill-defined but widespread phenomena, like patriotism, monarchism and imperialism. (Pugh, 1985, p. 3)

Lancaster's conservatism was silent, remaining unformed as doctrine or consciousness. Lancaster never had a popular Toryism like that of Blackburn or Birmingham: as we have seen, it was a Liberal town before 1914. Nor was it a place where paternalists cultivated a deferential, Conservative working class. There is not much evidence of positive Tory commitment on behalf of the workers of the town. Rather employer hegemony inculcated sentiments of anti-socialism or anti-Labourism, sentiments firmly based, as we have seen, on the material reality of the powerless position of the industrial proletariat in the area. This kind of political environment was still largely intact in the early 1960s so that it was no accident that the political alignment up to the end of the decade was 'anti-Socialists' versus Labour.

11.2 A decade of transition: the local political environment, 1963–73

The order established under the hegemony of the manufacturing employers was transformed during the 1960s. Industrial restructuring, de-industrialization and the growth of public sector employment brought changes in the class structure and an increased proportion of councillors who were welfare professionals. Unionization in the industrial sector saw the development of a more militant workplace culture. An increased female participation rate began to change the nature of gender relations in the town. At the same time the revitalization of the peace movement and the women's movement locally, the development of new left student political activism and the re-emergence of urban protest movements occurred, all part of a complex changing local environment. Subsequently, the reorganization of local government restructured local politics in the area. This section of the chapter examines the ways in which political life altered in the years up to reorganization in 1973/74. Changing partisan allegiance, mobilization over service issues, changes in the labour movement and the resurgence of campaigning by the women's movement and ecological movement introduced the elements of a new political environment.

Electoral politics prior to local government reorganization in 1973

The shifts in political allegiance in Lancaster in recent times are illustrated by changes in electoral behaviour. The low levels of Labour support in the earlier parts of the twentieth century are indicated by Figure 11.1 which

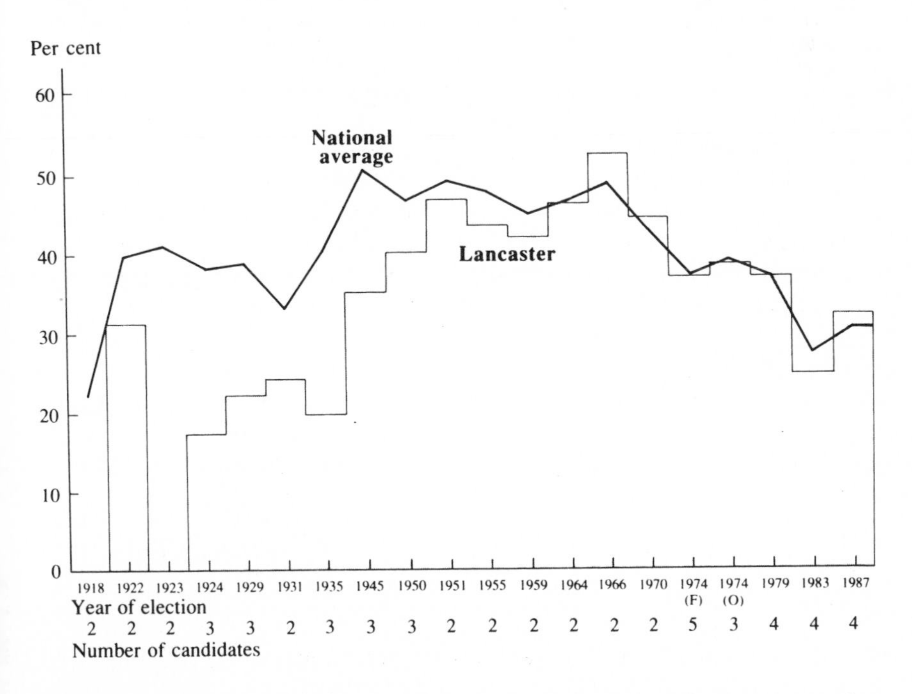

Figure 11.1 The Labour Party's share of the poll in general elections in the Lancaster constituency compared with the national average, 1918–87

compares the Labour share of the poll in general elections in Lancaster to the national average. Bearing in mind the class composition of the town it is apparent than the Labour vote was disproportionately low for much of the century. It was only very recently that Labour began to perform at all respectably; even when Labour won the seat for the only time in 1966, the party got 6 per cent fewer votes than would have been predicted by its class composition (Piepe *et al.*, 1969).

Trends in local elections show a somewhat similar pattern, with Labour's performance weak until the 1960s, but then improving quite considerably. From the late 1930s, when Labour first began to make an impact on the local council, until the late 1960s, the party alignment in the town was Labour versus anti-Socialists. This remained the way in which the Council, and the local press, viewed formal politics. Not until 1969 did the Conservative Party hold a majority on the Council in its own right; prior to that date it had always relied on the support of Independents. That the Independents had Conservative inclinations was shown by the fact that they never had to face Conservative opposition.

A build-up of Labour support locally is indicated by the fact that Labour ran steadily closer to the anti-Socialists as time went on, achieving a majority on the Council twice, in 1958 and 1963. On both occasions the majority was lost at the next annual election; and in both instances the changes in the ruling group on the council involved some contentious manoeuvres regarding the re-election of Aldermen.

Figure 11.2 shows levels of support for Labour locally in the 1960s. At the beginning of the decade it fills its customary minority position with support at around 40 per cent. The level rises from 1963–66, slumps in the period of unpopularity of the Wilson government at the close of the '60s, then increases very sharply in 1971. These trends probably indicate three developments: one, Lancaster seems to be responding more directly to national partisan movement than in the past; two, also in line with national trends, there is considerably volatility in support, especially if the fluctuations between 1966 and 1972 are considered; and finally, there is a

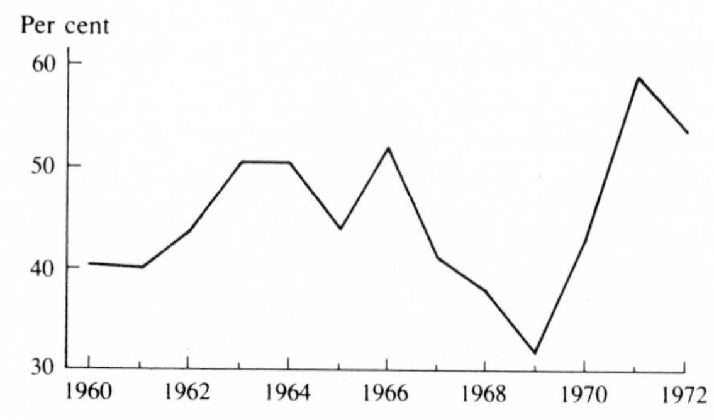

Figure 11.2 Labour's share of the poll in Lancaster Municipal Borough elections, 1960–72

significant break in the pattern of anti-Labourism in Lancaster: the electorate is no longer so blatantly dismissive of that party. These changes coincide with industrial restructuring in the town and with significant changes in the ethos of the parties locally.

In the late 1960s the anti-Labour environment began to disappear. Both Conservative and Labour politics underwent change. The Lancaster Division Conservative Association, for instance, experienced a high peak in membership in 1968 (*Lancaster Guardian*, 25 March 1970). By 1972 the local Conservative Party was making remarkably strong calls for political action. Tories needed to 'wake up and fight', claimed the Tory Agent, because Labour in Lancaster had undergone a metamorphosis from a reasonable and safe democratic organization to a militant, intellectual left-wing extremism. Lancaster Tories, he argued, had to be roused to 'fight for democracy as we know it in our city'.

> Attacking what he calls 'the militant and extremely vocal minority' among new members of the City Council, Mr Bottell [Tory Agent] claims that they are 'not so much interested in the city and the welfare of its people as the destruction of our democratic way of life both in Lancaster and the country as a whole . . . With the left-wing intellectuals now taking over the local Labour Party from the more solid and down-to-earth Socialists we are likely to see more and more of these irresponsible people serving on our City Council . . . that is unless we Conservatives are prepared to do something about it'. (op. cit., 21 April 1972)

Such rousing pleas seem to have had little effect. Although Lancastrians vote Tory in national elections, perhaps because of the 'silent' nature of local Toryism the local Conservative Party did not always even find it easy to get a full complement of candidates. In 1972, for instance, six Conservative councillors had decided to stand down and there was some difficulty in replacing them. There was no candidate in that year to fight in St Annes Ward.

If the Conservatives felt that their local opponents were undergoing a metamorphosis from good, solid, sensible Lancaster trade unionists to loony left lecturers, some Labour Party members felt the same way. In 1973 a man who had served as President of the Trades Council between 1950 and 1971 stood as an unofficial Labour candidate for the County Council elections, unofficial because the Labour Party had, in fact, selected someone else. One of his supporters claimed that he represented the disappearing virtues of an earlier Lancaster Labour movement:

> This man-of-the-people seems to me to demonstrate . . . a belief in the rights of the common man to seek a better deal for himself and the townsfolk without meekly bowing to 'the party' – whatever its colour. (*Lancaster Guardian*, 6 April 1973, p. 10)

The Labour Party in this period, as an effect of the process of deindustrialization, had an influx of new kinds of personnel who altered its social composition. Workers in education in particular were significant; health service workers seem to have had less of an impact on the labour movement. Later in the period an influx of workers from Heysham power station was to revitalize Morecambe Labour Party. One Lancaster City Councillor, who moved into the area in 1966, felt:

> 'The bulk of membership of the Lancaster Labour Party is in effect a white-collar membership. An awful lot of intellectual members, an awful lot of people in the teaching professions, a certain number in health and related professions. So we've very few in traditional working-class professions. That's been a gradual change. If you take the situation now and compare it with the situation as it was when I arrived 21 years ago then I think it's a reasonably striking change that a significant chunk of the membership then was made up of manual workers or the wives or families of manual workers. That's a very very small group now of the membership of the [Lancaster] Labour Party.' (Interview, Lancaster Labour City Councillor)

Another member of the Lancaster Labour Party felt that in the mid-1960s the Lancaster Labour Party was made up of 'two-thirds process workers, engineers and such like, with a third others, retired, academics or whatever'. Twenty years later the party had changed considerably with '. . . three-quarters or even more working in teaching or some allied occupation, and very few people who are working in manufacturing of any description' (interview, Lancaster Labour County Councillor, 16 October 1985).

The politics of housing

One of the major issues which contributed towards this shift away from a dominant and particularist local conservatism in the late 1960s and early 1970s was the classic 'consumption' issue of housing. (This issue was almost certainly implicated in a similar shift to Labour in the 1950s.) 1969–70 saw mobilization of tenants on several of Lancaster's council housing estates, with various types of actions carried out by the tenants' groups including petitioning, marches through the town and a rather cursory rent strike. The Lancaster branch of the International Socialists (IS) became involved with the tenants' mobilization, an involvement which was condemned from various sources but which almost certainly gave an edge to the Labour Group's support for the tenants – support which IS condemned as half-hearted. Although the issues at the heart of the tenants' mobilization were strictly housing issues, rent levels and the conditions of houses and other 'service' issues were linked in to the protests.

The housing issue was political, in the strictest sense of the term, with a clear division between the Labour and Conservative Groups on the council, a division by no means apparent over other service issues locally such as education. As the *Lancaster Guardian* put it in March 1970: 'the two political groups on the council are so sharply divided on housing matters that at the mere mention of them one can sense a wide gap developing' (6 March 1970, p. 13).

Different interest groups

One element of the divisions over housing in Lancaster concerned the issue of which groups such housing should be provided for. In February 1970, for instance, the Housing and Health Committee proposed that certain Lancaster flats should be let at rather high rents because they had decided '. . . to let the . . . flats to professional people because most of the Committee felt there was a problem for professional people seeking accommodation'. Alderman Eric Jones (Labour) complained about this. It was '. . . unfair because they allowed people who could afford them to jump the waiting list queue . . . [he] . . . would like to see these flats go into the ordinary housing points scheme', but his amendment was defeated by 11 votes to 20 (*Lancaster Guardian*, 27 February 1970). The Housing Committee's attitude on this was supported by a leader in the local paper which argued that the Council's policy of earmarking housing for key personnel was a good one:

> The ruling Conservatives and their Independent allies maintain there is a demand for such accommodation from people, possibly in professional positions, whose stay in the city might be limited . . . This is consistent with the attitude taken in the council over a period of years when the need for flats for single people or those in the city for a brief period has been stressed . . . Finding accommodation for key personnel might help the drive to bring more industry into the area. (ibid.)

A further issue concerned the marginalization of council tenants, who, it was alleged, were treated as second-class citizens simply as a result of their form of tenure. This position was argued by the tenants' associations, by IS and by the Labour Group on the council (the latter apparently contradicting its position laid out above that council housing should only go to the needy). Councillor J. Lodge, in the course of a debate on council housing, argued:

> . . . that council house tenants had become second-class citizens. They were harassed and hounded – regulated on the state of their gardens, the number of pets and the noisiness of their parties. There was a ghetto system with council estates far away from homes in private ownership. (*Lancaster Guardian*, 26 June 1970)

Similarly Marsh Tenants' Association, in the course of a protest about rent increases, based their call for mobilization on the general treatment of council tenants:

> It's about time we stood up and decided we aren't going to be second-class citizens any more . . . We need tenants' committees on every estate. We need to get the Tories out of the council. We need to resist the rent increases. We need to demand the renovation of our houses. (ibid.)

The view that council house tenants were second-class citizens was contested by other political groups, notably the local Ratepayers' Association, the Independents and the Conservatives. On the one hand the familiar division discussed by Dunleavy (1981) was made between ratepayers who *provided* council housing and tenants who *used* it. Cllr W. Parkinson, Chair of the Housing and Health Committee, argued against the tenants' associations' calls for council house improvements because '. . . council tenants were already subsidised by almost £100000' (*Lancaster Guardian*, 7 May 1971, p. 11). Similarly the Ratepayers' Association complained about the cost of schemes of renovation on Marsh estate in 1971 arguing that it would cost ratepayers too much money. Why, they asked, did the council not take advantage of its powers to sell such houses off (op. cit., 2 April 1971)? Not surprisingly tenants took issue with this. Marsh Tenants' Association argued that some council tenants had paid for their houses twice over and that owner-occupiers were more highly subsidized than council tenants (op. cit., 7 August 1970). A letter to the paper from a tenant argued '"Realist" thinks his rates help to pay council rents, council tenants can be sure their income tax pays "Realist's" rates' (ibid.).

A rather more unusual version of the consumption cleavage based on tenure was expressed by some Independents and Conservatives who argued that rather than council tenants being 'second-class citizens', owner-occupiers in Lancaster were worse off than council tenants and should not be expected to subsidize them any further. During a debate on a proposed rent rise for council tenants:

> There were Councillors like John Ball and Tom Shingler who represent St Annes, a ward with precious few council houses, who favoured the increase and compared the near slum conditions of private houses to the near elegance of the council house occupants, [whom] Cllr Ball referred to as the privileged classes. Others like Cllrs John Lodge, Abbot Bryning and Mrs J. Horner, who number many council tenants among their constituencies, took the opposite view . . . Many speeches lost a sense of proportion in an apparent attempt to divide the city into the 'haves' (with council houses) and the 'have-nots'. (*Lancaster Guardian*, 7 May 1971, p. 11)

The process of mobilization and the Labour Party

In 1970 rent reviews were held over until after the local elections, an action which the Labour Group complained was a political one (*Lancaster Guardian*, 1 May 1970). For its part the Labour Party were pushing service issues generally in the 1970 local elections, particularly housing, condemning the Conservative-controlled council's housing programme as feeble (ibid.). As Labour had prophesied, as soon as the election was over the council proposed to raise rents by 3 to 10 shillings a week. The Labour Group tried to prevent this move but were defeated 19 votes to 6 (op. cit., 26 June 1970). By late July tenants' associations had been activated. Tenants' associations had existed in the town from the late 1930s and had mobilized before over housing issues. However, the local paper felt that '. . . the rent issue has succeeded in unifying the city council's tenants for the first time' with tenants from a number of different estates joining a unitary protest (op. cit., 24 July 1970). The tenants had drawn up a petition signed by 3000 people and a protest march was planned to demand a better deal for tenants and no rent rises. In July 1970 a crowd of 300 tenants marched on the town hall and demanded a meeting with the Housing Committee. There were angry scenes when this was refused and when the mayor also refused to see them. Fifty people attempted to storm the doors of the Town Hall and there were a number of arrests. The local paper was critical of the stance taken by the council over this issue and laid the blame for the violent scenes at their door [sic]. The council should at best have consulted tenants about rent rises and at worst should at least have offered to meet the marchers. However, it was also claimed that '. . . a group of militants, some of whom were not council tenants and others not ratepayers were determined to cause a scene' (op. cit., 31 July 1970).

Following the demonstration a split took place between tenants on the different estates, some wanting a rent strike and others opposed to this move: Ridge tenants were more in favour of a strike while Marsh tenants were opposed (op. cit., 7 August 1970). In the event only about 40 members of the Ridge Tenants' Association went on rent strike (op. cit., 14 August 1970). The tenants lost this battle over rent increases but claimed victory in forcing a speeding up of the modernization programme (op. cit., 29 September 1970).

In the following year, 1971, the budget meeting revealed that there would be a large deficit in the housing account. This gave rise to speculation from the Joint Tenants' Action Committee (JTAC) that 15p rent rises would be an immediate outcome.

> Rent rises of this scale will cause widespread anger amongst council tenants especially after the steep increases passed last year. New rent increases will be particularly unwelcome because food prices are expected to rise by 10 per cent this year. Local unemployment soars to higher levels each week. (*Lancaster Guardian*, 19 March 1971)

The JTAC demanded to know the extent of any rent rises *before* the local elections. These were duly announced along with the details of an improvement scheme for Marsh estate with approximately £1200 being spent on each house. Electrical rewiring, full gas central heating, modern kitchens and upstairs bathrooms were to be provided. The cost in terms of rent increases would be between 40p–60p per week per tenant and an extra 12½p a week in rates (op. cit., 26 March 1971). These proposed rises may well have contributed to the Labour victory in the subsequent local elections. After Labour polled very well in the local elections in May 1971 the rent rise was reduced with no increase higher than 15p (op. cit., 25 June 1971). Alderman Eric Jones said:

> I suppose we can congratulate ourselves because when this increase was first mooted it was 50p and then a first [decision] reduced it to 20p and then, after we took note of the credit interest at the Housing Committee it went down to 15p. (*Lancaster Guardian*, 2 July 1971)

Just before the elections a year later in 1972 the Joint Tenants' Action Committee wrote to the Labour Group on the City Council to ask whether

Labour would refuse to collect rent increases imposed at the beginning of April and refuse to increase rents by a further 50p next October if it took control of the City Council (op. cit., 14 April 1972). Labour's reply was that they would refuse to raise rents. A leaflet distributed by them said:

> Under the Bill, we would be required to raise our rents by another 50p next April. We will refuse to do this. Furthermore, following an investigation of present rent levels . . . we will tell the National Rents Tribunal what we think fair rents should be. (*Lancaster Guardian*, 21 April 1972, p. 28)

They did duly make some attempt to refuse to implement central government dictates over council rents: in February 1973 the Town Clerk condemned the City Council for its 'irresponsible' behaviour in delaying a decision about the 50p rent rise (op. cit., 9 February 1973, p. 1). The Labour Group inevitably lost this battle with central government and in the event only 3 Labour councillors were prepared to defy the law (op. cit., 30 March 1973). One of these three was Cllr Corr, who criticized his own party's attitude to the Housing Finance Act. He:

> . . . berated the Labour Party, from the Parliamentary Party and the NEC down to the local group and also assailed the local Tenants' Action Committee. He wanted to know why they were not at the meeting howling their protests. (*Lancaster Guardian*, 6 April 1973, p. 11)

There is little doubt that the Labour Group lost a good deal of credibility by backing off this issue. However local government reorganization meant that the issue more or less disappeared off the election agenda in that year (possibly to the relief of Labour) and in fact never arose in the same form again.

[. . .] Up to the late 1960s it was difficult for the Labour Party to gain electoral support – particularly in view of the lack of a strong industrial wing of the labour movement. Where Labour did gain support in the town was over non-economic, non-industrial issues, and housing was one such issue. Mobilization around housing was significant in building some kind of base for Labour support in the town in the late 1930s. The same was true of both the 1950s and the early 1970s. This indicates the importance of 'urban politics' in understanding local political environments. Tenants' movements seem to have galvanized Labour into action on several occasions, often showing the way towards wider popular political participation and new modes of protest. The Lancaster Labour Party had not tended to organize public demonstrations, for instance, yet this was surely one way of reducing the apparent political inhibitions of groups in the town. Yet for its part Labour in Lancaster seems to have a poor record for capitalizing on these 'neighbourhood capacities' – which could have formed a basis of support – and in translating them into sustained electoral support. In spite of the stirrings of Labour in Lancaster in the late 1930s for instance, a Conservative MP was elected in 1945 by a surprisingly large majority (of 7723). One reason for the inability of any political party to capitalize on neighbourhood capacity may have been the absence of women from

Lancaster politics and the fact that Lancaster seems to have had, in the past at least, a strongly patriarchal element in the workplace and in domestic life [. . .]

Industrial politics

The local organization of the industrial wing of the labour movement was also in transition. After over sixty years of industrial quiescence, Lancaster's factory workers began to engage openly in industrial struggles. Strikes became frequent in the manufacturing sector after 1967. At Storeys labour was withdrawn by engineers in 1967 and 1971, by electricians in 1967 and by process workers in 1968, 1973, 1974 and 1976; at Lansils, by this time a branch plant of Monsanto, there was a three-week mass strike over pay and the establishment of a closed shop in 1969; and at Nelsons engineers were out in 1970 and many groups of workers were involved in a series of disputes in 1975. These new practices did not have a direct impact on local politics because, as often happens, industrial militancy did not extend past the factory gates for most workers. For instance, the sample of workers made redundant by Williamsons in 1967 and interviewed by Martin and Fryer (1973) were politically moderate (or, rather, ambiguous), although well disposed to trades unions. These men probably did not alter their political convictions radically, but the experience of employment shifts and job loss in manufacturing began to filter through to the labour organizations in the town.

Lancaster Trades Council changed abruptly in the late 1960s and early 1970s, adopting a more overtly political stance. This change arose from two causes: firstly, the influx of different types of workers (those in education seem to have played a particularly significant part); and, secondly, from the reduced passivity of workers in the traditional industrial base of Lancaster which followed from the extension of trade unionism. These two aspects co-existed uneasily and gave rise to internal strife within the trade union movement in the town. However, a lengthy period of inaction was broken and the Trades Council became a lively, if divided, forum in the early 1970s.

Early 1970 saw complaints from union delegates about the organization of the Trades Council: 'the local trades union movement', complained one TGWU rep., 'was not organized professionally as they would like . . .' (*Lancaster Guardian*, 9 January 1970, p. 1) and the Chair of the TGWU argued that most Lancaster workers had little faith in the Trades Council since most of the business conducted there was irrelevant. Making a very clear distinction between trade union and other issues he argued that:

> Biafra, Vietnam, double yellow lines, parking spaces, books for schools etc., all very commendable subjects I feel sure, debated by members of the WI . . . All very safe subjects requiring little effort from the leaders of the Trades Council, but certainly not subjects likely to stir the muddy depths to which Lancaster has sunk. No wonder there is so little interest and delegates do not attend in any great numbers. (op. cit., 16 January 1970, p. 12)

By contrast, what the Trades Council should concern itself with was the '. . . . plight of the working population of Lancaster . . . Surely they must realize how poorly paid the workers of Lancaster are.' Poor levels of pay in Lancaster were frequently linked by trade unionists to the weakness of the trade union movement there. The Chair of NUBSO (K shoe factory) also complained that the Trades Council consisted of 'puppets on a string'. 'It is high time the strings on this Trades Council were cut to give the people of Lancaster a well-deserved better deal', she argued (op. cit., 23 January 1970).

These criticisms coalesced around a critique of the Trades Council leadership, in particular the TGWU complained that USDAW members dominated the executive. The President of the Trades Council, an ex-Storeys worker, had been in office continuously since 1950 and in 1970 complaints were put to the TUC that he was no longer a delegate from a trade union branch (although he was then a member of USDAW). The TGWU, in particular, argued he should stand down. In March 1971 the presidency went to a new candidate breaking a 21-year-tradition. The new President in that year, Abbot Bryning, significantly did not come as a representative of the traditional economic base of Lancaster: he was a lecturer in economics at the local further education college. In 1974 a woman President, a delegate from the Musicians' Union, was elected (op. cit., 8 March 1974, p. 7) and in 1975 she was replaced by an ASTMS delegate, a Senior Lecturer from the university (op. cit., 9 January 1976, p. 15). These changes signify a break in the politics of the Trades Council which was accompanied by a resolve that the Trades Council should show more leadership in the fight to preserve the rights of unions, a decision which saw the Trades Council involve itself more in organizing marches and protest meetings (op. cit., 5 March 1971).

However, although the Trades Council did not become more involved in local political issue, staging marches and demonstrations against, for instance, the Industrial Relations Bill and the issue of increased council rents, involvement was very limited among the traditional Lancaster working class. In December 1970 it was announced that the Trades Council was to launch an offensive against the government's Industrial Relations Bill and an action day demonstration was held, but it was mainly students and staff from the university who turned out (about 300 men and women were on the demonstration). A *Lancaster Guardian* editorial said:

> The one-day strike called by militant left-wing factions on Tuesday made no impression on Lancaster industry and workers generally obeyed the advice of trade union leaders at local and national level to remain at their employment.

Support for a demonstration against the Housing Finance Bill in late 1972 was 'dismal'. On this demonstration, as on several others organized by the Trades Council around this period, not only did trade unionists not turn out but even Trades Council delegates were absent (op. cit., 9 February 1973, p. 19). In May 1973 only 45 factory workers in Lancaster stopped work for a day in support of the TUC's call for May Day protest against the government's Wages and Prices policy, but more than 700 workers at Heysham power station and 120 footplate men at British Rail Lancaster together with 40 ASTMS members at the university stopped work (op. cit., 4 May 1973, p. 1). A May Day March in 1976 was a 'near flop'. Although the Trades Council had organized it only 50 people turned up, representing Lancaster Communist Party, Young Socialists, the Lancaster Right to Work Campaign, the TGWU and the Campaign for Homosexual Equality (op. cit., 7 May 1976, p. 3). In 1977 the by now annual May Day March was reduced to only 30 people (op. cit., 6 May 1977, p. 7) (although in 1979 300 people were on it).

Against the backdrop of increased industrial militancy there was some involvement of IS and IMG (International Marxist Group) members in industrial action and this gave rise to complaints about socialist organizations claiming to speak for the official trade union movement. In 1969 a local TGWU official condemned a pamphlet published by a 'student-worker' group:

> We object most strongly to people from outside, whether students or not, attempting to intervene in industrial affairs which are of no concern to them. (*Lancaster Guardian*, 24 October 1969, p. 1)

The reply to such charges was '. . . what has the official trade union movement in Lancaster done to educate its members? Where is the campaign spearheaded by the Trades Council and backed by trade union branches to educate the membership . . .' (op. cit., 4 December 1970). By 1972 such complaints had extended to the Trades Council itself. The Storeys Branch of the TGWU complained that Lancaster Trades Council was being unduly influenced by bodies outside of the official trade union movement and called for the resignation of the executive committee. The TGWU representative alleged there had been 'an infiltration of anarchists' into Lancaster in the last two years and the Trades Council had been influenced by them. The executive had not acted honourably and this had reflected on local trade unionism generally.' His resolution was heavily defeated (op cit., 6 December 1972, p. 1) [. . .]

Students were involved in other incidents of industrial unrest in the town – at Storeys, at Lansils and among building workers at Heysham power station. Student politics was not 'discrete' and spilled over into other aspects of the local political environment, usually to the condemnation of politicians and trade unionists.

Although there were changes in the Trades Council and the trades union movement generally in Lancaster, these changes were highly circumscribed and were more to do with a new generation of trade unionists from a different occupational background rather than a change of heart on the part of the traditional union base. Despite there having been much more union activity in Lancaster in the late 1960s and early 1970s, the Labour Party appeared to have more success when it organized around service issues and there was not a great deal of translation of workplace militancy into political mobilization, as the failure to organize marches and demonstrations on issues outside the workplace demonstrates. Lancaster Labour Party has never had very strong union inputs. In the face of a traditionally weak trade union movement, trade union organizers have concentrated on workplace rather than wider political issues. 'If an area's not all that strong politically', as one councillor put it, 'surely it's much more important for them to work through the trade union movement to safeguard industrial matters' (interview, Lancaster Labour County Councillor, 16 October 1985). This situation has continued into the 1980s. In the late 1960s the TGWU was the dominant union on the Trades Council and in the local Labour Party. With deindustrialization the membership base of that union has declined and it is now a relatively minor force politically. Yet no other one union has replaced its influence within the Lancaster labour movement.

Social movements

The previous sections referred to the involvement of left-wing groups in both campaigns over housing and in the industrial wing of the Lancaster labour movement. Another significant development in Lancaster politics in the first half of the 1970s was the appearance of other types of social movements. This was, of course, a national phenomenon but such groups appear to have taken root more firmly in the Lancaster area than elsewhere – certainly the size and intensity of such movements is stronger in Lancaster than in the comparative six localities in the [Economic and Social Research Council's] Changing Urban and Regional System project.

In common with the left-wing socialist groups that developed in the area in the late 1960s and early 1970s, individuals associated with the university played an important part in these movements, usually students rather than university employees, although the transient nature of the student population means that local support must have been built up within them. Members of such movements interviewed had, on the whole, come to Lancaster as students and had subsequently stayed in the area because it offered wide informal political networks. But such networks shift and change. The local women's movement in particular, lacking the more structured institutional base of the ecology and peace movements, has at certain points waned as key households in such networks [have moved] off.

Within the national Women's Liberation Movement in the 1970s Lancaster was well-known for its strength. This almost certainly developed through the university since wider gender politics in Lancaster in the '60s and '70s and in the previous period was fairly patriarchal [. . .] As we have seen, a Socialist Women's Group was active in the early 1970s, although after about 1974 there was a marked increase in radical feminist activity in the town. Consciousness-raising networks were significant in this development, as were forms of politics developed in the American women's movement at that time and imported via the university, which significantly was the first in Britain to teach women's studies as part of its undergraduate degree programme. Both radical and socialist feminists were involved in the setting up of a Women's Refuge in the town in 1974, although subsequently this became entirely run by radical feminists, and indeed served as the centre for radical feminist activity in the area. Subsequent activity produced a Rape Crisis line, an Incest Survivors' Group, a Reproductive Rights Group, a Women in Education Group, a Lesbian Line and a Lancaster Women's Newsletter, together with various other groups. However, informal women's networks have been more important in the Lancaster women's movement than any institutional bases, and perhaps one of the distinguishing features of Lancaster feminism has been a politics dependent on informal networks and celebrated through the cultural sphere. Lancaster Women's Conferences have been significant, as have women's discos, feminist book fairs, writing groups etc. Such phenomena are, of course, to be found in large cities, particularly in metropolitan areas, but are more surprising in a town the size of Lancaster, particularly since the local council has given no support to such activities whatsoever.

Socialist feminism, working through the channels of the local labour movement, apart from the very early 1970s, has been less strong. There was a successful campaign around maternity provision in the early 1970s and some involvement in workplace disputes. On the whole, though, socialist and liberal feminism which might have been expected to produce campaigns around issues of equal opportunity and levels of public service provision – campaigns present in other localities – have not been much in evidence in Lancaster. One explanation for this may lie in the absence of women from political activity historically in the town. Local political parties and the local authority in Lancaster have proved particularly impermeable to pressure from women's groups. The Women's Refuge, for instance, unlike refuges in other towns, has had very little help or support from the local council and in fact there were several attempts to close it down in the 1970s. Women from the refuge have found it extremely difficult to get rehoused by the City Council and relations with local social services have been extremely strained. Even as apparently innocuous a demand as the setting up of a well-woman clinic was only met after something of a struggle in Lancaster, while political issues around reproduction, especially abortion, have been highly contentious [. . .]

[In 1985] a Women's Section of the Lancaster Labour Party [was] re-established. A Women's Section had existed between c1920 and 1970 but was then abandoned, apparently because women wanted themselves seen as equal within the Labour Party rather than requiring a special section (Interview, Lancaster Labour City Councillor). In 1984 a more feminist Labour Party Women's Section was set up, although this seems on the whole to have drawn on women already in the labour movement rather than feminists outside the labour movement locally.

If various aspects of the local political environment in Lancaster, notably the local authority, have been more hostile to feminist issues than in other areas, the peace movement and environmental politics have, by contrast, been thoroughly incorporated into the local political environment. In terms of the latter, for instance, a Lancaster branch of the Green Party has now developed, growing fast between 1984 and 1987 and putting up candidates in both general and local elections. Concern about the environment, particularly about the local environmental effects of Heysham nuclear power station and the geographically close nuclear reprocessing complex at Windscale, is now expressed by a variety of local institutions – from the health authority to local political parties – and this issue has become incorporated into mainstream politics locally, although there were apparently no voices raised against the original siting decision in the early 1960s. The peace movement locally has had a significant impact on the local Labour Party. One Labour Party Councillor felt: 'CND is clearly an important force in Lancaster and within the Labour Party it reflects the concern that I think perhaps wasn't there twenty odd years ago' (interview, Lancaster Labour City Councillor).

> '. . . the women's group is . . . the most rapidly growing bit of the labour movement. It is . . . hard to gauge its political impact as yet, because it is only . . . a year old. CND very easily created a political impact because the bulk of the new membership who have joined the Labour Party in the last few years have been members of CND and that's meant that on that particular issue the Labour Party now has moved to the left . . . Lancaster Labour Party is overwhelmingly pro CND.' (ibid., p. 12)

[. . .]

11.3 Summary: political developments in Lancaster

Our account of changes in the political environment of Lancaster has described the town as originally a place in which local employers exercised a local hegemony. This concerned more than simply the transmission of sets of values, but was rather a widespread and diffuse system of domination. It was only with the erosion of a particular form of material base – the removal of the structural conditions which had maintained the subordination of the local factory proletariat – that an 'anti-socialist' climate of opinion could be fractured. Looked at through the eyes of Offe and Wiesenthal (1980), the 'dialogic' organization of labour was made impossible from both ends: fear turning into a sense of powerlessness on the part of labour, and monopolization of channels of communication to impose silence rather than public political discourse upon the local working class. The removal or breaking up of the conditions of dependence was the first prerequisite of the transformation of the local political environment.

Those conditions were being breached to some degree as the Labour Party built up support from the late 1930s, ironically a support based in mobilization around service provision (housing) originally requested locally by capital. 'Consumption issues' made some space for dialogical discourse and democratic participation, but that space remained limited for so long as the economic power of local employers remained intact. That power was reduced as a consequence of unionization in the early 1960s and as an outcome of the demise of local ownership. Williamsons amalgamated with Nairns of Kircaldy in 1963, and Lansils were taken over by Monsanto in 1964 [. . .] There is a certain irony in local ownership of firms, since it was not until local ownership began to disintegrate that a labour movement could develop in Lancaster. Lancaster workers lost out all ways through local ownership of firms. On the one hand it effectively prevented mobilization in pursuit of higher wages and better conditions; on the other hand these firms showed little loyalty to local workers [. . .]

A second important feature of a complex of local changes was the undermining of the system of internal labour markets in the early 1960s as a consequence of a tight labour market and the location of public sector institutions in the town. The building of the power station at Heysham was one cause of declining long-service 'loyalty' among manual workers, as tradesmen and labourers moved away from traditional employers to obtain higher wages. The university, training college and expansion of the hospitals must also have afforded more alternatives to non-skilled manual workers. The exclusivity of employment opportunities faded out in the 1960s, as workers began to move much more freely between even the big manufacturing firms. The onset of redundancies in the major firms must also have broken any illusion or expectation of a job-for-life, which condition had in most respects been honoured by the manufacturing establishments from the 1920s to the 1960s. Instructively, in interviews with Lancaster workers, older interviewees, a number of whom had started their careers with either Storeys or Williamsons, felt that the best way to get on was to stay with one firm while younger workers felt moving between employers was a better way of getting promotion.

We should also consider the impact of national trends, both in industrial relations and party politics. The spread of unionization in the 1960s could hardly be prevented by the local employers in the general climate of inflation and effective bargaining by organized workers in the later stages of the long boom. The increased popularity of Labour in the mid-1960s brushed off locally, allowing the party to make a more significant electoral impact than, for instance, in 1945. Labour's marginal and unexpected victory in the General Election of 1966 itself was a way of further encouraging Labourism, a part of the changing counsciousness.

The parochialism of Lancaster politics was breached by the impact of popular national political movements, very largely imported by the changing personnel of the area. The university – its students rather than its employees – were prominent in some of the more overtly combative political incidents of the later 1960s. Certainly, before the location of the university in the area, Lancaster showed no signs that it was about to spontaneously generate anarchist, Trotskyist or radical feminist activists!

No matter how much we talk of shifts in the industrial base or the occupational structure, or the removal of structural constraints which reproduce worker dependence, without political mobilization established political practices would not cease. It is significant that in Lancaster key spheres of mobilization concerned service provision rather than industrial conflict. In Lancaster, municipal welfare provision was not given priority by any political party before the Second World War. The political environment, in particular local forms of gender politics, kept welfare provision low down the political agenda (see further Mark-Lawson *et al.*, 1985). The exception to this, interestingly, was housing. Lancaster was fairly advanced in terms of municipal house-building (Cullingworth, 1963), but this was not a Labour Party project. As in some other towns (for example, Luton and Dagenham) local employers had a strong interest in ensuring that this form of provision was adequate, especially in the context of a buoyant local economy and significant in-migration in the inter-war period, because lack of good housing and very high rent levels meant that skilled workers could not be attracted to the area. This argument was still being used by the Conservative City Council in the later 1960s as a justification for the construction of council houses.

In the local political environment of Lancaster many welfare services were provided under alternative sets of social relations (voluntarism especially). This made it difficult for the local Labour Party to develop electoral support, when many of its nationally defined policies were not on the local political agenda. But ironically, once municipal house-building was under way, the local political environment was changed and a new cleavage created which gave the party a new set of capactities on which to draw (see Mark-Lawson, 1987).

The conservatism of the labour movement elite in the 1950s and 1960s, who seemed content to be respectable and accommodative, was itself upset by new personnel and new activists in urban issues who appeared a threat to the Labour Party by their radicalism. The social composition of the Labour Party itself changed. In the early 1970s, when welfare professionals began to play an important part in Lancaster politics, and again in the early 1980s, when Thatcherite Conservatism and economic retrenchment drove many of the late 1960s left-wing radicals into that party, Labour recruited new groups of supporters. Many of these were public sector employees, and Lancaster is a supporting case for Dunleavy's claim that sectoral cleavages are of political importance currently. Industrial restructuring, especially the replacement of private manufacturing employment by public service jobs, has had an impact on the personnel of local politics. It has also had an indirect effect in the creation of a new territorial politics, with division of organized interest emerging between Lancaster and More-cambe.

11.4 Conclusions

Our account should serve to show one point above all, that local political environments are complex phenomena, configurations of a wide range of institutions and practices. It follows that the relationship between industrial restructuring and political change is an indirect, mediated one: there is no possibility of reading off political change from an economic base. Lancaster's experience is a powerful reminder of this. As a town with a large factory proletariat it exhibited strong anti-Labour sentiment; as it deindustrialized, collective sentiments swung against Conservatism.

We hope also to have demonstrated the value of looking at local politics in terms of the structural constraints on action rather than through the glass of political culture. Previous analyses of Lancaster politics (Gooderson, 1975; Myall, 1976; Martin and Fryer, 1973; Piepe *et al.*, 1969) have too easily interpreted worker quiescence and extensive support for the Conservative Party at general elections in terms of a Conservative culture built on a paternalist politics and a deferential labour force. Yet it is not clear that workers were either particularly deferential or committed Conservatives. It was, rather, the removal of conditions of material dependence that made space for resistance to develop. Dependence rather than conviction accounts for the development of the labour movement in Lancaster. Similarly, the role of spatial coalitions after 1974 indicates the manner in which material bases and particular institutional configurations constrain political practice. There are good grounds for thinking that capital's mobility and the reorganization of local government have combined to make local territorial politics particulary important in the last decade.

Examination of Lancaster also suggests at least two new considerations in explaining local politics. One is that issues of service provision – of urban protest – may be critical to the development of local partisanship. Though Labour has been the party of the working class, it did not necessarily gain support through class antagonism in the workplace. Lancaster also gives a powerful example of some of the mechanisms behind employer hegemony, of the way in which, without direct intervention in political affairs, employer dominance can be sustained (cf Lukes, 1974). Particularly interesting in this respect are the operation of exclusive internal labour markets and the ways in which employers collaborated locally, using the geographical feature of relative isolation to their joint benefit.

Acknowledgement

This paper is based on research by the Lancaster Regionalism Group as part of the ESRC Initiative on the Changing Urban and Regional System. We are grateful to other members of the Group, and to colleagues in other teams in the Initiative for their contribution to this paper. Supporting evidence for many of our claims, especially as regards economic restructuring, can be found in the Lancaster Regionalism Group's series of Working Papers [. . .]

References

CLARKE, P. F. (1971) *Lancashire and the New Liberalism*, Cambridge, Cambridge University Press.

CULLINGWORTH, J. B. (1963) *Housing in Transition: A Case Study in the City of Lancaster, 1958–1962*, London, Heinemann.

DUNLEAVY, P. (1981) *The Politics of Mass Housing in Britain: A Study of Corporate Power and Professional Influence in the Welfare State*, London, Oxford University Press.

GOODERSON, P. (1975) *The Social History of Lancaster 1780–1914*, unpublished PhD thesis, University of Lancaster.

LUKES, S. (1974) *Power: A Radical View*, London and Basingstoke, Macmillan.

MARK-LAWSON, J. (1987) *Women, Welfare and Urban Politics, 1917–1936*, unpublished PhD thesis, University of Lancaster.

MARK-LAWSON, J., SAVAGE, M. and WARDE, A. (1985) 'Women and local politics: struggles over welfare, 1918–39', pp. 195–215 in Murgatroyd, L., Savage, M., Shapiro, D., Urry, J., Walby, S. and Warde, A. (1985) *Locality, Class and Gender*, London, Pion.

MARTIN, R. and FRYER, R. H. (1973) *Redundancy and Paternalist Capitalism: A Study in the Sociology of Work*, London, George Allen and Unwin.

MOSER, C. A. and SCOTT, W. (1961) *British Towns: A Statistical Survey of Social and Economic Differences*, London, Oliver and Boyd.

MYALL, A. E. (1976) *Changes in Social Control in Lancaster 1913–38*, unpublished MA thesis, University of Lancaster.

OFFE, C. and WIESENTHAL, H. (1980) 'Two logics of collective action: theoretical notes on social class and organizational form', pp. 67–115 in Zeitlin, M. (ed.), *Political Power and Social Theory*, Greenwich, CT, Jai Press.

PELLING, H. (1967) *Social Geography of British Elections, 1885–1910*, London and Basingstoke, Macmillan.

PIEPE, A. *et al.* (1969) 'The location of the proletarian and deferential worker', *Sociology*, Vol. 3, No. 2, pp. 239–44.

PUGH, M. (1985) *The Tories and the People 1880–1935*, Oxford, Basil Blackwell.

TODD, N. (1976) *A History of Labour in Lancaster and Barrow-in-Furness c1890–1920*, unpublished MA thesis, University of Lancaster.

12 Local politics and the economy: the case of Sheffield

D. Blunkett and K. Jackson

Although local politics has been attempting to provide alternative examples for future national policy and influencing the political agenda, it has never suggested that a local approach could on its own provide the answer. There has been an emphasis on analysis and research which places the local economy in the context of international patterns of trade, ownership and control, the development of new technology and the availability and best use of resources.

Trade unions and community organizations have begun to develop a two-way process of communication. The debate on industrial decline and the re-emergence of large-scale unemployment has increased interest in the economic and social consequences for many people unconcerned with such issues for many years. The potential for raising consciousness and providing adult and continuing education opportunities has therefore re-emerged in a way not seen since wartime mobilization made such an exercise both necessary and possible. The numbers involved should not be exaggerated, but the opportunity to know and understand is just as important. For example, in its report, *Sheffield: The Second Slump* (1982), Sheffield Trades Council showed how employment and unemployment in Sheffield was increasingly determined by the decrease of multinational 'conglomerate' companies like Lonrho and RTZ. Special steel firms like Aurora were closed from a combination of rationalization and asset stripping.

Carrying out research and providing information [are] not enough in [themselves] to enable a debate to take place effectively. It is for this reason that local employment departments or units have backed trade union support groups, unemployed workers' centres, community groups and similar organizations as vehicles for seeking two-way communication between the local state and the community on economic issues. A particularly impressive example is the Merseyside Trade Union Resource Centre, funded mainly through Merseyside County Council and opened officially on 1 June 1985, whose objectives were 'to harness the enormous human potential in the area which has been ignored by successive governments, to integrate the activities of trade unionists and unemployed within a single collective endeavour'.

Large centres like these, where local authorities are sometimes backing up initiatives taken by the Trades Union Congress and local trade councils, are linked in some authorities to smaller local centres which provide neighbourhood facilities. It is a network that tries to prevent the unemployed from carrying the burden of industrial change as individuals, and gives both the unemployed and trade unionists in work an opportunity to contribute to local social and economic policy.

A different form of debate comes from councils joining workers in threatened industrial plants, as when the shop stewards committee at GEC Traction was faced with the proposed closure of their works at Attercliffe, Sheffield. Through the council's Employment Department, they made contact with workers in GEC's other plants, and developed a feasibility plan around a programme of investment in railway electrification and new rolling stock, that would have secured the future of their plant, and of course improved the country's rail network. Such plans were already available at British Rail headquarters, but frozen for lack of government capital borrowing approval.

The work gathered national interest, and a conference on railway electrification held in Sheffield on 10 October 1983 brought together all three main national rail unions, local branches and shop stewards committees of these and other unions in engineering, trades councils and local authorities, to consider the proposals and their implications both for the railways and their supply industries. Ironically at the point when the strength of the argument gained national credibility, the fight of the 750 workers at GEC Traction was coming to an end. The plant finally closed at the beginning of 1984, but the stupidity of the decision was clear.

[. . .] Local government today, as in the past, can offer its own entrepreneurship and enterprise in facing the enormous economic and social change which technology and industrial restructuring bring. As with the response to the Industrial Revolution and its aftermath in Britain, so in the late twentieth century local government has something to offer. The examples in the past of local government's role in providing electricity, gas, transport, telecommunications and construction, can all be reflected in the modern initiatives for meeting social need.

The free market is inefficient in matching supply and demand. Unless the form of demand can easily be turned to profit by a producer, it will be left unsatisfied. Democratic political institutions present an alternative way of providing for need, irrespective of the short-term gain to the producer.

Within the local authority the potential exists for workers themselves to generate enterprise. They can see what is happening to their jobs and recognize the obvious things which need to be provided, whether goods or services. They can see where goods purchased are inadequate for the task in hand or where they are simply not available at all. Skills, initiative, land, property and equipment all exist within the locality and yet often stand idle or are misused because an immediate profit cannot be made.

'Trade waste' is the business of collecting and disposing of any refuse from commerical or industrial premises, including major public facilities like hospitals. Councils have long been encouraged *not* to put this out to private contractors; Alec Douglas Home, later Conservative Prime Minister, was responsible in the 1950s for a report which showed the consequences of the operation of price cartels if it was left to private enterprise.

Until 1979 Sheffield City Council regarded the service as part of public health and provided it at no charge, but government policy changes required a direct charge to be levied by the council for the removal of trade waste. Hargreaves, Wimpey, Leigh and others started to expand into this area now that profits could be made. They could invest heavily in equipment and cut prices until a contract was secured and then steadily increase prices again as competition disappeared.

Sheffield's Cleansing Department began to lose contracts to the private sector, some of them big ones like the university. (Sixty-nine contracts were lost between May 1983 and April 1984.) The workforce, whose livelihoods were at stake, were worried. Management in the Cleansing Department wanted to compete but felt unable to match multinational companies in terms of investment. They talked around reducing pay and conditions and possibly the size of the workforce in order to reduce costs. The workforce argued for investment in sophisticated plant, symbolized for them by the private sector's 'big-bite' vehicles which were capable of easily shifting more than any council vehicle could. In the end, neither of these two approaches prevailed, yet contracts were won back and the city's capacity to deal with this public service was greatly improved.

Two trade unionists in the Cleansing Department, members of the local authority shop stewards' association, knew about the work of the Joint Works Group [. . .] and the City Employment Department's Public Sector Team. They made the necessary connections, and the entrepreneur in this case, therefore, was not an individual but a group of councillors, officers from a number of council departments, and trade union members. While recognizing the immediate problem a long-term view was taken. How could contracts be won on a stable basis and service firmly established? The answer was versatility, the ability to gain access to the widest variety of premises, and to cope as required with many different materials which large unwieldy vehicles had failed to do. By pooling experience a four-point strategy emerged based on capital investment in new equipment – bins, skips, miniskips, vehicles and adaptors; a low pricing policy; a co-operative approach to work reorganization; and lively promotion and publicity.

Within six months, £35 000 worth of work was won back, including that for the university and the health authority. Work-site meetings between councillors and the workforce threw up many suggestions about how improvements could be made and how work practices could be adapted to do a better job. Municipal enterprise has an old-fashioned ring to it but it showed itself here to be perfectly capable of competing effectively with the private sector [. . .]

12.1 Training, developing local skills and knowledge

A further area of intervention in which local politics has demonstrated a creativity absent at national level is the exploration of forms of training appropriate to the changing economic and social climate. But while there have been some useful experiments, these should not hide the enormous lack in Britain of local planning for training in line with known predictions of the demand for different skills. This kind of planning for relevant training can only be done through the development of employment plans for the local economy. Such local initiatives could then be integrated into national plans for job creation and the expansion of specific sectors of the economy [. . .]

In Sheffield it was felt important to develop the supporting resources first. In 1983 a Product and Technology Development Centre was established jointly by the city council and the polytechnic and the Centre for Advanced Manufacturing Technology was funded by the city polytechnic and a skills centre. This offers training on technologically advanced equipment along with support for its introduction in local industry. A Micro-Systems Centre also began work. In 1984 a Business and Management Development Programme was started, again a joint activity between the council and the polytechnic. Meanwhile discussions were under way with the university and Sheffield's five research associations so that their skills and resources could also be tapped.

The physical proposals – land and buildings – were developed as soon as the resource network began to come together. A number of secondments have been arranged from the polytechnic to the city council to ensure that key faculties – Technology, Business and Design – could play their full role. Presentations of the proposals to public and private sector agencies at regular intervals brought in their support and enabled them to contribute to the overall development.

The Sheffield Science Park provides a physical base for further development of the Business and Technology Support Network – for example in the Product Development Workshops which are run by SCEPTRE (Sheffield Centre for Product Development and Technological Resources). The park will also provide accommodation ranging from rent-a-desk up to attractive facilities for technology and science-based companies. Beyond this, work is in hand to link the Science Park with facilities in the Lower Don Valley New Employment Park in the east end of Sheffield where the rationalization of the steel industry has taken its greatest toll on jobs and the environment. As the environment in the valley improves, it should be possible to provide larger and permanent facilities for expanding firms, whether from the Science Park, the New Employment Park, enterprise workshops, or private sector developments, to facilitate the establishment of new firms in the city.

The links mentioned earlier between different educational institutions and research bodies form a fertile ground for product development. In 1985 Sheffield's Product Development Officer produced the following list of successful council-funded developments:

(a) the Tryad, designed ergonomically for disabled users (this is a shower unit which incorporates a WC and a washbasin);

(b) the washbasin for wheelchair users;

(c) shower chair, sink units and kitchen furniture for the disabled;

(d) a 'hearing aid' for the profoundly deaf (SESAD);

(e) early diagnostic equipment for deafness;

(f) orthopaedic implants such as hip joints;

(g) radiotherapy equipment such as the collimeter and syringe shields (Medical Equipment Manufacturers, Sheffield);

(h) hair-care products for the black community;

(i) the advanced dehumidifier to alleviate condensation problems;

(j) MEVA reading aid for the partially sighted (SCEPTRE);

(k) 'Audiocalc' spreadsheet software packages for blind users (SCEPTRE);

(l) Computer Numerically Controlled (CNC) lathe for schools (Abbeydale Engineering – small business);

(m) metal sensor (Parkway Instruments – co-operative).

Much of this work has been centred on SCEPTRE, linking good ideas with the ability to carry them through to production and marketing of the final article.

Many local authorities have acted as brokers and catalysts for new training and product development networks. The councils deploy their purchasing power, their limited investment funds and the infrastructure of educational and scientific institutions to provide a lever to gain the involvement of banking and industrial concerns. Universities and research institutes, private business and co-operative development agencies all contribute. London's technology network, Leed's training workshops, Sheffield's Centre for Product Development and Technological Resources, and the Enterprise Centre in a smaller district like Barnsley, are examples of variations on the theme.

In describing the relationship between economic policies and plans for meeting social need, we have outlined the importance of local government as a hub from which new initiatives and job creation measures can be built into the national framework. By providing a way of drawing together the needs of the consumers or users of services with those producing or delivering goods and services, local government in its new role can, in a small way, help the process of making sense of otherwise competing or conflicting interests which the unregulated market economy cannot do.

[. . .] At the heart of these programmes are the men and women who produce the goods and services. Local politics cannot easily overturn centuries of economic and political organization and power relationships in which the division of labour has produced major inequalities between workers and taken away creativity and control over their work. But somewhere a start has to be made.

Many enterprising policies have been destroyed or soured by resistance from the workers themselves, due to lack of adequate explanation and appreciation of what was intended. In addition, there is always the fear of adverse changes in working conditions, or even the fear of change itself. Lack of interest in the job is understandable from those on the lowest pay and working in the most unfavourable conditions. Sometimes trade unionists are guilty of exaggerated defensiveness and short-sightedness when responding to new proposals; sometimes there is political disagreement; but the main problem is poor pay, status and conditions among workers.

In 1985 Sheffield's employment department funded a project to improve and defend local authority services and jobs. Starting in two departments – parks/recreation and the cleaners and caretakers in the education department – shop stewards and workers were given time and resources to produce a report with the help of an independent national organization, Services to Community Action and Trade Unions (SCAT), with a brief to look critically at ways of improving both services and the quality of work. The first reports made compelling reading. The cleaners' report was called *We're Coming Out From Under The Carpet*. Levels of satisfaction with work were not high. The reasons were many – rushed jobs, corner-cutting bonus schemes, lack of materials, dirty unpleasant jobs and, again, low pay.

> 'Management should come out and look at the standard of work, instead of looking at good bonuses on work sheets.'
>
> 'Top management do not have the interest or sometimes the practical know-how.' (SCAT, 1985)

However, for some people, job satisfaction was high, particularly where there was good management and positive relationships with the workforce. The point was frequently made that more training and more opportunity to use talents and skills would be helpful. Darlington Shop Stewards' Committee carried out a similar exercise with SCAT, reporting in 1987, and the practice is spreading in local authority trade unionism.

Even with very restricted budgets, some local authorities are trying to include in their spending plans special sums for increasing the lowest pay and introducing equal status in holidays and conditions. Sheffield City Council, along with Glasgow and the London Boroughs of Camden and Islington, have pioneered policies on a minimum wage for their workforce and on equalizing conditions between white-collar staff and manual and craft employees. Sheffield City Council has gone farthest in this respect by raising the minimum wage to £100.20 for a basic week from 1 April 1987 and has been involved in campaigning for this important issue to become a key part of the Labour Party's anti-poverty strategy at national level.

The logic of increasing the attractiveness of work, removing the need for those in employment to apply for national and local benefits to supplement their income, and providing the status gained from adequate reward for a job done, is self-evident. For the national exchequer, the gains are also obvious. Benefit payments are reduced, and higher incomes yield both tax and national insurance income to the Treasury. Increased income results in increased consumption of goods and services of an essential nature which rarely include luxury items that threaten the balance-of-trade position.

Improving the quality of work also involves treating public-service workers as more than mere 'hired hands'. In Sheffield 'Take Ten', a programme of ten weeks on paid educational leave for a full day per week for non-vocational education, enables low-paid and manual workers in the authority to attend a specially designed course in the adult education service. It had its origins in a seminar provided for the council by the Northern College of Adult Education in South Yorkshire. The seminar debated Braverman's critical summary of scientific management in modern industry, which has been transferred to the public services with serious consequences. 'The manager assumes', Braverman reminds us, 'the burden of gathering together all of the traditional knowledge, which in the past has been processed by the work people, and then of classifying, tabulating and reducing this knowledge to laws, rules and formulae. All possible brain work should be removed from the shop floor and centred in the planning and laying out department (Braverman, 1974, pp. 112–13). 'Take Ten' is a small contribution to the process of liberating the creativity of local authority workers so that they can make the full contribution to society of which they are capable.

Of all the difficulties in creative local politics, extending and developing industrial democracy and worker involvement is probably the most difficult to surmount; it requires imagination, inventiveness from workers, trade unions and employers, and above all, a determination to press on. We shall need to turn to tried and tested practices elsewhere such as the worker self-management schemes pioneered in Yugoslavia. The pressure on local government to reduce costs results in those most vulnerable finding their earnings threatened as part-time work is cut back, overtime is reduced and short-term, temporary government job schemes replace long-term, permanent employment.

References

BRAVERMAN, H. (1974) *Labor and Monopoly Capital: The Degradation of Work in the Twentieth Century*, New York, Monthly Review Press.

SERVICES TO COMMUNITY ACTION AND TRADE UNIONS (1985) *We're Coming Out From Under the Carpet*, April, Sheffield, SCAT.

Section V
Changing bases of political support

Introduction

In the 1980s some of the previously dominant assumptions of British politics, particularly in terms of electoral analysis, have been sharply questioned. The relationship which appeared to exist between voting and occupational class has been dramatically undermined between the 1960s and the 1980s. A declining proportion of the working class is voting Labour. In that sense at least it is agreed that there has been a structural change in the British political system. The chapters in this Section begin to explore the implications of this, considering the extent to which it reinforces the importance of political ideas, communication and ideology. Like the arguments in Section IV, here there is a stress on the role of political actors (including political parties), but in this case with the main evidence coming from the national level.

Paul Webb, in Chapter 12, notes the declining relevance of union membership to voting in general elections even among the manual working class. Although he acknowledges that a subjective identification by individuals as part of the working class is a better guide to voting behaviour than occupational class he also confirms that union membership no longer generates a positive identification with class. In other words, Webb argues that trade unions do not play a major role in generating class consciousness. He is, however, reluctant to explain this in terms of broad processes of social change and instead points to the growth of instrumental attitudes which weaken the direct link of manual trade union members to Labour. To gain support from this group a political party needs to be able to provide the material benefits which its members seek.

But this also implies a potentially different role for unions and political organization. On this model no party can simply rely on passive support and unions may also have to become involved in more direct political campaigning on particular issues, rather than simply as supporters of one or other political party. In Chapter 13, in a rather different context, Dunleavy and Husbands also show the importance of political ideas and political communication at a time when basic allegiances can no longer be taken for granted. They argue forcibly that the press can have a significant influence on voting patterns and suggest that previous research which has indicated a high degree of self-selection at the level of the individual newspaper tends to underestimate the influence of the overall Conservative balance within the industry as a whole. Their analysis suggests that the broad ideological context set by the press is important in influencing electoral behaviour.

The final chapter looks explicitly at ideological change, and Heath, Jowell and Curtice stress that it cannot solely be explained in terms of social change. They argue that political parties help to shape values, but only within the constraints set by social structures and existing class values, and that change has been slower and more incremental than is often suggested. Heath *et al.* neatly set out the consequences of the ideological shifts they identify in the form of a 'map' (Table 15.5) which indicates that the distribution of gains and losses between political parties may be less clear-cut than is sometimes assumed. In particular, they have not simply favoured the Conservative Party at the expense of others. This suggests that the role of political leaderships in constructing coalitions of support is particularly important, above all for Labour whose 'heartland' (to use the terminology of Heath *et al.*) has declined while new potential voters identified (by the authors) have yet to be won over. In the 1980s, however, it has been the Conservatives who have been able both to consolidate their 'heartland' and maximize electoral support from their more marginal voters.

The chapters in this Section are those in the book which most explicitly look for political explanations for political phenomena, but they also refer back to social change with which political change interacts. There is little reference to economic processes, and none to spatial differentiation or uneven development. Yet their arguments cannot be divorced from the earlier Sections of the book and the arguments within them which set the context within which political decisions are made. At the very least they impose important structural constraints, and they may also more directly influence political processes. Certainly, the implication of some of the earlier chapters is that social and economic processes set political ones in train. Authors in this Section would be highly sceptical of such claims. It is not the intention of this book to set down any conclusion to this cross-disciplinary debate about the ways in which British politics ought to be analysed, so it is probably important to note that the inclusion of these chapters at the end of the book is not intended to imply that their emphasis is 'right' and the others 'wrong'. On the contrary, as we argued in the introduction, we believe that bringing articles from these different starting-points together should make it possible to achieve a more rounded picture of change in British politics and the state since the mid-1960s.

Allan Cochrane

13 Union, party and class in Britain: the changing electoral relationship, 1964–1983

Paul Webb

Despite the abundance of literature and comment upon the political involvement of British trade unions, surprisingly little work of any detail has been directed towards the impact that unions might have upon voting behaviour. (For a rare, and little publicized, example, however, see Freyman, 1980.) Yet, given that the burgeoning field of electoral studies has been indicating clearly for some time the widespread state of flux in which the British electorate finds itself, it is surely not unreasonable to assume that unions might comprise an element of this pattern of change. Andrew J. Taylor, in his interesting article on the growing politicization of non-partisan unions [. . .], summarizes what is perhaps a widely held view about this: 'There is, then, no inevitable connection between the citizen as union member and as voter, especially as the link between class, union and voter has weakened appreciably . . .' (Taylor, 1987, p. 8).

By implication, the declining incidence of Labour aligned working-class trade unionism means that, increasingly, it is the politics of non-partisan unions that will come to be of concern. But is the party–union–class nexus becoming irrelevant? For electoral analysts, Taylor's observation in many ways sums up the presumed obsolescence of the partisan identification model of voting behaviour with regard to trade unions. This 'traditional' view of union influence, since the pioneering work of Butler and Stokes in the 1960s, implies that union membership is likely, via a process of socialization, to reinforce the basic class loyalties and partisan attachments that determine voting choice (Butler and Stokes, 1969, Ch. 7). Whilst this orthodoxy has come to be challenged in certain quarters (see Dunleavy and Husbands, 1984, p. 9), there are others who appear to continue to regard it as the most useful way of understanding union effects for the present (see, for instance, Franklin, 1985, p. 17). The purpose of this article is to draw upon available British election study data to present some basic evidence that may help clarify the situation; just how far is it [. . .] reasonable to assert that the 'link between class, union and party has weakened appreciably'?[1]

13.1 Unionization, vote and partisanship between 1964 and 1983

Given that the voting decision of an individual most probably results from the interplay of a number of influences, both social and political, it might be useful to start by grasping some impression of the overall significance of union membership in such a context. A common approach to this sort of task involves the construction of a model of the major factors in the social background of an individual that are held to influence the way in which he or she votes. Typically, unionization would be one of the variables included in such a model.[2] [. . .] Given that the essence of social background effect in Britain since the war is commonly held to have been that of social class, it follows that the model should probably be one of class voting.[3] [My] analysis reveals that the [. . .] coefficient expressing the relationship between union membership and vote stood at .19 in 1964, but only at .09 in 1983. Thus, it can be confirmed that union membership does indeed appear to have lost some of its importance for determining the way that people vote.

Turning to Table 13.1, we notice an interesting aspect of this broad generalization: the erosion of the vote–unionization relationship appears to be restricted to manual workers only. This much is clearly demonstrated by the odds ratios presented on two party voting. These ratios highlight the distinctiveness of *unionists'* behaviour by dividing the odds on them voting Labour rather than Conservative by the odds on *non-unionists* doing so. (A ratio of 1:1 would indicate that the relative strengths of the two parties were identical amongst members and non-members alike.) Thus it is clear that union membership divides manuals less in 1983 than in 1964 (the odds ratio falling from 3.02 to 1.79), whilst its impact on non-manuals is virtually

Table 13.1
Vote by unionization for manual and non-manual workers, 1964 and 1983

	1964			
	Manual		Non-manual	
	Member	Non-member	Member	Non-member
Conservative	21	36	40	61
Labour	66	38	27	19
Other	4	13	21	14
Abstained	10	14	12	7
	100%	100%	100%	100%
Odds ratio	3.02		2.27	
	1983			
Conservative	22	30	34	50
Labour	41	31	22	12
Other	19	18	31	23
Abstained	17	21	13	15
	100%	100%	100%	100%
Odds ratio	1.79		2.75	

unchanged. Why should this be the case? One possible source of dealignment might be the changing occupational and social profile of union membership over the past decade or two. Whilst the most obvious single departure, the growth of white-collar unionism, cannot help explain changes in political alignment amongst *manual* workers, what about the effect of other notable changes in recent union recruitment? Researchers and commentators have, for instance, frequently referred to the feminization, de-skilling and public sector bias of modern union memberships (see, for example, Massey and Miles, 1984). Is it likely that any of these areas of membership growth are especially disinclined to offer Labour their support at the ballot box? Such evidence as has emerged from electoral study to date suggests, in fact, that this is not the case. To take the questions of gender, for instance, the clearest evidence as yet produced suggests that female manual unionists are decisively more *pro*-Labour than their male counterparts (Dunleavy and Husbands, 1985, p. 133). Thus, the influx of women recruits can hardly be said to offer a plausible explanation of the *anti*-Labour drift of manual trade unionists. And a similar picture emerges from the evidence on skill levels and production sector: Rose and McAllister have produced evidence which implies that the substitution of unskilled for skilled recruits would probably enhance Labour's standing within the ranks of manual unionists (Rose and McAllister, 1986, p. 58). Again, public sector employment is associated with support for Labour; in any case, production sector has so far only been shown to have any significant effect upon the voting behaviour of non-manual employees (Dunleavy and Husband, 1985, p. 132).

If social and occupational change alone does not appear to offer a promising account of Labour's decline within the heart of the trade union movement, it may be more propitious to consider a more narrowly 'political' explanation. For example, it is not inconceivable that it is precisely within the ranks of the traditional 'core' segments of Labour's support (which includes the manual unionist) that the sense of disillusionment with the party's performance over the past two decades is greatest. In this context, one thinks particularly of the effect upon the partisan affinity of manual unionists that the turbulent party–union battles over incomes policy might have had during the 1960s and 1970s. It is interesting that others have discovered that it was exactly this 'core' that was most susceptible to these events during the decade betwen 1964 and 1974; during the period of the 1964–1970 Labour governments, the party and the unions became estranged over the question of incomes restraint, only to be subsequently reconciled in the face of the new Conservative Government's Industrial Relations Act of 1971. Electoral behaviour in 1970 and 1974 corresponded closely to this pattern of events.

> The estrangement and reconciliation pattern of alignment was shown by unionists but not by non-unionists, by working class unionists but not by middle class unionists, by unionists who identified with the working class but not by those who did not, by stationary working class unionists but not by

> those who were upwardly mobile. In short, the more traditional unionist sectors most clearly showed the effects of political events during the decade. (Freyman, 1980, p. 314)

By 1979 party–union relations had once again foundered, this time on the lacerating rocks of the so-called winter of discontent. Therefore, the declining significance of union membership for voting choice over the period as a whole may well reflect Labour's precipitous loss of support amongst disillusioned manual unionists; a glance at Table 13.1 suggests the obvious plausibility of this notion. By far the sharpest change is that affecting the cell accounting for Labour-voting manual members.

It might be added that, unsurprisingly perhaps, where Labour's vote does seem to have held up best since 1964, is amongst those considering themselves to be 'very strong' Labour partisans; overall, the 7 percentage point drop in vote that the party registered in this group compares with a decline that was two to three times greater amongst its weaker adherents. This is worth bearing in mind with regard to unions since it provokes the question of how the strength of Labour's partisan following held up amongst unionists as compared to non-unionists. The brief answer seem to be 'not particularly well'; Table 13.2 clearly indicates that whereas the proportion of very strong Labour partisans has fallen by around 40 per cent within the unionized group of respondents since 1964, no commensurate change is discernible within the non-unionized group. Presumably, the factors which prevented manual unionists from voting Labour coincide with a weakened sense of general identity with the party.

13.2 Unions and class voting between 1964 and 1983

Historically, it has been assumed that the party–union link is the organizational expression of a social – i.e. class – phenomenon. For electoral theorists this has implied a union role founded upon the provision of a milieu that would reinforce class loyalty. But does it remain feasible to suppose that the trade union movement, taken as a whole, encourages working-class identity and class action at the ballot box? This is certainly not a picture that squares with the growing significance of non-partisan unionism. It would seem increasingly misconceived to think of the union movement as comprising a set of class typical institutions. Before the Great War trade union membership in Britain was 87 per cent manual; by the turn of the 1980s, this figure was a mere 56 per cent (Bain, 1983, p. 5). Indeed, Patrick Dunleavy has even demonstrated that with a control for production sector there is little overall association between class and unionization (Dunleavy and Husbands, 1985, p. 130). So what do the data reveal – is union membership especially associated with class-typical voting?

Table 13.2 Partisanship by unionization, 1964 and 1983

	1964		1983	
	Union	Non-union	Union	Non-union
Very strong Labour	34	14	14	10
Fairly strong Labour	23	16	22	13
Not very strong Labour	6	5	13	9
Other	13	17	23	23
Not very strong Conservative	3	6	4	10
Fairly strong Conservative	11	21	15	23
Very strong conservative	11	23	5	13
	100%	100%	100%	100%

Table 13.3 Two measures of class voting: occupational and subjective class voting amongst unionists and non-unionists, 1964 and 1983

	1964		1983	
	Union	Non-union	Union	Non-union
Occupational Class Voting				
Alford Index	38.2	19.1	18.8	19.2
Odds ratio	4.76	3.50	2.82	4.83
Subjective Class Voting				
Alford Index	40.9	36.1	25.9	23.7
Odds ratio	6.32	8.87	6.00	6.36

'Class voting' is a concept which has attracted considerable interest and not a little debate; in Table 13.3 two measures of occupational class voting are presented in terms of the simple manual/non-manual distinction. The widely employed 'Alford index' is calculated by subtracting the percentage of non-manual workers supporting Labour from the percentage of manual workers doing so; i.e., it is a simple comparison of support for Labour within the two occupational groups (Alford, 1963, pp. 79–86). As an alternative the odds ratio once again makes an appearance, this time comparing the odds on a *manual* worker voting Labour rather than Conservative, with the odds on a *non-manual* worker doing so. (For a debate on the technical advantages and drawbacks of the odds ratio as a measure of class voting, see Heath, Jowell and Curtice, 1985, p. 41; Crewe, 1986, pp. 623–30.) What seems clear from both measures is that, whilst union members were somewhat more likely than non-unionists to vote for the party 'typical' of their occupational class in 1964, this was no longer the case by 1983. The falling Alford index and odds ratio indicate this. The

Table 13.4 Subjective class by unionization for manual workers, 1964 and 1983

	1964		1983	
	Union	Non-union	Union	Non-union
Middle class	12	23	21	22
Working class	88	77	79	78
	100%	100%	100%	100%

incidence of class voting evidently declined within the group of unionized respondents; if anything, the reverse appears to have occured with non-unionists. However, it is possible that this approach to class voting is in certain respects too limited; Sartori, for instance, has argued that it is fundamentally erroneous to impute any form of class behaviour to individuals without knowing something about how consciously that behaviour is tied to perception and intention (Sartori, 1968, p. 13). Do people perceive the connection between class and their behaviour? Are they consciously acting out of a sense of class interest or loyalty? At the very least, therefore, we might insist that people can only be said to vote according to their class location when they are known to be *aware* of their class identity. Consequently, Table 13.3 also presents measures of 'subjective' class voting – that is, it defines class voting in terms of the propensity of people to vote according to their perceived class identity. Whilst the absolute levels of class voting do now increase, in one essential the picture remains unaltered: trade union members are no more likely to vote according to the identity of their self-perceived class than non-members are (and neither were they in 1964, we may add). Again, union membership does not appear to foster class voting.

This notwithstanding, we should not overlook the fact that class voting does increase in absolute terms when defined in terms of subjective class awareness. That is, in all cases subjective class voting levels are higher than simple occupational class voting levels, regardless of measurement technique. Class identity is important to class voting; more precisely, 'Labour requires class consciousness . . . the Conservatives do not' (Robertson, 1983, p. 86). Thus, if it can be shown that trade unions retain any impact upon class identity itself, then one might still be in a position to argue that they in some way encourage class voting. However, the data are unremitting; Table 13.4 indicates virtually no difference between the proportions of unionized and non-unionized manual workers who considered themselves to be working class by 1983. The insignificance of union milieu for class identity is, moreover, confirmed by a multiple classification analysis of subjective class; across the period, almost every other social background variable turned out to have a stronger impact on class identity than union membership.[3]

13.3 Conclusions

This chapter has briefly demonstrated that there is indeed evidence that the link between party, union and class has weakened, at least in so far as voting behaviour is concerned. The central problem that emerges is how to explain the heavy loss of support sustained by Labour amongst manual unionists. The simple fact that there has been an influx of certain types of member since the 1960s – such as women, the less skilled and public sector employees – does not seem to offer a promising way of understanding the change. Broader aspects of social change may well be informative, of course. Unions no longer have a distinctly manual profile, and the decline of traditional industries, changing patterns of residence and the geographic dispersion of unionism means that far fewer members now live in homogeneous occupational and cultural milieux (see Massey and Miles, 1984). In short, it seems virtually impossible to sustain the view that the union movement remains a class-typical organization which helps integrate its membership into a distinct sub-culture; the partisan identification model of voting, as far as union effects are concerned, has been rendered more or less obsolete.

Undoubtedly, then, processes of social change lie at the root of much that has happened to fracture the party–union–class relationship in the electoral context. Yet it is fundamentally dissatisfying for political science to rely on such baldly sociological explanations of what remain ultimately political phenomena. There is rarely, if ever, a one to one correspondence between social and political change. Hence, our understanding may be deepened by marrying sociological background with an account of more autonomous political level processes. In this respect, it was earlier suggested that the internal history of the Labour movement itself might not be unimportant. This calls to mind a general observation about the susceptibilities of parties that establish organic relationships with non-electoral organizations. Peter Mair has suggested that such parties 'lose control' of their established electoral bases to the extent that (*inter alia*) 'there is a weakening of links between parties and non-electoral organisations . . .' (Mair, 1983, p. 421). In assessing the usefulness of this explanation it is helpful to draw upon the theoretical and empirical work of industrial sociologists. An example is the classic (if not uncontroversial) work of Goldthorpe and Lockwood on working-class values. They concentrated upon manual workers employed in occupational growth areas; even in the 1960s they were able to pinpoint the fact that these 'affluent' workers bore a limited sense of communal loyalty. Despite identifying themselves as members of the working class, they shunned what Lockwood called a 'proletarian' or 'solidaristic' class perspective and focused inwards on their 'privatized' family situations (Lockwood, 1966; Goldthorpe *et al.*, 1969). Interestingly, they were found to regard the Labour movement itself in purely 'instrumental' and calculative terms. If this is an accurate picture of the attitudes of increasing numbers of manual workers during the past twenty years or so, the feasibility of our 'political level' explanation becomes clear: that is, rejection of the Labour Party is likely to follow relatively easily when basic affective loyalty has already worn thin. If the party proves unable to 'deliver the goods' by providing the economic and industrial environment best suited to their material aspirations, why should union members continue to support it? There remains no obvious reason, given the constraints of the 'instrumental' outlook. Ultimately, this sort of process may well have encouraged more and more manual union members to 'insulate their commitments', as Rose and McAllister have put it (1986, p. 59). To put it another way, we have the growth of 'non-partisan unionism'; thus, survey evidence tends to reveal that members approve of unions as economic interest representatives (Nielsen, 1985, p. 21), and may even approve of their occasional involvement in the political arena, but they rarely now support the 'direct and exclusive constitutional link with the Labour Party' (Torode, 1984, p. 21).

Finally, what are the broad implications of our findings for the role of unions in mobilizing electoral support in Britain? Although their general capacity to affect voting choice appears to have weakened, along with their significance for the socialization of class and partisan values, there is no necessary reason to conclude that their influence is waning terminally. Electoral theories other than the partisan identification model are suggestive in this respect. For example, Dunleavy and Husbands' 'radical' model implies that unions could have a role to play in the mobilization of a sectoral cleavage in British politics. Thus, certain unions could be significant in raising awareness about their members' interests as public sector employees; as yet however, there is little evidence to suggest that mobilization along sectoral lines of cleavage is strong, though this is not to say that we should blind ourselves to its potential (Dunleavy and Husbands, 1985, pp. 129–34). Alternatively, issue voting theorists might prefer the notion that unions could retain and develop a capacity to influence the assessments that voters make about important public issues (such as privatization, spending cuts). In this context it is arguable that the largely successful union campaigns on political funds demonstrate what might be possible. Alternatively, it may be that this presented union memberships with a very singular type of issue; many quite 'moderate' unionists seemed to resent an apparently heavy-handed attempt by the government to deny unions all access to the political area. Unions may not always be able to present the issues in such a clear-cut fashion. Moreover, Taylor drew attention to another limitation which a union like NALGO had already noted for itself: 'such campaigns should not coincide with general elections as the message is swamped and could have no impact on electoral behaviour' (Taylor, 1987, p. 10). Nonetheless, it would be unwise to discount entirely the potential that unions may have for influence in the context of an increasingly fluid and apartisan electorate.

Notes

1 The data sets employed are *Political Change in Britain, 1963–1970* (directed by D. Butler and D. Stokes), and the *British Election Study, 1983* (directed by A. Heath, R. Jowell, S. Field and J. Curtice). I gratefully acknowledge the ESRC data archive for making this material available to me.

2 Given the nature of the data that will be used here (which involves categorical level independent variables), an appropriate and simple statistical technique is that of *multiple classification analysis*. Using this procedure, derived from a straightforward analysis of variance, coefficients may be produced which summarize the relationship between unionization and vote, whilst controlling for the effects of other influences in the social background of an individual. (In some ways, these 'beta' coefficients, as they are called – based on the 'eta' statistic – are analogous to the beta weights of regression analysis (see Nie *et al.*, 1975, Ch. 22).) The class voting model employed here is based on that devised by Mark N. Franklin (see Franklin, 1985, p. 19). The independent variables were divided into the following categories: Occupation – Manual/Non-manual; Unionization – Member/Non-member; Housing – Council tenant/Other; Education – Minimum school leaving age/Other; Parental partisanship – Both Labour/Both Conservative/Other; Parental class – Father manual/Father non-manual. The dependent variable was the proportionate Labour vote.

3 The beta coefficients for unionization with subjective class as the dependent variable were just 0.04 for 1964 and 0.03 for 1983. The dependent variable was operationalized as a scale with the following values: −2=aware middle class; −1=unaware middle class; 1=unaware working class; 2=aware working class. ('Unaware' respondents initially replied that they 'did not know' to which class they felt they belonged, but chose between middle- and working-class identity when prompted by the interviewer.)

References

ALFORD, R. R. (1963) *Party and Society: Anglo-American Democracies*, Chicago, Rand McNally.

BAIN, G. S. (1983) 'Union growth: dimensions, determinants and destinies', in Bain, G. S. (ed.), *Industrial Relations in Britain*, Oxford, Basil Blackwell.

BUTLER, D. and STOKES, D. (1969) *Political Change in Britain*, Harmondsworth, Penguin Books.

CREWE, I. (1986) 'On the death and resurrection of class voting: some comments on *How Britain Votes*', *Political Studies*, Vol. 34, No. 4, pp. 620–38.

DUNLEAVY, P. and HUSBANDS, C. T. (1984) 'The social basis of British political alignment in 1983', paper to the annual conference of the Political Studies Association, Southampton, April.

DUNLEAVY, P. and HUSBANDS, C. T. (1985) *British Democracy at the Crossroads: Voting and Party Competition in the 1980s*, London, George Allen and Unwin.

FRANKLIN, M. N. (1985) *The Decline of Class Voting in Britain: Changes in the Basis of Electoral Choice, 1964–83*, Oxford, Clarendon Press.

FREYMAN, J. (1980) *When Labour Votes: The Partisan Alignment of British Trade Unionists, 1964–74*, Charlotte, NC, UMI Publications.

GOLDTHORPE, J. H., LOCKWOOD, D., BECHHOFER, F. and PLATT, J. (1969) *The Affluent Worker in the Class Structure*, Cambridge, Cambridge University Press.

HEATH, A., JOWELL, R. and CURTICE, J. (1985) *How Britain Votes*, Oxford, Pergamon.

LOCKWOOD, D. (1966) 'Sources of variation in working class images of society', *Sociological Review*, Vol. 14, pp. 249–67.

MAIR, P. (1983) 'Adaptation and control: towards an understanding of party and party system change', in Daalder, H. and Mair, P. (eds), *Western European Party Systems: Continuity and Change*, Beverly Hills and London, Sage.

MASSEY, D. and MILES, N. (1984) 'Mapping out the unions', *Marxism Today*, May.

NIE, N. H., HADLAI HULL, C., JENKINS, J. G., STEINBRENNER, K. and BENT, D. H. (1975) *SPSS: Statistical Package for the Social Sciences*, New York, McGraw-Hill.

NIELSEN, H. J. (1985) *British Attitudes Towards Trade Unions*, Copenhagen, Institute of Political Science Working Paper.

ROBERTSON, D. (1983) *Class and the British Electorate*, Oxford, Basil Blackwell.

ROSE, R. and McALLISTER, I. (1986) *Voters Begin to Choose: From Closed-Class to Open Elections in Britain*, London, Sage.

SARTORI, G. (1968) 'The sociology of parties: a critical review', in Stammer, O. (ed.), *Party Systems, Party Organisations and the Politics of the New Masses*, Berlin, IPW.

TAYLOR, A. J. (1987) 'The politics of non-partisan trade unions: the British case', *Politics*, Vol. 7, No. 1, pp. 8–13.

TORODE, J. (1984) 'The mood of the politically motivated', *The Guardian*, August 2.

14 Media influences on voting in 1983

Patrick Dunleavy and C. T. Husbands

Our analysis of media influence differs from other approaches in being informed by a wider range of theoretical perspectives, in particular, the radical approach to media analysis that stresses the importance of the overall climate of media values in influencing citizens' views into convergent patterns of thinking (Glasgow University Media Group, 1976, 1980; Philo *et al.*, 1982). From this perspective we should be less concerned about trying to gauge the political impact achieved by any one media source – such as a single newspaper – and focus attention instead upon the overall climate of media influence to which people have been exposed.

A first stage is to determine where voters obtain their political information. Table 14.1 shows that watching television was cited as their most important source of political information by more than twice as many respondents as referred to newspapers. However, if we broaden attention

Table 14.1 Voters' major sources of political information

Media source	Percentages citing source: As most important media source	Percentages citing source: In top two sources	Percentages citing source in top two media sources: Amongst newspaper readers	Percentages citing source in top two media sources: Amongst non-readers
Television	63	88	88	85
Newspapers	29	73	80	35
Radio	4	14	11	29
Personal contacts	3	12	9	27
Other	1	3	—	—
Total:	100	NA		
N:	1009		849	160

Major combinations of media souces (in percentages)

Primary source	*Secondary source*	
Television	Newspapers	45
Newspapers	Television	25
Television	Radio	8
Television	Personal sources	8
Newspapers	Radio	2
Radio	Television	2
All other combinations of sources		10
Total:		100

to include the top two sources of political information, and control for those respondents who do not read a daily newspaper, the apparent hegemony of television disappears. Almost the entire sample included television news in their top two sources of information. However, the same is true of newspaper readers as a group, once allowance is made for the 16 per cent of respondents who do not read a daily newspaper. On the other hand, radio serves as a primary source of news chiefly for people without television sets and a secondary source for non-readers of newspapers. Only a small minority of people seem to use personal sources as an important way in which to obtain their information about politics, despite our inclusion of three prompts about friends and neighbours, people at work and other members of the family.

There are no strong associations between people's major sources of political information and their political alignment. Those who cited newspapers as their most important channel of information are slightly more Conservative and disinclined to vote for the Alliance than those who cited television. However, for a more useful analysis we need to know in much finer detail which elements of media output structure people's political cognitions, information that is hard to obtain about television sources using survey methods. Most television presentation is so similar that there are few differences in political attitudes among those who rely on one programme source rather than another (Seymour-Ure, 1974).

By contrast, newspapers' highly partisan coverage of the election campaign and the events of the preceding four years (culminating in direct advice to their readers on how to vote) clearly creates a potential for political influence (Harrop, 1986). There is, in addition, a sparsely researched tradition of trying to gauge the influence of single newspapers upon their readerships (for example, Miller, Brand and Jordan, 1982). However, even if an association is established between reading a newspaper and adopting a congruent alignment, it is not clear which of these pieces of behaviour should be seen as the cause and which is the effect. People may use political criteria in deciding which newspaper to read in the first place, or they may decide what to buy on other grounds and be influenced by the newspaper's coverage into seeing political affairs from its perspective, or both processes may be involved in an observed association. Most studies have shown a linkage between press readership and voting behaviour, but not one strong enough to suggest that the partisan slant of news reporting is a dominant causal factor, after making allowances for a plausible level of self-selection into readership. Only Butler and Stokes (1969, pp. 265–300) followed through the development of newspaper readers' political views over time. They argued that there was a pronounced tendency for readers with views inconsistent with their newspaper's political slant to shift their allegiance so as to bring them into line.

From a radical perspective, however, the preoccupation with whether or not a single newspaper can influence its readers' politics is unjustified. It is unlikely that a gross effect such as a change in voting behaviour would correlate very closely with a finely graduated variable such as newspaper readership. Rather, our concern should be with the overall level of pluralism in the mass media messages to which voters are exposed. Given the increasing tendency for readers of 'popular' newspapers to read more than one title regularly (either because they buy two newspapers or because they swap papers with work colleagues), we can distinguish in quite a sophisticated manner between those press readers involved with a homogeneous or undifferentiated stream of political information from the press and those exposed to more mixed stimuli.

We may distinguish four types of press message:

1 The Tory press proper consists of those Fleet Street titles that consistently supported the Conservative government against other parties throughout its term and advocated voting Conservative in June 1983, namely, the *Sun*, *Daily Express*, *Daily Mail*, *Daily Telegraph*, *The Times* and the *Financial Times*, plus the London evening newspaper the *Standard*.

2 The Labour press consists of the *Daily Mirror* and in Scotland the *Daily Record*, the only titles consistently to criticize the Conservative government's record and directly to advocate voting Labour in 1983.

3 The 'non-Tory' press includes two Fleet Street titles that mixed their messages to readers over this period. *The Guardian* was broadly anti-Conservative throughout the period but did not clearly advocate either an Alliance or a Labour vote. The *Daily Star* was fairly clearly anti-Conservative in 1980–1, still critical in 1982–3 but reluctantly concluded that they could not support Labour (as too extreme) or the Alliance (as too inexperienced) in 1983, somewhat ingenuously advocating a vote for Thatcher's 'leadership' capabilities.

4 The 'other' press consists chiefly of regional daily morning or evening newspapers. Many of them are owned by national chains that produce overtly Tory papers on Fleet Street and so their preponderant colouring is again Conservative. This is significantly qualified, however, by their greatly reduced partisanship. While virtually all regional newspapers do have an explicit political line (unlike local weeklies, which cultivate a frequently bogus non-partisanship), this is usually restricted to formal editorializing. It rarely extends to the highly slanted presentation of lead stories and to the incessant propagandizing characteristic of the national popular press.

Our sample's exposure to press influences conforms closely to data on newspaper circulations and common-sense expectations of how different readerships cast their votes are broadly confirmed. Amongst the Tory press the Conservatism of *Daily Telegraph* readers is very marked, but in other titles around six out of ten readers vote Conservative and only one in six at most vote Labour. The (large) exception remains the *Sun*, where readers' political affiliations remain balanced, despite its uncompromising political line. Readers of 'other' daily newspapers show a lesser level of Conserva-

Table 14.2 Voting in the 1983 general election and newspaper readership

Newspaper	Vote in 1983 (%) Lab	Con	All	Con lead over Lab	N	1983 sales[1]	% of sample
Daily Telegraph	3	85	12	+82	67	1.28	7
The Times/ Financial Times	8	60	33	+52	27	0.48	3
Daily Express	15	63	22	+48	106	1.94	12
Daily Mail	16	58	26	+42	111	1.83	13
Sun	34	40	26	+6	177	4.15	23
All Tory press	20	55	24	+35	430	9.68	43
Other daily newspaper	27	49	25	+22	196	NA	24
Guardian	45	14	41	−31	49	0.42	6
Daily Star	48	21	31	−27	48	1.31	6
Non-Tory press	46	18	36	−28	94	1.73	*11*
Labour press (*Daily Mirror/Record*)	53	24	23	−29	199	3.27	24

[1] Figures for sales are in millions of copies and are the mean of monthly Audit Bureau of Circulation figures for the full year preceding the June 1983 general election.

tive predominance. Despite their very different composition in terms of social class, readers of the two non-Tory newspapers are very similar in their political views, with a healthy Labour lead over the Conservatives and stronger Alliance support. Finally, *Daily Mirror/Record* readers showed the strongest levels of Labour voting.

These data still include a good deal of multiple counting of people who read more than one daily newspaper. Controlling for mixed readership reveals that more than one in three voters read a single Tory press title. By contrast, although Labour newspapers were seen by nearly a quarter of our sample, only 11 per cent read no other daily newspaper, about the same proportion as depended on regional papers and around twice that of those who read only a non-Tory newspaper. Altogether, 58 per cent of voters depended on one daily newspaper, with 26 per cent reading two or more regularly and 16 per cent reading none. There is now an even clearer match between voters' political orientation and their press exposure, as Table 14.3 reveals. The Conservative vote and the Conservative lead over Labour are highest amongst readers of the Tory press and next highest amongst other press readers. However, both fall dramatically amongst people who either read no newspaper at all or are exposed to a Labour or non-Tory newspaper. Alliance voting increases sharply amongst people who do not read a daily newspaper and hence rely chiefly on the broadcast media. This is an especially interesting result when we consider the general

Table 14.3
Voting in the 1983 general election and type of press readership (in percentages)

	Lab	Con	All	Con lead over Lab	N	% of Three-party voters
Two Tory newspapers	9	65	27	+56	34	4
Mixed Tory newspapers[1]	16	62	22	+46	74	9
One Tory newspaper	16	60	24	+44	244	30
One other newspaper	20	54	26	+34	87	12
No daily newspaper	27	30	43	+3	129	16
Mixed Tory/Labour	45	32	23	−13	78	9
Mixed Labour/other	51	27	22	−24	37	4
One non-Tory newspaper	56	8	35	−48	48	6
One Labour nespaper	62	14	24	−48	84	11

[1] 'Mixed Tory newspapers' include the readerships of a Tory paper plus an 'other' or a 'non-Tory' newspaper (but not a Labour one).

lack of social distinctiveness in Alliance support. Readers of the non-Tory press and those taking a Labour newspaper are much the same in their political affiliations, except that Alliance voting is noticeably higher in the former group.

The relationship that we have traced seems too close to be attributable solely or even mainly to partisan self-selection into readership. We can further control for a selection effect by incorporating social background variables, of which the most important known correlate with readership behaviour is social class. We deploy a four-category measure of social class [. . .] We have also reformulated the readership categories given above into a new four-category variable, whose categories are as follows:

1 People exposed to predominantly Tory press influences (that is, Tory newspapers alone, or a Tory title and a regional daily) [Tory Predominance].

2 People exposed to more mixed or less partisan influences (that is, reading a Tory newspaper together with a non-Tory or Labour one, or reading only a regional newspaper) [Mixed Influences].

3 People who do not read a daily newspaper [No Newspaper].

4 People exposed chiefly to non-Tory or Labour messages (that is, reading a single newspaper in this group or any combination of titles involving a Labour or non-Tory newspaper without a Tory press title) [Non-Tory Predominance].

The control on social class further sharpens the differences that exist between people who are in the same social background but who receive different sorts of mass media messages and political information. Table 14.4 shows this clearly. Within all the class categories used the Conserva-

Table 14.4 Voting in the 1983 general election by press exposure and social class (in percentages)

Social class	Collapsed press category	Lab	Con	All	Con lead over Lab	N
Manual workers	Tory predominance	28	45	26	+17	125
	Mixed influences	44	29	28	−15	87
	No newspaper	50	16	34	−34	50
	Non-Tory predominance	71	9	20	−62	79
Non-manual workers	Tory predominance	8	64	28	+56	78
	Mixed influences	12	67	21	+55	42
	No newspaper	13	25	63	+12	40
	Non-Tory predominance	46	20	34	−26	39
Controllers of labour	Tory predominance	3	78	20	+75	80
	Mixed influences	16	58	26	+42	43
	No newspaper	14	46	39	+32	28
	Non-Tory predominance	46	20	34	−26	35
Employers etc.	Tory predominance	3	85	12	+82	34

tive vote is some 30 percentage-points lower amongst people primarily exposed to non-Tory messages than it is amongst readers of the Tory press, a high level of association that has few parallels amongst either social background or issue influences [. . .] The difference is even more marked when we compare the two extreme groups, those exposed to a predominantly Tory message and those receiving a predominantly non-Tory one; the differences in Conservative support range from 36 to 58 points.

Finally on press exposure, we need to take account of the role of the Sunday newspapers. Their potential electoral impact is clearly much less since voters saw just five issues in the 1983 campaign compared with twenty-eight daily issues. There is considerable continuity of readership habits across the two types of newspapers, produced particularly by 'family' titles. However, political news and coverage form a very small part of the output of 'popular' Sundays, especially the three largest circulation titles, the *News of the World*, *Sunday People* and *Sunday Mirror*, none of which ran the election campaign as a major lead story in more than one issue. The *News of the World* is a Conservative newspaper in editorial line but it regularly gives space to Labour and Alliance spokesmen. The *Sunday People* is chiefly 'non-political' with an anti-Conservative tinge, while the *Sunday Mirror* urged a Labour vote but without any of the elaborate propagandizing of its daily counterpart. For our analysis we have grouped all three into a 'non-political' category. By contrast, the 'quality' Sundays place a special emphasis on political coverage and weighty editorializing. The *Observer* is markedly opposed to the government and is the only Sunday title to qualify as a non-Tory newspaper in our analysis.

The *Sunday Telegraph* is an equally firm Tory title. Despite some more mixed reporting and a slightly equivocal endorsement of the Thatcher government's record, the *Sunday Times* has become consistently Tory, especially so since its change of ownership in 1981. In between are two semi-popular Tory newspapers, the *Mail on Sunday* and the *Sunday Express*, whose political coverage closely resembles that of the Tory dailies. There are therefore five Sunday titles in the Tory press. Finally, there are a number of regional Sunday titles, notably in Scotland, which constitute our final ('other') category. The key feature of Sunday readership patterns is the dominance of the 'non-political' popular titles, and the almost complete absence of a non-Tory press [. . .] Voting patterns in the 'non-political' group are very close to those we should expect, given the social class of their readers, and they certainly show no signs of a distinctive political influence from the newspapers involved. Labour had a 12 percentage-point lead over the Conservatives amongst *News of the World* readers (urged by that newspaper to vote Conservative) and only a 5-point lead amongst *Sunday Mirror* readers (urged by that newspaper to vote Labour) [. . .]

The real importance of the Sunday newspapers lies in the extent to which their different composition helps to produce any pluralization of the overall press 'line' to which most people are exposed. There is little evidence that it does. We distinguish five categories:

1 People exposed to 'solid Tory' press influence (that is, reading Tory daily and Tory Sunday newspapers, or a Tory daily with no Sunday newspaper) [Tory Influence].

2 People exposed to 'mainly Tory' influence (that is, reading a Tory daily with a Sunday newspaper other than a Tory title; or a mix of daily newspapers with at least on Tory Sunday title) [Mainly Tory].

3 People not exposed to any significant press influence (that is, reading no newspapers at all or only a Sunday newspaper) [Minimal or None].

4 People exposed to 'evenly mixed' influence (that is, reading a mix of daily newspapers but no Tory Sunday, or a non-Tory daily and a Tory Sunday) [Mixed Influences].

5 People exposed to 'non-Tory' influence (that is, reading a non-Tory daily alone or in combination with a non-political, regional or non-Tory Sunday) [Non-Tory Influence].

Nearly four out of ten voters are exposed to solid Tory press influence and 46 per cent to at least mainly Tory influence. Considering only actual newspaper readers, a clear majority fall into this category. On the other hand, only a fifth of the sample exposed to evenly mixed influences and even fewer to non-Tory influences; Table 14.5 shows the distribution among the five categories. We also show a breakdown by social class within each of the five readership categories but, since the number of categories for this analysis is one more, we distinguish only between manual workers

Table 14.5 Voting in the 1983 general election by social class and overall press exposure (in percentages)

Overall press exposure	Social class	Lab	Con	All	Con lead over Lab	N
Tory influence	Non-manual classes[1]	6	74	20	+68	192
	Manual workers	30	43	27	+13	113
Mainly Tory	Non-manual classes	17	54	28	+37	46
	Manual workers	26	52	22	+26	27
Minimal or none	Non-manual classes	13	39	48	+26	79
	Manual workers	50	16	34	−34	50
Mixed influences	Non-manual classes	25	48	27	+23	85
	Manual workers	49	23	28	−26	78
Non-Tory influence	Non-manual classes	48	22	30	−26	73
	Manual workers	71	10	19	−61	72

[1] Non-manual classes are non-manual workers, controllers of labour, and employers and petit-bourgeoisie.

and all other classes. There is again a very marked variation in political alignment according to media exposure. Eight times as many non-manual people vote Labour when exposed to non-Tory press influence as do those exposed to solid Tory influence. Amongst manual workers the level of Labour voting more than doubles across these two categories, while the Conservative vote falls by a factor of four. It is worth noting again the high level of Alliance support amongst people who read no daily newspaper or a Sunday newspaper alone. The more detailed data in Table 14.4 show that this support is concentrated especially amongst non-manual workers, over 60 per cent of whom in this readership group (out of a group of forty respondents in this class) voted for the Alliance.

References

BUTLER, D. and STOKES, D. (1969) *Political Changes in Britain: Forces Shaping Elections*, London and Basingstoke, Macmillan.

GLASGOW UNIVERSITY MEDIA GROUP (1976) *Bad News*, London, Routledge and Kegan Paul.

GLASGOW UNIVERSITY MEDIA GROUP (1980) *More Bad News*, London, Routledge and Kegan Paul.

HARROP, M. (1986) 'The press and post-war elections', in Crewe, I. and Harrop, M. (eds), *Political Communications: The General Election Campaign of 1983*, Cambridge, Cambridge University Press.

MILLER, W. L., BRAND, J. and JORDAN, M. (1982), 'On the power or vulnerability of the British press: a dynamic analysis', *British Journal of Political Science*, Vol. 12, No. 3, pp. 357–73.

PHILO, G., HEWITT, J., BEHARRELL, P. and DAVIS, H. (1982) *Really Bad News*, London, Writers and Readers.

SEYMOUR-URE, C. (1974) *The Political Impact of the Mass Media*, London, Constable.

15 Ideological change in the electorate

Anthony Heath, Roger Jowell and John Curtice

[. . . T]he class structure has been changing shape over the last twenty years with a contracting working class and an expanding salariat [so that we might expect f]ewer people than before [to] favour government intervention in the economy [. . . T]he expansion of higher education might [also] lead to a shift [where m]ore people than before [. . .] adopt liberal attitudes [. . .] On this account, there are gains and losses for both the Labour and Conservative Parties; Labour benefits from the [liberal] drift of the electorate but loses from the [rightward] drift while the Conservative Party makes the opposite gains and losses. The major net beneficiary of these movements is of course the Alliance with an expanded [right-liberal] area of the 'map' in which to search for voters.

[. . .] If we are correct, orthodox forecasts of the parties' prospects may be in need of substantial revision: the position of the Conservative Party may be less secure than is currently assumed while that of Labour may not be quite so dismal.

15.1 The class values

A standard question has been asked in [previous] election studies about one of the key class values, namely nationalization. Respondents were asked whether '[. . . M]ore industries should be nationalized', [. . .], 'no more industries should be nationalized, but industries that are now nationalized should stay nationalized', or 'some of the industries that are now nationalized should become private companies' [. . .] Table 15.1 shows the changing distribution of responses over time.

The major feature of Table 15.1 is the rather sudden change between October 1974 and May 1979. In 1979 for the first time more people favoured privatization than further nationalization, although the status quo was still (although only just) the most popular option. The balance tipped the other way in 1983, when privatization took over as the most popular option.

However, even though the same question wording was used in all the election studies, the interpretation of the answers is not wholly straightforward. The questions may have stayed the same, but the context – in particular the extent of public ownership – has not. Some companies have been nationalized, others privatized. The electorate may not have changed its mind at all about the preferred extent of public ownership; it may simply be reacting in a perfectly consistent way to the institutional changes. In other words, the changed responses to the nationalization question be-

Table 15.1 Attitudes to nationalization, 1964–1983

	Percentage favouring				
	Nationalization	No change	Privatization		
1964	28	51	21	100%	(N = 1604)
1966	29	49	22	100%	(N = 1631)
Feb 1974	28	47	25	100%	(N = 2103)
Oct 1974	32	46	22	100%	(N = 2109)
1979	17	43	40	100%	(N = 1751)
1983	18	40	42	100%	(N = 3486)

Source: British Election Study, 1983

tween 1974 and 1979 could be interpreted as a condemnation of the extension of the public ownership that had taken place under the 1974 Labour government, not as a true 'shift to the right'. It is not the public's liking for nationalization which changed, it could be argued, but the amount of nationalization itself.

It is not possible to check this interpretation in any definitive way, but a look at the recent history of nationalization is nonetheless illuminating. The major landmarks were as follows. In 1967 the Iron and Steel Act renationalized the industry, which had been first nationalized in 1949 by Labour and then de-nationalized by the Conservatives in 1953. This was the only major piece of nationalization carried out by the Wilson governments, which otherwise left things as much as they were. As Table 15.1 shows, public opinion also remained much as it was throughout the Wilson years.

The Heath government was also fairly modest in its accomplishments. The lame duck of Rolls Royce was taken into public ownership in 1971 following its bankruptcy but some modest privatization took place too. In 1971–2 some of BOAC's routes were allotted to British Caledonian, and in 1973 Thomas Cook's travel agency and the Carlisle state breweries were sold to the private sector. Overall, there was little change and public opinion too remained much as it was.

The Labour government which followed was much more active (as indeed its manifesto promised). Another lame duck – British Leyland – was rescued and the majority of its shares acquired by the government in 1975. The National Enterprise Board was also established in that year with the objective of playing an active, interventionist role in the economy. In 1977 the British National Oil Corporation was established and large sections of the aerospace and shipbuilding industries were taken into public ownership with the formation of British Aerospace and British Shipbuilders.

Although the 1974 Labour government has not normally enjoyed the reputation of being a radical, socialist administration, this was by far the

Table 15.2 Class and nationalization, 1964–1983

	Percentage respondents favouring privatization	
	1964	1983
Salariat	21	52
Routine non-manual	25	43
Petit bourgeoisie	35	66
Foremen and technicians	24	44
Working class	15	29

most extensive programme of nationalization since the 1945 government. Public opinion, however, 'responded' (although we should not assume that it was a simple matter of cause and effect) with a substantial swing in favour of privatization. It would not be implausible to infer that many people simply preferred the earlier status quo of the 1966 Wilson administration.

However, it is doubtful if the changes in attitude towards nationalization were caused purely by the institutional changes. Mrs Thatcher's administration in 1979 restored the status quo, but public opinion did not move back in step with the institutional changes. British Aerospace, Britoil, the National Freight Corporation, Amersham International, Cable and Wireless, and the British Transport Docks Board were all privatized (although British Airways, British Telecom and British Shipbuilders were left for the 1983 Parliament). But public opinion remained in favour of privatization. As Table 15.1 shows, the electorate did not revert to its earlier preferences. If Mrs Thatcher completes her programme, she will have pushed back the frontiers of public ownership behind their 1964 boundaries. It is quite possible that public opinion will swing back again, but at the time of writing (1985) we are forced to agree that there has been a net shift to the right on nationalization.

It is in theory possible that this net shift to the right is due simply to the changing shape of the class structure; a smaller working class means that there are fewer potential supporters of public ownership. However, as Table 15.2 shows, the shift between 1964 and 1983 is far greater than can be explained by the changes in the class structure alone. In all classes alike there have been shifts in favour of privatization. Mrs Thatcher, it would seem, has made converts to the free enterprise philosophy.

If this analysis is correct, we must not treat ideological change purely as a consequence of social change. We must avoid a naive 'sociological determinism'. Public attitudes can be shaped by political leadership as well as by social change. The political parties can perhaps help to define what counts as class ideology. Parties are not the prisoners of social change and social structure; they are probably one of the major agencies which help to shape subjective awareness of class interests and to translate these into class values. We would, for example, expect class values to take a rather different form in a country such as the USA where the two major parties have less conflicting class ideologies.

But while political parties may help to shape class values, they cannot shape them just as they please. A privatization programme of the kind espoused by Mrs Thatcher's Conservatives will fall on readier ears among the petit bourgeoisie or the salariat than in the working class. This can be seen from Table 15.2. Thus, although all classes have moved to the right since 1964 on nationalization, the movement is far from even. The working class has been relatively immune to the blandishments of free enterprise with an increase of only 14 points in favour. The petty bourgeoisie and the salariat have responded more enthusiastically with increases of 32 and 31 points. The shift to the right could perhaps be described as a successful attempt by the Conservatives to articulate the latent interests of their natural supporters.

However, we must not place too much weight on a single question if we wish to measure ideological change. On some of the other questions which make up the class axis there was much less *net* movement. We do not have comparable data over time on attitudes towards job creation, but since 75 per cent of our respondents in 1983 favoured government intervention to create jobs, it is rather more likely that there has been a move to the left than to the right – again perhaps in response to the actual rise in unemployment.

There is rather firmer evidence on income distribution. Similar questions were asked on this in 1974, 1979 and 1983. In 1974, 56 per cent favoured redistribution, and this fell, but only modestly, to 55 per cent in 1979 and 47 per cent in 1983. The net change of 9 points is more in keeping with the small change in the shape of the class structure over the ten years in question (although it cannot wholly be explained by structural change).

These results suggest that while nationalization may have become increasingly unpopular to many voters, support for other elements of working-class ideology is both higher and more stable. By focusing on nationalization, we highlight the movements at the extremes of the ideological continuum. But we should not forget that this affects only a minority of people. Even in the case of nationalization the overall dissimilarity of 21 points between the 1964 and 1983 distributions is quite small. It is a lot smaller for example than the dissimilarity between working-class and petit bourgeois respondents in 1983. It means that there must be a great deal of overlap between the two distributions. The extent of ideological change must not be exaggerated therefore. If we take into account the other class values (particularly income redistribution and job creation), our estimate of ideological change will be further reduced.

Our interpretation therefore is that the majority on the far left of the ideological continuum has declined somewhat in size while that on the far right has grown proportionately. But the bulk of the electorate remains in the centre, favouring some measure of job creation and income redistribution but with ambivalent views towards both nationalization and privatization.

Such an interpretation has rather less momentous implications for the political parties than one which concentrates purely on nationalization. Attitudes to the latter may show the most dramatic change, and it is true that (in a cross-sectional analysis) they are the best predictors of vote, but the other class values are not wholly unimportant and they appear to have been more stable.[1] Moreover, even in 1983 more people shared Labour's views on income redistribution than shared the Conservatives', just as there were still more people in the working class in 1983 than in the salariat. A *shift* to the right is not the same as a *majority* on the right.

15.2 The liberal values

The best time-series available on the liberal values consists of respondents' changing attitudes towards the death penalty. Questions about this were asked in four of the election studies, although the wording necessarily changed after 1969 when the death penalty was finally removed from the statute book.[2] The time trends are shown in Table 15.3.

The picture is quite different from that of Table 15.1 on nationalization. There is a slight drift from 1966 to 1979 in favour of abolition followed by a more marked shift, in the same direction, in the course of the last Parliament. Despite Mrs Thatcher's views in favour of the restoration of the 'ultimate deterrent', the electorate showed no sign of following her on this as they did on privatization. Instead, as we would expect from the growth of sixth-form and higher education, the balance of movement has been away from the authoritarian end of the continuum and towards the liberal one.

The rather abrupt change between 1979 and 1983, it must be admitted, is greater than can be explained in educational terms alone, although the overall change from 1966 is more in line with educational expansion. We have no specific explanation for the abrupt change, but it is quite plausible that values will in general change abruptly rather than smoothly. Values must be thought of as *social* phenomena rather than *individual* ones. There needs to be some social process in order to crystallize a change. The rhetoric of a political party may perform this function, but other processes could do the same job. For example, values may also be shaped by the development of new social networks, as with the university expansion of the 1960s and the spread of more 'permissive' values at that time.

As with the class values, however, we should not rely on a single question to measure change. This is particularly important as the death

Table 15.3 Attitudes to the death penalty, 1966–1983

	Percentage favouring			
	Abolition	Retention/ restoration		
1966	18	82	100%	(N = 1783)
1970	19	81	100%	(N = 1094)
1979	25	75	100%	(N = 1713)
1983	37	63	100%	(N = 3515)

Table 15.4 Changes in social attitudes, 1979–1983

	Percentage agreeing that changes had gone too far		
	Equal opportunities for women	Equal opportunities for blacks and Asians	Abortion on the National Health Service
1979 (minimum N = 1714)	23	30	44
1983 (minimum N = 3287)	9	20	32

penalty is one of the least 'politicized' of issues [. . .] We repeated a number of questions that had been asked in the 1979 Election Survey about issues that might be regarded as liberal ones. These confirm the picture given by the death penalty question of a clear shift in a liberal direction. As in 1979 we asked our respondents whether a number of social changes had gone too far. We asked [. . .] about 'attempts to give equal opportunities to women in Britain' [. . .], 'attempts to give opportunities to black people and Asians in Britain' [. . .], and 'the availability of abortion on the National Health Service' [. . .]. The results for 1979 and 1983 are given in Table 15.4.

In all three cases the movements are of very similar magnitude to those with the death penalty question and are in the same direction. Interestingly, there was little movement (again in all three cases) in the percentages who thought that the changes had *not* gone far enough. Rather, the increase was in the proportion who felt that the changes were about right. It is the status quo, not radical change, that has become popular.

A longer, although technically less satisfactory, time-series can be constructed on attitudes to tax cuts and spending on social services. Government spending on the welfare state may seem an unlikely candidate for measuring liberal values as, at first sight, it would seem to have more in common with the interventionist-free enterprise values. However, there is an important distinction which must be made between the universal benefits, such as health, education and pensions, which are available to everybody at some stage of their lives and the selective ones, such as supplementary benefit, which go only to those with specific needs. The universal benefits tend to be much more popular than the selective ones. For example, 64 per cent of our sample in 1983 thought that government spending on education had not gone far enough, while only 28 per cent thought that welfare benefits had not gone far enough.

It is not difficult to explain the difference in popularity. The universal benefits appeal to everyone's self-interest; and they go to the salariat as much as, if not more than, to the working class. The selective benefits on the other hand go only to a minority, mainly the working class, and appeal to the altruism rather than the self-interest of the bulk of the electorate. In line with this, we find that attitudes towards the selective benefits are quite closely related to class position, whereas those towards the universal benefits are not. For example, in response to our question on welfare benefits there was quite a marked difference between the classes: 40 per cent of the working class though that 'welfare benefits . . . have not gone far enough' [. . .] whereas only 22 per cent of the salariat gave the same answer. But on education spending the differences were almost non-existent, 69 per cent of the working class and 66 per cent of the salariat agreeing that it had not gone far enough, while on pensions and the Health Service there were modest class differences.

It is a mistake therefore to treat the welfare state as a single entity or to regard it as a straightforward class issue [. . . S]pending on health and education were two of the questions on which Alliance voters were closer to Labour than to the Conservatives, and we are inclined to see these particular aspects of the welfare state as ones which to some extent cross-cut class interests.[3]

Unfortunately, because of the wording differences, we cannot directly compare the welfare state question in the 1966 survey, which asked about spending on 'social services' with the 1979 question on 'government spending' or the 1983 question on 'health and social services' [. . .] The questions suggest a modest increase in support for spending – from 40 per cent in favour in 1966 to 45 per cent in 1983 – but we cannot read too much into this.

Fortunately, there is some more direct evidence. The proportion of the electorate saying that the government spends too little on the health service increased from 30 per cent in 1960 to 66 per cent in 1979 to 85 per cent in 1983. And the proportion agreeing that 'government services such as health, education and welfare should be extended, even if it means some increase in taxes' increased from 39 per cent in 1978 to 50 per cent in 1983.

As with nationalization, these changes could reflect changes in government expenditure rather than real changes in people's values. There were much publicized expenditure cuts under both the 1974 Labour government and the 1979 Conservative government, so again people may be expressing their opposition to these changes rather than altering their values. But while this may be part of the story, particularly of the last few years, it is unlikely to be the whole of it. Over our period as a whole, from 1964 to 1983, government spending has increased from 36 per cent of Gross Domestic Product to 47 per cent, and within the total the proportion given to education and health has stayed fairly constant. Our interpretation is that this increase in spending has met with general approval and that attempts to reverse it are disliked.

We suspect, then, that very different processes have been at work with nationalization and government spending. In the case of nationalization, there has been increased support for cutting back on public ownership; in the case of welfare-state spending there has been increased opposition to cut-backs. There is, we believe, nothing inherently inconsistent in these divergent trends. In principle there is no reason why trends on the first question should run parallel with those on the second.

15.3 Changing contours of the map

Our assumptions, therefore, that there have been net movements of the electorate to the [. . .] right on the class axis of our ideological map and to the [more liberal end of the liberal axis] appear to be sound. They have almost certainly been helped by the changing class structure and the expansion of higher education, but equally certainly they have not been purely passive consequences of social change. Government action and political conversion have played a part too.

It is difficult to make any accurate estimate of the actual amount, rather than the direction, of change. If we take the two questions on which we have the best time-series, namely nationalization and the death penalty, we obtain the picture of change [shown in Table 15.5.] This shows the change in the proportions of the total samples who favoured each possible combination. Thus is 1966, 20 per cent of the total sample were in favour *both* of further nationalization *and* of the retention of the death penalty. By 1983 this had fallen to 9 per cent of the total sample, giving us our figure of −11 in the [bottom left-hand] corner [. . .]

Too much weight should not be placed on individual figures, but the relative decline of population in the [bottom left] and the growth in the [top right] is clear enough. Table 15.5 also makes clear that the changes have not been entirely to Labour's disadvantage. While Labour's heartland has contracted (although only slightly) and the Conservatives' has expanded, the areas immediately adjacent to the heartlands show a different pattern: potential Conservative recruits [along the bottom] have dwindled in number while potential Labour recruits [along the top] have grown.

We should not exaggerate the impact of these changes, since attitudes towards the death penalty are very weakly related to voting behaviour. Even if we use the alternative, more politicized criterion of defence for

Table 15.5 The changing map, 1966–1983

nationalize private companies	no change	sell off nationalized industries	
−1	+6	+10	oppose death penalty
0	+1	+4	no change
−11	−17	+7	favour death penalty

← class axis → (horizontal); ↑ liberal axis ↓ (vertical)

measuring the second axis [. . .] it still proves to be only of secondary importance. In other words the increased numbers of people who share their attitudes on the class values have been a more valuable asset to the Conservative Party than the increased numbers of like-minded people on the non-class issues have been to Labour. Labour have not gained as much on the roundabouts as they lost on the swings.

But the main beneficiary of the ideological shift towards the [top right] of our map is likely to be the Alliance [. . . T]his area of the map seems to be the Alliance heartland. We can attempt to estimate the size of the Alliance gain by assuming that the preferences of the inhabitants of each area of our ideological map had remained constant but that the numbers in each area changed in the way they actually did. Our best estimate is that the Alliance vote has been increased by between a minimum of 1 point and a maximum of 5 points by this drift to the [top right].[4] Such Alliance gains would have been drawn more from Labour than from the Conservative Party, but only just. If the Alliance had gained the full five points, we estimate that three would have come at Labour's expense and two at the Conservatives' expense.

Notes

1 Nationalization and trade union legislation are the two best individual predictors of Conservative or Labour voting, but the questions on income redistribution and job creation make further quite substantial increments to variance explained.

2 The death penalty was abolished temporarily in 1965. After a review period it was permanently abolished in 1969. In the 1966 and 1970 studies the wording was 'Did you want to see the death penalty kept or abolished?'. In 1979 it was 'I am going to read out a list of things that some people believe a government should do. For each one you can say whether you feel it is: very important that it should be done, fairly important that it should be done, it doesn't matter either way, fairly important that it should not be done, very important that it should not be done . . .

What is your view about bringing back the death penalty?', and in 1983 'Please say whether you agree or disagree with each of these statements, or say if you are not sure either way: . . . Britain should bring back the death penalty.'

3 It is quite possible that there has been a trend against welfare benefits (as with the other class issues) but in favour of health and education.

4 Unfortunately the results of this exercise are not very robust. Estimates of the likely benefits to the Alliance are rather sensitive to the assumptions we make about preferences.

Index